RUTH
SONG OF SONGS
ESTHER

A Commentary in the Wesleyan Tradition

Ruth
Sarah B. C. Derck

Song of Songs
Joseph Coleson
Sarah B. C. Derck

Esther
Elaine Bernius

BEACON HILL PRESS
OF KANSAS CITY

Copyright 2020
by Beacon Hill Press of Kansas City

Beacon Hill Press of Kansas City
PO Box 419527
Kansas City, MO 64141
www.BeaconHillBooks.com

ISBN 978-0-8341-3873-5

Cover Design: J.R. Caines
Interior Design: Sharon Page

Unless otherwise indicated, all Scripture quotations are from the Holy Bible, New International Version® (NIV®). Copyright © 1973, 1978, 1984, 2011 by Biblica, Inc.™ Used by permission of Zondervan. All rights reserved worldwide. www.zondervan.com. *Emphasis indicated by underlining in boldface quotations and italic in lightface quotations.*

The following version of Scripture is in the public domain:

King James Version (KJV)

The following copyrighted versions of Scripture are used by permission:

The Common English Bible (CEB), copyright 2011. All rights reserved.

The Contemporary English Version (CEV). Copyright © 1995 by the American Bible Society.

The ESV® Bible (The Holy Bible, English Standard Version®), copyright © 2001 by Crossway, a publishing ministry of Good News Publishers. All rights reserved.

GOD'S WORD® (GW). Copyright © 1995 by God's Word to the Nations. Used by permission of Baker Publishing Group. All rights reserved.

The New American Standard Bible® (NASB®), copyright © 1960, 1962, 1963, 1968, 1971, 1972, 1973, 1975, 1977, 1995 by The Lockman Foundation. www.Lockman.org.

New JPS Hebrew-English Tanakh (NJPS), © 2000 by The Jewish Publication Society. All rights reserved. *Emphasis indicated by italic.*

The New King James Version® (NKJV). Copyright © 1982 by Thomas Nelson, Inc. All rights reserved.

The Holy Bible, New Living Translation (NLT), copyright © 1996, 2004, 2015 by Tyndale House Foundation. Used by permission of Tyndale House Publishers, Inc., Carol Stream, IL 60188. All rights reserved.

The New Revised Standard Version Bible (NRSV), copyright © 1989 National Council of the Churches of Christ in the United States of America. All rights reserved. *Emphasis indicated by italic.*

The Revised Standard Version (RSV) of the Bible, copyright 1946, 1952, 1971 by the Division of Christian Education of the National Council of the Churches of Christ in the USA. All rights reserved.

Library of Congress Cataloging-in-Publication Data

A complete catalog record for this book is available from the Library of Congress.

The Internet addresses, email addresses, and phone numbers in this book are accurate at the time of publication. They are provided as a resource. Beacon Hill Press of Kansas City does not endorse them or vouch for their content or permanence.

COMMENTARY EDITORS

General Editors

Alex Varughese
  Ph.D., Drew University
  Professor Emeritus of Biblical
    Literature
  Mount Vernon Nazarene University
  Mount Vernon, Ohio

George Lyons
  Ph.D., Emory University
  Professor Emeritus of New Testament
  Northwest Nazarene University
  Nampa, Idaho

Section Editors

Robert Branson
  Ph.D., Boston University
  Professor Emeritus of Biblical
    Literature
  Olivet Nazarene University
  Bourbonnais, Illinois

Kent Brower
  Ph.D., The University of Manchester
  Vice Principal
  Senior Lecturer in Biblical Studies
  Nazarene Theological College
  Manchester, England

Alex Varughese
  Ph.D., Drew University
  Professor Emeritus of Biblical
    Literature
  Mount Vernon Nazarene University
  Mount Vernon, Ohio

George Lyons
  Ph.D., Emory University
  Professor Emeritus of New Testament
  Northwest Nazarene University
  Nampa, Idaho

CONTENTS

GENERAL EDITORS' PREFACE

The purpose of the New Beacon Bible Commentary is to make available to pastors and students in the twenty-first century a biblical commentary that reflects the best scholarship in the Wesleyan theological tradition. The commentary project aims to make this scholarship accessible to a wider audience to assist them in their understanding and proclamation of Scripture as God's Word.

Writers of the volumes in this series not only are scholars within the Wesleyan theological tradition and experts in their field but also have special interest in the books assigned to them. Their task is to communicate clearly the critical consensus and the full range of other credible voices who have commented on the Scriptures. Though scholarship and scholarly contribution to the understanding of the Scriptures are key concerns of this series, it is not intended as an academic dialogue within the scholarly community. Commentators of this series constantly aim to demonstrate in their work the significance of the Bible as the church's book and the contemporary relevance and application of the biblical message. The project's overall goal is to make available to the church and for her service the fruits of the labors of scholars who are committed to their Christian faith.

The *New International Version* (NIV) is the reference version of the Bible used in this series; however, the focus of exegetical study and comments is the biblical text in its original language. When the commentary uses the NIV, it is printed in bold. The text printed in bold italics is the translation of the author. Commentators also refer to other translations where the text may be difficult or ambiguous.

The structure and organization of the commentaries in this series seeks to facilitate the study of the biblical text in a systematic and methodical way. Study of each biblical book begins with an *Introduction* section that gives an overview of authorship, date, provenance, audience, occasion, purpose, sociological/cultural issues, textual history, literary features, hermeneutical issues, and theological themes necessary to understand the book. This section also includes a brief outline of the book and a list of general works and standard commentaries.

The commentary section for each biblical book follows the outline of the book presented in the introduction. In some volumes, readers will find section *overviews* of large portions of scripture with general comments on their overall literary structure and other literary features. A consistent feature of the commentary is the paragraph-by-paragraph study of biblical texts. This section has three parts: *Behind the Text*, *In the Text*, and *From the Text*.

The goal of the *Behind the Text* section is to provide the reader with all the relevant information necessary to understand the text. This includes specific historical situations reflected in the text, the literary context of the text, sociological and cultural issues, and literary features of the text.

In the Text explores what the text says, following its verse-by-verse structure. This section includes a discussion of grammatical details, word studies, and the connectedness of the text to other biblical books/passages or other parts of the book being studied (the canonical relationship). This section provides transliterations of key words in Hebrew and Greek and their literal meanings. The goal here is to explain what the author would have meant and/or what the audience would have understood as the meaning of the text. This is the largest section of the commentary.

The *From the Text* section examines the text in relation to the following areas: theological significance, intertextuality, the history of interpretation, use of the Old Testament scriptures in the New Testament, interpretation in later church history, actualization, and application.

The commentary provides *sidebars* on topics of interest that are important but not necessarily part of an explanation of the biblical text. These topics are informational items and may cover archaeological, historical, literary, cultural, and theological matters that have relevance to the biblical text. Occasionally, longer detailed discussions of special topics are included as *excursuses.*

We offer this series with our hope and prayer that readers will find it a valuable resource for their understanding of God's Word and an indispensable tool for their critical engagement with the biblical texts.

Roger Hahn, Centennial Initiative General Editor
Alex Varughese, General Editor (Old Testament)
George Lyons, General Editor (New Testament)

ABBREVIATIONS

With a few exceptions, these abbreviations follow those in *The SBL Handbook of Style* (Alexander 1999).

General

→	see the commentary at
AD	anno Domini (precedes date)
ANE	ancient Near East(ern)
AT	Greek Alpha Text
BC	before Christ (follows date)
ca.	circa
cf.	*confer*, compare
ch(s)	chapter(s)
ed.	edited by; editor; edition
e.g.	*exempli gratia*, for example
Eng.	English
esp.	especially
et al.	*et alii*, and others
etc.	*et cetera*, and the rest
f(f).	and the following one(s)
fem.	feminine
Gk.	Greek
HB	Hebrew Bible
Heb.	Hebrew
ibid.	*ibidem*, in the same place
i.e.	*id est*, that is
lit.	literally
LRWP	long-range wordplay
LXX	Septuagint (the Greek translation of the OT)
masc.	masculine
MT	Masoretic Text (the Hebrew text of the OT)
n(n).	note(s)
NT	New Testament
OT	Old Testament
p(p).	page(s)
pl.	plural
repr.	reprint, reprinted
sg.	singular
v(v)	verse(s)
vol(s).	volume(s)
vs.	versus
Vulg.	Vulgate (Latin translation of both the OT and NT)

Modern English Versions

CEB	Common English Bible
CEV	Contemporary English Version
ESV	English Standard Version
GW	God's Word
KJV	King James Version
NASB	New American Standard Bible
NIV	New International Version
NJPS	Tanakh: The Holy Scriptures: The New JPS Translation according to the Traditional Hebrew Text
NKJV	New King James Version
NLT	New Living Translation
NRSV	New Revised Standard Version

Print Conventions for Translations

Bold font	NIV (bold without quotation marks in the text under study; elsewhere in the regular font, with quotation marks and no further identification)
Bold italic font	Author's translation (without quotation marks)

Behind the Text: Literary or historical background information average readers might not know from reading the biblical text alone

In the Text: Comments on the biblical text, words, phrases, grammar, and so forth

From the Text: The use of the text by later interpreters, contemporary relevance, theological and ethical implications of the text, with particular emphasis on Wesleyan concerns

Ancient Sources

Old Testament

Gen	Genesis	Dan	Daniel	**New Testament**		
Exod	Exodus	Hos	Hosea	Matt	Matthew	
Lev	Leviticus	Joel	Joel	Mark	Mark	
Num	Numbers	Amos	Amos	Luke	Luke	
Deut	Deuteronomy	Obad	Obadiah	John	John	
Josh	Joshua	Jonah	Jonah	Acts	Acts	
Judg	Judges	Mic	Micah	Rom	Romans	
Ruth	Ruth	Nah	Nahum	1—2 Cor	1—2 Corinthians	
1—2 Sam	1—2 Samuel	Hab	Habakkuk			
1—2 Kgs	1—2 Kings	Zeph	Zephaniah	Gal	Galatians	
1—2 Chr	1—2 Chronicles	Hag	Haggai	Eph	Ephesians	
Ezra	Ezra	Zech	Zechariah	Phil	Philippians	
Neh	Nehemiah	Mal	Malachi	Col	Colossians	
Esth	Esther	(Note: Chapter and		1—2 Thess	1—2 Thessalonians	
Job	Job	verse numbering in the				
Ps/Pss	Psalm/Psalms	MT and LXX often		1—2 Tim	1—2 Timothy	
Prov	Proverbs	differ compared to		Titus	Titus	
Eccl	Ecclesiastes	those in English Bibles.		Phlm	Philemon	
Song	Song of Songs/	To avoid confusion, all		Heb	Hebrews	
	Song of Solomon	biblical references follow		Jas	James	
		the chapter and verse		1—2 Pet	1—2 Peter	
Isa	Isaiah	numbering in English		1—2—3 John	1—2—3 John	
Jer	Jeremiah	translations, even when		Jude	Jude	
Lam	Lamentations	the text in the MT and		Rev	Revelation	
Ezek	Ezekiel	LXX is under discussion.)				

Apocrypha

Bar	Baruch
Add Dan	Additions to Daniel
Pr Azar	Prayer of Azariah
Bel	Bel and the Dragon
Sg Three	Song of the Three Young Men
Sus	Susanna
1-2 Esd	1-2 Esdras
Add Esth	Additions to Esther
Ep Jer	Epistle of Jeremiah
Jdt	Judith
1—2 Macc	1—2 Maccabees
3—4 Macc	3—4 Maccabees
Pr Man	Prayer of Manasseh
Ps 151	Psalm 151
Sir	Sirach/Ecclesiasticus
Tob	Tobit
Wis	Wisdom of Solomon

Josephus

Ant.	*Jewish Antiquities*

Secondary Sources: Journals, Periodicals, Major Reference Works, and Series

JSOT	*Journal for the Study of the Old Testament*

Greek Transliteration

Greek	Letter	English
α	alpha	a
β	bēta	b
γ	gamma	g
γ	gamma nasal	n (before γ, κ, ξ, χ)
δ	delta	d
ε	epsilon	e
ζ	zēta	z
η	ēta	ē
θ	thēta	th
ι	iōta	i
κ	kappa	k
λ	lambda	l
μ	mu	m
ν	nu	n
ξ	xi	x
ο	omicron	o
π	pi	p
ρ	rhō	r
ῥ	initial rhō	rh
σ/ς	sigma	s
τ	tau	t
υ	upsilon	y
υ	upsilon	u (in diphthongs: au, eu, ēu, ou, ui)
φ	phi	ph
χ	chi	ch
ψ	psi	ps
ω	ōmega	ō
ʽ	rough breathing	h (before initial vowels or diphthongs)

Hebrew Consonant Transliteration

Hebrew/ Aramaic	Letter	English
א	alef	ʾ
ב	bet	b
ג	gimel	g
ד	dalet	d
ה	he	h
ו	vav	v or w
ז	zayin	z
ח	khet	ḥ
ט	tet	ṭ
י	yod	y
כ/ך	kaf	k
ל	lamed	l
מ/ם	mem	m
נ/ן	nun	n
ס	samek	s
ע	ayin	ʿ
פ/ף	pe	p; f (spirant)
צ/ץ	tsade	ṣ
ק	qof	q
ר	resh	r
שׂ	sin	ś
שׁ	shin	š
ת	tav	t; th (spirant)

RUTH

Sarah B. C. Derck

DEDICATION

for Charlotte and Lynnette,
mothers in life and faith

ACKNOWLEDGMENTS

Like many novice Hebrew students, I began by translating Ruth. It was such a joy that I changed my focus of study from the New Testament to the Old. What a pleasure to return to Ruth in this volume! I owe deep gratitude to the professors under whom I have delighted to study the word of God, especially Melanie Kierstead, Stephen Lennox, and Dwight Swanson. Seneca's maxim, "While we teach, we learn," has proven true. I have learned from my students over the years and want to mark the contribution to this current work of the members of my Ruth classes at Houghton College. We have reasoned together over the meaning of this tale. Any mistakes are my own.

The *hesed* of Ruth's story is the reigning voice in my parents' home, where Joseph and Charlotte Coleson taught me how to rightly divide the word of truth. My own *'iš gibbôr ḥayil*, Joshua, and our children, Joseph and Miriam, have held me up and filled my heart through the challenges of writing. May these and all who read this find refuge under Yahweh's wing.

BIBLIOGRAPHY

Bauckham, Richard. 1997. The Book of Ruth and the Possibility of a Feminist Canonical Hermeneutic. *Biblical Interpretation* 5:29-45.

Beattie, D. R. G. 1974a. Kethibh and Qere in Ruth IV 5. *Vetus Testamentum* 21:490-94.

_____. 1974b. The Book of Ruth as Evidence for Israelite Legal Practice. *Vetus Testamentum* 24:251-67.

_____. 1978. Ruth III. *Journal for the Study of the Old Testament* 5:39-48.

Berger, Yitzhak. 2009a. Ruth and the David-Bathsheba Story: Allusions and Contrasts. *Journal for the Study of the Old Testament* 33:433-52.

_____. 2009b. Ruth and Inner-Biblical Allusion: The Case of 1 Samuel 25. *Journal of Biblical Literature* 128:253-72.

Berman, Joshua. 2007. Ancient Hermeneutics and the Legal Structure of the Book of Ruth. *Zeitschrift für die alttestamentliche Wissenschaft* 119:22-38.

Bernstein, Moshe J. 1991. Two Multivalent Readings in the Ruth Narrative. *Journal for the Study of the Old Testament* 50:15-26.

Black, James. 1991. Ruth in the Dark: Folktale, Law and Creative Ambiguity in the Old Testament. *Literature and Theology* 5:20-36.

Bledstein, Adrien J. 1993. Female Companionships: If the Book of Ruth Were Written by a Woman . . . Pages 116-33 in *A Feminist Companion to Ruth*. Edited by Athalya Brenner. Vol. 3 in *The Feminist Companion to the Bible*. Sheffield: Sheffield Academic.

Bush, Frederic. 1996. *Ruth, Esther*. Word Biblical Commentary 9. Dallas: Word.

Campbell, Edward F. 1975. *Ruth*. Anchor Bible 7. New York: Doubleday.

Clarke, Adam. 1966. *Joshua to Esther*. Vol. 2 of *The Holy Bible Containing the Old and New Testaments with a Commentary and Critical Notes*. 8 vols. 1810-26. Repr. 8 vols. in 6, Nashville: Abingdon.

Coxon, Peter W. 1989. Was Naomi a Scold? A Response to Fewell and Gunn. *Journal for the Study of the Old Testament* 45:25-37.

Davies, Eryl W. 1981. Inheritance Rights and the Hebrew Levirate Marriage, Part 2. *Vetus Testamentum* 31:257-68.

Derck, Sarah B. C. 2011. Love in the Old Testament: Insights from Ruth and the Song of Solomon. Pages 241-56 in *The Bible Tells Me So: Reading the Bible as Scripture*. Edited by Richard P. Thompson and Thomas Jay Oord. Nampa, ID: SacraSage.

Dijk-Hemmes, Fokkelein van. 1993. Ruth: A Product of Women's Culture? Pages 134-39 in *A Feminist Companion to Ruth*. Edited by Athalya Brenner. Vol. 3 in *The Feminist Companion to the Bible*. Sheffield: Sheffield Academic.

Driesbach, Jason. 2012. *Ruth*. Cornerstone Biblical Commentary 3. Carol Stream, IL: Tyndale House.

Eskenazi, Tamara Cohn, and Tikva Frymer-Kensky. 2011. *Ruth*. JPS Bible Commentary. Philadelphia: Jewish Publication Society.

Fewell, Danna Nolan, and David M. Gunn. 1990. *Compromising Redemption: Relating Characters in the Book of Ruth*. Eugene, OR: Wipf and Stock.

Franke, John R., ed. 2005. *Joshua, Judges, Ruth, 1-2 Samuel*. Ancient Christian Commentary on the Scripture: Old Testament IV. Downers Grove, IL: InterVarsity.

Galpaz-Feller, Pnina. 2008. The Widow in the Bible and in Ancient Egypt. *Zeitschrift für die alttestamentliche Wissenschaft* 120:231-53.

Hubbard, Robert L. 1988. *The Book of Ruth*. New International Commentary on the Old Testament. Grand Rapids: Eerdmans.

_____. 1991. The *Go'el* in Ancient Israel: Theological Reflections on an Israelite Institution. *Bulletin for Biblical Research* 1:3-19.

James, Carolyn Custis. 2008. *The Gospel of Ruth: Loving God Enough to Break the Rules*. Grand Rapids: Zondervan.

Kapelrud, Arvid S. 1968. The Number Seven in Ugaritic Texts. *Vetus Testamentum* 18:494-99.

LaCocque, André. 2004. *A Continental Commentary: Ruth*. Minneapolis: Fortress.

Leggett, Donald A. 1974. *The Levirate and Goel Institutions in the Old Testament: With Special Attention to the Book of Ruth*. Cherry Hill, NJ: Mack.

Levine, Amy-Jill. 1992. Ruth. Pages 78-84 in The Women's Bible Commentary. Edited by Carol A. Newsom and Sharon H. Ringe. London: SPCK.

Linafelt, Tod. 1999. *Ruth*. Berit Olam: Studies in Hebrew Narrative and Poetry. Collegeville, MN: Liturgical Press.

Meyers, Carol. 1993. Returning Home: Ruth 1.8 and the Gendering of the Book of Ruth. Pages 85-114 in *A Feminist Companion to Ruth*. Vol. 3 in *The Feminist Companion to the Bible*. Edited by Athalya Brenner. Sheffield: Sheffield Academic.

_____. 1999. "Women of the Neighborhood" (Ruth 4.17): Informal Female Networks in Ancient Israel. Pages 110-27 in *Ruth and Esther*. A Feminist Companion to the Bible, Second Series. Edited by Athalya Brenner. Sheffield: Sheffield Academic Press.

Moore, Michael S. 1997. Two Textual Anomalies in Ruth. *Catholic Biblical Quarterly* 60:203-17.

_____. 2001. To King or Not to King: A Canonical-Historical Approach to Ruth. *Bulletin for Biblical Research* 11:27-41.

Nielsen, Kirsten. 1997. Ruth. Old Testament Library. Philadelphia: Westminster.

Parker, Simon B. 1976. The Marriage Blessing in Israelite and Ugaritic Literature. *Journal of Biblical Literature* 95:23-30.

Phipps, William E. 1992. *Assertive Biblical Women*. Contributions in Women's Studies 128. Westport, CT: Greenwood.

Sakenfeld, Katherine Doob. 1999. *Ruth*. Interpretation. Louisville, KY: John Knox.

Sasson, Jack M. 1978. The Issue of *Ge'ullāh* in Ruth. *Journal for the Study of the Old Testament* 5:52-64.

_____. 1979. *Ruth: A New Translation with a Philological Commentary and a Formalist-Folklorist Interpretation*. Johns Hopkins Near Eastern Studies. Baltimore: Johns Hopkins University Press.

Trible, Phyllis. 1978. *God and the Rhetoric of Sexuality*. Overtures to Biblical Theology 2. Philadelphia: Fortress.

_____. 1992. Ruth, Book of. Pages 842-47 in vol. 5 of *Anchor Bible Dictionary*. Edited by David Noel Freedman. 6 vols. New York: Doubleday.

Walton, John H., Victor H. Matthews, and Mark W. Chavalas. 2000. *The IVP Bible Background Commentary: Old Testament*. Downers Grove, IL: IVP Academic.

Wesley, John. 1975. *Explanatory Notes upon the Old Testament*. Salem, OH: Schmul.

TABLE OF SIDEBARS AND EXCURSUSES

INTRODUCTION

Ruth was an unusual woman, and her book is no less so. It joins Esther and Jonah as the only short stories in the Protestant Bible. Only Ruth and Job are non-Israelite protagonists; only Ruth and Esther feature women. In the OT, even Ruth's happy ending is rare.

This last feature can overwhelm the reading of Ruth. It is hailed as the Bible's great love story, following the typical plot of that genre: desperate woman finds salvation in the arms of noble man. However, a deeper look reveals Scripture's central themes in this complex little book: love of others and enemy, God's great welcome and provision, and redemption.

A. Composition of Ruth

The story's origins are debated. Lacking explicit attribution or strong internal evidence, we face a situation in which questions of authorship, dating, and purpose are integrally connected. What prompted the telling of this little story? Who had reason to write it, and when?

1. Authorship

Like most ancient Near Eastern (ANE) narratives, the book of Ruth is anonymous. As a short story, it is a strong candidate for transmission via oral tradition, the formalized storytelling of a society lacking universal literacy, until finally codified as sacred writing. Scholars have proposed many sources.

The rabbinic tradition favoring Samuel is untenable. Samuel died before David's rule was even established, let alone momentous enough to inspire veneration of his family history. Ruth is framed as looking into the distant past (1:1; 4:7), and Samuel came on the scene only three generations later, before such framing was needed for readers (Driesbach 2012, 497). Still, an author with royal connections is plausible; given the obvious literary skill, perhaps a royal scribe preserved the origin of Israel's greatest king. This tale is exceptional in its artistry and emotive effect, though, and does not read like an official chronicle.

The narrative quality of Ruth has convinced some it is the work of professional storytellers, a class well-known in the ANE (Campbell 1975, 18-23). Its sympathetic portrayal of Ruth and Naomi, and unusual focus on their share in an officially male concern (preservation of the male line), may suggest a female hand at work (Hubbard 1988, 24; Bledstein 1993; LaCocque 2004). Some have proposed a professional wise woman or community of such, preserving a tale of two women who embody wisdom (van Dijk-Hemmes 1993).

2. Dating

Ruth's dating occasions as much debate; the possibilities range from the tenth to fourth century BC. Commentators in recent decades argued over whether the linguistic features support a date in the early monarchy, exilic, or postexilic eras. The issues include unusual Hebrew vocabulary and syntax, the presence of Aramaisms, and an unusual series of disagreements between the gender of verbs/pronouns and their nouns (see Bush [1996, 18-30] for detailed treatment of the question). The linguistic data is complex, contested, and ultimately inconclusive for dating the book. Other considerations need attention, but turning mostly on Ruth's audience and purpose, they are treated in the next section.

3. Purpose

Good stories do many things. They entertain, but they can also instruct and exhort, and when preserved over generations, can shape a group's identity and values. What then does Ruth teach? How does it shape an audience, and what audience did the storyteller have in mind?

If Ruth belonged to the repertoire of professional storytellers, what use did it serve? Campbell suspects these traditions served, in part, "to interpret to the people of the countryside what was going on in high places"; in the case of Ruth, "interpreting the fact that the great King David had a Moabitess for an ancestress" (1975, 20). He suggests the tradition of Ruth became fixed ca. 873-849 BC during Jehoshaphat's reform (2 Chr 17—20), which was concerned with "right judgment and care for the unfortunates" (ibid., 28). Hubbard also favors a preexilic date, seeing in Ruth an attempt to legitimate David and his royal line as Yahweh's choice, demonstrating how divine providence brought him from this unlikely union, consistent with Yahweh's modus operandi in Israel's ancestral generations (1988).

Ruth twice breached Deuteronomy's prohibition against Israelites marrying foreigners (7:1-4) and possibly the ban on Moabites entering the worship assembly (23:3-6 [4-7 HB]). Her story challenges the Ezra-Nehemiah tradition, which demanded the divorce of all foreign wives after the return to Jerusalem, by appealing to the example of Ruth's own descendant, Solomon (Ezra 10; Neh 13:23-27). If Israel's greatest kings descended from a Moabite, maybe the divorce decree was unwarranted. Likewise, Ruth's story supports the perspective of the later Isaiah tradition, which promotes inclusion of non-Israelites in Yahweh's favor and purposes. She is a pointed illustration of how foreigners can be incorporated into Israel.

Is this complexity of biblical voices a goal of Ruth's creator(s) or only the result of canon history? Ruth enters a compelling argument for the validity of mixed marriages, against strident nationalism. However, it is unsettling to regard this finely crafted tale only as political polemic. As Hubbard argues, "The simple, elegant story has nothing disputatious about it" (1988, 35-36), and one is hesitant to claim one effect as "proof" of conversation with Ezra-Nehemiah and Second Isaiah.

Ruth functions in another important way: it provides a credible vision of women's lives in ancient Israel. It is women's literature, in the sense that "the text genuinely reflects women's experience and convincingly adopts a woman's perspective" (Bauckham 1997, 30). As such, Ruth challenges those who insist the Bible is exclusively androcentric. Its inclusion in the canon, Bauckham argues, provides internal critique of the canon's own male focus, and so invites readers to a more nuanced encounter with ancient Israel. In this and many more senses, Ruth is more subversive than polemical (Moore 2001, 35).

The ubiquity of law in this short story is intriguing, an effect intensified by social and historical distance. Its gleaning, redeemer, levirate marriage, and other legal motifs plead for Israel to adopt the spirit of the law: generosity and welcome. In this view it functions as an illustration of Israelite law at work (Bauckham 1997, 34; Berman 2007).

Other purposes for Ruth draw on its major themes. These might be called the theological purposes: an exhortation to *ḥesed* love, an illustration of redemption, and a call to trust Yahweh's providential provision. These will be explored below and in the commentary.

We noted above that a good story does many things at once, and Ruth is a good story. With Trible we conclude that to narrow its scope to one particular purpose, theme, or even era is to miss the point entirely:

> Many levels of meaning intertwine—social, political, religious, and aesthetic. A representative list includes: to maintain Israelite customs, inculcate legal duties, integrate law and daily life, legitimate David and his monarchy, tell a good story, encourage proselytes, promote universalism over against

nationalism, elevate the virtues of friendship and loyalty, glorify family ties, preserve women's traditions, and witness to God at work. (1992, 846)

B. Structure and Features

Ruth is an ideal of its type: a short story finely crafted, rewarding a reader with endless discoveries. Each chapter displays a clear pattern: journey-dialogue-home, with each section developed to varying degrees from chapter to chapter. The genealogy in 4:18-22 is an epilogue to the action: not narrative, but not at all superfluous. Each chapter opens with someone in need, prompting a journey:

1: Elimelek's family needed food; they went to Moab.

2: Ruth and Naomi needed food; Ruth went to the fields.

3: Ruth needed a home; Naomi sent her to the threshing floor.

4: Naomi needed a redeemer; Boaz went to the city gate.

Each chapter advances the quest through extensive dialogue (fifty-five of eighty-five verses) and ends in a conversation with Naomi at home.

In fact, the story is told from Naomi's point of view. Her need prompts the main action in every chapter, eliciting extravagant effort from Ruth and/or Boaz on Naomi's behalf. Each chapter closes by returning the attention to Naomi, in a chiasm of conversations between her and:

A: the women of Bethlehem (1:19-22)

B: Ruth (2:18-23)

B^1: Ruth (3:16-18)

A^1: the women of Bethlehem (4:13-17)

The final solution, Obed, landed in Naomi's lap, not Ruth's. Even his celebration and naming revolved around Naomi, not Ruth.

Why is the book named for Ruth, then? In a clever tactic, the author's distribution of action centers Ruth: she is the subject of twice as many verbs as either Naomi or Boaz. Naomi and Boaz never met or spoke together in the text; Ruth was their go-between, which keeps her central (Campbell 1975, 18). Ruth was the chief vehicle of Naomi's redemption, so tradition has named it her story, as "the means by which the problem in the story is resolved" (Bush 1996, 49).

The author's skill extends to vocabulary. A careful reader of the Hebrew text will observe a series of seventeen words, used only two to four times and always at a distance from one another. Campbell calls them "long-range word-plays" and notices eleven (to which we add six) at key plot points that "constitute brackets, . . . from difficulty to be overcome to resolution of that difficulty" (1975, 13-14). They are labelled LRWP (long-range wordplay) in the commentary. Another set of inclusios uses chiasm: six *pairs* of words repeated, always in reverse order the second time (ibid., 14).

Ambiguity and double entendre are also favorite techniques, "the conscious, intentional employment of multiple levels of meaning" at the same time (Bernstein 1991, 16). Examples include single words such as *dābaq* ("cling" [1:14]) and *kānāp* ("wing," "extremity" [3:9]) and whole statements such as Naomi's blessing in 2:20 (is "he" Yahweh or Boaz?). All this adds up to a story shaped by marvelous artistry.

C. Ruth in the Canon

The Christian Bible places Ruth in the historical books, a chronological account of Israel in the land, from settlement/conquest to exile/return. Ruth opens with the chilling phrase, "In the days when the judges ruled" (1:1). The story of those judges precedes Ruth, and it did not end well. Israel claimed a king would stem the rising tide of violent chaos and civil war among the tribes. First Samuel answers that need by introducing the kingmaker, Samuel; by the end of 2 Samuel, the Davidic monarchy was firmly established.

Sandwiched between anarchy and monarchy is this rich tale of David's great-grandmother. Ruth provides a break in the national action, a chance to revel in Yahweh's astounding provision, to linger in a little village where everyone does what is right for once. Of course, it also foreshadows the potential answer to Israel's chaos: a king.

In the Hebrew canon, Ruth follows Proverbs in the Writings, where a fascinating textual thread emerges. Proverbs ends with that lofty poem in praise of *ēšet hayil*, *a woman of valor* (31:10). This is the rare feminine counterpart of the common phrase *'îš gibbôr hayil*, *a mighty man of valor*, and refers to a person of strength and standing. The *ēšet hayil* occurs only in Prov 12:4, 31:10, and Ruth 3:11, as Boaz accepts Ruth's marriage proposal. The Hebrew order strikes a rich chord, asking rhetorically at the end of Proverbs, "Who can find an *ēšet hayil*?" and answering with Ruth, an *ēšet hayil* in the flesh.

Ruth also leads the Megillot, "scrolls," a section of short books read aloud on Jewish holy days. Ruth belongs to Shavuot (Feast of Weeks, or Pentecost), a late spring festival celebrating the wheat harvest (Exod 34:22). It completed the counting of seven weeks from Passover in Lev 23:15-21, a passage followed directly by the instruction to leave harvest gleanings for people exactly like Ruth and Naomi: "the poor and the foreigner residing among you" (23:22). This instruction is central to the plot of Ruth. In Jewish tradition, our little love story turns out to be a profound liturgical text.

Ruth reverberates throughout the canon, from Genesis, to David, to Matthew, where the Gospel writer lists Ruth with Tamar, Rahab, Bathsheba, and Mary—all five sexually suspect from the viewpoint of traditional morality—in a genealogy of Jesus, the eternal fulfillment of the Davidic covenant. Looking backward in the timeline of Israel, allusions in Ruth to Lot's daughters (Gen 19) and Tamar (Gen 38) have long been argued on the basis of a shared plot point: in all three accounts, a woman seduced an older relative to secure the family lineage. Lot's daughters are further linked to Ruth: their tale is the biblical origin story of Ruth's own nation, Moab. Tamar's story shares with Ruth the levirate marriage motif, and the Bethlehem townsfolk invoked Tamar as they blessed Boaz (Ruth 4:12).

Looking forward, connections emerge between this story and David's life. Ruth hovers in the background of 1 Sam 25 when readers meet David's wife Abigail (Berger 2009b). Both women literally bowed down to the ground before a powerful man; both asked for more than was due them, saving their families. In each case, their boldness elicited favor and admiration from the man, and both married the men of whom they asked so much.

Not every comparison between Ruth and David is favorable. Berger reads Ruth and Boaz as foils to the ignominy of their progeny's treachery with Bathsheba in 2 Sam 11 (2009a). The contrasts are suggestive:

a. Ruth and Boaz were selfless and righteous; David fed his laziness and lust, resorting to murder to cover his tracks in arrogance.

b. Ruth and Boaz's union brought life; David and Bathsheba's brought death.

c. Ruth and Boaz acted autonomously, partnering together in a "blessed alliance" for Naomi's redemption (James 2008, 31); David wielded absolute power, making Bathsheba, Uriah, and Joab party to or victims of his sin.

Naomi's grief and redemption resonate with other important texts. She was bitter but expressed her anguish in the same words and tone as the lament psalms (44:9-12 [10-13 HB]; 60:1 [3 HB]; 74:1) or wisdom literature (Job 7:11-21). Indeed, her words could have come directly from the lips of the most famous sufferer in the world: Job. Both lost everything; both saw their suffering as from Yahweh's hand; both experienced surprising redemption and abundant restoration (Ruth 4:14-15; Job 42:10-17). These canonical connections prevent readers from dismissing Naomi as a bitter whiner; instead she provides an important female portrait of suffering and redemption in the larger biblical context.

D. How Should We Read Ruth?

Given its beguiling complexity, how shall we approach Ruth? Trible's list above is instructive; the church would benefit from attention to every item. Unfortunately, in recent decades, Ruth has been treated in two rather divergent ways. To oversimplify, the academy studies its technique, while the church dismisses it. A profusion of literary and feminist scholars has expanded the literature on Ruth vastly since the 1960s, while churches use it only as a source for sermons on marriage or the lineage of Christ, or sequester it in women's Bible study groups.

As noted above, Ruth *is* women's literature, a story about women told from their viewpoint. This dare not prevent sustained, public, and corporate attention to such a complex part of Scripture, however. Both men and women need tales of strong and triumphant women in Scripture, for myriad reasons.

Androcentric priorities in the church are not the only danger to Ruth's inclusion in the functional canons of most congregations. The current disparity between scholarly and ecclesial attention to Ruth is due also to its form. Even when it comes to the Bible, short stories get short shrift, considered lightweight literature. Who dares to suggest Ruth is on a theological par with Genesis?

A remedy lies in recovering the ability to engage a finely wrought tale, which is dependent on at least two things. First, readers must suspend their familiarity with the outcome; everyone knows Boaz rescued Ruth and they lived happily ever after. But when that knowledge is suspended, the reader instead discovers *Ruth* was the rescuer, recruiting Boaz in her rescue of Naomi. This engagement also requires a prolonged gaze and attention to detail. There is plenty of detail to notice, but much depends on access to the Hebrew text, study of the literary form, and exploration of the historical setting; hence this volume.

E. Theological Themes

1. *Ḥesed*

The love incumbent upon Israelites is best described by the Hebrew word *ḥesed*. Difficult to translate because it entails so much, *ḥesed* is shown in every chapter of Ruth. It is extravagant faithfulness on the beloved's behalf, loyalty inspired but not required by relationship. It is love performed; in Hebrew, one "does *ḥesed*."

In Ruth, *ḥesed* describes Ruth and Orpah's posture to their family even before the men died (1:8, translated as "kindness" throughout). It is Boaz and God's provision and protection in the harvest (2:20). It is Ruth coming to Bethlehem, laboring in the fields, and visiting the threshing floor, all for Naomi (3:10).

Ruth calls readers to this *ḥesed*, valiant love in action, on behalf of those who need it most. The most vulnerable people in the story, Naomi and Ruth, were the primary recipients of *ḥesed*. The people of Israel were meant to be the conduit of God's *ḥesed* to all creation. In Ruth, everyone eventually got it right, able to participate in God's redemption of Naomi because they demonstrated *ḥesed*.

2. Providential Provision

Though invoked in blessings and oaths throughout Ruth, God acted directly only once in the whole book, giving conception in 4:13. This illustrates a key theme: God usually acts behind the scenes, rather than through explicit intervention. Thus, the widows returned at the opportune moment, "as the barley harvest was beginning" (1:22). Ruth would have gleaned "behind anyone" (2:2), but "as it turned out" she ended up in a family field (v 3); and "Just then Boaz arrived" (v 4); she only learned he was a relative when she returned to Naomi (v 20). In settling the legal arrangements, Boaz arrived at the gate "just as the guardian-redeemer he had mentioned came along" (4:1). All was apparently coincidental, but the reader knows better. The effect is to highlight the skill and sophistication with which God lavishes abundant provision when willing human partners are at hand.

3. Redemption

God's providential provision united with Ruth and Boaz's *ḥesed* to accomplish Naomi's redemption, filling her emptiness, renewing her life. Redemption is an unmistakable theme. The Hebrew root *gāʾal*, "to redeem," occurs twenty-three times in eighty-five verses, always with Naomi as the understood object.

Lest we jump right to the spiritual sense of *gāʾal*, we note its actual usage in Ruth is uniformly pragmatic. The needs of this aged widow were concrete, physical, and urgent, and the emptiness she suffered was material. Naomi's redeemers, both divine and human, cooperated to save her life first, with only one possible mention of her soul. Food, security, and a permanent home were the responsibilities her redeemers assumed willingly and beyond what was required. Only once these were obtained, and not until the end of the story, was *gāʾal* used in a way that could rise above the realm of practical provision (4:14).

This point is vital precisely because of the nature of *hesed* described above. Perhaps especially in a Wesleyan understanding, love is always embodied by action on behalf of the other, in the meeting of human need. Redemption cannot be only spiritual, because God has always employed embodied humans in providential ways to lavish redeeming *hesed* upon the world. In Ruth, *hesed*, providence, and redemption coalesce into one and the same, both means and end.

COMMENTARY

I. HOW ELIMELEK'S PLAN WORKED OUT: RUTH 1:1-22

BEHIND THE TEXT

Despite its reputation as a peaceful country tale, Ruth is set in an era of upheaval and increasing violence in Israel. After the partial conquest and settlement of the promised land under Joshua, the twelve tribes dispersed to their territories, governed by tribal leaders and judges.

According to Judges, this system was effective as long as a righteous judge was in office. When he or she died, the tribes fell into idolatry and violence, conquered by enemies until the next judge liberated them. By the era's end, the tribes were fighting among themselves. Judges 17—21 describes the situation in chilling detail.

The effect of this turbulent setting cannot be overstated. It factors into the desperation that drove an Israelite family into Moab. It accounts for the potential of a foreign widow facing harassment or violence in a Bethlehem field. It turns Ruth's trip to the threshing floor into one fraught with risk. It even suggests how Boaz was able to arrange things in Ruth and Naomi's favor by conflating and extending two separate legal customs; in an era of centralized rule, negotiations may not have gone so smoothly.

Moab, located directly east of the Judean hills, beyond the Dead Sea, is the setting of the main story of ch 1. Israel's contact with their kin in Moab was fraught and often sexually charged; Moabites were suspect, if not always enemies. Moab was born of incest (Gen 19:30-38). At Shittim, Israel's men slept with Moab's women, who led them into idolatry; 24,000 died as punishment (Num 25). Moab controlled Israel for eighteen years (Judg 3:12-30). A Moabite wife was part of Solomon's downfall; he built a temple to her god and worshipped with her (1 Kgs 11). In one battle between the nations, Moab's king sacrificed his son on the city wall (2 Kgs 3). The prophets spoke judgment against Moab (Jer 48; Amos 2:1-3). Moabites were among the wives divorced in Ezra-Nehemiah. Given all this, a Moabite *sojourn* by an Israelite family was most unsuitable, let alone a Moabite *heroine*.

Bethlehem, a village in Judah, is where the story of Ruth 1 begins and ends. Bethlehem is also the setting of the remainder of the story of Ruth. It is six miles south of Jerusalem (in that era, a non-Israelite town called Jebus), in the Judean hill country with all its bounty, on the edge of the rain boundary. The town overlooked almost fifteen miles of arid wilderness east to the Dead Sea, with Moab on the other side. Surveys of the site indicate prehistoric occupation. It has long been home to farmers and shepherds, and profited from proximity to major inland trade routes. Though called a "town" in the NIV, Bethlehem fits Meyers' description of Iron Age settlements in Israel: "Most had no public buildings and were little more than fortified villages . . . inhabited by farming families (peasant farmers) that worked the surrounding lands" (1999, 116).

Bethlehem was a significant location in Israelite tradition as the environs of Rachel's tomb (Gen 35:19; 48:7). Two Bethlehemites figured in the breakdown of Israel described at the end of Judges: the Levite priest for hire who fell in with rogue Danites (chs 17—18), and an unnamed concubine, whose horrific gang rape and dismemberment launched a civil war (chs 19—21). Bethlehem later became known as the hometown of David and finally the birthplace of Jesus, but romantic notions of a sleepy little hamlet derive more from modern, Western Christmas traditions than from biblical texts.

IN THE TEXT

A. Loss after Loss (1:1-5)

■ **1** **In the days when the judges ruled** is a menacing first line. The Hebrew describes the judges judging (*špṭ*) rather than ruling (*mlk*). Judges in Israel were associated with legal disputes and military leadership, not rule. The loosely organized tribal federation of the thirteenth to eleventh century BC is the proper backdrop of this story. This vague time indicator is a feature of Ruth's narrative artistry, compared to the historical concerns of Samuel, Kings, and Chronicles. It indicates the storyteller was looking back to a time that no longer was, like the English "once upon a time," but more ominous.

A famine in the land is the second dire tone struck by the opening verse. An already dark time was made worse by famine. This is terrible irony: the land of milk and honey fell into famine, engulfing even **Bethlehem (*house of bread* in Hebrew)**. Ancients always viewed such disasters as the work of divine hands. Early Jewish interpreters saw this famine as the result of the tribes' sin. Later exegetes tried to find cause in the era's history; Clarke, for instance, says of this phrase, "Probably occasioned by the depredations of the Philistines, Ammonites, &c., carrying off the corn as soon as it was ripe, or destroying it on the field" (1966, 192).

This raises a question: exactly what **land** was suffering famine? All of Israel, only the southern tribes, or was this just a local phenomenon? Other biblical texts do not mention famine in Israel during this era, but most commentators suggest periodic droughts were likely in this region straddling the fertile hill country and the arid desert. The vagueness of **land** also serves the stylized opening, widening its appeal beyond those concerned with the tribe of Judah.

The first installment of our journey-dialogue-home pattern unfolds (→ Introduction): due to the famine, **a man from Bethlehem in Judah** took his family to live **in the country of Moab**. Though the NIV translates simply **Moab** from v 2 on, the Hebrew throughout is *śĕdēh / śĕdê mô'āb,* **the field(s) of Moab.** This phrase is an idiom signifying a nation or its territory. However, the literal translation is preferable in Ruth, as it magnifies for English readers the theme of famine/fulfillment, and maintains continuity with the many other occurrences of *field*. Ruth's labor in the *field* (seven times in ch 2) and Naomi's sale of the *field* (ch 4, twice), together with the *fields of Moab* (seven times), remind us this is an agricultural tale.

The first thing we know about this man is his hometown. **Bethlehem in Judah** distinguishes it from Bethlehem of Zebulun (Josh 19:15) and marks the characters' tribal connection. If we have suspended our familiarity with the tale, and are reading canonically, this part of the verse rings a final, ominous bell. According to the previous book, Bethlehemites who left home found only trouble (the Levite, Judg 17—18) or violation and death (the concubine, Judg 19).

It is enough for now to absorb the import of this plan. A hungry family from the House of Bread left behind their barren portion of the promised land **to live for a while** in Moab. The verb *gûr* leaves open the possibility of return, denoting a stay of indefinite duration rather than permanent emigration. Such sojourns figured in the ancestral narratives: during earlier Canaanite famines, Abram went to Egypt for food, as did Jacob's sons (Gen 12, 42—43), and Isaac to Philistia (Gen 26).

However, each of those instances predated Israel's settlement of the land. After several generations tending their own plot, the hopelessness driving this family to Moab must have been acute. The provisions in Israelite law for the care of desperate relatives were apparently insufficient (maybe even unavailable) to this family. Maybe the devastation was so widespread, no one in the clan was able to help. A horrible situation has been set up in just one verse: tumult and famine led a family of refugees to seek sustenance in a hostile land.

Names in Ruth

As etymological studies have shown, the six personal names in Ruth are plausible, and some occur in extrabiblical sources (Hubbard 1988, 88-90; Campbell 1975, 52-56). This has led some to dismiss their meanings as immaterial, apart from Naomi, which is an object of overt wordplay (1:20-21). Bush says the etymologies "are of no relevance for the meaning of our story" (1996, 64).

While the names were not symbolic inventions, a heavy-handed attempt to forecast the fate of each person, we will not ignore their subtle effects on the Hebrew reader. Given the storyteller's striking fondness for wordplay generally, and ambiguity in particular, the names read as part of that technique. Several of the meanings are uncertain, so we do not assert more than can be supported by the data, but neither must we relinquish connotations where they are sound.

■ **2 Elimelek** means "my God is king" (combining the Heb. ʾel, "God," and melek, "king"), ironic for a man who sought refuge in another god's land. **Naomi** comes from nāʿēm and means either "pleasant one" or "my pleasant one." This name conjures tragic irony even before Naomi says so out loud (vv 20-21). The pleasant one is already living a life decidedly unpleasant when we meet her: running from famine to Moab.

The sons' names are less certain in meaning. **Mahlon** likely derives from mḥl, but as this root occurs only in other personal names, its meaning cannot be established conclusively. The common proposal that it is from ḥlh ("to be weak") is enticing given Mahlon's fate, but dubious. **Kilion** is as likely to mean "little vessel" (from kĕlî) as "completeness" or "annihilation," both from kālâ. Such uncertainty is grounds for caution against asserting *intentional symbolism* for each name, but as Moore has argued in reference to other texts in Ruth, the connotations aroused by words that sound alike is a characteristic technique in Ruth (1997, 237-43).

Ephrath was the name of Caleb's second wife, whose descendants settled Bethlehem (1 Chr 2:19; 4:4), and is sometimes used as another name for the town (Gen 35:19). **Ephrathites from Bethlehem** is not mere repetition, then. Hubbard posits that here **Ephrathites** denotes the village's founding clan, and high social standing (1988, 90-91). A shocking decline in fortunes, indeed: members of the village's oldest family fled starvation. The opening action is now summarized: **they went to Moab and lived there.**

■ **3** Moab was no guarantee against trouble, though, and disaster struck again: **Elimelek, Naomi's husband, died.** This statement is notable for two reasons. First, it is harshly succinct, with no detail about the circumstances of death. We are not told how he died, how long after their move, or how the family coped. Second, the phrase identifies the husband by relationship to his wife. More usual would be to read, "Elimelek died, and his wife, Naomi, was left." The order places Naomi in primary position, Elimelek in secondary. Already the spotlight is moving away from the opening setting toward the main action and characters.

36

Elimelek fades even further into the background with **she was left with her two sons**. Not "his sons," as expected in an androcentric culture, and as they were called in vv 1-2; Naomi was now a single mother, widowed in a foreign country. In contexts of death, the verb *šā'ēr* ("to be left behind") indicates bereavement. It stuns with its starkness, but the desolation was not over; the verb occurs again in v 5.

■ **4** We do not know the sons' ages when they left Judah, but they grew old enough to marry. **They married Moabite women** is literally, *they took for themselves Moabite women*; the verb *nāśā'* means "to lift," "to carry," "to take (as wife)." In the context of marriage, the verb usually described dubious unions: when the marriage was to a foreigner (Ezra 9:2) or forced (Judg 21:23) or the number of wives was excessive (2 Chr 11:21). The verb *nāśā'* figures in another idiom in this chapter; in Ruth 1:9 and 14, *nāśā'* denotes the lifting up of one's voice (NIV: "wept aloud"). The wives *taken* soon *take up* their own voices in lament. This is our first long-range wordplay (LRWP), stretching over the next chapter. The verb *nāśā'* in ch 1 signals negative developments (marriage to Moabites, then death), but its last use is a step toward redemption ("she carried barley" [NIV] or "she took grain" [CEV, ESV, etc.] in 2:18).

For Naomi, these marriages marked another sorrow: her sons broke the Israelite law against foreign wives. Some commentators have seen in these marriages the cause of the coming misfortune. For example, John Wesley comments, "Either these were Proselytes when they married them, or they sinned in marrying them, and therefore were punished with short life, and want of issue" (1975, 880).

This is a possible reading, though it is hard to see how Naomi could have prevented it. A widow in a foreign land, she lacked the wherewithal to get brides from Judah (see Gen 24; 28). She may also have lacked authority to prevent her sons from marrying whomever they wanted or to impose obedience to Israelite law in Moab. It is worth noting that the text makes no explicit connection between the sons' breach of law and their deaths. Instead, these foreign wives are only ever praised for their actions (Ruth 1:8; 2:11-12; 3:10-11; 4:15).

Orpah is introduced first, then **Ruth**; the order is odd on two counts. We might expect the main character first, but in a clever twist, Orpah disappears by chapter's end, never to be mentioned again. Second, we are not told who married whom. The fact that Ruth was Mahlon's widow is revealed only at the end of the story (see 4:10). In ch 1, the women are introduced in reverse order, forming a double chiasm with their husbands, the first of seven word pairs appearing in chiasm (Campbell 1975, 14):

(A) Mahlon and (B) Kilion (v 2)

(B¹) Orpah and (A¹) Ruth (v 4)

(A) Mahlon and (B) Kilion (v 5)

The marriages are deliberately vague. They simply did not matter except to set up the main action of the story—Naomi's destitution and redemption via her daughter-in-law Ruth—and ended in the next verse anyway.

37

Tradition relates **Orpah** to the Hebrew ʿôrep, meaning "back of neck" and by extension "obstinate" (a rabbinic pun invented to vilify Orpah's choice to turn back). Without this proposed symbolism, however, there is no cause for thinking so poorly of Orpah, as we shall see. Just as plausible is that Orpah, like the others, was a personal name from the era. **Ruth** most likely comes from the Hebrew root rwh (meaning "to be satiated," "drink one's fill"), a pleasing play on the book's theme of emptiness/filling. The common claim that it means "friendship" (from the Heb. root rʿh) is suspect (Sasson 1979, 20-21).

The final clause in the verse, literally *and they lived there about ten years,* raises questions: who lived there that long? Elimelek's whole family? Naomi and sons? Naomi, sons, and their new wives? If this is a summary statement, meaning **ten years** composed the total length of this family's sojourn in Moab, it was an odd choice to summarize before the sons' deaths in the next verse.

More convincing is that **ten years** indicates the length of the marriages—the immediate topic of the sentence, after all—before the wives became widows. Ancient hearers would have realized the import of this statement immediately: ten years of marriage with no children was a tragedy in the ancient world. Later rabbinic law even made ten years' sterility grounds for divorce (Sasson 1979, 21).

■ **5** The final blow was the death of Naomi's sons, and by the end of this verse we sit in mourning with her, **left without her two sons and her husband**. This phrase offers the second instance of chiastic word pairs. The male nouns appear here in reverse order from v 3, her husband "died . . . left with her two sons."

However, in a sophisticated twist, rather than **sons** (bēn, as in vv 1-3), the Hebrew here is **boys** (yeled). This is unusual: yeled was not used of full-grown, married men. With one word, we are invited into the keening grief of a mourning mother who had survived so much already (famine, exile, widowhood, barren children), only to bury her boys. In yeled we also find another LRWP. Naomi lost her **boys** in this verse; in 4:16 she regained a **boy** when Obed was put in her arms.

The final clause lacks names. *The woman* (the NIV inserts **Naomi**) strips Naomi of all her identifying relationships. Now dead, the **sons and her husband** are not named again in the chapter. Orpah and Ruth are not even mentioned here, let alone named, reducing them from co-mourners to shadowy burdens. In only five verses, the spotlight has shifted permanently from Elimelek, the proffered protagonist, to his desperate widow. Elimelek's plan and the ensuing journey to Moab did not work out; Moab was not kind to them, and it was up to his widow to make a plan and journey of her own. It is now resolutely a woman's tale.

B. Three Widows, Then Two (1:6-18)

Widows in Israel

Widows were vulnerable in ancient Near Eastern (ANE) societies. Caring for widows was one of the cardinal duties of Yahweh's people (Exod 22:22-24 [21-23 HB]; Deut 10:19), but a widow's fate depended on her situation. For a lucky few, bride-price (money given by the groom, set aside for the bride's use) or dowry (the bride's portion of her family inheritance, given at the marriage) was enough for independence. A childless widow could return to her parents to remarry (Gen 38:11; Lev 22:13) or remain in her husband's household by marrying his brother and bearing heirs (Deut 25:5-10, discussed below). A widow with young children could expect support from her husband's family, as the children belonged to his lineage, but this did not always materialize (2 Kgs 4:1-7). A widow with grown children could expect to live with them.

■ **6-7** The first mention of **Yahweh** (LORD) occurs here in juxtaposition to **Moab**. This would have caught the ancient ear; Moab was the domain of the god Chemosh. In *his* territory, an Israelite refugee heard rumors of *Yahweh*, but the divine intervention was complete by the time Naomi caught wind of it.

Yahweh's provision of **food** (lit. *bread*) is the first good news in the story. As the ancients attributed famine to divine retribution, so its reversal was divine favor. Yahweh had **come to the aid of** [*pāqad* in Hebrew means "to visit, attend, or remember"] **his people** again and brought the famine to an end. This verb is used in the OT to describe Yahweh's visitation to bring judgment or punishment (Jer 6:15), salvation (Job 10:12), and once, even pregnancy (Gen 21:1). Bread had returned to the House of Bread (Bethlehem), and Naomi was quick to respond.

That both Naomi's **daughters-in-law prepared to return** with her is interesting. Fewell and Gunn suggest Orpah and Ruth were following a custom of accompanying a departing traveler to the edge of town (1990, 27, 31); this is unlikely given their genuine resistance to leaving later (Ruth 1:10-14). Hubbard suggests Naomi let them come away so they did not urge her to stay in Moab, always intending to send them back (1988, 102). In any case, Naomi was content with their company for the moment. The tone of the upcoming dialogue hints at a simple reason: there was a sincere, though laden, bond between these women.

This is the first of fifteen occurrences of the word **return** (*šûb*) in the Hebrew text of Ruth. It is a major motif of ch 1, appearing twelve times, escalating the urgency of Naomi's plight. If she could just get back home, **return** where she belonged, there might be rest from all the tragedy, if not hope of restoration.

We are not told where in Moab **she had been living** (v 7), because it does not matter to the story. Notably, Orpah and Ruth are still not named, highlighting Naomi's emotional limbo: she had daughters-in-law but no longer the sons who brought them into her life. Narratively they have functioned only as props so far, not autonomous agents in the action, which remains focused firmly on Naomi's plight.

■ **8** Here begins the first of the extensive dialogues by which the action is advanced in each chapter. After setting out together, Naomi tried to send Orpah and Ruth back. Whenever she decided on this, her motives deserve consideration. Their company granted safety on her journey; it was one hundred miles on foot through treacherous landscape in a tumultuous time, likely to take a week. Once in Israel, two young women could lend strength and energy to her survival. On the other hand, taking them meant an ethical responsibility for their livelihood, a real burden for a destitute widow. It was also thorny to bring home evidence of her sons' illicit marriages. There is no accounting for the complex emotions tormenting Naomi, but we need not infer any deception or hard feelings between the women.

Naomi's opening words are the first speech in the book, entreating them, **Go! Return!** (Go back), each to her **mother's home**. This rare phrase (Gen 24:28; Song 3:4; 8:2) is a variation on the more common "house of the father" (*bêt ʾāb*), referring to the household unit, the family of origin, not a literal building. It does several things here. First, it distinguishes between mother and mother-in-law, freeing them to embrace loyalty to their own families again after ten years in her household. Second, it conjures the possibility of future marriages. The other uses of **mother's home** revolve around love and marriage, suggesting the mother's dwelling as the emotive realm for such arrangements (Hubbard 1988, 102). This hope becomes explicit in the next verse. Third, it reminds the reader Ruth is unabashedly a woman's text (Meyers 1993).

Naomi continued her plea with a blessing that witnessed to both women's **kindness**, a rather tame translation of *hesed*, which she called down upon them from Yahweh. *Ḥesed* is fiercely loyal love based on, but not demanded by, relationship (→ Introduction). This is a major clue to the reader that Orpah was no less noble than Ruth. Naomi freely acknowledged the *hesed* both women gave their **dead husbands** and herself, over ten years of life as a family. The NIV inserts **husbands**, where the Hebrew says only *the dead and me*, a stark statement reflecting the isolation of grief. Having lost all hope of meaningful life, Naomi aligned herself with the dead.

At the end of the next chapter, Naomi attributed to Yahweh this same *hesed* toward her and her dead menfolk (2:20). By her own account, then, the Moabite widows paralleled the Israelite God in their *hesed*. With a third occurrence, *hesed* forms our next LRWP; responding to Ruth's marriage proposal, Boaz praises her *hesed* (3:10). This frames *hesed* as the solution to Naomi's problems, pairing Ruth and Yahweh as partners in redemption.

■ **9-10** After a general blessing of *hesed*, Naomi continued with the specific hope that Yahweh would provide her daughters-in-law **rest** in new marriages (1:9). The Hebrew *měnûḥah* in this context means security, safety, knowing one is provided for. It forms our next LRWP: here it is a general hope for their future, but in 3:1, Naomi takes it upon herself to find *měnûḥah* for Ruth by getting her a husband in Bethlehem.

At this point, though, the best chance for a safe future lay in Moab. Seeking remarriage through their own families' efforts was easily the wisest choice for Orpah and Ruth. Ten years of marriage with no children was a liability on the marriage market, but a savvy matchmaker could argue the fault lay with the grooms: two brothers, neither of whom begat heirs, suggests the women were not to blame. Such a matchmaker was easier to find in Moab, their native society. In Israel, foreign brides were not only suspect, but forbidden.

Naomi's advice was wise and her tone can be read as caring, even if desperate. She dared to bless them in Yahweh's name, even though she fully expected that future to unfold in the land of Chemosh. She ended her speech with a farewell kiss, **and they wept aloud** (lit. *they lifted up their voices and wept*; → 1:4 above). This can refer to the younger women's response, or to all three weeping together; in any case, they shared real affection for one another.

Following cultural wisdom, Ruth and Orpah should have turned back, while Naomi carried on alone. Instead, they used Naomi's own words, **go back** (*šûb*, return), insisting their home was with her and her people. It was not actually a return for them, but in this declaration, they expressed solidarity with Naomi.

Levirate Marriage (Deut 25:5-10)

The levirate law compelled the brother of a deceased, childless man to marry his widowed sister-in-law, to conceive an heir for the dead brother. Though part of the legal background of Ruth's story, no one in Ruth was required to fulfill the role of levir, brother-in-law. The specific case law in Deut 25 was predicated on living brothers residing together (Davies 1981), and crucially, they must be sons of the same father, not mother (Sasson 1979, 24). Further, the expectation upon the levir was never absolute, as is sometimes portrayed; the law itself provided a way out for unwilling brothers.

No levir was available to Ruth and Orpah, as both Elimelek's sons were dead. Even if Naomi remarried and miraculously bore sons, they would not be eligible levirs, being of her new husband's blood, not Elimelek's. In the only other story related to the levir, it was not Er's brother, but his father, Judah, whom Tamar tricked into the role of levir, and the sons she bore were accounted as Judah's children, not Er's, though Judah himself still had a living son (Gen 38; 46:12).

Neither situation in Scripture where the responsibilities of a levir are performed fits the relationship specified in Deut 25. In neither are the resulting children recorded as heirs of the deceased man, but of their physical fathers. Simply put, no one was required to preserve Elimelek's line. Boaz claimed the role of levir as part of his shrewd negotiations in Ruth 4, but no one in the story expected this law to save these widows. In fact, this was part of the tragedy: there was no way to save Elimelek's line.

■ **11** Deliberations between the women were not over, however; Naomi pled with them again, **Return home**. Instead of the narrator's legal term (*kallâ*, "daughter-in-law"), she used the more affectionate **my daughters** (*bĕnōtâ*, three times in vv 11-13). Claiming their family bond as grounds for a hearing, she launched into a series of rhetorical questions intended to highlight the absurdity of casting their lots with her.

Her argument employed a variation on the complex theme of levirate marriage (→ "Levirate Marriage" excursus, above). By so lampooning the one legal provision even tangentially related to their situation, Naomi's rhetoric intended to convince Orpah and Ruth they had no future with her. In the first place, the levirate law did not apply to their situation. In the second place, even if it had, Naomi was too old to conceive. Her second rhetorical question, **Am I going to have any more sons . . . ?**, is vivid in Hebrew, *Do I still have sons in my womb?*

■ **12** Naomi repeated her plea a third time, reversing her original *Go! Return!* (v 8), with, *Return! Go!* (**Return home**; our third chiasm). In case the rhetorical question in the previous verse was not clear, Naomi made her reproductive status explicit. **I am too old to have another husband** in Hebrew is *I am too old for belonging to a man* and conveys the idea that she is too old for intercourse or conception (as in Hos 3:3; see Sasson 1979, 25).

■ **13** Naomi's rhetorical questions continued: **Would you remain unmarried for them?** Even if she could bear more sons, who agreed to marry Orpah and Ruth, it was ludicrous for young women in their prime to wait so long for the pleasures of the marital bed. Using again the same phrase meaning intercourse, the Hebrew is forthright about the self-denial involved: *Would you shut yourself off, to not belong to a man?* The verb ʿāgan ("to shut oneself off") occurs only here in the OT. Naomi concluded by answering these questions herself: **No, my daughters**. Her hope for their potential remarriages involved the security and pleasures of marriage, not heirs for Elimelek.

After pleading for Orpah and Ruth to see sense, Naomi succumbed to her sorrow. She had shown tacit trust in Yahweh, responding to the famine's end by leaving for home, and blessing Orpah and Ruth in his name. There had not been a word of blame or bitterness, but then she compared her situation to the potentially safe futures of her daughters-in-law. The Hebrew, **It is more bitter for me** *because of you* (**than for you**), can also be read to mean that Naomi was grieving on their behalf (Eskenazi and Frymer-Kensky 2011, 16). The KJV reads it this way: "It grieveth me much for your sakes." Either way, Naomi was suffering greatly.

She expressed despair as any ancient would. The Israelites viewed **the LORD's hand** as the source of all blessing *and* all loss. When Naomi attributed her loss to Yahweh, she was acknowledging reality as it was perceived. In this worldview, there was no contradiction in asking the same Yahweh who **has turned against me** to show kindness to others (→ vv 8-9). In fact, it would be wise for the younger women to distance themselves from someone Yahweh had evidently singled out for suffering (Driesbach 2012, 517). Naomi would soon sink lower in her own bitterness, but she was still holding out hope for others.

John Wesley on Ruth 1:13

It is with *me*, that God has a controversy. This language becomes us, when we are under affliction; tho many others share in the trouble, yet we . . . hear the voice of the rod, as if it spake only to us. (Wesley 1975, 881)

■ **14** Back in v 9 "she kissed them goodbye and they wept"; here the weeping came first, then the kissing, in our fourth chiasm. **They wept aloud again** is literally, *they lifted up their voices and wept* (the third use of *nāśā'*; see vv 4, 9; 2:18). This conjures the practice of ululation, the piercing trills of mourning women in the Middle East and some African and Asian cultures. These were not quiet tears.

At the moment of decision, the younger women are named again, for the first time since their introduction. **Orpah** was convinced to take the way of wisdom and **kissed her mother-in-law goodbye**. The LXX adds here "and she returned to her people," but the kiss is Orpah's last action in the Hebrew text. We do not hear of her again, but Orpah's choice is not worthy of the vilification she has endured. It was the smart thing to do, and done with affection, after ten years of laudable *ḥesed*.

Ruth clung bodily to Naomi, as though to convey her resolve physically. The Hebrew verb *dābaq* ("to cling") is common in the OT to describe close relationships, physical proximity, or dedication (Gen 34:3; Deut 11:22; 2 Sam 20:2); many also see here an echo of Gen 2:24. *Dābaq* figures in our next LRWP: Ruth clung to Naomi against all sense, putting herself at great risk. In the next chapter, she clung very sensibly to the women working Boaz's field and so found safety (Ruth 2:8, 21, 23).

■ **15** Naomi spoke directly to Ruth, urging her to follow Orpah's **going back** [*šûb*] **to her people and her gods**. Orpah's people and gods were Ruth's as well; it seems more compelling for Naomi to have said, "your people and your gods." Perhaps she had already begun to realize Ruth's determination to stay with her, though that is made clearer in the next verses.

■ **16-17** The intensity of Ruth's reply parallels that of Naomi's words to her. She made clear that staying in Moab was not an option for her. **Urge** translates the Hebrew verb *pāga'* ("to entreat," "to meet," "to encounter"), which is our next LRWP (→ 2:22, where this verb is used in the sense of meeting others). **Leave you** translates the verb *'āzab*, which has an intensity here (*forsake*). Some translate "abandon you" (Trible 1978, 172; Campbell 1975, 61). In Ruth's eyes, obeying Naomi would actually be betraying her. She built rhetorical momentum by repeating the key word in this conversation (*šûb*, **turn back** or **return**). The phrase could be translated *to forsake you, by turning back from following you*. This sets up another LRWP, as *'āzab* will recur three times in ch 2 (vv 11, 16, 20).

In these beautiful lines in 1:16-17, Ruth pledged herself to Naomi with an astonishing, lifelong vow. Framed in sparse, poetic parallels, Ruth turned her back on the safety of a potential remarriage. These two widows were bound forever. Ruth's vow began by acknowledging the uncertainty of their future, **where you go**. They had already set off and would continue at least as far as Bethlehem, but there was no guarantee Naomi's hometown was their final destination.

Where you stay furthers the uncertainty by the temporary nature of the verb *lûn* (**spend the night**). We expect something more permanent like "dwell" or "live," but Ruth anticipated a potential future of poverty-driven nomadism. *Lûn*

43

also figures in the next LRWP. Ruth pledged to **stay** the night with Naomi from now on, wherever that might be, but at Naomi's urging she later "stayed the night" with Boaz (3:13). The effect of this first pairing, **go** and **stay** might be rendered colloquially, *Wherever we end up, we'll be together.*

Ruth pledged not only her company but also ethnic and religious solidarity: **Your people will be my people and your God be my God**. This was courage itself, perhaps even foolhardiness. Naomi's **people** might well reject this Moabite widow, so leaving her own people was a great risk. Jewish and Christian readers see wisdom in pledging allegiance to Yahweh, but from Ruth's own perspective, this was risky. For all she knew, Yahweh, Naomi's God, might be hostile to Moabites. Yahweh might not even be reliable; after all, Naomi's whole family had been followers of this God and they were not spared from immense suffering. Naomi herself had no qualms about laying the blame at Yahweh's feet; could Ruth trust this God?

Ruth again expressed her solidarity with Naomi by pledging that even in death they would be inseparable (1:17). The place of Naomi's death, wherever that may be, would be the place of her own death and burial. Ruth next moved beyond all expectations. Generally speaking, vows in Israelite law were binding only as long as both parties to the vow were alive. Even Christian wedding vows apply only "until death parts us." Ruth pledged herself *beyond* Naomi's death, to her own, meaning she would oversee Naomi's burial, and whenever Ruth died, her bones would eventually join Naomi's in the same tomb. Not **even death** would part them.

Sasson sees here a formal, legal commitment, "Ruth practically indenturing herself to Naomi" (1978, 52; 1979, 123-25). As many have noticed, this vow took no account of future family and did not even mention her dead husband; this vow was strictly, starkly, only about two widows (Eskenazi and Frymer-Kensky 2011, 18). Remarriage impinged on this vow, as a married Ruth could not follow Naomi or continue lodging with her or be buried with her instead of with a husband. Put another way, this vow curtailed Ruth's chances of remarriage: no man in Israel would marry a foreign, barren widow who came with another, older widow.

From this point forward, all Ruth's actions must be read in light of her pledge. Her options going forward were: (1) never remarry, (2) marry someone who would take Ruth's former mother-in-law into his household, or (3) dissolve the vow; there were legal ways of doing this. Sasson sees Boaz's "acquiring" Ruth in 4:5 as the legal dissolution of the vow before he married her (1979, 119-36).

As it turned out, Ruth's marriage became a way to keep this vow (informally, if Sasson is right), providing for Naomi all her life and eventually preserving Naomi's name into perpetuity. If our primary view of the book has been a love story between Ruth and Boaz, we would do well to remember Ruth spoke these rousing words to her mother-in-law. The relationship in focus here was between a pitiful old woman and her stalwart daughter-in-law.

Ruth sealed her vow with the name of her new God, **the LORD (*Yahweh*** in Heb.). Where Christian tradition appropriated her words for weddings, Jewish tradition made them the declaration of a proselyte in a conversion ceremony. However, the extent to which Ruth's vow represents conversion to Israel's God is ambiguous. The story continued to designate her—sometimes quite conspicuously and awkwardly—as a Moabite (1:22; 2:2, 6, 21; 3:5, 10). This was the only time Ruth spoke Yahweh's name, inviting him to punish her **ever so severely** if she violated her pledge.

Others in the story invoked Yahweh's name: Boaz and his servants in the field (2:4); the townspeople in their blessing and celebration (4:11-13); even Naomi eventually came to bless Yahweh again (2:20). Where Boaz specifically invoked *Yahweh's* protective wings over Ruth (2:12), she cheekily sought refuge under *Boaz's* wing (3:9). We read this vow as Ruth's first step toward Yahweh, anticipating she would grow in faith as she kept faith with Yahweh's people.

■ **18** In the face of such resolve and fortitude, Naomi was struck dumb. The Hebrew reads, *she stopped speaking to her* (she stopped urging her), but this need not indicate total silence for the rest of their journey, much less an emotional withdrawal in resentment from Ruth (Fewell and Gunn 1990, 74); simply that on this topic, there was no more to be said. Already overcome by grief, the extent of her destitution, and the perilous journey before her, Naomi was stopped in her tracks by Ruth's insistence. There was no point in arguing further.

C. Home with Naomi (1:19-22)

■ **19** With the cast of characters winnowed down, and Naomi's return firmly established, there was no need to linger in Moab, even narratively. The progress of the women's travel, with all the effort and tension it undoubtedly entailed, is compressed into half a verse. Everyone in town noticed their arrival. The population of Bethlehem at this time was likely fewer than two hundred people (Walton, Matthews, and Chavalas 2000, 278). In keeping with the nature of Ruth as women's literature, we notice **the whole town** reacted to their arrival, but only **the women** spoke. This pattern is repeated in every chapter: the action closes with Naomi back home, speaking to or being spoken to by other women (2:22; 3:18; 4:14-17).

The villagers' awed question might have several causes, but the narrative is indefinite as to its tone. **Stirred** is a rare verb in the OT (*hûm*), sometimes indicating great celebration (1 Sam 4:5), sometimes great panic (Deut 7:23). Maybe the villagers were delighted to see their long-lost friend or surprised to see her arrive without menfolk, accompanied by a strange woman. Naomi's suffering, grief, or aging may have changed her beyond recognition; we do not know how long she had been away. Insightfully, Linafelt sees here an example of the author's penchant for "ambiguity and double-meanings . . . negotiating a delicate balance between the poles of blessing and curse" (1999, 18). However it was meant, the question paved the way for Naomi's voluble grief and bitterness to erupt.

■ **20-21** Seizing on their use of her name, **Naomi** rebuked them (Ruth 1:20), for its connotation ("pleasant," → 1:2) conflicted with her experience of life. In a despairing outburst, she chose **Mara** (bitter) to characterize **the Almighty**'s treat-

45

ment of her. She complained to the women about God, outlining her charges against him.

Shaddai vs. Naomi

Almighty is the traditional rendering of *šadday* ("Shaddai"), one of the OT's names for Yahweh. For decades, scholars have argued the most likely origin is not the Hebrew root *šdd* ("deal violently") but either the Akkadian *šadû* ("mountain") or Hebrew *šad* ("female breast"). In some OT texts, Shaddai was a judge with the power to bless/curse (Gen 17:1; 43:14; Job 5:17). In others, Shaddai was the one who blessed Israel with fertility (Gen 28:3; 35:11; 48:3-4; 49:25) and protection (Ps 91:1). Shaddai is particularly prominent in Job, where its connotations of judgment and nurture find resonance in lament. For Naomi, it may reflect a view of her loss as divine judgment. If the intended connotation is nourishment and fertility, Naomi used the name almost as an accusation; Shaddai should nurture life, not strip it away!

Naomi claimed to have had a **full** life at her departure from Bethlehem, but she was fleeing famine, after all (Ruth 1:21). In any case, **the LORD** took it all and **brought** her **back empty.** This is a dispiriting complaint in light of Ruth's astounding pledge; Naomi's grief clouded her vision, and the reader feels for Ruth. It also sets up two LRWPs. Here Naomi was **brought . . . back** (*šûb*) by Yahweh; in 4:15 the bringer-back (of life) was Obed. Here Naomi was **empty** (*rêqām*) both of food and family; in 3:17, Ruth was not allowed to return to her "empty-handed."

However, those restorations were not yet known to Naomi, so her complaint grew, rising almost to a fever pitch. First she rejected her name, then she questioned why anyone would use it for her. We can hear her voice choking with the biting sarcasm of this question. She gained steam and leveled two more charges, reversing her previous use of God's names: **the LORD . . . afflicted** and **the Almighty . . . brought misfortune.**

Like a wounded child who runs crying to her mother's arms, Naomi found release in the bosom of her hometown. Sounding just like Job or a psalmist, Naomi employed the rich Israelite habits of lament, startling modern readers with her unashamed expressions of grief and anger. She was bold in her fervor but deflated quickly with no response from the listening women, who perhaps knew better than to mollify her.

■ **22** The first word in this final verse lets us know Naomi's lament, though substantive, did not reflect the ultimate reality of her life. The narrator did not allow her the name she claimed but returned her to **Naomi;** Mara is never mentioned again. For though Naomi had suffered, she came full circle in a beautiful inclusio. In v 1, she left for Moab with her three menfolk. Now she **returned from Moab** (another *šûb* to drive the theme home), having lost the men but gained Ruth.

After being completely ignored by both Naomi and the townspeople in the homecoming scene, Ruth was reinstated in the recap of the action. She was described paradoxically as both **the Moabite,** emphasizing her outsider status, and

her daughter-in-law, reiterating her familial connection. Ruth was crucial to Naomi's coming redemption, and both parts of her identity were factors.

A second element in Naomi's redemption was completely underplayed. The last clause plays on our theme of providence, foreshadowing the direction from which salvation came. A final *šûb* is present in the Hebrew but missing in the NIV, **they returned, arriving in Bethlehem**, and then the tantalizing detail: they came just **as the barley harvest was beginning**. Harvest was the most advantageous season for destitute widows and foreigners in Israel, and the barley harvest, beginning in April-May, kicked it off. Ruth and Naomi had weeks and weeks of opportunity and provision ahead of them.

FROM THE TEXT

God's Providence: Our introduction to Naomi and her problems has been both heartbreaking and exhilarating. We have plunged to the depths of her loss and desperation, but also soared on the hope that God was at work behind the scenes. The return of plentiful food did not fall directly in Naomi's lap in Moab; she only heard about it from others, and then in time—after the crops had grown and were ready for harvest—she returned to the place where she could get what she needed. Ruth was not sent directly from God like a prophet with an oracle; she was merely left over after the family dissolved. Providentially, this leftover daughter-in-law turned out to be the strongest, boldest champion a desperate woman ever needed. Even the townspeople were waiting in the background rather than conjured up for the occasion, a social structure already in place to support the restoration of this destitute widow. God's action on Naomi's behalf was subtle and complex, accomplished mainly through others.

The Seeds of Ḥesed: Two models of faithfulness in love are already emerging in this opening chapter. Naomi displayed an honest, intimate, though tattered faith, declaring her trust in God by her very words of lament, not to mention her return to Judah. She also sought the good of her daughters-in-law instead of keeping them bound to her, setting them free for a new future with blessing and commendation. Her love might be wounded and limping, but this portrayal showed Naomi to be a woman who both practiced and inspired *ḥesed*.

Orpah and Ruth were both involved in setting up the second model of faithfulness, in their acts of daughterly *ḥesed*. First, they had a history of *ḥesed* toward their husbands' family that prompted praise and goodwill from their mother-in-law. Second, they wept with Naomi in their shared grief and wanted to stay with her. Finally, of course, Ruth's path of *ḥesed* deepened and strengthened in her refusal to abandon Naomi, binding her life to the old woman's. At this point, the *ḥesed* of these daughters has been described and promised, and Ruth has completed the travel portion of her pledge, but much more *ḥesed* is to come.

Care for the Needy: The story set up in this chapter promises an exhibition of love in a Wesleyan direction: God's love of the poor and vulnerable. The main characters, Naomi and Ruth, were vulnerable in multiple ways: women adrift, financially poor, widowed with no immediate family, childless, and foreigners (one in Moab, one in Israel). Any one of these circumstances placed them firmly in the category of "needy" according to OT standards; they occupied all at once, leading to absolute destitution. The story has already begun to hint at the ways God met their needs: the binding of their lives together, the harvest, and the townspeople of Bethlehem. By the end, we will know exactly what it looks like when the people of God engage in the work of God.

The Canonical Effect: These twenty-two verses have already challenged expectations about what constitutes a proper scriptural narrative. The Israelite men were swept offstage in the first five verses, leaving behind three insignificant women in great need. There was no voice from heaven, no holy servant, not even a male speaker in the whole chapter! There was no miracle done, no oracle given, and only a rumor of divine action very much in the wings. Instead of these usual salvation motifs, three poor women had one thing going for them: they knew how to love each other. From the perspective of the wider canon, this story not so quietly subverts and nuances all notions of what is worthy of our attention in this world. The needs of an old woman were worthy of a book in the Bible.

Ambrose and Jerome on Ruth I

Ambrose: [Ruth] deserved to be counted among the honored figures in the Lord's genealogy, chosen for kinship of mind, not of body, [and] is a great example for us, because she prefigures all of us who were gathered from the nations for the purpose of joining the church of the Lord. We should emulate her, therefore.

Jerome: Naomi, fleeing because of famine to the land of Moab, there lost her husband and her sons. Yet when she was thus deprived of her natural protectors, Ruth, a stranger, never left her side. And see what a great thing it is to comfort a lonely woman: Ruth, for her reward, is made an ancestor of Christ. (Franke 2005, 182)

II. HOW RUTH'S PLAN WORKED OUT: RUTH 2:1-23

BEHIND THE TEXT

Bethlehem was a small village, a tight-knit community of a few hundred souls, and an agrarian society: life revolved around crops and livestock. Harvest was a highlight of their year, a prolonged season involving feasting, religious celebrations, and the satisfaction of hard work finished, side-by-side with all one's family and neighbors. It was also an opportunity for righteous Israelites to fulfill the oft-repeated commandment, "Remember that you were slaves in Egypt" (Deut 24:22). This reminder of Israel's past was to prompt their provision for the needy and vulnerable among them.

Israel was to harvest crops in particular ways, leaving produce for those who needed food but lacked the land to grow it themselves: widows, orphans, foreigners, and the poor. The harvest laws required a farmer to leave crops standing around the edges of every field, for harvest by these needy ones (Lev 23:22; Deut 24:19-22). A farmer should never count on the full yield of a field; the edges belonged by law to those in need!

Further, if in the process of gathering the cut grain or produce in the middle of the fields, a grain stalk or grape cluster was dropped on the ground, it must not be picked up by the farmer, but left for the poor. If while carrying the sheaves, or bundles, of grain off the field, one was accidentally forgotten, it too must be left. Thus, the needy had the right to harvest for themselves all the standing crop around the edges of a field, as well as to glean what was dropped or left behind by the farmer and hired laborers in the main portion of the field. In this way, those without fields of their own could still count on food to get them through the coming year.

Of course, that is how it was supposed to be. If Israel was faithful, the culture of a given community ensured provision and dignity for their poor, without harassment or persecution. In a small town like Bethlehem, there may not have been many foreigners in need, but a handful of the community's widows and orphans probably expected to glean every harvest season.

However, this was the era of the judges, and not a good time to be a woman on her own in Israelite society, as she could not count on her personal safety. This was also the first harvest after a famine, and most farmers were likely desperate for every stalk of grain that grew. When Naomi (an Israelite widow) and Ruth (a foreign one) arrived in Bethlehem, each had the legal right to harvest and glean over the upcoming season, but they could not be sure it would be granted.

A Moabite in a Judahite village, Ruth faced prejudice, even intimidation or abuse. Naomi may have expected censure from the villagers. After all, she had fled, while they endured the famine; she had not managed to keep even one of her family alive. She had let her sons marry outside the faith, and then brought back one of those idolatrous wives, and the community was expected to help them survive? It did not promise to be an easy homecoming or smooth transition to life in Bethlehem.

IN THE TEXT

A. Seeking Food (2:1-3)

■ **1** **Naomi** is the first and last word in the Hebrew of ch 2: **Naomi** (v 1); "mother-in-law" (v 23). This reminds us the book is about her. Ruth and Boaz were the main actors, but Naomi's need drove the action.

The storyteller employs foreshadowing; the import of the first verse (there was a decent relative in town) has no immediate effect on the action. It is a clever setup, anticipating the one Ruth met that day, but Boaz did not actually *need* to appear until v 3, when Ruth arrived at his field.

This preamble reveals crucial facts about the man who became Ruth's partner in redemption. Suspending our familiarity, we do not yet know Boaz held the legal position of redeemer; he was just Naomi's **relative** (*môda'*) through marriage. This general term appears twice in Ruth, forming our next LRWP. Here, *môda'* confirms the famine did not wipe out Elimelek's clan in Bethlehem. *Môda'* appears again in 3:2, where its generality is key to the drama on the threshing floor.

Boaz's name has prompted much comment, but like others in our story, its origin is unclear. It is probably from a root meaning **strength**, but occurring nowhere else in the OT than as the enigmatic name of a temple pillar (1 Kgs 7:21; 2 Chr 3:17). It could also be related to an Arabic root meaning "lively," "vigorous" (Sasson 1979, 40-41).

More interesting is **man of standing**, which translates the Hebrew *'îš gibbôr ḥayil* (lit. ***mighty man of valor***). This common term is usually rendered "mighty warrior," connoting military prowess (Judg 11:1; 2 Kgs 5:1; 1 Chr 28:1). In a few instances, it signifies wealth or social standing (1 Sam 9:1; 1 Kgs 11:28; 2 Kgs 15:20). Most have presumed the less common connotation here, since our narrative portrays Boaz as a leading man in Bethlehem: he owned fields, had workers who respected him, and commanded respect at the town gate. In a clever pun on the other occurrence of his name, Fewell and Gunn call Boaz "a pillar of the community" (1990, 40).

The two meanings of *'îš gibbôr ḥayil* are not mutually exclusive, so this might be another instance of the author's love of ambiguity. There is no reason to rule out an early career as one of Judah's warriors. A soldier with years of active service, such as the judges' era demanded, could accumulate wealth and property and be a man of standing in his town. It may even explain why Boaz appears unmarried: he was not home enough to establish a family during his early adulthood in an era of chaos and famine. Traditional explanations, that Boaz was a widower or polygamist, are more speculative than simply accepting the usual implications of the Hebrew term. In any light, Boaz was a hopeful development.

The ***mighty man of valor*** sets up our next LRWP, and one of the most delightful. In the next chapter, just when readers might be tempted to condemn Ruth for her risqué behavior, Boaz called her a ***woman of valor*** (*'ēšet ḥayil* [3:11]). This brilliant wordplay has a third layer, however: in the last chapter, the ***mighty man of valor*** and the ***woman of valor*** created *ḥayil*, standing and reputation in Bethlehem (4:11).

■ **2** With Boaz waiting in the wings, the action begins the second installment of our journey-dialogue-home pattern. **Ruth the Moabite** did the planning in this scene; the narrator plays with irony by highlighting her foreignness. The outsider initiated a risky and laborious scheme. The Hebrew verb form **Let me go** is not a polite request, but a polite demand (Campbell 1975, 91; Hubbard 1988, 136). **Pick up the leftover grain** translates Ruth's intention to make use of the provisions for foreigners and widows, but destitute people do not expect a warm reception, so Ruth anticipated needing to try several fields, to work **behind anyone** who let her. Juxtaposed with the clues about Boaz in v 1, her words hint at a providential outcome.

Whoever might let Ruth work in their field, she was prepared to see it as more complicated than just receiving her due. Her hope of finding **favor** implies awareness that all might not go smoothly—the villagers might not let her glean; if someone did, it would be a kindness. **Favor** (*ḥēn*) is our next LRWP: Ruth knew it would take *ḥēn* for someone to let her glean, and in v 10, Boaz's *ḥēn* actually exceeded what she asked. In v 13, Ruth hoped for even more *ḥēn*, foreshadowing their future together. In its first occurrence, *ḥēn* was something hoped for; in its last, *ḥēn* had been given, and more was on the way.

Why was the foreigner left to solve their hunger? We find a clue in Naomi's stark response, **Go . . . , my daughter**, the same words she had already said to Ruth three times to no avail (1:8, 11, 15). She had no energy for more: no thanks, no warning of the evident danger, no offer to join Ruth in the field, though her presence would clear Ruth's path. At the end of the last scene, Naomi expected nothing good, and her dismissal of Ruth in claiming emptiness (1:21) revealed despondency. She did not think anything would come of Ruth's efforts. Their timely arrival (1:22) would have been wasted if not for Ruth.

■ **3** With no further words, Ruth left. The first clause summarizes the coming action, **So she went out, entered a field and began to glean behind the harvesters** (lit. *she went, and she came, and she gleaned in the field behind the reapers*). In the second clause, the narrator's tongue-in-cheek approach to coincidence and providence is overt. All the fields being situated side-by-side around the perimeter of the village, Ruth picked Boaz's. **As it turned out** translates the Hebrew *her chance chanced upon*. For simplicity, the NIV translates the Hebrew *tract of the field* as **field**, but this obscures another LRWP. *Ḥelqâ* (tract) here identifies Boaz's parcel of land as meeting Naomi and Ruth's immediate need of food. In 4:3, Boaz will raise the issue of Naomi's *ḥelqâ* to solve her long-term need of redemption.

John Wesley on Ruth 2:3

It was a chance in reference to second causes, but ordered by God's providence. . . . Many a great affair is brought about by a little turn, fortuitous as to men, but designed by God. (Wesley 1975, 883)

B. Finding Favor (2:4-17)

■ **4** The details of Ruth's day begin with the narrative marker *hinnēh* (**behold**) followed by a pleasing alliteration in the Hebrew, *bôʿaz bāʾ* (**Boaz arrived**). Bush renders this "And wouldn't you know it, Boaz came" (1996, 111), which captures the providential nuance of the scene nicely. Boaz's arrival **from Bethlehem** reflects the trip from the village to the fields on its outskirts. He was wealthy enough to leave the harvest of his field in others' hands but, being a responsible landowner, came to monitor progress.

The exchange of blessings in Yahweh's name (**The LORD be with you! . . . The LORD bless you!**) reflects pious convention between boss and workers. As Boaz's first speech, it suggests at least a publicly upright man. We cannot be sure the harvesters' blessing reflects genuine faith, as we suspect some of them pose a danger to Ruth in the field.

The last time Yahweh was invoked, the destitute Naomi was blaming him for her trouble; here the fortunate Boaz named him as the source of blessing. Narratively the tide is turning, and these greetings in passing help mark the shift. This exchange in the context of harvest also helps to make sense of the enigmatic ending of Ps 129, where this same greeting is denied to one whose wickedness has made them into grass that does not last to be harvested (vv 6-8).

■ **5** Boaz noticed Ruth immediately, asking his overseer literally, **Whose is this young woman?** Lest we assume Boaz was predatory, or thought of women as property, Bush reminds us of the same question directed to men in Gen 32:17 [18 HB] and 1 Sam 30:13 (1996, 112-13). This question fits with Israel's group-oriented culture, in which one's identity came from family connections. It was thus a natural query in Bethlehem's small community, where Boaz may reasonably be expected to know everyone in town. The "man of standing" wanted to know the newcomer's connections before he spoke to her.

The question alone, but also its pronoun **this** (not **that**) suggests physical proximity and helps unravel part of the puzzle of Ruth 2:7. If Ruth were already out in the field, gleaning among the rest of the villagers, she would barely have been distinguishable in the bright sun. As our reading of v 7 concludes, Boaz noticed Ruth at once because she was standing there, awaiting his arrival.

■ **6-7** The overseer's response was telling, but so was his designation by the narrator. In v 5 and here, he was called *na'ar*, which can mean either **young man** or **servant**, and in both verses, Ruth was called by the feminine of the same noun, *na'ărâ* (**young woman**). The *na'ar*, scandalized by the *na'ărâ*'s Moabite origin, mentioned it twice in one breath: the Moabite [in Heb.: *the Moabite young woman*] **who came back from Moab.** The narrator, however, kept Ruth on an even footing, denying the overseer's attempt to disparage her by pairing him *with* her; they were *both* young people, at least with respect to Boaz. **The Moabite . . . with Naomi** further degraded Ruth by ignoring her place as daughter-in-law to a Bethlehemite.

Boaz knew all about Ruth (v 11), and this discovery of her in his own field marks a significant advance in the plot. Boaz also knew something critical to Ruth's future: she had made contact with one of her family's redeemers. Readers know only that Boaz was a relative, but Ruth did not even know that much, and would not until she returned home; Boaz revealed nothing of their relation all day long. From this point on, though, Boaz knew he was dealing with a member of his extended family, for whom he was responsible as a redeemer (→ "The *Go'el*" excursus at v 20). We can expect this to inform his treatment of Ruth.

The remainder of the overseer's report in v 7 is fraught with difficulty in the Hebrew. She asked to **glean**; as both a foreigner and a widow, this was Ruth's right, but it was still wise for a newcomer to ask permission. The second part of Ruth's request occasions vigorous debate. At issue is how to interpret **gather among the sheaves behind the harvesters.** Was it simply further explication of her overall request, to glean as she had right (Linafelt 1999, 32; Bush 1996, 113-15)? Or was it a bold appeal, going beyond the law, even beyond what she told Naomi she was planning? Was she asking for access to the part of the field where the harvesters were still working (Campbell 1975, 94-96, 147-49; Sasson 1979, 47-48)? A savvy owner or overseer would not let gleaners in until **the sheaves,** the piles of harvested stalks, were carried off that portion of the field, lest a desperate gleaner snatch a handful or two from every sheaf they passed.

We are convinced of the latter reading. The verb *watta'ămôd,* **and she stood** (**remained here**), is clear, and we agree with Sasson that to render "on her feet" (NRSV) is a dubious extension of meaning (1979, 48), made in order to support a particular reading of the last, unintelligible part of the verse (see below). Further, why did Ruth react so strongly to Boaz's permission (v 10), if she were only asking what she was owed by law?

Ruth asked something the overseer could not grant on his own, so she **remained here from morning till now,** awaiting Boaz's arrival. Sasson suggests Ruth asked the extra privilege precisely in order to meet Boaz (1979, 47-48). A tantalizing idea, but according to a plain reading of the text so far, from Ruth's perspective, Boaz was still the unknown "anyone" of v 2. Another motive is more likely: facing exactly the kind of prejudice posed by the overseer, and tied to a listless Naomi, things were getting desperate. Ruth needed more than the meager yield of a day's gleaning, so with nothing to lose, she asked for more.

The second half of v 7 reads literally **then she came and she stood from then the morning until now, this her sitting the house little.** The final clause is simply unintelligible, resulting in more than twenty proposed emendations (for details, see Hubbard 1988, 147-52; Campbell 1975, 94-96). The NIV's **except for a short rest in the shelter** is as likely as many other renderings. It also does not demand the untenable rendering of *watta'ămôd* (**and she stood**) mentioned above, which the NRSV's "without resting even for a moment" does. Even given the incoherent Hebrew, the effect of the verse is to portray Ruth as a woman who respected custom by asking permission to glean, dared to ask for more, and gained the consideration of a wary overseer and his wise boss, overturning her previous invisibility to the villagers (1:19-21).

■ **8-9** Boaz responded to Ruth directly. Calling her **My daughter** (2:8), as Naomi did in 1:11-13 and 2:2, situates Boaz similarly in the reader's mind as older than Ruth, who was likely in her twenties after ten years of marriage. There is nothing that suggests Boaz was truly old. This conventional address from elder to younger person in the ancient world signals approval, even affection (Gen 43:29; Josh 7:19; 1 Sam 3:6, 16; 4:16; 24:16 [17 HB]; 2 Sam 18:22, etc.).

Boaz's instructions did more than give permission; they attached her to him and his field, offering protection and connection. **Don't go** was a striking reversal of all the times Naomi tried to send Ruth away! Gleaners worked as many fields as they could; asking her to stay in his field showed willingness to meet her need.

Together with **listen to me, Don't go** conveyed urgency, and now we begin to sense the danger lurking in the field. Boaz's directions are more fervent in Hebrew: **cling to my young women, your eyes on the field they reap, and go after them,** *for I am commanding the young men not to touch you*. The nouns and pronouns alternate between feminine and masculine, and we can imagine Boaz pointing out to the field at the groups of workers as he speaks: stay with them, the *young women* (fem.); watch where *they reap* (masc.); follow *after them* (fem.); they won't touch you, the *young men* (masc.). He wanted her to stay *with* the women harvesters, *away* from the men. Ruth clung (*dābaq*) once before, to Naomi, showing her determination; now her clinging to other women provided safety.

Boaz's concern for Ruth's safety might seem an overreaction, an intrusion in the happy harvest scene. However, we have already met an inhospitable overseer, and it apparently took specific orders to keep the male workers from harassing her! Boaz related his order to Ruth so she knew she was protected. Considering the tumult of the era (see Judg 19, the debauched attack on the Levite's concubine just ten miles away in Gibeah), and Ruth's vulnerability—as a widow and a hated Moabite, with no man to avenge her—these were viable concerns. Trouble in the field was a real and present danger and suggests a very good reason Ruth wanted to wait until she'd spoken to the field's owner: she needed to know she was safe.

Boaz's instructions to Ruth and his orders to his men established him as her male protector at least for the day (Sakenfeld 1999, 43). No one would interfere with a woman shielded by an *'îš gibbôr ḥayil* (→ Ruth 2:1). This allowed Ruth to feel safe in partaking of the water supplied for his own workers, a privilege the average gleaner would never assume, and one for which she had not dared ask.

Boaz did not explicitly grant Ruth the right to gather among the sheaves here, but his instruction to attach herself to his own women harvesters implied consent. She could not stay close to them without going among the sheaves. He sanctioned her request explicitly after the meal, but to others (vv 15-16). As he gave Ruth no other instructions, and as she did actually glean in the way she had asked to, Ruth must have understood his permission from this.

■ **10** Ruth's response makes some readers uncomfortable, as though she debased herself by groveling. In that honor-shame culture, however, where the disparity between Ruth and Boaz's social positions is hard for us to fathom, it made sense. With nothing to offer, Ruth had overstepped her social boundaries. In return, Boaz offered not rebuke, but all she asked and more. He extended extraordinary privileges, but also social standing.

Ruth found more **favor** than she was looking for (v 2), and couldn't help but ask, **Why . . . notice me—a foreigner?** This noticing, *nākar*, sets up our next LRWP. Ruth wondered at Boaz's *nākar*, and she was likely tentative, still unaware of his being a relative. In those menacing days, a man might expect certain "favors" in return for such notice and protection, especially with no one to protect her. By the time *nākar* is used again (v 19), this tension was dissolved: all doubt of Boaz's character was gone, so even Naomi was jolted out of her despondency into blessing the giver of "notice."

Nākar also forms a pun with **foreigner** (*nokrîyyâ*); why did Boaz *nākar* a *nokrîyyâ*? These words come from related but not identical roots. While in the common perspective, Ruth was fortunate indeed, her question strikes an ironic note, a tacit censure of the state of things in Israel. If anyone should be expected to notice and show favor to a foreigner, it was an Israelite!

■ **11-12** Boaz's answer relieved all worry; he had no treacherous motive. He arrived at his field that morning already knowing of Ruth and her loyalty to Naomi, but now he had a face for her name. Even before he was prompted by her bold gleaning request, even aside from their family connection, or any personal attraction, Boaz was predisposed to notice and favor Ruth because of what she had done for Naomi (though we admit this was also the motivation most fit for public conversation). Meeting Ruth fanned his predisposition into action.

Boaz's description of Ruth evoked Yahweh's first instruction to Abram (Gen 12:11), with one important difference: Ruth had no promise from Yahweh (Trible 1978, 173). His is our second use of *'āzab* ("to leave," "to forsake"; Ruth 2:11). Boaz honored Ruth's forsaking her parents and homeland so as not to forsake Naomi (1:16). Boaz made no mention of their family connection, at precisely the point where it would have made sense to do so. It gave him a natural reason to favor her, and pointed to an obvious reward for all Ruth had forsaken in Moab: her family was Naomi, but also included the kind man in front her.

One dynamic of their culture explains why Boaz kept the family connection to himself. Israel practiced endogamous marriage, choosing spouses from outside the household, but within the clan, to preserve identity cohesion. In this system, and in a small town like Bethlehem, Boaz and Ruth were obvious and immediate candidates for one another. She was a vulnerable woman, he had a lot to give; she an experienced wife, he an older man. His standing in the community might even curb the effects of her foreignness. But even better, they were kin!

Revealing their family connection to Ruth in front of Boaz's workers would set tongues wagging. Silence on this point, at least for the day, amounted to kindness. Ruth needed food; she did not come to the fields looking for a husband. Having protected her already from untoward advances by his workers, Boaz would not say anything to raise the idea of marriage.

Boaz's blessing was warm but not too personal. Having testified to Ruth's great loyalty, he called upon Yahweh to **repay** her, that she be **richly rewarded by . . . the God of Israel**, acknowledging her transition from worshipper of the Moabite gods to inhabitant of Yahweh's territory. He named her care for Naomi as bringing Ruth under the **refuge** of Yahweh's **wings** (*kānāp*), our next LRWP. In Boaz's blessing, **wings** provide safety. Ruth herself took up this word in 3:9, challenging Boaz to answer his own prayer. The moving image of Yahweh, a mother hen who shelters chicks under her wings, is used only in Ruth and Psalms (17:8; 36:7 [8 HB]; 57:1 [2 HB]; 61:4 [5 HB]; 63:7 [8 HB]; 91:4). As a feminine image of God, perhaps it is particularly at home in Ruth.

Levine notices here the reversal of a common biblical scene. Like Jacob (Gen 24) and Moses (Exod 2:15-22), Ruth journeyed into foreign territory, where she encountered someone who gave her water, whom she later married. This scene is more than just a nod to that literary convention, though. Boaz framed Ruth's commitment to Naomi in appropriately weighty terms for the reader: "Although the women of Bethlehem will recognize Ruth's value in the context of the child she bears, Boaz sees the full extent of her *chesed*" (Levine 1992, 81).

■ **13** Despite Boaz's kind reserve, and even without echoes of other texts, marital possibilities hovered over the field that day: an eligible man of standing treated a young widow kindly, protected her from other men, and favored her publicly. Even a novice reader could guess where this might lead. Ruth hoped Boaz's **favor** would not end, and assured by his care and refusal to take advantage of her, she brought the prospect playfully into the open.

Her tone was evocative: Ruth called him **my lord** (*'ădōnî*: **my lord/Lord**) a form of address playing on his reference to Yahweh, but also used between wives and husbands (Gen 18:12; Judg 19:26; Ps 45:12 [13 HB]). She thanked him for **speaking kindly to your servant**, in Hebrew the tender phrase, *you have spoken to the heart of your maid*. **Maid** (*šipḥâ*) is reminiscent of Hagar, Bilhah, and Zilpah, each a *šipḥâ* who slept with their masters (Gen 16:1; 29:24, 29); it anticipates Abigail, who called herself "maid" and David "my lord," then married him (1 Sam 25:24ff.). Even Ruth's last statement, outwardly humble, was double-edged: since she was not his hired woman, she might qualify as his wife. One of these ambiguities alone might not mean much, but all in one speech, in that time and place, they could not but plant subliminal seeds, in Boaz and the reader!

■ **14** Boaz did not respond to Ruth's playful speech directly; instead, he offered her food. **Bread** is still a staple of Middle Eastern diets. **Wine vinegar** was bitter if drunk, but as a sour liquid for dipping bread into, refreshed laborers without upsetting stomachs in the heat.

With the LXX and Vulgate but against most modern commentators, we follow the natural sense of the Hebrew word order (if not the MT's pausal pointing), reading **At mealtime** as Boaz's words to Ruth, not as marking an interlude between Ruth's words and Boaz's invitation to eat: *And Boaz said to her, "At mealtime, come over here."* The primary objection to this seems to be an inability to envision Boaz responding to Ruth's daring speech with talk of food (Campbell 1975, 102; Sasson 1979, 55).

On the contrary, it is perfectly credible that Boaz, having shown reserve on this possibility, was flustered by her teasing, and grasped whatever neutral subject was at hand to cover his abashment. Leading her over to the lunch site, offering food, bought him time to recover while still proving she had not repulsed him. Indeed, his actions showed approval, generosity again beyond what a gleaner could expect. As in v 8, Boaz did not answer Ruth's bold approach directly, but by making room for her among his people.

On this reading, the interval between conversation and meal (shorter than commonly proposed) occurred in the middle of v 14, precisely at the shift from speech to action. Bush calls such a reading "a clumsy break in the flow of the action" (1996, 125). In fact, it preserves the continuity of their conversation to its end, before moving to the action of sitting down to eat.

The almost universal construal—Ruth spoke, Boaz kept quiet, she went to the field to work, he later called her over to eat, she sat down and ate—is unnecessarily choppy and reads the Hebrew syntax oddly. It also presents a doubtful vision of Boaz; would he make *no* response to Ruth's speech? Against any attempt to pair Boaz's supposed silence with Naomi's (1:18), it must be pointed out that Naomi's silence was at least reported (1:18), and while Naomi's next speech made no mention of Ruth (1:20-21), Boaz's next words were spoken *to Ruth*. It is a dubious parallel.

If the overseer's report of Ruth waiting "from morning till now" made any sense (2:7), she must have waited several hours. Thus, the midday meal was imminent, especially as grain harvesters were eager to start work as early as possible, to let the cut grain dry before loading, and to get off the fields before the late afternoon sun became oppressive. If Ruth did any work before sitting down to lunch, it cannot have been much.

When she sat down with the harvesters, Ruth found herself honored by a place among Boaz's workers, a move meant to establish respect from the people who could prevent or promote her efforts. Boaz distinguished her further, serving her **roasted grain** in addition to the bread and wine vinegar; the form this dish took is unclear. **Offered** translates the Hebrew verb *ṣāvaṭ*, which occurs only here in the OT and could mean "to heap" or "pile up." In any case, the provision was more than enough for a hungry gleaner, as she **had some left over.** This was Boaz's last recorded interaction with Ruth until ch 3.

■ **15-16** As Ruth headed for the field, Boaz addressed **his men** (*nĕʿārîm*). This could refer to the *young* men, against whom he warned Ruth earlier (2:9), but masculine plural nouns often refer to mixed groups in Hebrew, especially when feminine plural nouns are missing (→ vv 8-9). In this case, *nĕʿārîm* means **workers,** both male and female, since these orders were just as binding on the women as on the men.

Once Ruth was out of hearing, Boaz gave strict instructions. She was allowed to **glean among the sheaves** (explicit approval of her earlier request), without **reprimand** for working where gleaners usually did not. His next instruction went even further: they were to intentionally **pull out some stalks** of grain and **leave them** (use of *āzab* again) for her to find. The harvesters were to *forsake* some of Boaz's yield to honor Ruth's forsaking of her home and refusal to forsake Naomi. This order not being spoken in Ruth's hearing, we must imagine her response when she began to find more "leftover" grain than good workers should leave behind, especially given the recent famine.

Boaz showed wisdom, knowing even with his permission in place, Ruth might face resentment over these privileges, and he forbad any verbal censure: **don't rebuke her** (v 16). He wanted Ruth to know no shame as a needy Moabite in his field. We can be sure, too, that Ruth's feisty speech and Boaz's flustered response stirred ideas in the minds of his workers, which might result in insults and innuendos. He would have none of it, especially if his own thoughts were beginning to move in that direction.

■ **17** With all obstacles removed and multiple privileges in place, **Ruth gleaned**. This summary verse omits the special circumstances of her gleaning arrangements. Wanting to make the most of her afternoon, Ruth gathered grain from lunch until evening, then **threshed** it.

Small quantities of grain were threshed by beating the heads of the stalks with a stick to loosen the individual kernels from the ear. The kernels were then scooped into bundles or baskets for carrying, while the stalks were used as straw. Depending on how one calculates an **ephah**, Ruth collected either twenty-nine or fifty pounds of kernels after threshing! Either way, this was an amazing yield for a gleaner, testifying "both to Boaz's generosity and to Ruth's industry" (Hubbard 1988, 179).

C. Home to Naomi (2:18-23)

■ **18-19** The action turned from the field to the village, as Ruth headed home. This is the second instance of a chapter's action closing with Naomi, at home talking to a woman. The Hebrew of the first clause is simply *she lifted up and she went to the town* (v 18). It features our final use of *nāśā*, closing the LRWP that began when Ruth was *lifted up* as a bride back in Moab (1:4), and then *lifted up* her tears with Orpah (1:9, 14). Since English requires an object for this verb, the NIV has **She carried it** (2:18). Hubbard's "She loaded up" is pleasing and allows for a smoother division between the closing line of the previous scene (v 17) and Ruth's departure from the fields (1988, 180).

Her **mother-in-law** is noteworthy; rather than naming the woman absent from the drama at the field, **mother-in-law** allows a gradual reentry into Ruth's home situation. With a potential suitor back there in the field, she still had a mother-in-law at home, one to whom she had pledged herself. The narrator called her **mother-in-law** three times in two verses, and not by her name until v 20!

Ruth displayed her haul, then handed over the leftovers from her lunch. Not only were they provisioned for the next few weeks, but the old woman also had supper. This did not match her complaint that she was empty and as good as dead, with even Yahweh against her (1:21).

The abundance provoked wonder: who was so generous? Her rapid-fire queries, **Where did you glean today? Where did you work?** (2:19), seem redundant until we notice its effect compounded with the rest of the verse. Before Ruth could answer, the older woman continued with her first positive words since she blessed Orpah and Ruth (1:8-9): **Blessed be the man who took notice of you!** (lit. *your notice-taker*). The LRWP of **notice** (*nākar*; → v 10) is continued here; Ruth and her mother-in-law used the same term for the kindness of the field owner.

The double questions are matched by redundancy in Ruth's answer. The Hebrew reads: *she told her mother-in-law the one she worked with and she said, "the name of the man who I worked with today."* Two questions, a blessing, and two tellings: these intentional redundancies by the storyteller prolonged the moment until Ruth finally revealed the name that held no significance to her: **Boaz**.

■ **20** At this, **Naomi** was restored both to her own name and to *Yahweh*'s. Interestingly, Ruth became again **daughter-in-law**. Even with Ruth moving toward a new marriage, the narrator did not allow the women's relationship to become secondary.

Our LRWP with *āzab* ("forsake") is brought to a magnificent conclusion, and the forsaking ended (v 20). Another LRWP continues: in 1:8, Naomi was happy to send *ḥesed* off with Ruth and Orpah, but here, she found *ḥesed* had returned. The reader knows she was never without it. In Hebrew, the blessing is ambiguous: **Blessed is he by Yahweh who has not forsaken his *ḥesed* to the living and the dead.** Who did not forsake his *ḥesed*, Boaz or Yahweh? Both readings make sense narratively and grammatically. Naomi may have meant Yahweh had reversed his policy of afflicting her (1:21); she may also have been praising Boaz in exactly the terms she praised Ruth and Orpah (1:8). One of the luxuries of literary ambiguity is that both meanings can operate upon the reader simultaneously.

Theodoret of Cyr on Ruth 2:20

With a heart thankful for the remembrance of kindness, Naomi rewarded the absent benefactor of her daughter-in-law with a blessing. For she said, "May he who has acknowledged you be blessed, for he has filled an empty soul by doing what he did. He took notice not of poverty but only of the Lawgiver, who ordered that widows be shown care." (Franke 2005, 186)

Another layer of meaning is added to Naomi's words by recognizing an allusion to another passage. When Abraham's servant Eliezer met Rebekah, and knew by a sign from Yahweh she was the one to marry Isaac, he said, **Blessed be Yahweh . . . who has not forsaken his *ḥesed* and faithfulness to my master** (Gen 24:27). With this textual echo, readers cannot help but wonder if Naomi suddenly saw Boaz as a potential husband for Ruth. She did later send Ruth to the threshing floor to force the issue; was this the lightbulb moment?

Naomi knew this man. She called him first *qārôb lānû*, **near to us**, or **our close relative**. This is a different term than the narrator's *môda'* in v 1, but neither signifies a specific type of relative. At this point, two people in the story (Boaz and Naomi) knew the relative was also a redeemer, though it was not yet spoken aloud. Naomi's final revelation, however, introduced new dynamics into Ruth's day: *one of our redeemers is he* (he is one of our guardian-redeemers). The implications of Boaz's status as redeemer (*go'el*) will be explored below and in the following chapters. For now we will observe that her statement suggested an implicit reason for Boaz's largesse in the field. Hearing it was Boaz, Naomi understood better than Ruth at least one reason he was so kind: it was his *job* to look out for them.

Naomi's repetition of **our** is important. She had called Ruth "my daughter" every time she spoke to her, but given the common use of that address discussed above, and her despondency, we could never be sure she was not using it generically. Indeed, she was at pains to isolate herself from this daughter (1:13*b*, 20-22; 2:2). The return of *ḥesed* resurrected her ability to connect, and for the first time, she acknowledged Ruth unequivocally as belonging to her family: **our close relative . . . our guardian-redeemer.** Naomi was now engaged, and she and Ruth were in this together (Trible 1978, 179).

The *Go'el*

Reading Ruth well means understanding the duties of a **guardian-redeemer** (*go'el*). Many misconceptions center on the conflation of two distinct roles: the levir, or brother-in-law (→ "Levirate Marriage [Deut 25:5-10]" at 1:9-10), and the *go'el*, or redeemer. As shown above, there was no levir for Naomi or Ruth; *go'el* duties (below) had nothing to do with marriage. Boaz was a *go'el*; neither he nor anyone else in Bethlehem was required to marry Ruth. Commentary on chs 3—4 will explore how *go'el* and levir figured there. (For more detail, see Hubbard [1988, 188-89; 1991] and Leggett [1974].)

A *go'el* could be one's brother, uncle, uncle's son, or anyone of the same blood, from the whole clan (Lev 25:49). One's *go'el* acted in at least the five situations below. If a person:

1. sold land or house to raise money, a *go'el* was to buy it or buy it back for them (Jer 32; Ruth 4; Lev 25:25-34).
2. indentured themselves, a *go'el* was to buy their release (Lev 25:47-55).
3. was owed restitution but died before it was paid, a *go'el* was to receive payment (Num 5:8).
4. was killed, a *go'el* was to pursue justice (Num 35:12-27).
5. went to court, a *go'el* could plead their cause (inferred from poetic texts: Ps 119:154; Prov 23:11; Jer 50:34; Lam 3:58).

Only the first duty informed Naomi's situation directly. In at least some duties, a closer relation gave one *go'el* precedence over others, but in every case, a *go'el* acted only *if they were able and willing.*

A thorough survey of *go'el* in the OT reveals a broad sense of family responsibility. In short, a *go'el* was any of a pool of relatives who could be called on to redeem an Israelite from poverty or injustice. The case laws above specify how redemption played out in those situations, but they are not the limit of the concept. When Naomi and Ruth called Boaz a *go'el* (Ruth 2:20; 3:9), they were drawing on this broader sense of his belonging to a group of relatives who could be depended on as gracious benefactors. Boaz was already a proven *go'el*, after one day in the field!

■ **21-22** Why call her **Ruth the Moabite?** (v 21). The narrative has been gradually assimilating Ruth into Israel: she bound herself to an Israelite, then literally moved from Moab to Israel (ch 1), then found acceptance in an Israelite field (to replace the *fields of Moab* she left [1:1]). Naomi just affirmed Ruth's place in her Israelite family. Eventually Ruth became wife to an Israelite *'îš gibbôr ḥayil*, and mother to his son, absolute proof of belonging. However, the incorporation was not final yet, and raising her foreignness again recalled not only her astonishing welcome but also that more favor and *ḥesed* were yet needed.

Stay with my workers echoed Boaz's instructions (and features the third use of *dābaq*, "cling"), but replaced the *young women* of 2:8 with *young men*. Ruth probably meant it as the inclusive noun representing the whole group (→ v 15), but the idea of clinging to young men prompted a corrective from Naomi: in Hebrew, *It would be better for you, my daughter, to go with the young women who work for him*. Why? Men (or people in other fields) might *pāga'* her; the LRWP that opened in 1:16 with "urge" closes here with "harm." The verb's root meaning is "meet" or "encounter" (so, "meet with a request" = urge). Here it carries negative nuance, "meet with hostility," "attack" (Judg 15:12; 2 Sam 1:15), which many commentators soften to "bother" or as the NIV, **harmed** (Ruth 2:22). Ruth did not want to meet with urging from Naomi in Moab; Naomi did not want Ruth to meet with harm in the field. Now concerned for Ruth's safety, Naomi was emerging from her grief at last.

An interesting addition to Boaz's welcome was now revealed: it had been extended through the whole harvest season. He did not hire her, but offered to prolong the extra gleaning privileges. This is apparent from Naomi's response, which anticipates that Ruth might go to **someone else's field**; she would only do that if she were still gleaning.

The narrator did not include this offer in the midday encounter, so we do not know when Boaz extended the invitation, but presumably in another conversation later in the day. There is no need to see mischief on Ruth's part (Fewell and Gunn 1990, 39). This is a common narrative technique, to reveal part of a conversation between two characters by reporting it to a third. We've seen it in the overseer's report to Boaz, and we will see it again in 3:17. It serves the style of a short story well, rather than the extended repetition of conversations or events sometimes used in longer narratives (see Gen 24; 41; Exod 11—12).

Something else omitted in Ruth's report was Boaz's praise and blessing of her. As encouraging as it must have been for Ruth, she could hardly repeat it, lest it shame Naomi as an object of public pity in the village. Wesley comments at this point, "Humility teaches not only not to praise ourselves, but not to be forward in repeating the praise which others have given us" (1975, 885). Humility leads to kindness.

■ **23** This summary statement closes an LRWP, as well as the chapter. Ruth once "clung" to Naomi on a dusty road (*dābaq*, 1:14); she now *clung* (**stayed close**) to Boaz's women in a dusty field. She gleaned through two harvests, approximately seven weeks of backbreaking labor from late April through early June. If she maintained her rate of yield from the first day, she likely gathered enough to see them through the year. Her tenacity was serving them well.

And she lived with her mother-in-law returned Ruth from the fields to her home each night. Rather than a cozy picture of domestic bliss, this was an intentional anticlimax. With Boaz that first day in the field, with all the trappings of a betrothal scene, a removal from her home looked possible. But after weeks of daily encounters, nothing materialized in that direction. Ruth and Naomi were home and well-fed, at least for now, and restored to each other as partners in their mutual survival. However, there was no permanent solution in place; they were still dependent on the Israelite "welfare system," so the story must go on.

FROM THE TEXT

Partners at Last: After the roughest of beginnings in ch 1, the second episode of Naomi and Ruth's saga began by separating them—one at home, one in the field—and by introducing a third partner in redemption. The spotlight moved away from Naomi to see how Ruth might fulfill that magnificent oath she made back on the road. Ruth's day took her from uncertainty to welcome, away from potential danger, through extraordinary attention and the frisson of attraction, to hard work and home.

Lest the reader forsake the old woman for these new possibilities, the narrator kept reminding us of Naomi: (1) The overseer's identification of the stranger, "who came back . . . with Naomi" (2:6); (2) Boaz's familiar address to Ruth, "My daughter" (v 8); (3) his praise of Ruth's care for Naomi (v 11). These subtle cues culminated finally in Ruth's physical return to Naomi loaded down with food, and Naomi's satisfying reattachment to the younger woman. The chapter as a whole proved the hollowness of Naomi's claim to emptiness in 1:21; as long as Ruth was around, Naomi was full. These events moved them from the isolation of grief to the strength of partnership.

A Harvest of Ḥesed: Naomi testified to Ruth's capacity for *ḥesed* in 1:8. Ruth staked her own life on it in 1:16-17. Would it be enough? Could she live up to that? As ch 2 began, these were open questions, but the events on Boaz's field dispelled all doubt.

Ruth's way of gleaning pushed boundaries, shined a light on their need, and called out the best in Boaz. Love bears fruit, and Ruth's love in action did exactly that. She carried home the literal fruit of her laboring love for Naomi, having secured them a powerful ally by her efforts. Would Ruth's *ḥesed* be enough? This bounty of grain and goodness made Naomi herself answer the question: Ruth's *ḥesed* called forth Boaz's *ḥesed*, and together they proved Yahweh's *ḥesed* (v 20). The harvest was well under way, and not just on the field.

This chapter reminds us that the love that is to characterize the people of God can be sweaty and uncomfortable work. If Ruth's *ḥesed* only went as far as her words, or if Boaz had cared too much about people's opinions, we wouldn't know their story. Naomi needed food, not words; Ruth needed someone to let "that good-for-nothing Moabite" onto his field. *Ḥesed* is loyalty that is willing to take risks, look foolish, and work hard.

Wesley on Taking Stock of *Ḥesed*

Where hast thou gleaned today? It is a good question to ask ourselves in the evening, "Where have I gleaned today?" What improvements have I made in grace or knowledge? What have I learned or done, which will turn to account? (Wesley 1975, 884)

III. HOW NAOMI'S PLAN WORKED OUT: RUTH 3:1-18

BEHIND THE TEXT

The structures of chs 2 and 3 are similar. Both begin with a conversation between the two women, after which Ruth departs for the main location. A summary statement reports her departure and describes the action at the main location (2:3; 3:6). Each summary statement is then followed by the first action of Boaz (2:4; 3:7), which leads to extensive dialogue between Ruth and Boaz. Boaz then gives Ruth food and exits the scene; Ruth goes home to Naomi, where she reports the outcome of their encounter.

The main action of ch 3 occurred at Bethlehem's threshing floor, a flat, communal tract of land outside of town. Large quantities of grain were threshed with carts, sledges, or animals treading over them. Then the kernels needed to be separated from the rest of the stalk so they could be ground, roasted, or stored. The best way to do that was winnowing: tossing the threshed grain into a breeze, the stalks and chaff blew out, and the kernels fell down together. Everything was then gathered, the kernels for food, the rest for fuel or animal feed. This process marked the end of the growing cycle, and so was a merry time with festivities and ritual celebration (Exod 23:16; 34:22).

The author's penchant for ambiguity, double entendre, and even innuendo, reached its summit in this chapter. Without being bawdy, the nighttime encounter on the threshing floor was rife with sexual tension. It served a more important function than vulgar entertainment, though. By the end, Ruth and Naomi had secured their future by securing Boaz's commitment. Critical to this chapter is a consideration of the role of levir vis-à-vis redeemer. We refer the reader back to the excursuses on these laws in Ruth 1 and 2 ("Levirate Marriage [Deut 25:5-10]" at Ruth 1:9-10 and "The *Go'el*" at 2:20).

Recognizing the undertones of this scene, and allowing their full weight in our interpretation, is not, as some would have it, prurient. Instead, it restores to the canon an entry that resources healthy theologies of human sexuality. As argued below, Ruth and Boaz preserved their sexual integrity, even if they did consummate their marriage that night, as is possible but not certain. Refusing to ignore the directions in which the text intentionally points will lead, in the end, to a richer theological reading of this infamous chapter.

IN THE TEXT

A. Risking All for a Mother-in-Law (3:1-6)

■ **1** **Naomi** emerged from her despair during the harvest, able at last to look into the future. In our third installment of the journey-dialogue-home pattern, Naomi set about planning a journey for Ruth. Ruth's vow had been effective so far, but from Naomi's point of view, it did not guarantee Ruth lifelong security. As Phipps discerns, "If [Naomi] were to die, even the marginal security that Ruth has in Bethlehem will be jeopardized, for an alien childless widow with no neighboring relatives has virtually no place" (1992, 57).

Naomi's purpose was clear: to **find a home** for Ruth. **Home** here translates *mĕnûḥah*, the same state of marital rest Naomi urged on her daughters-in-law back in 1:9. The obvious candidate, Boaz, had not yet followed through on their promising beginning, so Naomi set about to raise the issue in a way that could not be ignored.

■ **2** **Boaz** again was called *môda'*, **relative**. The endogamous marriage practices of this culture made a relative the preferred spousal choice. Boaz's specific status as *go'el* was irrelevant, because Naomi was not pursuing *levirate* marriage for her daughter-in-law; her concern was Ruth's marriage to a relative, and not her own redemption. The first use of the noun *môda'* confirmed other clan members were still alive in Bethlehem (2:1). Here it confirmed an eligible spouse in Bethlehem, one of their own family.

Naomi's mention of the **women** harvesters helped lay the groundwork for her astonishing plan. Ruth knew these women by now and had watched them interact with Boaz; he could be trusted to protect the women under his care. He was a known entity.

Winnowing barley (instead of the second crop, wheat) seems to conflict with 2:23, wherein Ruth gleaned "until the barley and wheat harvests were finished" and *then* "lived with her mother-in-law" (Bush 1996, 149). Since the Hebrew syntax is awkward, **winnowing the threshing floor of the barley**, Campbell reads "gates" instead of **barley** (the Hebrew nouns are nearly identical). He translates "winnowing the threshing floor near the gate," citing the threshing floors found just outside the gates of some towns (1975, 117-19). This is a viable solution, though not without issue, as Bush points out.

Sasson reads chs 3 and 4 as occurring after the barley harvest, but before the wheat was completely gathered. This fits his views that Naomi wanted to secure Boaz before harvest ended (1979, 63), and that Boaz wanted to secure the field before the other *go'el* might be at leisure to stake his claim (1979, 130-31). We take his point about a narrative timeline not needing to be precisely linear, and both needs for haste make sense. However, if as Sasson argues, Ruth's betrothal was arranged and made public before the wheat harvest was over, would she have continued to glean as a widow (2:23)? Driesbach suggests that with the whole town harvesting, and only one threshing floor, there might still be barley to winnow after both crops were gathered in (2012, 531). This solution has the advantage of being plausible without needing to amend the text.

Naomi's proposed location for the encounter is our first hint that her plan was unusual. The **threshing floor**, in addition to being a public place, was a festive one during the harvest season. After long days in the sun, harvesters relaxed by eating and drinking (3:3), possibly in ritualized celebration as part of the annual harvest rites (Sasson 1979, 65). In at least one other text, the threshing floor is a scene of sexual behavior (Hos 9:1). Even without knowing specifics, it was dangerous in this era to send the foreign Ruth alone into the night.

■ **3-4** Naomi's instructions form a remarkable chain of imperatives, in Hebrew: ***Wash, anoint, put on, go down, do not make known, take note, go, uncover, lie down***. Naomi's rapid-fire commands were impressive. She gave Ruth no time to question or falter, and did not stop to elaborate or clarify any of them. They were to be taken at face value by Ruth.

The intention was unmistakable. Ruth was to **wash** and **perfume** her body, then wrap in a ***cloak***. With most commentators, we read the MT's notation of the singular noun *śimlâ* ("cloak," "garment"), not the plural (**clothes**). **Best clothes** stretches the meaning of the plural noun, which is usually found in contexts where the person dressing was in a lowly state (Gen 37:34; 44:14; Exod 19:10; Josh 7:6; Isa 4:1).

The grooming here was reminiscent of the bride in Ezek 16:9-10, and of Esther (2:12), and Sasson finds further parallels in Mesopotamian texts (1979, 67). Against this connotation, Bush complains Ruth's ordinary garment does not match the finery in these texts (1996, 152). While correct, he ignores the glaring discrepancy between their lavish contexts and a poor widow's resources. His proposed parallel with the same sequence of verbs in 2 Sam 12:20, in a context of emerging from mourning, is compelling and fits Ruth's situation. It does not negate the sensory impact of a clean and scented body in the dark, though. It might be more than the text can bear to see Ruth as a bride preparing for her groom, but these were deliberate preparations nonetheless. She was to go **to the threshing floor** and stay hidden ("do not be known by the man," Fewell and Gunn 1990, 117), until Boaz fell asleep.

When he lies down . . . where he is lying . . . lie down. Three times in Ruth 3:4, seven in the whole chapter, the author used the verb *šākab*. In many other instances, *šākab* means to lie with, sexually (Gen 30:15; 39:7; Exod 22:15 [14 HB]; 44). In most of our seven uses, it cannot mean that, but the third use here and Ruth 3:14 are more suggestive. The author teases with terms that have explicit sexual meanings elsewhere, but *probably* do not carry that connotation here. It is a brilliant way to portray the tension, through vocabulary choices rather than heavy-handed explication (e.g., "and feeling nervous and excited, Ruth offered herself to Boaz").

Uncover his feet and lie down. He will tell you what to do: the final instructions were shocking. Remember, Naomi's goal was to get Ruth married. She was to show up at the dark threshing floor, freshly bathed, then uncover a sleeping man, *šākab* next to him, and do whatever he said. Uncover (*gālâ*) opens our final LRWP. Its use here brings the reader up short; Naomi cannot mean that? Ruth took her at face value and followed this instruction, not knowing what the reaction would be (v 7). *Gālâ* occurs a third time with a similar sense of suspense, but in a very different context. Here it was used as part of Naomi's plan in the dead of night; there it helped Boaz uncover his own plan in the light of day (see "bring the matter to your attention" or "inform you" [NKJV] in 4:4).

His feet was at least innuendo, if not euphemism. Our noun *margĕlōtāyw*, **the place of his feet**, is a rare form of *regel*, **foot**, which sometimes operates as a euphemism for genitalia:

1. Judg 3:24; 1 Sam 24:4 [5 HB]: **covering his feet** means urinating
2. Ezek 16:25: **you spread your feet** is an accusation of promiscuity
3. Deut 28:57: the afterbirth comes out **from between her feet**
4. Isa 7:20: shaving the head, the beard, and **the hair of the feet** as an act of humiliation

Fewell and Gunn suggest Naomi employs *margĕlōtāyw* instead of *regel* precisely because she could not bear to say aloud what she really meant (1990, 127). The narrator maintained this minor diversion, using *margĕlōtāyw*, **the place of his feet**, through the rest of the chapter (Ruth 3:7, 8, 14). Nielsen pursues another approach, noting the verb **uncover** here is not followed by the usual direct object marker, and citing the usual sense of *gālâ*, uncovering nakedness as a euphemism for sex (Lev 18:6-19; 20:11-21). She argues for a translation something like **uncover yourself at the place of his feet** (1997, 67-71).

We find these readings compelling, but maintain the author's intention was to be indistinct, to suggest connections never confirmed. Whether Naomi intended anyone's skin to be exposed or not, her instructions positioned a freshly bathed woman next to a sleeping man to wake him up in the middle of the night. The implications were unavoidable, but they remain implications.

Threshing Floor Morals

Even if one does not grant that Naomi instructed Ruth to uncover either Boaz's body or her own, there can be no doubt Naomi thought they would have sex. The standard objections to such readings are based on the premise that respectable women like Ruth and Naomi would never undertake such a brazen plan, and that a righteous man like Boaz would be properly repulsed by such debauchery. Two examples are representative of the vast majority of commentators. Bush declared it "so inconsistent with the character of Ruth as portrayed in the story as to be utterly implausible" (1996, 153). While acknowledging the sexual sense of the scene without hesitation, Hubbard is confident that "[Boaz] would not take unfair sexual advantage of the situation" (1988, 204).

Predicated on the dominant sexual ethic of the Judeo-Christian traditions, of course they are right. But mitigating factors were at work here. First, we will argue below that Boaz and Ruth were betrothed this night, not the next morning. As I have discussed elsewhere,

> One must understand that the point at which a couple was considered married and intercourse permissible was different in the ancient world than in Christian communities today. Israel's law tacitly acknowledged that men and women sometimes slept together before the public wedding ceremony. It was more concerned to keep a man from abandoning the woman after physical union or from having sex with a woman betrothed to someone else (Deut 24). Therefore, sleeping with one's betrothed was not in quite the same moral category as it is for most Christians today. We may consider Ruth and Boaz as having acted honorably within the moral constructs of their own day, whether or not intercourse occurred that night. (Derck 2011, 247)

We refer the reader to our treatment of Song of Songs in this volume. In many passages, sexual activity is clear, and though wedding imagery is present in the poems, any proposed definition of the lovers' marital status is tenuous at best.

To insist Ruth and Boaz *did not* have intercourse because righteous people *would not* is, first, circular reasoning, and second, anachronistic. Further, it repudiates the author's overt playfulness. As Sakenfeld says so cogently, "Never is there any indication of the consummation of sexual relations, yet the choice of words keeps that possibility always before the reader. The storyteller creates an atmosphere of ambiguity and mystery" (1999, 54). To insist either way is to deny the storyteller his or her own creation.

■ **5-6** Ruth's answer was brief and unquestioning. Sasson reads this as the proper obedience of one who has indentured herself to Naomi (1979, 124). Even while accepting that Ruth's vow in ch 1 was not just a loving outburst, but a formal commitment sworn by oath, the dynamic between them did not deny Ruth's choice. She showed initiative from the beginning. Her resistance to Naomi trying to send her back, and her assertiveness at the field, proved she was not a woman to be cowed into blind submission. Perhaps instead, she was flabbergasted; this audacious plan likely took her by the same surprise it does the reader. Just as previous speeches have provoked intense reactions (1:18; 2:10, 14), Naomi did not stop for breath, and Ruth's response to the plan reads like one stirred to action by its very daring.

Verse 6 of ch 3, like its counterpart transition statement in 2:3, forecasts the main action of the chapter. However, it is playfully broad; as we will learn, Ruth followed Naomi's instructions in her own way, taking even more initiative than Naomi had devised. We dare not overlook the risks Ruth willingly undertook; though Naomi planned this encounter for Ruth's benefit, Ruth dared more, as she had done with her gleaning.

B. Ruth and Boaz's Extreme Obedience (3:7-15)

■ **7** Boaz's evening unfolded just as Naomi predicted, suggesting she knew the habits of the threshing floor. Modern readers want more explanation. Why did Boaz need to spend the night? Various reasons have been suggested by interpreters: to utilize the late and early breezes for winnowing, to guard the grain, or to join in harvest celebrations. All are plausible, and each likewise has its limits. The story either assumed the readers' knowledge or deemed it irrelevant; we just aren't told.

Was Boaz alone? Modern readers hope so, recoiling at the idea of Naomi instigating such an intimate meeting in public. Most ancient peasant families slept all in one room, though, and notions of privacy were different. Avoiding discovery was part of the reason for Naomi's cautions, but to what end? Stay hidden until Boaz (and everyone else?) was settled (v 3); take note of where he lay down (v 4), to avoid waking the wrong man? Boaz wanted her to get home without being seen (v 14). What did discovery risk? Danger? Shame? Ruining the next day's negotiations? Perhaps all three.

We likewise refrain from speculating on the nature of Boaz's meal, and how much of what drink he consumed (quiet repast or merry feast?). The phrase **was in good spirits** translates *his heart was good*, an idiom of satisfaction and merriment in similar contexts (1 Kgs 8:66; Prov 15:15; Eccl 9:7). Many commentators follow Campbell's suggestion that Naomi needed Boaz to be sufficiently mellow to be receptive to her plan (1975, 122), suggesting wine helped him achieve the state. She had no hand in how much he ate or drank, however, and his alacrity in responding (both that night and first thing next morning) does not sound like a man intoxicated.

In any case, Boaz was in a good mood and went to sleep in a fortunate location, **at the far end of the grain pile**. The reader does not need to "note the place where he is lying" (→ v 4) as Ruth did, so why was this detail included? Sasson suggests the perimeter of the grain pile provided maximum privacy in that public place (1979, 73). They did, in fact, get through the night without detection. It strikes the chord of providence early in this scene, which was so fraught with tension, and together with Boaz's mood, which Naomi did not specifically anticipate in her instructions, hinted that all was well.

Once Boaz was asleep, Ruth followed Naomi's final instructions, uncovered **his feet** (with the same grammatical construction and interpretive possibilities as v 4), and **lay down**. So far all had gone to plan, but this was the point where Naomi's instructions left off, allowing Boaz to take charge. Ruth's faithfulness to Naomi led her to a compromising situation. If we did not already trust Boaz because of his kindness in the field, we might fear for Ruth's safety, having gotten into bed with a man of influence, to whom she owed a great deal, in the time of the judges.

■ **8** The effects of Ruth's presence were not immediate. Boaz was sleeping soundly, the inevitable result of hard work in the fresh air and a good meal, even without wine. With Linafelt, we find the common claim that he was roused by the air on his uncovered body unconvincing (1999, 53). As argued above, we cannot be certain whether Boaz or Ruth was uncovered. The text also described his waking as violent, not the kind of slow surfacing from sleep equated with one who has lost their blanket. Ruth's moment finally came, but Boaz did not wake gently.

The middle of the night is not a peaceful time in OT narratives (Gen 32:22-32 [23-33 HB]; Exod 12:29; Judg 15:3). Sasson's theory of a prevailing fear of nighttime demons is promising, though unprovable: it was common in Israel's neighbors, and in the Judaism of Jesus' day, and may be read in the Hebrew of Isa 34:14 (1979, 74-78). More than that we cannot say.

The verbs described Boaz's waking as intense. **Startled** translates *hārad*, **he trembled** or **was terrified**, as one might well be, when woken suddenly from a deep sleep to find someone there in the dark. **He turned** renders an obscure verb, *lāpat*, which occurs in only two other passages. In Judg 16:29, Samson **grasped** the pillars to which he was chained and pulled them down. In both Job 6:18 and our passage, that meaning is nonsensical; none of the dozens of theories in the literature about this verb's meaning have achieved consensus. The clause that follows this enigmatic verb reads quite starkly in Hebrew, **and behold: a woman lying at "the place of his feet."** There is more shock in this verse than the NIV's exclamation point can convey.

■ **9** Boaz's "good spirits" were startled out of him, and he could choke out only the question, **Who are you?** There's a delicious irony here: Boaz asked this question once before about Ruth, in broad daylight. In the dark, he could not distinguish her face, but the end of v 8, and his use of the feminine form of **you**, indicate she was recognizably female.

The question fit the clandestine nature of the meeting. Ruth emerged from her hiding place in the dark, "approached quietly" (v 7), and then uncovered either him or herself. The Hebrew text of ch 3 has not even called her by name until now. She was anonymous and generic, "her" (v 1), "she" (vv 5-7), or "a woman" (v 8) all along, until she revealed herself, **your servant Ruth**. This was the first time her name was spoken aloud by anyone (Black 1991, 28); in fact, it was the first of only three times someone in the tale spoke her name (4:5, 10).

Much has been made of the switch to *'āmāh*, another word for **maid**, from *šipḥâ* (2:13), though the terms are used interchangeably in many passages. Sasson and others claim a *šipḥâ* occupied the lowest position in a household, an *'āmāh* slightly higher (1979, 53). Thus, he argues that Ruth used *šipḥâ* to express obeisance in ch 2 but that with *'āmāh* she hinted the social gap between them was closing (1979, 80-81). As we are not convinced any difference between *šipḥâ* and *'āmāh* has been proved, this interpretation seems an overreach. We look instead to their parallel effects in Ruth: both expressed deference to Boaz, and both refer in other passages to women who married the men to whom they were maids, suggesting a subtle allusion to the future she was offering him.

This debate has typically obscured a remarkable absence. Ruth did not call herself "Ruth the Moabite," like the narrator (1:22; 2:2, 21), the overseer (2:6), and even Boaz (4:5, 10). She did not identify herself as Naomi's "daughter-in-law" (1:6, 7, 8; 2:20, 22; 4:15), or as Mahlon's widow (4:5, 10), though either would lay the groundwork for her subsequent reference to *gŏ'el*. Instead of "her daughter" or "his widow," **your servant** was a term of deference claiming connection to the man of whom she was about to ask so much.

In the natural course of events, and in Naomi's mind, this was the point at which Boaz would know "what to do" (v 4) with a young woman who came and lay down next to him in the middle of the night. Instead, Ruth charged past everyone's expectations and upped the ante. Instead of going quiet, Ruth kept speaking; instead of letting him tell her what to do, she told him what to do: *Spread your kānāp over your maid* (Spread the corner of your garment over me).

This phrase rang two bells. *Kānāp* was the same word Boaz blessed Ruth with (2:12), closing the LRWP that opened in their first encounter. The basic meaning of the word is "extremity," so "wing" when referring to birds, or "skirt" or "corner" when referring to a garment (1 Sam 15:27). She challenged Boaz to answer his own prayer, to provide the "refuge" he ascribed to Yahweh.

Kānāp, and even the whole idiom *to spread a kānāp*, occur in other passages where a marriage relationship is in view (Deut 22:30 [23:1 HB]; 27:20; Ezek 16:8). That Ruth employed an established formula for a marriage proposal is more than can be supported, but it is nonetheless clear she was asking a permanent commitment of him, proposing they marry. Boaz knew nothing of Naomi's instructions, but this was not going to be just a lucky harvest encounter.

Since you are a guardian-redeemer (*gŏ'el*) has been read almost unanimously as the crux of the matter, the linchpin that secured Boaz's compliance. We have argued no one in Bethlehem was legally obliged to marry Ruth, and Boaz's remit as *gŏ'el* had nothing to do with marriage (→ "Levirate Marriage [Deut 25:5-10]" at 1:9-10 and "The *Gŏ'el*" at 2:20). If correct, then why did Ruth mention *gŏ'el* in the context of her proposal? In other words, Ruth didn't need a *gŏ'el* for a husband

(Boaz admitted as much in his response), so why prevail on that particular sense of responsibility in the way she proposed marriage?

We are convinced by Sasson, who answers this question by arguing that Ruth's proposal actually contained two separate requests. He should marry her *and* redeem (Naomi and her field, yet unknown to the reader), instead of marrying her *because* he was redeemer (1979, 81-82). Sasson's argument depends on reading the Hebrew *kî* as corroborative ("indeed") instead of causal (**since**). Though Sasson has not gained much support here, it makes the most obvious sense of Boaz's thoughts turning to another *go'el* in vv 12-13.

Modern readers do not know yet, but Ruth, Boaz, and Naomi all knew of the field. It was a small town, and everyone's land was adjacent. An ancient audience, on hearing Ruth ask Boaz to act as *go'el*, and knowing it was nothing to do with marriage, would say to themselves, "Oh, there must be property that needs dealing with." On this reading, the request to redeem brought specifics to Boaz's mind (and the original audience), which were not spelled out for the reader until ch 4.

Why raise redemption at such a time as this? Naomi hadn't asked her to, and it did seem to be mixing business with pleasure. Reminding Boaz of his general obligation to Naomi's family connected the two women in his mind. If he were willing to help either woman, the other stood a good chance of being received well.

Loyal and capable as she was, Ruth still brought three major liabilities to the marriage market. She was a widow, not a virgin; she was apparently barren; she was a Moabite. If she also came with a needy mother-in-law, was that a further strike against her? Ruth never shied away from asking the impossible, but only someone generously inclined would overlook all this to marry her anyway.

To put it crassly, Boaz was a good bet. Beattie, who also denies any obligation to marriage for a *go'el* (though with different arguments), sees *go'el* "as descriptive of Boaz in the part he has already played in the story" (1978, 44). Ruth prevailed on Boaz's already proven record as *go'el* in the general sense, before asking him to assume the mantle of *go'el* legally.

■ **10-11** Boaz's positive response took a circuitous route, not immediately answering her questions (as at 2:8, 14). It was, however, full of praise. This is a crucial corrective to those who would judge Ruth, even subliminally, for utilizing her sexuality as she did. Boaz's response was unequivocal: he considered Ruth's move as flattering evidence of her good character. Ruth gained an immediate sense of his answer, though he did not get to his agreement just yet, blessing her first with the same phrase Naomi used to bless him (2:20), **The LORD bless you** (3:10). This was the last speech in which he called her **my daughter**, as their relationship was moving to a new plane.

Boaz praised her *hesed*, **kindness**, closing the LRWP that began in 1:8. There, Naomi tried to send off her daughters-in-law with thanks for their *hesed*, believing she was now beyond its reach. In 2:20, she proclaimed *hesed* revived through Boaz and Ruth's collaboration at the field. Here, Boaz confirmed Naomi's experience of Ruth's *hesed*.

Scholars debate which **kindness** Boaz referred to. Sasson reads this statement as saying Ruth's second request, to redeem Naomi, was even better than the first, to marry Ruth (1979, 84). Boaz could be referring to at least three things: Ruth's return with Naomi, which he praised once before (2:11-12); her work in the field, which we assume he admired since he protected her in that work; her valiant approach to a marriage partner in uncomfortable conditions. Given that the last time they talked together, he specifically praised her return with Naomi, it makes sense to read that as the **kindness** she **showed earlier** (3:10). In other words, Boaz referred back to their previous conversation, subtly assuring her she was not forgotten in the meantime. Boaz defined the last kindness for us with his next words, *by not going after* other men (a complementary infinitive construct in the Hebrew).

Boaz's good opinion of Ruth revealed two things. He did not expect to be approached like this. As a corollary, Ruth was not required to marry him, but free to marry anyone, **rich or poor**. This negates the theory that Ruth was obligated to marry a *goʾel*, or vice versa. As Sasson says, she was "a free agent in her search for a mate" (1978, 64 n. 2).

Don't be afraid is a common phrase in the OT (Gen 21:17; 35:17), but it strikes a humorous note here, because it is exactly what we expected to hear Ruth say when Boaz was scared awake (Ruth 3:8). Nonetheless, it assured Ruth that she had not offended Boaz. In fact, he agreed to her proposal in every particular. His phrasing, **I will do for you all you ask** (v 11), is a complete reversal of Naomi's expectations, but almost an exact copy of what Ruth herself said to Naomi before setting out into the night (v 5). Ruth's compliance was repaid with Boaz's; he made no caveats or provisos.

Boaz paid one more compliment, calling her *ʾēšet ḥayil*, **a woman of valor** (→ 2:1). To the reader, this marks a perfect match; the man and woman of valor would do well together. His mention of the townspeople lifted Ruth out of the ignominy of foreignness into the realm of public respect.

■ **12** Boaz turned here to the second part of Ruth's request, the duty for which his legal status as *goʾel* came into play. As mentioned in ch 2, in at least some *goʾel* duties, the order of relationship mattered. Apparently, in considering the redemption of land, another of Naomi's relatives had priority. Are we to assume Ruth and Naomi did not know this? Again, Bethlehem was a small town, and Naomi had proved herself a shrewd woman; she surely knew the order of her family's redeemers. On the other hand, redemption was not part of Naomi's plan that night, but Ruth's idea.

■ **13-14** **Stay here for the night** closes the LRWP set up in Ruth's own vow (1:16). She pledged to stay (*lûn*) with Naomi, wherever they could lay their heads, but at Naomi's urging she would **stay** (*lûn*) with Boaz (3:13; → v 4). It connotes a temporary lodging and does not carry the sexual implications of the verb *šākab* scattered throughout this chapter. However, we posit that this invitation confirms for the reader that the marriage between Boaz and Ruth was going forward, regardless of the other man's claim to the field.

No "man of standing" would allow Ruth to spend the rest of the night with him in those conditions—harvesttime on the threshing floor, with all its atmosphere and connotations—if he could not confirm their betrothal (→ "Threshing Floor Morals" at 3:3-4). In Jewish law, a betrothal was as binding as marriage; it even required a divorce to dissolve. Being of age, with Ruth's father out of the picture, they could contract a betrothal on their own by verbal consent. If they were discovered at this point, Boaz could reveal the betrothal and all would be well.

It also proves they had no thought of the other *go'el* marrying Ruth. They could not hope to arrange a marriage to someone else the next day after spending the night together there. Even if no sexual activity occurred, public speculation would have been enough to ruin hopes of marriage to anyone but Boaz.

If he wants to do his duty . . . let him. Some insist Boaz's use of the singular **you/your** means the *go'el* must have something to redeem for Ruth, not Naomi (i.e., marry her). However, we read this as Boaz evincing the same idea of redemption already adopted by the two desperate widows. Naomi considered them as partners in need ("our *go'el*" [2:20]). Ruth did too: Naomi sent her off to get a husband, which she would not do without securing an ally for Naomi at the same time. Boaz displayed the same perspective here.

The Hebrew does not specify how the **duty** might be fulfilled (Beattie 1978, 45). So far, no field was mentioned by anyone, but that is the only one of the law's conditions that *could* apply to Naomi. Boaz could marry Ruth no matter who redeemed Naomi's field, but another buyer would not prevent Boaz from fulfilling the spirit of Ruth's request to redeem Naomi. Simply arranging the field's fate was an act of redemption, even if someone else bought it. Having accepted Ruth, Boaz could redeem Naomi's life in every other way. Even without her field, he could extend his protection and provision, and had already agreed to do so (v 11).

Boaz sealed his submission to Ruth's requests with an oath **on the life of Yahweh**. He then repeated, **Lie here until morning** (3:13), this time using *šākab*. With a betrothal in place, now solemnized by an oath, the talking was over for the night, and *she lay at the place of his feet until morning* (*margĕlōtāyw*, again).

We decline to draw a conclusion either for or against consummation of the marriage at this point. It is more faithful to the text, both in its use of suggestive words and its lack of explicit confirmation, to leave the question open. The tone of playfulness that the author has so carefully crafted is ignored, even violated, by an insistence in either direction.

Ruth rose in the early darkness to get home undetected. **Before anyone could be recognized** closes another LRWP (v 14). In ch 2, Ruth and Naomi were deeply grateful for Boaz's *nākar*, "notice" (vv 10, 19). As the wordplay closes here, Boaz's notice of Ruth had developed far enough that she did not need anyone else to notice, or recognize her.

With a formal betrothal in place, Boaz's caution cannot stem from worry over their reputations (against Phipps 1992, 59). We suggest, instead, their agreement was one of Boaz's points of leverage in the negotiations later that morning, and premature discovery would ruin its efficacy (we will argue that case in our treatment of ch 4). In the meantime, Ruth's departure in the dark was a fitting counterpart to her arrival.

■ **15** Before Ruth left the threshing floor, Boaz gave her more **barley**. The measurement here is less discernible than Ruth's yield in ch 2. The Hebrew reads literally *six barleys*. We appreciate Sasson's comment, "to load a young woman with a large quantity of barley is certainly no way to insure her discreet return home" (1979, 95). The desire to go unseen, together with her **shawl** as the container, suggests a manageable amount; on the other hand, it was enough that Boaz had to place **the bundle on her**. Such ambiguity fits the chapter's tone.

Many reasons for this gift have been suggested, several of which are plausible (Sasson 1979, 97-98). If Ruth were seen, it gave a reason for her coming from the threshing floor: she was bringing home her grain (Hubbard 1988, 222). Ruth's statement in v 17, "Don't go back to your mother-in-law empty-handed" could be read thus, Boaz's way of saying, "Have your hands full as you go, so no one suspects."

The more usual reading of v 17 sees the grain as a gift for Naomi, but such a gift could function in two ways. The grain could serve as a material but discreet pledge of the betrothal, a symbolic bride-price, since Naomi was in no legal position to demand one (Sasson 1979, 98). As Boaz had shown himself willing to do more than what was required, that is plausible. It might also communicate his intention to incorporate Naomi into his care of Ruth.

Boaz's departure **back to town** before Ruth prevented further risk of discovery. It also echoed his departure from the frame in ch 2, where Boaz and Ruth had no reported interaction after he piled her with "roasted grain" (v 14).

C. Home to Naomi, Again (3:16-18)

■ **16-17** This scene continues the pattern of closing the action with Naomi, at home talking to a woman. Ruth's return occasioned a query from Naomi, **How did it go, my daughter?**; literally, *Who are you, my daughter?* This cannot be Naomi's inability to make out the identity of her visitor in the dark, since she called her **my daughter**. Though we have said that address was a conventional one from an older to a younger person, Naomi still had to know it *was* a younger female. This question forms a clever trio with two previous verses. In 2:5 Boaz asked, *Whose is this young woman?*, seeking her familial connection. In 3:9 he asked, "Who are you?", not knowing what woman was lying next to him. Here, Naomi asked with the language of Boaz's second question, but the sense of his first. Naomi was asking what Ruth's familial connection was after her night at the threshing floor. Going forward, was she going to be known primarily by her connection to Naomi or to Boaz?

As we have seen before, the report is here condensed into a summary statement, and adds a detail absent from the narrative of the dialogue (→ 2:21). Ruth's explanation of the grain again reports words of Boaz to which the reader was not privy. With Naomi, we only heard about it after the fact.

Empty-handed closes another LRWP. On her arrival in Bethlehem, Naomi complained of being "empty." It was not really true then, but now the proof was in her hands: grain, given by her new son-in-law, brought by her faithful daughter-in-law. Ruth's last words in the book place her activity at the threshing floor firmly in the realm of redemption, in which she engaged Boaz as partner.

■ **18** Naomi's response reflected satisfaction and trust. In another man, there might still be reason to worry. Would he leave Ruth compromised by their nighttime rendezvous or bring it to an honorable conclusion? Naomi knew Boaz would **not rest** before it was all **settled**. Time was of the essence; Boaz needed to arrange things before talk of their night together got around. It was to his advantage if Boaz approached the other *go'el*, instead of waiting until the other man raised the subject of the field himself, for reasons we will discuss in the next chapter.

FROM THE TEXT

Boldness on Behalf of Others: Naomi cooked up a daring plan. If it went as she expected, she would be giving up her partner in survival, to a man who had no legal obligation to take her into his home. She was effectively releasing Ruth from her vow.

Why do all this at night? As a destitute widow, Naomi stood little chance of being able to arrange any marriage for Ruth through the usual matchmaking channels. They had nothing for a dowry, no social prestige with which to negotiate, and several serious obstacles to Ruth's value. It would take a man just like Boaz, and it would take an unusual approach, since he had not pursued Ruth himself. Just as Ruth's bold requests on the field leveraged the pressure of a public audience upon a "man of standing," Naomi's bold plan leveraged the pressure of intimacy upon a man of honor. Naomi was willing to give up her only aid to survival, to secure rest for Ruth.

Ruth's boldness was astounding. To risk everything—person and reputation—on her mother-in-law's crazy plan, took mettle. Never content with the status quo, Ruth took things two steps further. She made marriage the terms by which she would belong to Boaz (not a given, considering her vulnerability as a foreign widow; many men could have tried to take advantage). Then she made Naomi's need part of her own. Ruth declined the release Naomi offered her, risking the outcome of the whole plan by keeping their fates tied together.

Sexuality and Faithfulness: Christians today should not base their betrothal practices on Ruth 3. As Adam Clarke said in 1826, "The experiment . . . was dangerous, and should in no sense be imitated" (198). However, that raises two crucial points. First, we must be willing to read the Bible for what it *does say*, not for what we *think it should say*. Moral constructs around sexuality and gender have always been particular to time and place, and the scriptural witnesses are no different. One of the primary reasons Ruth's approach is unadvisable today is because it would not have the same ramifications in our world as it did in ancient Israel. We must read Scripture with an eye for the gaps between their cultures and ours, or we risk misreading the word of God.

Second, some women in the Bible found themselves with very little to work with in achieving the things their societies valued. Some resorted to uses of their womanhood that are distasteful to modern readers: Sarah's complicity in Abraham's sister-wife deceptions (Gen 12:10-20); Sarah, Leah, and Rachel's use of their maids as surrogates (Gen 16; 30:1-13); Rachel and Leah's child-birthing competition (Gen 29—30); Tamar's deception of Judah (Gen 38); Rahab the prostitute sheltering Israel's spies (Josh 2).

Ruth worked within the context of her culture and law, but pushed boundaries in order to obtain security for herself and her mother-in-law. These kinds of efforts, often judged by readers as morally dubious, saved the family of God over and over. That Ruth's deeds resulted in the reward of a lineage was God's ruling, but it was not a guaranteed outcome from her perspective. Ruth was not salacious or promiscuous, but neither was she meek, or even "appropriate"; however, she was blessed by the one who knows our hearts.

Human sexuality, so often viewed as a liability, is part of God's good creation. As such, it should be used with all our other resources in the service of God, to pursue God's will. Any accounting of Ruth's faithfulness that denies either the valiant use of her sexuality, or Boaz's corresponding commendation, is a feeble reading of this book. Oh, that we would learn to let God judge the goodness of womanhood.

Ephrem on Ruth

Ephrem the Syrian praised Ruth along these same lines. His fourth-century AD hymn addressed to Christ is worth excerpting:

> By you honorable women made themselves contemptible, [you] the One who makes all chaste. . . . Ruth lay down with a man on the threshing floor for your sake. Her love was bold for your sake. She teaches boldness to all penitents. Her ears held in contempt all [other] voices for the sake of your voice. The fiery coal that crept into the bed of Boaz went up and lay down. She saw the Chief Priest hidden in his loins. . . . She went gleaning for love of you; she gathered straw. You repaid her quickly the wage of her humiliation: instead of ears [of wheat], the Root of kings, and instead of straw, the Sheaf of Life that descends from her. (Franke 2005, 192)

IV. HOW BOAZ'S PLAN WORKED OUT: RUTH 4:1-22

BEHIND THE TEXT

This chapter brought the work of Ruth and Boaz on Naomi's behalf to its climax and conclusion. Many readers are dissatisfied by the apparent absence of Ruth and Naomi from the action. However, it has been one of the narrator's frequent techniques to advance the action with dialogue that did not involve every person concerned. In ch 2, Ruth and Boaz interacted, with Naomi recalled by the overseer (v 6) and Boaz (v 11). In ch 3, Ruth and Boaz interacted, alluding to Naomi in their plans for her redemption (vv 9, 12-13) and the gift of grain (vv 15, 17). In ch 4, then, Boaz talked with Mr. X and the townspeople, with overt mentions of Naomi or Ruth in eleven of the seventeen verses (vv 3, 5, 9-17, not counting the genealogy in vv 18-22).

Neither woman uttered a word in the chapter, but theirs were the needs filled. In fact, a clever denouement was achieved even by Naomi's silence. As Coxon observed, there was an "obvious comparison . . . between the loquacious complaining Naomi of ch. 1 and the serenely silent and satisfied Naomi of ch. 4" (1989, 30).

79

In what is argued below, much of our reading of the legal and social conditions is supported by others, but some is novel. We have tried to take careful account of both the words and the world of the text. We invoke Adam Clarke: "Other meanings, of which I am not ignorant, have been derived from these words; those who prefer to follow them have my consent" (1966, 202).

IN THE TEXT

A. Boaz the Shrewd (4:1-6)

■ **1** With Ruth and Naomi waiting at their home, Boaz set out to accomplish the business of redeeming Naomi. The prominent return of providence is delightful. With divine timing, he arrived **just as the guardian-redeemer he had mentioned came along.** Sasson's translation catches the tone effectively, "No sooner had Boaz gone up to the gate to wait there" (1979, 102).

The town gate was the center of social connection and commerce in ancient towns, in addition to being the locus of security for the inhabitants, and the boundary that marked arrivals and departures. Market stalls operated, business and legal transactions were formalized, and agricultural activity was conducted there in at least some towns (→ 3:2). As Boaz had business that required ratification by the town elders, he settled in, expecting the other *goʾel* to make the typical morning visit to the gate.

Boaz addressed the other *goʾel* by the melodious term *pĕlōnî ʾalmōnî*, which translates literally as **So-and-So**, the equivalent of the modern designation Mr. X (**my friend** in some translations, including the NIV). Boaz knew the man's name, but it was not to be recorded in this tale, in a scene concerned with preserving another man's name. Mr. X forms a parallel to Orpah in ch 1, a secondary connection of the family who did the wise thing in discontinuing their responsibilities. Another parallel is that Orpah and Mr. X each served as a foil to the main character who was their closest counterpart. We learned about the valiance of Ruth by comparing her to Orpah, who took the safe route. We learn about the selflessness of Boaz in contrast to the self-interest of Mr. X. One important difference is maintained between these secondary figures: we know Orpah's name!

■ **2** Boaz assembled **ten of the elders of the town,** revealing several cogent details. First, their immediate compliance with his simple request reflected Boaz's influence in the town. Second, his action established a public audience for the proceedings, which he needed. As the other villagers noticed the elders gathering, they came to watch the proceedings (vv 9, 11), and their presence provided social pressure in the negotiation. Third, the elders served as a jury of peers in situations where judgment was required. Whatever Boaz was planning, then, was something that needed their adjudication. The simple redemption of a field by purchase was not likely such an occasion and could have been arranged within the family.

Inheritance in Israel

In Israelite law, one could not sell or purchase land permanently, because it belonged to Yahweh. The sale of land was essentially a long-term sublease from its human tenant (Lev 25:23-34; Hubbard 1991, 7-8). Every fifty years, the Jubilee returned all land to its original owners, giving families a viable living in perpetuity.

Israelites could only obtain land permanently by inheritance. Property passed from fathers to sons, or daughters if there were no sons (Num 27). If no children lived to inherit one's property, it went to his brothers, then uncles, then nearest blood relative (Num 27:9-11). Elimelek's field was inherited first by Mahlon and Kilion. On their deaths, with no children of their own, it would go to an uncle or blood relative in Bethlehem. This much is clear from OT law.

In what follows, we admit this open question: Boaz spoke of Naomi selling Elimelek's field, but there is no solid evidence Israelite widows could inherit or sell their husbands' property (Galpaz-Feller 2008). Boaz referred to the field as belonging to Elimelek (Ruth 4:3, 9, 10) but being sold by Naomi (vv 3, 5, 9). How could Naomi sell a field bound for a male heir? We cannot solve this puzzle any more than others have, and must accept Boaz's words at face value, observing that he proceeded on a basis that does not match what we know of Israelite law but was acceptable to Bethlehem's elders.

Boaz wanted to redeem Elimelek's field for Naomi (v 4). In this case, redeeming meant purchasing the land from Naomi, giving her capital in exchange (Jer 32:1-15). The purchase was not permanent, but the *go'el* had land rights until the next Year of Jubilee, when it would be released to Naomi if alive, or transferred to the next heir in line.

In redeeming Naomi's land, any *go'el* would do. Boaz did not need the field, either to marry Ruth or for his own gain. Why did it matter then, whether he or Mr. X redeemed it for Naomi? We propose the risk was not *who* redeemed it but whether it was *redeemed for Naomi* or *immediately inherited by another*, passing out of Elimelek's line. With no levir, oblivion was Elimelek's fate, but the field suggested one last option to Boaz.

We draw tentative conclusions about two points in the dynamics of the negotiations. The first is the status of Elimelek's field on Naomi's return. The inheritance was not claimed yet, because the field was still accounted as his. The heir had not pressed his claim, and we do not know exactly why. Confirmation of Mahlon and Kilion's deaths without heirs was unavailable until Naomi returned with reliable evidence. When she did come, everyone was occupied with harvest, and the inheritance claim needed to wait long enough to confirm Mahlon's widow was not carrying his child.

Our second inference is the identity of that heir. Boaz described "another who is more closely related than I" (3:12), and said to Mr. X at the gate, "no one has the right to do it [redeem] except you, and I am next in line" (4:4). These statements endorse the prospect that Mr. X was Elimelek's nearest kinsman in both senses: the *go'el* with prior right to redeem the field, and the blood relative first in line to inherit.

That was the rub for Boaz. Mr. X had only to claim his inheritance, and the field was gone forever from the line of Elimelek. However, if Boaz convinced Mr. X to redeem it instead of inheriting it, or let Boaz redeem it, Naomi would have its redemption price. More importantly, redeeming kept the field in trust for the second part of Boaz's plan, to volunteer as *levir* and conceive an heir for Elimelek with Ruth.

If Boaz stood any chance of success, he had to get Mr. X to renounce his claim, especially since volunteering as *levir* was an unprecedented extension of the law. In the elders' view, a rightful heir may have a stronger claim to the land than a voluntary *levir*. How to force Mr. X's hand, then? Boaz's hopes depended on beating him to the punch with a bold, two-step strategy employing public pressure and timely revelations.

■ **3-4** No one at the gate knew of Boaz's betrothal to Ruth, so to them, Naomi was just a poor widow with nothing but a Moabite daughter-in-law and a field she was about to lose. Having set the scene, Boaz began by recalling the journey of **Naomi** from **Moab**, alluding to her loss and desolation. He described her as **selling the piece of land** (another tragic circumstance; v 3), which closes the LRWP from 2:3. There, Boaz used his own *tract* (*ḥelqâ*, "field") to fill Naomi's stomach and cupboards; here he used her **piece** (*ḥelqâ*) to negotiate a longer-lasting legacy. This announcement was the first explicit mention of the field (→ 3:9).

After opening his case in terms that recalled Naomi's misfortune, Boaz moved forward with the weight of public sympathy for the desperate widow behind him. A subtle jab might be intended with **I thought I should bring the matter to your attention** (v 4). The Hebrew is an idiom, **uncover your ears**, suggesting the man in first position had not hurried to help the poor widow. This closes our LRWP from 3:4 and 7, where "uncovering" figured in Naomi's risky instructions to Ruth. This gentle chiding helped Boaz's cause as he bet on an extension of the legal principle of property redemption. Along with the questions raised above about the legality of a widow selling her husband's land, we doubt Naomi could technically claim redemption for the field herself. Undeterred by such concerns, Boaz maintained they had a responsibility to the widow, and challenged Mr. X to do a nobler thing by *redeeming* the field for Naomi (instead of *inheriting* it from Elimelek).

Such an extension fits the general pattern of the book. Ruth sought an expansion of the gleaning laws; Naomi and Ruth sought expansion of the marriage customs; and Boaz later sought expansion of the levirate law. Using the verb *ga'al*, **redeem,** four times in one sentence, he implied that as her *go'el*, Mr. X should take the high road, paying Naomi the purchase value of the field so she had money to live on, before it transferred to him permanently on her death.

Next, Boaz increased the pressure by asserting his own intention to redeem the field if Mr. X would not. Mr. X was trapped. His claim on the land as heir was valid, but with the "noble opportunity" to redeem it now raised in front of the elders and everyone else, refusal to pay Naomi for the field was shameful. Saving face, Mr. X agreed to redeem the field.

■ **5** At this stage in the negotiations, Mr. X was still the acknowledged heir of the field, so the next step was crucial. Boaz had to get Mr. X to give up all future claim on the field by handing off his redemption rights to Boaz, thereby conceding the ethical superiority of redemption over inheritance in front of everyone, and simultaneously clearing the path for Boaz's unorthodox plan to be levir. This would ensure Mr. X could not later press his claim as heir.

A perfectly timed revelation was the trick up Boaz's sleeve. With many, we read the Hebrew of the phrase **you also acquire Ruth the Moabite** according to the Ketib, not the Qere. So: **On the day you buy the land from Naomi,** *I am acquiring Ruth the Moabite,* **the dead man's widow, in order to maintain the name of the dead with his property** (Beattie 1974a, 1974b; Sasson 1979; Nielsen 1997; LaCocque 2004). As others have argued, if a *go'el* was required, or even expected to marry Ruth, he would have known agreeing to redeem the field included an obligation to marry Ruth. However, upon being supposedly informed of this, Mr. X backed out (v 6). What reason for his change of heart, if "everybody knew" a *go'el* had to marry a widow?

Instead, Boaz was announcing *his marriage* to Ruth, and intention to establish that marriage as a levirate one. If a child resulted from the union (not a guaranteed outcome between an older man and potentially barren woman), Boaz would designate him as heir to Mahlon, thus providing someone to inherit the field. The social pressure of the moment gave Mr. X no room to refuse. With such a noble gesture by the *'îš gibbôr ḥayil*, Mr. X had to back down. Insisting on his right to inherit over the needs of a widow to whom he was *go'el* was further than a decent Israelite could go.

■ **6** It worked. Mr. X backed out, crying, *I am unable to redeem for myself, or I would ruin my inheritance.* The property he had been expecting to inherit any day was now publicly designated for Elimelek's future heir. To redeem it himself at this point meant an outlay of initial capital, and years of labor investment, until it reverted to Naomi or her grandson anyway. He could not take that risk and gave up all claim. Boaz won the day, even convincing the redeemer this expansion of the levirate law was defensible.

B. Sealing the Deal (4:7-12)

■ **7-8** The narrator here inserted an interpretive gloss to help the reader understand the upcoming interaction. **In earlier times in Israel** echoes the opening line of the book "In the days when the judges ruled" (1:1). It explained a custom already unknown when the book was written down. We note with Hubbard though, it does not actually explain much, "Who gave the sandal(s) to whom?" (1988, 250), and why a sandal?

We know of another sandal ceremony, of course, to do with widows and levirs (Deut 25:5-10). That ceremony was also to take place at the gate in the presence of the elders. Such a resonant parallel has led many to interpret what actually happened in Ruth 4:8 as a version of the events prescribed in Deut 25:9.

As we deny any requirement of levirate marriage in Ruth, we can hardly assume such an interpretation. Further, the narrator tells us this sandal ceremony was about property redemption, the very issue Boaz raised. In fact, **redemption** in this verse is the twelfth occurrence of the root in the chapter so far. It is inconceivable that after driving home the theme of redemption so emphatically, the term would now mean something to do with the marriage of Ruth.

Black on the Shoe Ceremony

Perhaps the shoe ceremony is the narrator's humorous gesture, as if to say, "If this canny dealer *were* in the position of being asked to be a levir, he would be as self-protecting in that situation as he is in this: off with his shoe!" (1991, 30, emphasis his).

We suggest the explanation prevents any mistaken connections to Deut 25, as though the narrator were saying, "Now, in case anyone knows about Deut 25, *this sandal ceremony* was different." A key difference is found in the effect of the ceremony: in the case of a levir, the whole point was to shame the unwilling brother. In this case the whole point was, as the narrator said, **the method of legalizing transactions**. Mr. X might be chagrined, but there was no shame in ceding his rights to help members of his own family.

As we have argued, Boaz forced the hand of Mr. X to get to just this point: the handing over of rights to the field, in front of the elders and the townspeople. The ceremony introduced, it then was performed. We note a similar lack of clarity in its performance. Which man, Boaz or Mr. X, **removed his sandal?** Hubbard helpfully concentrates on the effect of this interlude in the dialogue: "The break allowed the audience to absorb the momentous significance of v 6" (1988, 248). It also allowed Mr. X to exit the scene, fading into obscurity. We never hear of him again. Whereas Boaz did all in his power to perpetuate the name of Elimelek, Mr. X did only as much as he had to. So, we remember Boaz.

■ **9-10** Boaz announced the conclusion of the negotiations to **the elders and all the people** (v 9). This was their chance to challenge the outcome of the proceedings, if they had any problems with how it worked out. **Today you are witnesses** (repeated twice), together with the crowd's positive response (v 11), renders the proceeding binding. From this point on, if someone were to challenge the decision, any of the ten **elders,** or one of **all the people**, could be called to defend Boaz.

What Boaz asked the people to attest expanded from the original negotiations: **All the property**, not only the field, and not only of Elimelek, but also of Kilion and Mahlon. With Mr. X no longer an obstacle, Boaz made use of the community's goodwill while he had it, to secure Elimelek's whole family and all their possessions into his care.

The names attached to the redemption have been imprecise throughout the negotiation. The land was Elimelek's in v 2, but possibly Mahlon's in v 5; "the dead man's widow" must refer to **Ruth the Moabite**, suggesting **the name of the dead** to be maintained was Mahlon (v 10). On the other hand, Ruth could be the vehicle through which her *father-in-law*'s name was maintained, as in the case of her predecessor, Tamar (Gen 38). In Ruth 4:9, the land was associated with all three dead men by name, the sons for the first time since 1:5 (but in reverse order, one of Campbell's chiasms). When Boaz asked the people to attest the nature of his marriage in v 10, the legacy was focused on Mahlon. The reader finally learns which son of Elimelek was Ruth's original husband!

A dynamic is at work here that parallels one we noticed on the threshing floor. Boaz spoke there of redeeming Ruth and Naomi together (vv 10–13). Here the formal attestation encompassed Elimelek's sons in the perpetuation of **the name of the dead with his property**. For Boaz, redemption was a family affair; he would not care for one member to the exclusion of the others.

The reason Boaz recorded, **so that his name will not disappear from among his family or from his hometown**, creates a deep irony. None of these men were mentioned again in the book, and in fact, they were expunged from the genealogies, appearing nowhere in the Bible outside Ruth. The son born to Ruth was counted as Boaz's heir, not Elimelek's (v 21; 1 Chr 2:10; Matt 1:5; Luke 3:32)! In the opening chapter, the narrator refused Naomi her choice of the name, Mara (Ruth 1:20). Likewise, despite all Boaz's efforts to uphold Elimelek's line, the narrator overruled him. In the end, this was not about the names of the family's men, but the security of the family's women.

■ **11-12** **The elders and all the people at the gate** gave their consent, **We are witnesses**. The order of these terms is reversed in Hebrew, *people/elders*, forming another chiasm with their order in v 9. The emphasis created by the Hebrew order is worth noting, as it suggests the onlookers' eagerness overtook the elders' solemn responsibility. By his skillful negotiating, Boaz succeeded in gaining the popular vote, so to speak, sweeping aside all potential criticism of either his marriage to a Moabite or his extensions of law.

More importantly, they gave a blessing. The blessing was addressed to Boaz (**your home . . . May you . . . your family**), but covered Ruth too. The blessing did not mention Elimelek, Naomi, or their sons, and so directed attention toward the new family of Boaz and Ruth.

Parker identifies this as a rare example of a marriage blessing in the ANE and finds parallel elements in a Ugaritic blessing: a focus on fertility and an invoking of the ancestors (1976). The blessing mentioned six ancestors: **Rachel and Leah,**

4:11-12

Israel (Jacob), **Perez**, **Tamar**, and **Judah**. Boaz was aligned with **Israel, Perez,** and **Judah**, while Ruth was blessed in the name of three matriarchs.

The connotations of these ancestors deserve comment. **Rachel and Leah** exhibits the typical reversal of their age and marriage order, reflecting a preference for Rachel in the tradition. Leah was the older and more prolific of the two sisters (seven children to Rachel's two), but she was unloved and suffered in the shadow of Rachel's beauty. Rachel had the love of Jacob, and through triple tragedy (her father's marital trickery, excruciating barrenness, and death in childbirth) became the more revered heroine (Gen 29—30; 35:16-26).

The attribution **who together built up the family** is doubly ironic. It makes no mention of Bilhah and Zilpah, the maids who added four sons to **the family**. It also draws a curtain over the bitter rivalry between the two women, whitewashing their legacy for posterity. No reader with any affection for Ruth would want for her the kind of dysfunctional family life these women endured! We hope, too, Boaz was a better husband to Ruth than **Israel** was to his wives.

The reference to **Perez** is intriguing. The older twin born to **Tamar** by her father-in-law **Judah** (Gen 28), Perez was notable only for his birth story and his lineage. At the point of birth, Perez apparently pushed his brother out of the way to emerge from the womb first (Gen 28:27-30). He further supplanted his older brother Shelah, being remembered as the primary descendant of Judah in the genealogies and the one through whom the royal line of David was traced at the end of Ruth (4:18-22), and throughout the Bible. Ironically, Boaz himself supplanted Elimelek as the father of Obed in those genealogies.

Given Boaz and Ruth's encounter the night before, the reference to **Tamar/Judah** may have struck a nerve, though the townspeople did not know it. Many commentators have drawn parallels between the two couples, not only for the levirate connotations of their two stories, but for the unorthodox uses of their sexuality both women employed to secure an older husband, establishing his family lineage in the process. Again, we would hope for Ruth a better husband in Boaz than Judah.

Standing in Ephrathah was ironically directed to Boaz, the *'îš gibbôr ḥayil* who already had **standing** (→ 2:1). This phrase closes our LRWP with *ḥayil*, opened at 2:1 with Boaz's introduction and picked up again in 3:11 in his commendation of Ruth. Likely, **Ephrathah** referred here to Boaz's legacy in the clan, not to his social location in the village (→ 1:2). **Famous in Bethlehem** is an awkward translation, as "famous" has connotations in Western culture not meant here. The blessing was not about celebrity but about the reputation of Boaz in his village and his continuing legacy.

Parker is convincing, that the three parts of the blessing (Rachel/Leah/Israel, Ephrathah/Bethlehem, Perez/Tamar/Judah) all had the same focus: fertility for the couple (1976, 29-30). The well-wishers invoked ancestors whose extraordinary reproductive tactics built and preserved the nation and their particular tribe. **Rachel, Leah,** and **Israel** were progenitors of all Israel, but **Ephrathah, Bethlehem,**

Perez, **Tamar**, and **Judah** narrowed the focus to a locally appropriate blessing. Ancient understandings of standing and reputation also implicate fertility: family worthiness was measured by the number and honor of descendants.

Bernstein notes such lavish wishes for fertility were interesting in light of the groom's age and the bride's ten years of childless marriage. However, like so many previous Israelite women, Ruth's barrenness was overcome. A vivid effect of this blessing was to enfold Ruth into the Israelite community, totally and finally. This blessing swept away all vestiges of Ruth's foreignness. Just prior to the blessing, Boaz called her **Ruth the Moabite** for the last time in the book (v 12). The blessing "unnamed" her: she was called only *iššâ*, *wife/woman*, and *na'ǎrâ*, *young woman*. When she married Boaz, she became fully, finally, only "Ruth" (v 13). Blessing Ruth in the names of Israel's mothers turned Ruth into a mother of Israel, at least rhetorically.

C. A Home for Naomi (4:13-17)

■ **13** The public negotiations over, the scene changed, from the town gate to the new couple's home, from official transaction to personal relationship. As a result of Boaz's efforts, connections between the three main characters were rearranged. Boaz was now Naomi's official *go'el*, free to redeem her field and assume responsibility for her person and property. This arrangement allowed Ruth to maintain her relationship with Naomi, to fulfill her vow from the Moab road. If Ruth had a son, then as Elimelek and Mahlon's heir, he would replace Boaz in caring for Naomi when he came of age; a widow with a grandson did not need a *go'el*. Her future was secured.

Before turning to Naomi's final conversation with women, however, the narrative settled, for a peaceful moment between the crowd at the gate and the women of the neighborhood, on the couple themselves. **Boaz took Ruth** uses the usual verb for marriage, *lāqaḥ*, **to take as wife**. The first marriages in the book were tainted (by foreign context, grief, and breach of law), and so used the more pejorative *nāśā'* (→ 1:4). Whereas Mahlon's Moabite marriage created problems for Naomi, Boaz's marriage to the same Moabite solved many problems for Naomi. Boaz did not sit under judgment for marrying a Moabite, either in the story or in the tradition.

The traditional explanation of this difference refers to Ruth's vow as a conversion, making her second marriage to an Israelite man acceptable. As we have argued, her incorporation into Israelite society was not likely so smooth, and certainly was not accomplished on the Moab road. In other words, in the eyes of the villagers, Ruth was a Moabite even at her marriage. Aided by the position of her husband, her mother-in-law's restored condition, and the birth of a son, she eventually joined her own line of foreigner-cum-Israelites.

He made love to her translates a phrase that strikes an impish note in the Hebrew. It reads **he went to her**, forming a playful reversal of ch 3, when Ruth went to Boaz. This time we know they **made love**, and **the LORD enabled her to**

conceive. This phrase is interesting on several counts. It was the first direct action of Yahweh in the whole book. In 1:6, Naomi heard rumor of fertility returned to the land. Here, fertility was returned to Ruth.

We cannot know whether Ruth's lack of children was due to her body or Mahlon's. None of the Hebrew words or phrases for a woman's barrenness is used of Ruth. Even the *fact* of her lack of children was only implied by the text, never stated.

This phrase is similar to the conception formula used in the barren women narratives, but is not the same. In those instances, Yahweh was the subject of verbs that mean "attended to her" or "opened her womb" or "remembered her" or "listened to her," but the woman herself was the subject of the verb for conception (*hārâ*, "she conceived") (Gen 21:1-2; 25:21; 29:31-35; 30:17-19, 22-23; 1 Sam 1:19-20; 2 Kgs 4:17). Here, conception is a noun: **Yahweh gave to her conception**. The effect of this phrasing is striking: **Boaz took . . . Yahweh gave**. It reminds the reader that despite the overwhelming focus in the following verses on the benefit to Naomi, the birth was a gift to Ruth from Yahweh.

■ **14-15** Naomi was the focus of the narrative from this point on. Ruth and Boaz did not speak or act again, but each was mentioned once more (Ruth in v 15, Boaz in the genealogy in v 21). According to the reaction of **the women** and Naomi's response, the benefit of the child was all on Naomi's side (v 14). Instead of ending the book like a fairy tale would, at v 13, with the happy couple settled into their new life, the narrator continued. Who were these **women**? They spoke on Naomi's return to Bethlehem (1:19), but we haven't heard from them since. We will hear from them again in 4:17.

Praise be to the LORD is the seventh and final blessing in Yahweh's name (1:8-9; 2:4, 12, 20; 3:10; Naomi blessed Ruth's "notice-taker" without it [2:19]). This one acknowledged the fulfillment of Boaz's promise to designate a son as heir for Elimelek. **Guardian-redeemer** could refer to Boaz or the baby. Boaz was Naomi's *go'el*, and the baby was her heir and grandson; in adulthood, he would be responsible for her through an even closer connection than a *go'el*. On the other hand, the less formal sense of *go'el* used by the women all through the tale makes sense here too (→ 2:20; 3:9). The child, though not in a *go'el* position to Naomi, could still provide the kind of redeeming care an old widow needed.

Guardian-redeemer could even refer to Yahweh as Naomi's *go'el*, playing again on the same question from 2:20. Just as it may have been either Yahweh or Boaz who had not forsaken his *ḥesed*, here the women may be ascribing to Yahweh the redemption of their friend. The ambiguity continued through the next two statements. The hope that **he become famous** repeats in the same words the blessing from 4:11, extending it from "Bethlehem" to **Israel**. Again, it could refer to either Boaz or the son, but there is also a corollary concern in the OT for Yahweh's name and reputation (2 Sam 7:26; 1 Kgs 8:42; Ps 76:1 [2 HB]; Mal 1:11).

Renew your life and **sustain you in your old age** are, again, activities that described the benefits of her new heir, but also spoke to Yahweh's attention to

Naomi. In fact, **renew your life** translates a word Naomi used of Yahweh before. In 1:21, she accused Yahweh of "bringing her back" empty; here, in closing the LRWP, the women pray that he (Yahweh?) would *be to you a bringer-back of life.*

Lest the reader forget the immediate source of this great blessing, the women reminded Naomi that Ruth, her **daughter-in-law**, was responsible for all the bounty that came her way. **Who loves you** sums up the narrator's assessment of Ruth's efforts. Naomi and Boaz called them *ḥesed,* sacralizing Ruth's staunch dedication in *action,* at moments when she was in danger of being dismissed as overly emotional (grieving in 1:8, proposing to Boaz in 3:10). The English word **love** is usually understood emotionally, and while the Hebrew word here, *ʾāhēb,* can express emotional love, it also carried covenantal overtones in many contexts (Deut 6:5). The author chose a word here connoting both affective love and covenantal love in action. Ruth's love was judged to be thoroughly Israelite.

The NIV reverses the last two phrases; the Hebrew order is **has given him birth, she who is better to you than seven sons.** This is preferable, as it maintains the author's intention that the last word regarding Ruth be not childbirth, but the greatest blessing known in ancient family life (1 Sam 2:5). Seven being a favored number in Semitic cultures, and especially Israel, it represented a number of things in differing contexts: completion, fertility, creation, divinity, fate, fullness, and so forth (Kapelrud 1968). In the Ugaritic marriage blessing Parker cites, the gods blessed the groom thus: "The girl you are bringing into your court will bear you seven sons" (1976, 26). Ruth received even higher approbation, as Bledstein explains, "In the ancient world it was believed that seven sons secured a man's well-being in the underworld. With no little irony, these women give the ultimate in praise to one daughter (in-law)" (1993, 130).

■ **16 Naomi took the child** closes the LRWP with the longest span in the book. Back in Moab, Naomi mourned the loss of her *yĕlādîm,* her **boys** (1:5), but now she had another *yeled* to hold **in her arms.** Whether or not this verse intended an official adoption of the boy by Naomi is an issue of great debate in the literature. It is not necessary to understand it in that light. Naomi did not need to adopt him, as Boaz had arranged the legal attestation of him as her heir.

Neither do we claim this was only a tender picture of a doting grandmother; Naomi had a legally established relationship with the child, after all. As she likely entered Boaz's household along with Ruth, we see no need to read here any usurpation of Ruth as his mother (against Fewell and Gunn 1990). Driesbach suggests a nuance in the next verse that is appropriate here: "to imply the full acceptance of Ruth's child into Israel" (2012, 546). In other words, if anyone balked at accepting this child of a mixed marriage, they had Naomi to deal with.

Over-literal readings of the Hebrew *and she put him on her bosom,* suggested to some earlier generations that Naomi served as the boy's wet-nurse, despite the fact she described herself as too old for childbearing (1:11-13). As Campbell points out, the Hebrew vocabulary does not support that reading at all (1975, 165-66). The noun *ḥēq* refers to that portion of the upper torso, the bosom, symbolic home of comfort (Isa 40:11), secrets (Prov 21:14), or even anger (Eccl 7:9), where anyone, man or woman, might clasp someone beloved. When discussing breast-feeding, the OT used *šad*, which always means the female breast (Job 3:12; Hos 9:14). The second phrase **and cared for him** uses the participle form of the verb *'āman* ("support," "uphold," etc.). The KJV rendered "nurse," but the Hebrew here intends it in the sense of a caretaker or guardian (2 Kgs 10:1; 2 Sam 4:4). Here, too, there was another word to use, were breastfeeding in view: *yānaq*, "to suckle."

■ **17** **The women living there** have the last words of speech in the book, and they are odd. The **son** was attributed to **Naomi**, not to Ruth. We have no name for the boy yet, because the text did not reveal his name in the usual place. We expected the naming formula immediately after his birth in Ruth 4:13, even a pun between his name and the circumstances of his birth (Gen 21:3; 25:25-26; 29:31-35). But the narrator placed the naming here with no pun, and even more unusually, in the mouths of the women instead of his parents!

In this construction, even with all the jubilation over his birth, **Obed** was not significant in himself (we know nothing about him besides his existence). As the culmination of the story, though, he marked the total satisfaction of all Nao-mi's emptiness. He filled her need for an heir, but also served as a symbol of the whole people of God who rallied around this widow, from the foreigner Ruth to the women of Ruth's new home. Herein lies the significance of his name: Obed, *he who serves*.

Some complain of Ruth's absence at the end of her own book and read ten-sion between Naomi and Ruth into the celebration of the boy (Fewell and Gunn 1990). Arguing as we have that the book is about Naomi, Ruth's explicit absence does not strike us as problematic. Every chapter ended with Naomi; why should the last be different? Further, as we believe in the ability of two strong women to live together without jealousy (as these two have all along), we would argue that rivalry is not the inevitable result of Naomi's connection to Obed. As Black observes so beautifully:

> The narrational intention clearly is to show joy triumphing over strict logic, while at the same time making the illogicalities logical. The child Obed ob-viously is Ruth's, yet he also is everyone's in spirit and by customary right. Ruth and Naomi are indivisible, because "thy people" and "my people" have lost all distinction. (1991, 33)

The child of a Moabite and an Israelite, Obed "served" as a summary of all the story has to tell. Thus understood, the scene closed with that favorite technique of our author: a brief statement that both recaps the past action (**Obed**), and antici-pates future action: **father of Jesse, the father of David.**

D. Epilogue (4:18-22)

■ **18-22** This **family line of Perez** was not merely a scribal addendum to legiti-mate the tale of two widows. Nor was it a sloppy duplication of the end of v 17. Rather, it was a clever final statement of the importance of the themes and content of the narrative. After this story, even the existence of a **family line** attested to victory over the tragedy that washed over Naomi, wave upon wave at the beginning of her story. The specific details of the lineage have their own work to do too.

Perez, already mentioned in the townspeople's blessing of Ruth and Boaz, was a byword for the royal lineage. Beginning with Perez, instead of with Judah his *father*, cleared space for his *mother* to emerge from the shadows. But who was his mother? Tamar, invoked by name in v 12, but who also has hovered in the background of this story at so many points: that other foreigner who preserved the lineage through overt transgression of "proper" womanhood. Is this the family line of Perez, or of Tamar? Attached to a tale so stubbornly focused on the women, the latter possibility emerges.

Such a possibility was strengthened by other women in the shadows of the genealogy. Matthew follows this same order and brings the women out of the shadows (1:5-6). **Salmon** was married to Rahab, another foreigner of suspicious morals. After four chapters of such drama, the reader cannot encounter **Boaz the father of Obed** *without* thinking, too, of Ruth and Naomi. Likewise the unavoidable connotation of **David** with his wives Bathsheba, through whom this lineage continues; and Abigail, whose story shared some striking parallels with Ruth's (→ Introduction and 2:13). Fresh off the experience of dwelling with Ruth and Naomi over the course of their redemption, it is impossible to see this particular genealogy as only a list of men. If the story has done its work in us, our reading habits have been subverted to leave us always asking, what about the women?

FROM THE TEXT

It is impossible to read Ruth without recognizing the intersections of this little story with vast swaths of law and life in Israel. In the space of only eighty-five verses, we have delved into conventions that regulated the making of vows (1:16-17; 3:10-13), harvest and gleaning (chs 2—3), widowhood (ch 1), marriage and betrothal (chs 2—4), inheritance (ch 4), redemption / *go'el* responsibilities (chs 3—4), levirate marriage (chs 1, 4), and the adjudication and ratification of transactions (ch 4).

Absent from this tale was any obvious connection to the formal religious practices of Israel. This suggests a major theme of the piece. The life of faith, or keeping the covenant (as the Israelites would have put it), is *always* expressed in relationship with others. All relationships are governed by custom and law, and for the family of God, *hesed* is the ethic characterizing our practice of those laws and customs.

We have noticed over and over that these complex and faithful people sought to fulfill not the letter of the law but its spirit. Ruth's vow to Naomi was unusual even in existing, but then she chose an unprecedented expiration date: after death! Her way of gleaning pursued abundance for Naomi, not just survival. Boaz's protection and season-long invitation to his field were more than anyone should offer a Moabite.

In the second half of the story, this dynamic of pursuing *ḥesed* at all costs only intensified. Naomi's betrothal plan for Ruth thumbed its nose at convention, but also at her own future. Ruth's inclusion of Naomi in her proposal to Boaz stipulated the right thing at exactly the wrong moment. Boaz's unhesitating acceptance of Ruth saddled the man of standing with two needy women. Boaz adopted a view of both redemption and levirate law that expanded their reach and led others to see that expansion as virtue.

The lesson of Ruth, even down to its genealogy, ironically, is that redemption is not primarily about name or lineage, but relationship. The field turned out to be useful, but incidental. Every legal concern was turned on its head. Even the legacy of the original husband, which drove so much of the action on the public surface, turned out to be a temporal concern. What mattered instead was how *ḥesed* was performed: bodily, thoroughly, with mighty effort and not much concern for public opinion. On the Moab road, in the barley field, at the threshing floor, and in the gate, loyal love in action, not legal obligation, filled Naomi's emptiness.

SONG OF SONGS

Joseph Coleson
Sarah B. C. Derck

DEDICATION

For Charlotte, in every sense my darling and my beautiful one, JEC

For Joshua, my beloved, my friend, SBCD

ACKNOWLEDGMENTS

It is a rare privilege to open to our brothers and sisters this marvelous portion of the Bible. We owe special thanks to our editor, Alex Varughese, whose scholarship, editorial wisdom, and patience have made it possible for us to complete the work. Of course, remaining errors and other shortcomings are ours.

We are grateful for the generous assistance and encouragement of our home institutions, Houghton College and Nazarene Theological Seminary.

Countless others have formed and inspired us along the way: teachers and other mentors, colleagues, and students at institutions of higher learning on four continents; scholars whose writing has informed and inspired us, many we count as friends; members of the congregations we have been privileged to serve and worship with.

Of course, no author blessed with family could bring any lengthy work to fruition without both the active help and the patient forbearance of family members. Thus, we gladly thank our spouses, Joshua and Charlotte. Our children have borne the demands on our time with patience and grace. More important even than their patience through the writing process, their presence in our lives has made us mindful always that we write for them and their generation.

Over the years of writing this commentary, we have observed the uniqueness of a father/daughter team of scholars exegeting the Song of Songs together. It has been a rare privilege, and our partnership has helped us to think well about the Song. Much might be mended in the world today if more families could talk with frankness about a text such as this, as we have been able to do in our writing.

We come around again to where we began: grateful humility is the only proper response to the awesome reality of God's passion for the creation in every aspect. May God bless your study and incarnation of this portion of instruction (*torah*), as God has blessed ours.

BIBLIOGRAPHY

Brenner, Athalya, ed. 1993. *A Feminist Companion to the Song of Songs*. Sheffield: JSOT Press.

Cantrell, Deborah O'Daniel. 2011. *The Horsemen of Israel: Horses and Chariotry in Monarchic Israel*. History, Archaeology, and Culture of the Levant. Winona Lake, IN: Eisenbrauns.

Carr, G. Lloyd. 1984. *The Song of Solomon*. Tyndale Old Testament Commentaries. Downers Grove, IL: InterVarsity.

Coleson, Joseph E. 2012. *Genesis 1—11*. New Beacon Bible Commentary. Kansas City: Beacon Hill Press of Kansas City.

Davis, Ellen F. 2000. *Proverbs, Ecclesiastes, and the Song of Songs*. Westminster Bible Companion. Louisville, KY: Westminster John Knox.

Exum, J. Cheryl. 2005. *Song of Songs: A Commentary*. The Old Testament Library. Louisville, KY: Westminster John Knox.

Fishbane, Michael. 2015. *Song of Songs*. JPS Bible Commentary. Philadelphia: Jewish Publication Society.

Garrett, Duane. 2004. *Song of Songs*. Word Biblical Commentary. Nashville: Thomas Nelson.

Goulder, Michael D. 1986. *The Song of Fourteen Songs*. Journal for the Study of the Old Testament Supplement Series 36. Sheffield: JSOT Press.

Hess, Richard S. 2005. *Song of Songs*. Baker Commentary on the Old Testament. Grand Rapids: Baker Academic.

Jenson, Robert W. 2005. *Song of Songs*. Interpretation: A Bible Commentary for Teaching and Preaching. Louisville, KY: Westminster John Knox.

Keel, Othmar. 1994. *The Song of Songs: A Continental Commentary*. Translated by Frederick J. Gaiser. Minneapolis: Fortress.

King, Philip J., and Lawrence E. Stager. 2001. *Life in Biblical Israel*. Library of Ancient Israel. Louisville, KY: Westminster John Knox.

Lewis, C. S. 1996. *That Hideous Strength*. New York: Scribner. First published 1945.

Longman, Tremper. 2001. *Song of Songs*. New International Commentary on the Old Testament. Grand Rapids: Eerdmans.

Mazar, Amihai, and Nava Panitz-Cohen. 2007. It Is the Land of Honey: Beekeeping at Tel Reḥov. *Near Eastern Archaeology* 70:202-19.

Murphy, Roland E. 1990. *The Song of Songs*. Hermeneia: A Critical and Historical Commentary on the Bible. Minneapolis: Fortress.

Pope, Marvin H. 1977. *Song of Songs*. The Anchor Bible. Garden City, NY: Doubleday.

Pritchard, James B., ed. 1969. *Ancient Near Eastern Texts Relating to the Old Testament*. 3rd ed. Princeton: Princeton University Press.

Trible, Phyllis. 1978. *God and the Rhetoric of Sexuality*. Overtures to Biblical Theology 2. Philadelphia: Fortress.

Walton, John H., Victor H. Matthews, and Mark W. Chavalas. 2000. *The IVP Bible Background Commentary: Old Testament*. Downers Grove, IL: IVP Academic.

Wesley, John. 1975. *Explanatory Notes upon the Old Testament*. Salem, OH: Schmul.

Wright, J. Robert, ed. 2005. *Proverbs, Ecclesiastes, Song of Solomon*. Ancient Christian Commentary on the Scripture: Old Testament IX. Downers Grove, IL: InterVarsity.

TABLE OF SIDEBARS AND EXCURSUSES

INTRODUCTION

The first line of the Song of Songs reads, ***The song of songs, which is Solomon's***. The Hebrew expression "X of X-es" designates "the best one of all." Thus, "Song of Songs" means, "the best of all songs." This small book certainly deserves such a superlative title, both for its exquisite poetry and for its revelation of the heart of God for creation.

A. Date and Authorship

If "Solomon's Song of Songs" is the intended sense, the title may be naming Solomon as the author, though most scholars believe the title is a later addition. Alternatively, it may designate him as the author of some individual lyrics, the compiler or editor of others, or the arranger of the whole. Given ancient conventions of both poetry and literary patronage, other translations also are accurate: "The Song of Songs, in the style of Solomon"; "The Song of Songs, Dedicated to Solomon" [or "to the memory of Solomon"]. In short, we cannot name Solomon as author from the title alone.

In fact, there are good reasons to think Solomon had little to do with the Song in its final form. His reputation as a patron of wisdom in Israel is well established (1 Kgs 4:29-34 [5:9-14 HB]), but so is his profligacy as a lover (1 Kgs 11:1-8), and the apostasy and dissolution of Israel that resulted from his one thousand marriages (1 Kgs 1:9-13; Neh 13:23-27). His history does not inspire confidence in Solomon as writer of *this* Song, which after all extols the virtue of sustained attention to a love of personal and public integrity.

Further, each mention of Solomon in the Song functions only figuratively, rather than invoking the historical Solomon in the action (→ 1:5; 3:7, 9, 11; 8:11-12). The Song uses Solomon as a stereotype, much like the figures of Don Juan or Casanova might be used in Western literature. In fact, the last chapter censures Solomon as a negative foil to the fidelity of the Song's male lover (8:11-12), an unlikely choice if Solomon himself penned these lines.

By the first century AD, Jewish rabbis attributed the writing (or possibly editing) of the Song to "Hezekiah and his company" (Mishnah, Baba Bathra 15a). Israelite literature certainly proliferated from that era onward. Modern scholarship is famously varied in its conclusions about both the dating and authorship of the Song. Proponents abound for every viable option: early (Solomonic reign, tenth century BC); middle (Hezekiah's reign or later, eighth to sixth century BC); and late (postexilic, fifth to third century BC). It cannot be later than this, as four fragmental copies of the Song were found in the Dead Sea Scrolls. In some cases, scholars cite the same evidence in support of opposing conclusions (e.g., "Tirzah" in 6:4). With Longman, we remain agnostic on both questions (2001, 2-9, 19).

B. Content

1. Anthology or Story?

Even the casual reader notices the Song of Songs is a collection of love poems. For more than a century, those who interpret it as an anthology have increased in number. By definition, an anthology is a collection. This one collects love poems: some original, some borrowed or adapted. If the Song is only an anthology, it would not surprise us to see it exhibit little or no structural coherence.

But is it *only* an anthology? Certain streams of both Jewish and Christian traditions have read the Song as a love *story*, with a plausible beginning, coherent development, and a satisfactory ending. This entails discerning the number and identities of its speakers; where each poem or fragment begins and ends; and to whom each may be ascribed. These tasks have exercised the ingenuity of commentators for generations.

We view the Song as a song cycle: a series of songs with both thematic and narrative coherence, in the sense that each poem considers the "story" of these two lovers, but without the definitive beginning, plot development, and ending many describe in the Song. A woman and a man find love together. Like most lovers, they make a series of loverly discoveries, and they overcome various obstacles. It certainly displays what Exum deems an "artistic unity" (2005, 37). However, the poems lack clarity about any timeline of their relationship, and this is where we find a definitive plot untenable.

2. Keeping Track of Speakers

This series of poems features two lovers. The woman often is identified as a maiden from an Israelite country town, at a distance from urban centers such as Solomon's Jerusalem. The man is similarly a country peasant, described as a shepherd (1:7-8). Though he speaks fewer lines, he is no secondary character.

It is critical to notice the Song is entirely dialogical; except for 1:1, every line is one of direct address. The woman speaks about 60 percent of the lines, most of them to the man, and the man's speeches are directed mostly to the woman. Several times the woman speaks to unidentified "Friends" (NIV), and they speak a few lines.

Nowhere in the Hebrew text is any of these speakers identified by a narrator. As English does not distinguish singular/plural or masculine/feminine forms of "you," translation without comment may leave a reader confused about speakers' identities, and the beginnings and endings of speeches. In the Hebrew text, these details are usually clear in the person, number, and gender of pronouns and verbs. Because English readers need them, the NIV adds italicized identifiers, usually pronouns.

3. Structure

Viewing the Song as a poetic celebration of two lovers, rather than the developing plot of a modern "love story," we see its primary structure as follows:

1:1 Title
1:2—2:7 Harbingers and Tastes of Love
2:8—3:5 Presence and Absence: Ways of Love
3:6—5:1 Celebrating and Consummating Love
5:2—8:4 Absence and Presence: Vicissitudes of Love
8:5-14 Enduring Love, Hers to Give

C. Literary Forms and Features

I. Parallelism

Hebrew poetry is defined by parallelism between successive lines (usually two, but it may extend to three or four). Important elements of the first line appear in some way in the second line. Partly, parallelism lies in grammar and syntax: both lines may begin with a verb, followed by a subject and a direct object. Partly, it lies in the meanings of corresponding words: "beams . . . rafters," "cedars . . . firs." Elements may be absent from one of the lines, or their order may differ, without destroying this parallelism. This definition vastly simplifies the variations and complexities of parallelism. An example of a two-line parallelism is 1:17:

The beams	of our house	are	cedars;
Rafters	our	are	firs.

2. Metaphor

Metaphor mentions, characterizes, or pictures one entity by naming it as another; for example, in 2:16 the woman says her "beloved . . . browses among the lilies." Human males do not eat lilies; she is picturing him here as a gazelle or stag (v 17). The reader understands that her "browsing" lover is not eating food, and here "lilies" are not flowering plants. The subject is lovemaking.

One subset of metaphor—simile—is common in the Song: "dark like the tents of Kedar" (1:5); "his eyes are like doves" (5:12); "love is as strong as death" (8:6). Both metaphor and simile compare two entities, helping the reader understand one more completely, because she already understands the other well.

Metaphor lends meaning through a point of comparison. In 4:1, "flock of goats" is the *lender* of meaning; "hair" is the *receiver* of meaning. This metaphor is famously dissonant to Western ears, because we do not know the point of comparison intended by the ancient author. The man was not calling the woman a goat, but comparing the waves of her tresses with the undulant grazing of a flock of black goats down a hillside. This is a beautiful sight (as we personally have observed), giving the reader a vivid vision of the woman's glorious hair. Metaphor most often entails but one or two points of comparison, though these may be complex, even multivalent.

Animal metaphors: The frequency of animal metaphors in the Song surprises some. A modern woman's first thought, upon being compared with a mare (1:9), a dove and a flock of goats (4:1), or gazelle fawns (7:3 [4 HB]), would not be that she had received a high compliment. Yet, in cultures where humans and animals live together in mutual dependence, animals are highly valued, and if we understand the point of comparison in each metaphor, there is no insult.

Architectural metaphors: The Song's use of building imagery is similarly unfamiliar to modern readers. Few women today want to hear, "Your neck is like the tower of David" (4:4), nor would a man hope for his love to tell her friends, "His legs are pillars of marble" (5:15). Again, when we understand their culturally sourced and inspired points of comparison, these also compliment the one described.

Euphemism: Much of the lovers' praise of one another, and celebration of their sexual activity, is expressed in euphemism, which we may treat as a subset of metaphor. For example, the woman's invitation of 4:16, "Let my beloved come into his garden," and his response, "I have come into my garden" (5:1), have nothing to do with gardens, everything to do with the delights of lovemaking. Couched as euphemistic metaphor, this dialogue is acceptable to a general audience, yet effectively communicates between the lovers intimacies not readily aired in public.

3. *Wasf*

Thrice the speakers praised their beloved in a specialized song, describing his or her person in some detail, using metaphor almost exclusively (4:1-7; 7:1-7). In the first, the man's description moved *explicitly* from her head to her breasts; *implicitly*, nearly to her feet. The second progressed from her feet to the crown of her head. In 5:10-16, the woman moved from head to foot in exuberant praise of her lover's body.

This genre of love song is known today by an Arabic name, *wasf*, "descriptive song." Western scholars first recognized it as they came to know Arabic cultures. This connection is not central to the Song, as some thought, partly because the *wasf* is not reserved to a village wedding context. Still, any detailed knowledge of a specific song form aids our understanding.

4. Wisdom Literature

The Song of Songs as wisdom literature is a foreign concept to many. In the Bible, and the ANE generally, wisdom literature comprises a questioning exploration of and common-sense orientation to everyday life, from the big questions of meaning to the nooks and crannies of human experience. If that is true, we should expect—rather than be surprised by—the Bible's inclusion of the Song. It explores love between a woman and a man, a main feature of life for most people throughout history.

This has ramifications for understanding the Song. One important conclusion emanates from the text from first to last, but never explicitly. Thus, it easily is missed: Appropriate, real sex, as celebrated in the Song, rescues both men and women from the all-too-common view of women that casts them in only two roles: "madonna or whore." This view has even been reflected in some interpretations of the Song over the centuries: Pseudo-Dionysius claimed, "in the Songs there are those passionate longings fit only for prostitutes" (Wright 2005, 293). Read rightly, the Song calls women and men to see themselves and each other as equally human, created fully *in imago Dei*, gifted together with sexuality they are meant to use, redeemed together, and privileged to work together fostering *shalom* (wholeness and well-being) across God's good creation.

Thus, on literary as well as theological grounds, we take issue with allegorical approaches to this book. The Song's understandings and treatment of its own real subject does give rise to a "better love for God" as a beneficial, but unintended, byproduct. (We may say the same of much of the Bible's other nonlegal, nondidactic content.) However, the embodied human experience of love and sex matters for its own sake, theologically, not primarily as an analogy for relationship with God.

D. Interpretive Approaches

1. The Song as Allegory

An irony of both the Jewish and the Christian canons is that neither would include the Song, had the rabbis and the early church interpreted it *only* at face value. While not denying its overt sense as a starting point, both saw its real meaning as "spiritual." Jews read it as an allegory of God's love for Israel; Christians, as an allegory of Christ's love for the church. If the man is Solomon, as many have thought, the Song also is typological, with Solomon as a type of Yahweh or Christ.

We agree with Jenson: the Song is not precisely an "allegory," but even "spiritual" readings, traditional and modern, still follow allegorizing lines (2005, 4-8). The allegorizing tendency is to find "spiritual" import in each detail: the overt sense of the text must lead to "spiritual" truth about God's relationship with God's people, and the exegete's task is to find it.

One example will suffice: early Christian expositors identified the woman's breasts in 1:13 as "the Old and New Testaments," or as "belong[ing] to the holy soul," or even as "those of Christ's dear Mother" (Pope 1977, 352; he cites many more). The natural question, "Which is it?" highlights a central problem with the methodology. Many early interpreters were downright opposed to reading the Song at face value.

Theodoret of Cyr

My view is that when they read this composition and noticed in it unguents, kisses, thighs, belly, navel, cheeks, eyes, lilies, apples, nard, ointment, myrrh and the like, in their ignorance of the characteristics of the divine Scripture they were unwilling to get beyond the surface, penetrate the veil of the expression, gain entrance in spirit and behold the glory of the Lord with face unveiled. Rather, they gave the text a corporeal interpretation and were drawn into that awful blasphemy. (Wright 2005, 289-90)

Not all older readings were spiritual/allegorical, and some modern readings are. Still, most today set aside all but the most general of "spiritual" conclusions as eisegesis, rather than exegesis.

2. An Anthology of Love Songs

By far the most common reading among scholars today is that the Song is an anthology, a collection of Hebrew love songs, with very little theological import, if any. Not all the poems need have been Hebrew compositions originally. Some may be adaptations of works from the substantial library of love poetry from across the ANE/eastern Mediterranean worlds. To date, Egyptian love poetry is best known, but the Sumerian/Akkadian examples from Mesopotamia and some passages from the epic poetry of Canaan (preserved in Ugaritic) also are impressive. Some who date the Song later suggest influences from the Aegean (Greek) world.

Important to this approach is the reality that no story line proposed through two millennia of reading the Song is consistent and convincing throughout the text. Soon or late, each becomes muddled in inconsistency or contradiction. Thus, while multiple narrative strands are woven through the Song, a plot developed to a climax and resolution simply is not present.

3. Drama: Two- or Three-Person Love Story

Many who *do* see a plot have read the Song as a three-person love story. The Shulammite maiden had a local beau. Solomon, visiting his domains (8:11), saw and tried to woo her, but the faithful maiden rejected him. At one time, if this view did not dominate, it held its own. Today, one would be pressed to find a commentator on the Hebrew text espousing it.

Those reading the Song as a two-person love story are on firmer ground, finding only one man rather than two. Some identify him as Solomon, and some see him as a type of Yahweh or Christ. Others, remembering Solomon's promiscuity and apostasy, think the unnamed local lover a more suitable hero.

Some exegetes take the next step of framing the Song formally as a drama. This takes ingenuity in identifying minor *dramatis personae*, assigning lines, and so forth, but the most telling point against it is that drama of this kind is a Greek invention, introduced to the Jewish people too late for it to have inspired the Song.

4. Liturgies, etc.

Some readings at face value have a more exotic flair. A few identify the Song as a ceremony (or liturgy) for a royal wedding (one of Solomon's?). Similar proposals see it as a ceremony for a divine marriage or a liturgical reenactment in Israel's (or a neighbor's) cult. Chaim Rabin (1973; discussed in Pope 1977, 27-33) saw sources in South Indian Tamil poems finding their way to Solomon's Israel.

For our approach, → "Content," above.

E. Theological Themes: An Invitation to Celebrate

The "big idea" is simple: the Song celebrates God's gift of love between a woman and a man. This couple shows that love's sexual expression can be uncomplicated and pure, when partners relate in mutual love and honor.

1. The "Rightness" of Sex

The rightness, the virtue, of sexual expression is a given in the Song's every line. Both partners initiate; both partners receive. The joy in their mutuality is unstinting and unabashed. Each rejoices in the other's presence; each rues the other's absence. Their sex talk is candid. Euphemism is employed to heighten, not disguise, their pleasure in each other.

Procreation hardly features at all. In the Song, sex is all about the loving relationship between these two, with no consideration of potential descendants. The woman of the Song is almost unique in the OT, with no mention made of her motherhood, potential or otherwise.

2. Gender Equality in Sexual Expression

In the Song, the joys of sexual love are celebrated *first* by the woman, and then also by the man. Throughout the Song, the woman speaks more lines and is as apt to initiate both love speech and lovemaking as is the man. In Gen 3:16, God revealed (*not* decreed) to the woman that the man's propensity would be to rule over her, in sexual expression as in many other life arenas. The Song shows this up as the unnatural, unstable state of affairs it is. Neither is it inevitable, this couple teaches us: it can be unlearned and undone, to the benefit of all.

3. The Beauty and Delights of God's Creation

Readers marvel at the trysting-places of this couple: indoors and out, within city walls and in sylvan countryside, often secluded but sometimes encountering other persons. All nature, it seems, takes joy in their love. Most commentators point out that for a small book, the Song names a notable array of ancient Israel's flora and fauna. This is yet another way of affirming that all God's creation is "very good" (Gen 1:31).

4. Necessary Safeguards

We live in a world beset by alienation. Of necessity, we institute safeguards around such primary functions as sexual expression. Naturally, we assume and often read these safeguards into the text of the Song. These two were married, weren't they? Or if they weren't in the beginning, certainly they were by the end of the Song? They did not consummate their sexual relationship until after they were married, did they? We refer readers to the excursus, "Threshing Floor Morals," in the commentary on Ruth 3:3-4 in this volume.

We think the Song, read most naturally, reports this couple's complete sexual enjoyment of each other, often in startlingly vivid detail. Equally noteworthy is that the Song never mentions "safeguards" of any kind in place. Marriage is hardly mentioned, though the man does refer to the woman as "my bride" six times in a single section (4:8-12; 5:1). In these, "bride" is neither a caution (We have to get married first!), nor a justification (Oh, we *are* married!). It is an endearment, a pet name used across the ANE. We tend to infer their marriage as his reason for calling her "my bride," but this is a modern inference, not the text's own statement. It is important to notice the man pairing "my bride" with "my sister," another endearment that also should not be read literally.

Pontificating, moralizing, even friendly advice-giving are not in the Song. Exegeting the Song as a morality tale actually diminishes its power. Some things are best set forth well, then left alone. The "moral understatement" characterizing the Song invites the reader to the conversation, as it were. Pondering the Song and making it our own is more powerful and more enduring than any moralizing the poet could have included. This wise poet allows us that privilege.

5. An Embrace of Embodiment

The Song was not written as "theology," but everything carries theological import in God's world. Gnosticism had not gained currency in the Israelite-Jewish world when the Song first appeared, but by the time the OT canon was finalized, Gnosticism was a serious issue. In that context, the Song became an important witness.

A bit too simply: Gnosticism teaches that the material creation either is evil and must be overcome by the spiritual person, or merely appears to be real and is transcended as the soul realizes its "true" identity. Gnosticism denies the biblical teaching that God's material creation is good, including the universe in all its physical aspects. The Song is a poignant case study; everything about it flatly denies Gnosticism. Far from being evil or shameful, sexual love is one of God's gifts, to be celebrated with our good bodies, in joy and gratitude.

F. The Place and Function of the Song in the Canon

In the Hebrew Bible arrangement, the Song of Songs usually follows Ruth as the second book of the Megillot, the (Festival) Scrolls. The Song is the liturgical reading highlighted at Passover, the beginning of ancient Israel's agricultural year (in some Jewish traditions, it is read every Sabbath). Most Christian Bibles, following the LXX, place the Song after Qohelet (Ecclesiastes) and before Isaiah. In either placement, it is important to recognize the Song as a Wisdom book of a very special, practical kind.

The Song is unusual in the biblical canon for many reasons, but prominent among them is its contribution to biblical views of women and of sex. A dominant Christian reading of the canon, in both its narrative and its didactic portions, is that sex is primarily for the purposes of procreation. Sexual encounters in biblical narratives usually result in pregnancy (Gen 4:1; 16:1-4; 19:33-38; 29:21—30:24; 34:1-4; 38:2, 16-18; Exod 2:21-22; Ruth 4:13; 1 Sam 1:19-20; 2 Sam 11:1-2; 12:24). In many cases where they don't, the encounter itself was/is viewed as illicit or problematic (Gen. 12:17-20; 38:8-9; Judg 19:25-29; 1 Sam 2:22; 2 Sam 13:1-20).

Procreation is, of course, one of God's good gifts, and a treasured part of many couples' sexual life. But viewing children as the *only* purpose for sex is an incomplete picture of the biblical witness and distorts the dynamics of a relationship, placing more pressure on childbearing than that experience can bear. An unintended consequence is that women are positioned as objects for the purposes and pleasures of men, and in androcentric or patriarchal societies, men's reproductive priorities. The countervailing canonical voices (e.g., Gen 2:22-25; Prov 5:15-20; the Song) have not been sufficiently pondered and heeded.

In the Song, the woman's sexuality is on full display, with never a hint that she is deviant. Rather, the sexuality of both partners in the Song is a means to, and a function of, intimacy, connection, and belonging. *Both* partners give and receive pleasure; *both* partners initiate encounters. Shame, manipulation, and ulterior motive are nowhere to be seen. Neither is there any overt reference to the woman's motherhood, potential or otherwise, making her almost unique in the cast of OT women. The total silence of the Song on the subject is particularly revealing. The Song simply celebrates at length God's good and many-splendored gift of sex between a woman and a man.

Absent the Song in the canon, many of the faithful would miss the biblical teaching that sex is sacred and beautiful, to be enjoyed for its own sake, celebrated, even named in our litanies of thanksgiving. Would we spare our younger brothers and sisters the griefs of our modern culture of promiscuity? Would we encourage Christians, instructing them in *how* to "rejoice in the [spouse] of [one's] youth"

(Prov 5:18)? In an age addicted to sex, but terrified of true sexuality, the Song is God's gift to the church. Will we, charged to impart *all* God's counsel, find the will and the means to end this neglect and distortion?

COMMENTARY

I. TITLE: SONG OF SONGS 1:1

IN THE TEXT

■ **1 Solomon's Song of Songs.** These opening words function as the title. The NIV reflects one translation tradition; some render, a bit more literally, "The Song of Songs, which is Solomon's" (NRSV). (→ Introduction: Date and Authorship.)

II. HARBINGERS AND TASTES OF LOVE: SONG OF SONGS 1:2—2:7

OVERVIEW

Carr notes regarding the Song, "Any division is somewhat arbitrary" (1984, 45). His restraint commends itself, and we follow his broad outline of the Song. This first major section begins with the woman's first long speech (1:2-7), addressed primarily to her lover, secondarily to women bystanders. A dialogue ensues: the man's first speech (1:8-11), her response (1:12-14), followed by a back-and-forth: He, 1:15; She, 1:16; He, 1:17; She, 2:1; He, 2:2. A longer speech of the woman (2:3-7) concludes this section with the charge, **Do not . . . awaken love** (2:7). Two other major sections also close with this admonition (3:5; 8:4).

A. She: Take Me Away! . . . Where Can I Find You? (1:2-7)

BEHIND THE TEXT

The Song's first detail signals its message and purposes as a whole: The woman utters its opening words. This is easily overlooked; new readers do not yet know she is its central persona. Yet, from its very first word, the Song celebrates the woman as protagonist and initiator. As the poem unfolds, it becomes plain that her role is as large in scope and lively in nature as the man's; neither is passive.

IN THE TEXT

■ **2** The woman began by addressing a not-yet-identified group of bystanders, but referring to her lover, **Let him kiss me with the kisses of his mouth**. Here, the hoped-for inception of active sexual expression is a kiss, followed by more kisses. Voicing her desire so publicly marks her already as bold, though this is not a negative judgment (→ Introduction: Theological Themes). Her next words prompt the reader to visualize her turning from the group to her lover, saying, **for your love is more delightful than wine**.

Delightful translates Hebrew *tôb*, usually rendered "good." Expressing her desire for his kisses, the woman has invoked already three senses: touch, taste, and smell are all involved. Her song evokes the senses thoroughly and deeply, from her first word, giving each in turn its due.

■ **3** The Hebrew text begins with the preposition *lĕ*, which we ought not ignore. Modifying Pope only slightly (1977, 291, 299-300), we translate vv 2*b*-3*a* together:

> *For your love is better than wine,*
> *[Better] than the fragrance of your fine perfume oils.*

Perfume in the Ancient World

With infrequent bathing, and lacking other hygienic measures industrial cultures take for granted, ancients rich and poor used perfumes. Rather than the sprayed liquids common today in the West, these were oils, balms, or even solids, usually rubbed into the skin, and sometimes applied to clothing and bed coverings. In Israel, perfumers used olive oil as the base of their products. Common ingredients included extracts or resins of plants: aloe (not *aloe vera*; → 4:14), cassia, frankincense, myrrh, and nard (spikenard). The latter three were more expensive because they were imported from Arabia or beyond.

This young woman found **delightful** both the taste of fine wine (v 2*b*) and her lover's use of fragrant perfumes (v 3*a*), but his love itself was **better**. As **wine** is enjoyed in its taste, and the delight of *perfume* is in its **fragrance**, her comparisons again highlight the senses through which we enjoy our world.

Verse 3*b* is metaphorical, but the Hebrew text does not express it as a simile. We may translate: ***Perfuming oil poured out is your name***. In this usage, **name** functions as synecdoche, representing her lover's presence, his whole self. Even the usual very small juglet of perfume, if **poured out**, wafted fragrance on every side. Such was her lover's encompassing presence to this young woman.

Name also denotes reputation; hence her observation, **No wonder the young women love you!** This does not imply the other young women were "in love" with him or that her lover was promiscuous. Rather, she knew other women understood her attraction; their admiration validated her own judgment.

■ **4** It would be difficult to overstate the urgency of the woman's plea—or demand—in v 4*a*; we could render, ***Draw/pull me along after you; let us run!*** The Song presents strong physical desire as good, whether evidenced by the woman or the man.

Let the king is grammatically possible and makes sense of a complex set of lines. However, we cannot take this as evidence that the man was Solomon; in many western Asian contexts down to the present, the groom is "king" and the bride is "queen" on their wedding day. Identifying the man requires more evidence than this clause provides. As it is common for lovers to portray each other in metaphorical terms, this usage does not prove, either, that the Song depicts a wedding day, nor a wedding feast lasting a week.

Where did she wish her lover to take her? In wealthy households, the master's **chambers** often comprised a suite of rooms. Later in the Song, outdoor venues are described or intimated. Here at the beginning, however, the woman expressed her ardor as intense longing for him to bring her into **his chambers**, his bedroom, the "normal" home of lovemaking.

The plural verbs of v 4*b*, **We rejoice . . . we will praise**, require an interpretive decision. With others, we take the woman here as using the "royal" we, speaking only to her lover (though the bystanders also heard her), and only of herself. Parallels occur in other ancient Near Eastern (ANE) love poems (see Pope 1977, 303-4).

The woman had invoked the reality of other admirers of her lover (v 3*c*), so the NIV's decision to identify them as the speakers, while not ours, is plausible. This would mean that speaking as a "chorus," these women approved of him, and joined in public celebration of the man as an eminently suitable partner. (Both **you** and **your** are singular masculine here, so refer to the man.)

Now the sense of hearing is brought to the fore. She **will praise** him; not only he, but all within the sound of her voice will hear. **More than wine** begins closure of this subsection as the woman began it in v 2. Though wine and other revelry may be thought to enhance the joys of sexual union, in the end the couple's intimacy leaves all else behind.

The last phrase can be translated ***Rightly do they love you***, since the woman repeated the final verb of v 3, "the young women love you." There, she viewed other women's admiration of her lover as "no wonder." Here, she approved, understanding they expressed the **right** kind of love, as loving friends looking on the lovers with goodwill.

■ **5-6** As many have noted, these verses pose the Song's first major set of interpretive options; decisions here influence (or even determine) those taken later. We translate:

> v 5a ***Black am I, and beautiful,*** O daughters of Jerusalem,
>
> v 5b **Like the tents of Kedar, like the tent curtains of** Salmah.
>
> v 6a **Do not stare at me because I am** *black,*
>
> v 6b ***Because the sun has looked on me*** [*to blacken me*].
>
> v 6c ***The sons of my mother*** were angry with me; *they set me maintaining the vineyards.*
>
> v 6d ***My vineyard—which is mine—I have not maintained.***

We note first an artistic conclusion and a dramatic turn. Completing the recital of the senses unifying this first set of stanzas, the woman foregrounds the sense of sight with her assertion that she is ***black***. The apparent "prohibition" of v 6a means only that those who see her sun-darkened skin should not **stare** askance at her; these words *invite* all to see her. She has employed each of the physical senses, by turns.

Verse 5a also is a dramatic "hinge" (Hess 2005, 58). Implicitly, the woman's words continue to include her lover; explicitly, they begin a short speech to the **daughters of Jerusalem** (vv 5-6). Seven times she used this title (1:5; 2:7; 3:5, 10; 5:8, 16; 8:4); in 3:10-11, it is paired with "Daughters of Zion." This group certainly included "the young women" she referred to as admiring her lover (vv 3-4). Some take **daughters** to comprise all the women of **Jerusalem**. Whether a small or large group, these women function in the Song similarly to the chorus of classical Greek dramas. Sometimes they were "only" her sounding board; sometimes they responded verbally.

Kedar was a confederation of Arab tribes east of biblical Edom (today, southern Jordan and northwestern Saudi Arabia). Pastoral nomads, they lived in **tent**s woven from black goat hair. The woman expanded her opening assertion with a simple simile, doubled in a parallelism for emphasis. She was ***black*** . . . **like the tents of Kedar, like the tent curtains of** ***Salmah***.

The tent curtains of Solomon is an understandable mistranslation resulting from a different vowel pointing of the Hebrew text. However, with Pope and others, we read ***Salmah***, an Arab tribe preceding the Nabataeans in and around Petra, beyond the Dead Sea, south-southeast of Jerusalem (1977, 320). The **curtains**—the exterior walls, the interior dividing curtains, or both—designate the whole. Kedar's tents were black; Salmah's tents were black. By a simple parallelism, the woman compared herself to both.

Modern readers may respond reflexively, "Of course, black is beautiful!" However, the woman was not self-identifying as African, nor even as Egyptian. Ancient Israel's world did exhibit prejudice and social stratification, but not based on racial notions of skin color. Neither was she presenting herself as a nomadic princess (contra Goulder 1986, 51-52).

The Song as a whole includes compelling evidence that this woman was probably from the rural north of Israel, perhaps from Shunem/Shulam (see 6:13 [7:1 HB]). Never in history were the inhabitants of this region viewed as social equals by their urban neighbors. At least some of these **daughters of Jerusalem** would have scorned any country woman, because village life required women to work long, hard hours, often outdoors in the sun. By contrast, upper-class urban women usually did little or no physical labor; they had servants. They were paler of skin, and she darker by comparison, and she anticipated the derision that greeted a peasant's deeply tanned complexion. But if some in this group dismissed the woman as a "peasant" because of her sun-darkened skin, she turned it into a badge of worth and honor. This is the point of the woman's simile.

The woman explained the reason for her color, blaming **My mother's sons**, not calling them her "brothers" because they treated her harshly. Giving neither reason nor context, she said only that in their anger, they set her to work the **vineyards**. That this was not an isolated incident, the reader may infer from their overbearing "protection" in 8:8-9.

This whole verse builds a complex chain of wordplays, allusions, and assonances. No explanation could be both clear and brief, but today she may have said it this way: "Don't **stare** at me like that! My skin is **burned black** because the sun has stared at me for days on end, and has burned me black. That's because my 'brothers' **burned with anger** against me, and made me **keeper** of our family **vineyards**, so I couldn't **keep** my own **'vineyard,'** for myself. A deep healthy tan may not be *your* idea of beauty, but where I come from, it is. I'm black, *and* I'm beautiful."

Reading vv 5 and 6 together confirms v 5 as the woman's own positive self-assessment, expressed with confidence, even defiance. Embracing, drawing attention to, and celebrating her dark beauty (v 5), then explaining but not apologizing for it (v 6), she rendered disdainful stares impotent.

■ **7** The young woman turned her attention to her lover, addressing him as *whom my life loves*. Hebrew *nepeš* ("self, being") denotes the higher sensate creatures, including humans, as whole and entire living beings (not the Greek concept of soul). She loved him in and with her whole self, all her "person."

Both her questions open with **where**; she did not propose to stay and tend her mother's vineyards. *Where do you pasture [your flock]?* was a request for directions: Where should she go to find him leading and guarding his grazing animals that day?

Her second question concerns the midday; its Hebrew expression is very poetic: *Where do you cause [your flock] to recline at noonday?* Sheep and goats need rest for rumination (part of the digestive process) between grazing times. The shepherd also needs a noon meal, and a short nap if the place is safe for it. Many days the midday scene is the most idyllic, as shepherd and flock rest in the

1:7

shade of a clump of trees, a "mighty rock" (Ps 62:7 [8 HB]), or a vertical rock face at the side of a wadi.

Why should I be like a veiled woman? is a literal translation of her third question. In Israel, only prostitutes wore veils daily (see Gen 38:13-26). Other women reserved veils for weddings or other special occasions. The point of her question is, "Tell me where to find you, so I won't be like a veiled prostitute who has come upon your **friends** tending their **flocks**, trying to drum up business." As we shall see, much of the Song is set outside the walls of house and town. Already though, the woman was careful to be seen for who she was: the faithful love, desiring and heeding no other.

FROM THE TEXT

Reading through the Song, many times our most helpful takeaways will be, "What she said!" "What he said!" Using what this woman and this man said to and about each other, we can assess and adjust our understanding of God's full intentions for the gifts of human sexual love. As this unit ends with the woman's question of where she would find him, we may ask not, "Where can I *find* a love such as theirs, such as they were for each other?" but, "How can I *be* such a love as these two were, a love *worth* finding?"

B. He: Most Beautiful of Women (1:8-11)

BEHIND THE TEXT

A number of commentators take v 8 as the friends' response to the woman's question of v 7. On this view, they knew her lover was not within hearing, and suggested where she could look for him. We view v 8 as the man's response to her questions, and thus as the first words of the Song uttered by him. His next lines (vv 9-11) attest that she found him, after following his directions.

Both his praise (vv 9-11) and the woman's reply (vv 12-14) are three poetic lines. Each of the man's next three replies (1:15; 1:17; 2:2), and the woman's next two (1:16; 2:1), comprise a single line in Hebrew. The woman's fourth reply (2:3ff.) is the first of the longer, reciprocal acclamations characteristic of the rest of the Song.

IN THE TEXT

■ **8** We should read the first clause, **If you do not know *for yourself.*** The Hebrew epithet, ***the beautiful one among the women***, is stronger and more eloquent than the NIV renders it. All women are beautiful, but in her lover's eyes, this woman was ***the beautiful one*** among them all.

The man's first words form the protasis (If . . .), to the apodosis, [***then***] ***you yourself go out along the sheep-tracks, and pasture your kids*** [young goats] by

the tents of the shepherds. His implication: "To answer your question, 'Tell me where?' *there* is where you will find me."

Some read this as though he were instructing her to do what she already had objected to doing (v 7). She did not wish to be alone in the presence of shepherds she did not know, but this is not only his answer to her request for directions but also his promise that when she found the *place*, she would find *him*. She need not worry; in his company, none would harass her.

The sheep-tracks in the Judean countryside are very narrow, horizontal tracks made by sheep grazing along the slopes of hillside pastures, usually two to three feet apart on the slope face. They are grazed most heavily from early winter through spring, enough to make the tracks permanent throughout the year. In dry weather, humans can walk them safely. The young woman needed only to take the direction her lover indicated, grazing her own **goats** along the way, until she came to the **shepherds** in their **tents**. There she would find her lover.

In the animal husbandry of western Asia, sheep and goats always have been paramount among both pastoral nomads and settled agriculturalists. It follows that flocks and their increase carried a religious significance for faithful Israelites, and their pagan neighbors. Because of this, many invest this response to the woman's query with both religious and erotic significance. Such weights of innuendo and double entendre are more than we should ask *this* verse to bear, however. She asked where to find him; he told her, with the tenderness of a lover.

■ **9** The Hebrew text begins with the prepositional phrase **to a mare**. It is not "to my mare," as some propose. (The final vowel [*hîreq yôd*] is a nonpronominal genitive, not a 1cs dependent pronoun.) Not even Solomon, noted as an international dealer in horses and chariots (1 Kgs 10:28-29), would have said one of his mares was **among Pharaoh's chariot horses**. His horses were not in Egypt, and Solomon was never at war with Egypt. With respect to the **mare**, she was not one of the team harnessed to his chariot, nor his own mount; this was any fine mare among the best-caparisoned chariotry within ancient Israel's horizons.

With **Chariot horses**, the NIV correctly translates *rekeb* as referring to the teams of two or three stallions harnessed to pull each chariot, and not to the wagons of war called chariots. The mare is pictured among the males of her kind, and Egyptian chariot horses were considered the best.

But what is the point of this metaphor? Proposals are varied; Pope has an interesting collection (1977, 336-40). Could a mare have pulled a chariot? Cantrell notes that pregnant mares do not excite stallions and so could be put to harness between weaning one foal and birthing the next, about a five-month period (2011, 24). However, mares were usually kept for breeding. Carr expresses the point of this metaphor succinctly, "The comparison here underscores the girl's attractiveness. A mare loose among the royal stallions would create intense excitement" (1984, 83). As healthy stallions cannot ignore a healthy mare, the man could not ignore his **darling**.

The Power of a Mare

An episode from a campaign of Pharaoh Thutmose III (mid-fifteenth century BC) illustrates the reality behind the metaphor. The tomb inscription of the
soldier Amenemheb includes this account, "When the Prince [of Qedesh-on-
the-Orontes] sent out a mare, which [*was swift*] on her feet and which entered
among the army, I ran after her on foot, carrying my dagger, and I (ripped) open
her belly" (Pritchard 1969, 241). The mare's soft underbelly was her only real vulnerability; Amenemheb's quick thinking saved the Egyptian chariot horses from
ruinous distraction, and Thutmose from defeat.

In many contexts, Hebrew *ra'yātî* is rendered "friend," but here, he calls
her **my darling** (*my friend*) as a term of endearment. In ancient Israel, where the
intimacy of friendship was usually enjoyed with others of one's own gender, it pro-
claims his honor and respect for her. This is the first of nine occurrences: 1:9, 15;
2:2, 10, 13; 4:1, 7; 5:2; 6:4; the NIV renders each, **my darling**. *Ra'yātî* is the man's
term of address to the woman, never hers to him. Used about once per speech—
more than any other of his endearments—*my friend*/my darling is the man's preferred way of addressing his love. Second most frequent (first in 4:9 [→]; also →
Behind the Text for Song 4:8-15 with sidebar, "Carr on 'Sister'"), **my sister, my
bride** also connotes love, honor, and respect. Together, these terms demonstrate
that ancient Israel viewed mutuality between a man and a woman as possible,
admirable, and desirable; this is not a modern construct imposed anachronistically
upon an ancient text.

■ **10-11** A passive form of *'āvâ*, "desire," begins the first line, and is understood
in the second line of v 10, a common technique of Hebrew poetry. **Beautiful** is a
justifiable translation: the man found the woman's **cheeks** and **neck** desirable (*desired*) because he found them **beautiful**. Hess comments, "Rather than a necessity
to create an attraction that is not there naturally, [the **earrings** and **jewels**] serve
to make more beautiful what is already desirable. They also . . . form appropriate
adornments for one so noble and beautiful" (2005, 65).

The plural noun translated **earrings** means "round, turned things," and they
set off the woman's **cheeks**. A sampling of translations makes clear the imprecise
state of our knowledge: "bangles" (Pope 1977, 291); "pendants" (Murphy 1990, 130);
"ornaments" (Keel 1994, 56); "jewelry" (Garrett 2004, 140). Probably gold pendant
earrings (v 11), they framed and highlighted the beauty of the woman's face.

Strings of jewels (v 10) translates a plural noun meaning "pierce[d]." Poetic
parallelism pairs this and the descriptive phrase of v 11, **studded with silver** (*with
pierced beadwork of silver*). This could be any multi-strand necklace of silver
beads, perhaps strung with precious or semiprecious stones, as often found in
artistic representations of both women and horses from ancient Egypt and Mesopotamia.

Some take the plural **We will make** (v 11) as an interjection by the friends. It may be more natural as the man's declaration of purpose: to celebrate his beloved's beauty, he would commission other fine pieces for her.

FROM THE TEXT

First voiced in this short section and repeated through the Song, the man's terms of endearment express love, honor, *and* respect for his beloved. Among the first questions wisdom bids a couple ask: Do we respect each other? Do we *show* our respect by the terms we use in addressing each other?

C. She: My Beloved Is (1:12-14)

BEHIND THE TEXT

The man had begun with a simile ("I liken you" [v 9]). Conversationally skilled, the woman began her response with a "true" metaphor: "the king" here *is* her beloved. She referenced him here, not as king of Israel, but as her lover, "king" of her heart and life.

IN THE TEXT

■ **12** *Mēsab* is not the usual noun for **table**, but means literally "that which surrounds." Carr renders, "among his own surroundings," noting, "The broader context is a combination of bedroom motifs (1:4, 16f.) and banquet motifs (2:1-5), and this translation preserves the ambiguity of the original" (1984, 84).

Her **perfume** was nard ("spikenard," KJV), a loanword from Sanskrit via Persian, as the plant is native to India's Himalayan regions. Its distant origin and rarity made it expensive. In its Indian homeland, as in western Asia, nard was used in aphrodisiac preparations.

All three lines are metaphorical, laced with erotic innuendo. As befits such verbal love-play, they raise tantalizing questions: Is this man really the king, or only her "king" by virtue of love? Is the place of "his own surroundings" his table? His bed? Both? Was she really wearing a **perfume** of expensive *nard*, or was the *nard* her own bodily scent? The natural scent of a lover can be erotic, and while myrrh and henna are mentioned in the following two lines, she really wore neither; metaphorically, her lover was both.

■ **13 Myrrh** is an aromatic resin from several species of trees related to balsam. In antiquity, the myrrh of the Arabian Peninsula was more highly prized than that from East Africa or India. Like nard, myrrh was a luxury of international trade.

Allowed to harden, solid myrrh could be used in a **sachet**, a small cloth bag tied with a cord. Hung around her neck, or fastened to her inner garment, the woman could wear it as she said, **resting between** her **breasts**. As her body heat softened the myrrh in the sachet, it gave off a pleasant fragrance.

Here, though, she disavowed physical myrrh; her **beloved** was her **sachet of myrrh**. **Resting** lessens the intimacy of the Hebrew verb, when we should highlight it: *spending the night between my breasts*. She contemplated the joy, the excitement, of embracing her **beloved** the whole night through. We should be circumspect, but we may not downplay: the Song celebrates human love in all its intimate aspects.

This is the woman's first use of **my beloved** (*dôdî*). In the Song's eight chapters, this endearment is on her lips nearly thirty times, always referring to him.

■ **14** Verses 13-14 form what is called popularly a synthetic parallelism:

> *A sachet of myrrh / my beloved is to me /*
> *spending the night between my breasts.*
> *A cluster of henna blossoms / my beloved is to me /*
> *from the vineyards of En Gedi.*

The final element of the second line (v 14) is neither a repetition of nor a variation from the first line (v 13), but introduces a different thought or image, multiplying the poetic possibilities.

Henna is known also as cypress (not that of v 17, below) and camphor/camphire. Growing up to ten feet tall, the shrub is native to ancient Israel. Nard and myrrh were imported and expensive; henna was local and readily available. The dried leaves are processed to make a red-orange cosmetic, still used to color hair and nails. **Henna blossoms** are bluish-yellow and grow thickly together; hence, the term **cluster** (*'eškōl*), used also of grapes and dates (→ 7:7-8). The flowers were processed into a perfume, much as roses were (Pope 1977, 352).

En Gedi, "the spring of the kid," is a copious spring above the western shore of the Dead Sea, sustaining a large oasis at the edge of the Judean Desert. From at least the late Judean monarchy onward, En Gedi was an important source of dates, grapes, balsam, and henna. All could be identified as coming **from the vineyards** [orchards, plantations] **of En Gedi**.

All three lines feature the sense of smell. In v 12, her nard dispersed its scent for her lover. In vv 13-14, *he* is her aromatics: a sachet of myrrh between her breasts; a cluster of the most fragrant henna blossoms, from En Gedi's verdant oasis. The ancients knew the power of erotic scents.

FROM THE TEXT

Such an immersion in metaphor and double entendre invites us to infer the woman's ardent fantasies, impelling persons of goodwill to applaud her and her lover. We are not invited into the chamber with them; if we are persons of normal decency, we will not wish to be invited. As we pass by their door, we will bless them, together with their modern counterparts of our acquaintance, in the name of the God who created and blesses all loves of integrity.

D. A Repartee of Love (1:15—2:2)

BEHIND THE TEXT

These verses record a witty exchange: he, she, he, she, he. It is the most rapid-fire dialogue of the Song. Some of its themes will surface again.

The Song does not restrict itself to Yahwistic imagery. Though we first see the metaphorical representation of the dove (v 15) in pagan settings, we are not obliged to view the Song's poet as pagan. In every age, such metaphors move beyond their original settings into general use.

IN THE TEXT

■ **15** These are the man's words. Hebrew *hinnēh*, used in positive contexts such as this, evinces wonder and awe. Using a comparable English idiom, we may translate, *Ah, you are beautiful, my darling! Ah! You are beautiful!* Your eyes are doves. This is the lover's attempt to combine realistic assessment with appreciative awe that such a woman was glad to be in his presence, intricacies of love that ultimately surpass expression in any language. Even saying it twice is inadequate, but further repetition would diminish rather than enhance his praise.

Your eyes are doves is a simple, direct metaphor, but what is the point of this one? Many suggest the dove's seeming softness and gentle nature; others, the appealing luster of its eyes; still others, the mutual affection and apparent faithfulness of a dove pair. Not uncommonly, commentators conclude the specific comparison intended by this metaphor is indiscernible (e.g., Carr 1984, 86; Murphy 1990, 135).

As often happens, the archaeology of ancient Israel's cultural horizons clarifies the issue. Keel reminds us that for well over a millennium the dove symbolized Ishtar/Astarte, the Mesopotamian/Canaanite goddess of love, and her Greek counterpart, Aphrodite (1994, 69-73).

The symbolism broadened, and the dove became a symbol of love itself. Keel includes eight representative works from Syria, Israel, and Greece, in which doves function as the symbol of, and invitation to, love. When the meaning is "invitation," the goddess or woman usually is depicted sending a dove (or doves) in flight toward the god or man. Keel summarizes, "When Cant. 1:15b speaks of 'eyes,' what it really means is 'glances.' . . . [O]ne can see the doves only as messengers of love. Thus the sentence would mean: 'Your glances are messengers of love!'" (1994, 71). The man saw not only beauty in his **darling** but also love and welcome in her look.

■ **16a** The first words of the woman's response reflect her lover's words. Her exclamatory *Behold!* repeats his. She used the same adjective (*yāpeh*, **handsome**) with which he had lauded her (*yāpâ*, **beautiful**). Finally, she responded to his *ra'yātî* (**my darling**) with her own *dôdî*, **my beloved**.

1:15-16a

123

Next, though, instead of a repeated *yāpeh* (as the man had done with *yāpâ*, v 15), the woman used a different adjective and preceded it with *'ap* (**Oh**), a particle of strong assertion. To reflect the building, emphatic timbre of her tone, we may translate the whole, ***Behold! How handsome you are, my beloved! Yes! More than that! How delightful!***

Here, the Hebrew *nā'îm* is more deeply insightful, and much more passionate, than the NIV's **charming**. ***Captivating*** reflects the unreserved passion of her love for him (as would "enchanting" or "enthralling"). Anyone could see he was **handsome**, or encounter and experience him as **charming**. However, only one who *knew* him could praise him, in the romantic/sexual context of this exchange, as *nā'îm* (***captivating***).

■ **16b** This clause belongs to the woman's speech, since she introduced it also with *'ap*. Moreover, the NIV's **And** is not nearly strong enough. Our translation above, ***Yes! More than that!*** would be appropriate here, as well. In this poetic context, her characterization of **our bed** is as important as her assessment of her lover.

Most commentators rightly take this clause as the first of a triplet. The second and third (v 17*a* and v 17*b*) feature nominal predicates; exegetical prudence calls for taking this one also as a substantive (noun), not as an adjective. We may read, ***Our bed is verdure.*** What that *means*, we must consider with the parallel clauses of v 17.

■ **17** Do these three clauses belong to the woman or the man? Commentators espouse three positions: (1) the woman spoke all three; (2) the woman spoke the first, the man the second and third; (3) the man spoke all three. As noted (→ v 16*a*), the woman introduced her exclamatory ***How delightful!*** with *'ap*. The next clause also begins with *'ap*; the two clearly belong together as the woman's words.

In the context of this dialogue as a whole (1:9—2:2), it seems best to take v 17 as spoken by the man. In this section, each introductory "speech" is three verses: the man, vv 9-11; the woman, vv 12-14. From that point, the dialogue comprises alternating, rapid-fire utterances: each is one Hebrew line, each a quick-witted, warm, and loving response to the last. If this reading is apt, taking v 17 as the man's words carries the pattern through to the end (2:2) uninterrupted.

As noted, we must consider v 16*b* together with v 17, to understand the whole:

[She]: ***Yes! Our bed is verdure!***
[He]: ***The beams of our houses are cedars;***
     Our wainscoting is firs.

The literal referents are straightforward. A **bed** is for lying on, whether to sleep or to make love. It may be plain, ornate, or anything in between, according to the householder's station. ***Verdure*** refers to the luxuriant foliage of forest or garden: the leafy branches of trees and shrubs, the stems and leaves of other plants and grasses. The ***verdure*** they have fashioned into, or appropriated as, an eminently suitable ***bed***.

In antiquity, as today, **beams** rested on bearing walls to support roofs. **Cedars** were the building material par excellence, an expensive import from Lebanon (1 Kgs 5:6-12 [20-26 HB]; 7:1-3).

Wainscoting, decorative paneling of interior walls, reflects ancient building practices (and perhaps also the etymology of the Heb. *rāhîṭ*) and is better than the NIV's **rafters**. Moreover, **rafters** is redundant: not all **beams** are **rafters**, but here **rafters** would have to be **beams**.

To say that *běrôṭîm* (**firs**) is used only here is true, but could mislead; this is the northern dialect (and Aramaic) plural form of *běrôš*, common in the OT (Isa 37:24; Hos 14:9 [10 HB], etc.). Translations include "cypress," "juniper," "fir," and "pine." The various junipers belong to the cypress family, and the "fir" in question is the Aleppo (or Jerusalem) pine. Though not as prized as cedar, all can be of a quality to make excellent *wainscoting*.

Various interpreters read here: (1) a normal, if luxurious, human dwelling; (2) a temple, or other divine sanctuary; (3) an outdoor bower of love, in the garden or the forest. It is helpful here to remember that most ancient dwellings (especially peasant ones) did not include separate bedrooms for each couple in the family. Instead, family members slept in common spaces, with bedding cleared away for daytime hours. As a result, intimate trysts outside the home were more common, and considered less "deviant," than in some modern societies. These two lovers meeting in the outdoors, then, is a reasonable, if not a necessary reading.

We take the lovers to be describing their outdoor trysting-place in the terms of the house where most of a couple's romantic encounters would take place over the years of a marriage. Taking seriously the woman's exclamation, **Our bed is verdure** (not **verdant**), the thick, soft groundcover or freshly cut boughs laid down *is* their bed for this encounter.

Whereas cedars must be harvested, sawn, and lifted into place as the beams of a house, the cedars above them are living beams; towering, majestic, conducive of love. Likewise of wainscoting: in a house the trees have been harvested, sawn, planed, and placed. In forest or garden, the living trees are the walls enclosing them in privacy, even scenting their bower as a further, generous gift of nature, and of nature's God.

Two further observations are persuasive. One, often noted, is that much of the Song is set outdoors, celebrating human, sexual love as part and parcel of the abundance of joys with which God imbued all creation. That this lively dialogue should be set also outdoors fits the ambiance of the Song as a whole.

The second observation also is noted, then usually dismissed. The man begins (v 17a), **The beams of our houses** (not **house**). Carr takes an enclosed garden to be the lovers' trysting-place, then observes, "The couple is not restricted to secret chambers behind solid walls and closed doors for their lovemaking—they have the whole garden with its many-shaded bowers at their disposal" (1984, 87). In the man's metaphorical language, each separate bower is a "house." The plural *houses* also can be read as referring to recurrent trysts: *the beams of our houses are [always] cedar.*

■ **2:1** The woman extended the outdoor metaphors, comparing herself to two strikingly beautiful flowers. The identities of both have been subjects of discussion.

None of the plants commonly known as roses today can be the **rose of Sharon** (v 1a). What we know as a rose "apparently was brought in at a later period from Armenia and Persia" (Pope 1977, 367). Some argue for the crocus or meadow-saffron, but Keel suggests the wish to see in the woman a "chaste and modest maiden" prompts them to read her as comparing herself to "one of the modest spring flowers . . . , and to the purity of the lily" (1994, 78).

However, as *šôšannat* in v 1b is the *lotus* rather than the **lily**, so *ḥăbaṣṣelet* in v 1a is not some small, little-noticed bloom, either. This is confirmed by its only other occurrence, where it is a bold, joyous harbinger of eschatological renewal (Isa 35:1). Anyone familiar with its striking blossoms, and remarkable adaptations to its rugged habitat, would agree the *sea daffodil* is a strong candidate (Keel 1994, 78). It is worthy of the character of this woman, and of its pairing with the lotus in her self-assessment.

The second flower is the *lotus*, a water lily ranging across the ANE. Both Hebrew *šôšannâ* and Akkadian *šešanu* are loanwords from Egyptian *ssn*; in Egypt, without question, this was the lotus. Keel asserts that today both a white and a blue water lily grow in Israel; that the Sharon plain was marshy in antiquity; and that the lotus was a prominent motif in ancient Israelite art and architecture (1994, 78-82). He is correct on all three counts.

We may translate, then: *I am the sea daffodil of the Sharon, the lotus of the valleys.* This is not particularly melodic in English, but the Hebrew text is most poetic! The **Sharon** is the coastal plain, from the Yarkon River north of Jaffa to the Carmel headland. Mostly swampy and malaria-ridden in antiquity, it was lightly inhabited. Many points along its sandy beach fronts would have provided excellent habitat for the *sea daffodil.*

We note that *the valleys* (*hā'ămāqîm*) is plural. Used here as a common noun, it could designate any or all of the following: the Sharon Plain; the Jezreel Valley/Plain, also a swampland in antiquity, inhabitable only around its periphery; several segments of the Jordan Valley, from above Lake Huleh almost to the Dead Sea; and several smaller valley/plain regions in northern Israel. The lovers could have known the *lotus* in many places.

■ **2** Her lover affirmed her self-assessment, repeating the second metaphor. By comparison with his love, any other woman was as appealing to him as a thorny, woody *bramble* (NIV: **thorns**). Of course this is hyperbole but, on some levels, it also will strike many as an appropriate feeling and attitude for someone deeply in love. He calls her again **My darling** (→ Song 1:9). In this context, Hebrew *habbānôt* denotes primarily **the young women** of marriageable age.

Many passages in the Song affirm without comment the goodness of all God's creation. That their intent is not to counter Gnosticism only strengthens their impact in doing so. Cumulatively, they show Gnosticism not only as incompatible with biblical teaching but also simply as untenable.

Both general and special revelation (creation and the Bible) proclaim and celebrate the innate goodness of *all* aspects of God's creation. More than that, they invite God's people to an active "junior partnership" in restoring what was lost or marred in the alienation of Eden. That this includes the joys of sexual love comes in the Song as good news indeed!

E. She: Like an Apple Tree (2:3-7)

BEHIND THE TEXT

In some areas of the ANE, worshipping the goddess of love involved cakes made with raisins, formed in her likeness, or representing her in the shape of female genitalia (see Hos 3:1; Jer 44:19). Apples also were associated in various ways with lovemaking. We do not mean this woman was a goddess worshipper. She simply appealed here for the **raisin cakes** and apples commonly associated with love and lovemaking, prompted by the acts of love she figured here with masterful imagery, simultaneously allusive and direct.

IN THE TEXT

■ **3** In Hebrew, the single line of v 2 and the first line of v 3 are parallel in grammar and syntax:

(2) *Like the lotus among the brambles,*
so is my darling among the daughters.
(3a) *Like the apple among the trees of the woodland,*
so is my love among the sons.

The lowly bramble bears no comparison with the beautiful and sensuous lotus of the wetlands. Just so, the woman replied, the woody denizens of the forest uplands are valueless compared with the apple. Her parallelism is complete, through the last word. As **the daughters** means primarily the younger women, so **the sons** means primarily the younger men.

Though some suggest *tappûah* refers to another fruit tree, neither apricot, orange, nor lemon were present in the area at this time, and the quince does not have the pleasing smell the Hebrew name requires, whereas the apple does (Pope 1977, 371). Moreover, the apple features in love lyrics from neighboring regions well before the time of the Song. The *tappûah* is the apple.

We translate v 3*b*:

In his shade I delight and I remain,

And his fruit is sweet to my palate.

To be sure, this imagery is sexual and erotic, but it is more. ***In his shade*** is first in this compound clause for emphasis; *he* is her focus. The first verb is a *pi'el*, an intensive, and its nuances overlap; we should translate, ***I greatly desire and I greatly delight.***

The image of sitting in the shade of an apple tree evokes the senses. She has likened him to an apple tree because the smell of both is sensuous. Going further, she pronounces **his fruit is sweet** to her ***palate*** (NIV: **taste**).

When Lovers Rest in Each Other

The woman has evoked the physical pleasures of sexual love deeply, graphically, fully. At the same time, and just as importantly, she has pictured the breadth of love that goes beyond satisfaction of physical desire. Hess's insight here is comprehensive and compelling, worth pondering at length: "He shelters her as she sheltered him in 1:13," when she described him as "resting between my breasts" (2005, 78). Their contentment in and with each other is complete. Insofar as one human can be a source of *shalom* for another, they are.

■ **4** We translate:

> *He brought me to the house of wine,*
>
> *And his intention [look] concerning me (was) love.*

As Carr observes, "Idiomatically, the 'house of wine' could be the place where wine is grown (i.e., a vineyard), manufactured, stored, or consumed" (1984, 90-91). Given the near-ubiquitous presence in the Song of vineyards, wine, and sexual metaphors of vineyard, grape, and cup, we understand this place to which he brought her as a vineyard, or perhaps as a booth often built in vineyards, accommodating romantic trysts, among other purposes (with Carr, ibid.; see also Hess 2005, 79 and n. 79).

The meaning of the second line hinges on its first noun, *degel*. All but one of its biblical uses occur in Numbers, where they denote the standards or banners of the respective tribes of Israel as they prepared to leave Mount Sinai. Thus, its use here has seemed straightforward, but not so. Hebrew *degel* is a cognate of (or possibly a loanword from) Akkadian *dagalu*, "to look." In Numbers, each tribal standard was the emblem toward which people looked, identifying the tribes and their encampments by their "banners." Warriors looked to their banners to lead them into battle. Here in the Song, though, a battle standard hardly seems a fitting symbol of **love**.

If we return to the meaning of "look," used as a noun, the verse makes excellent sense. The woman had asked for her lover to take her away to his chambers (1:4). Now he did so, but to a trysting place in the vineyard. She had asked for his love; he would give it soon. Verse 7, below, tells the reader the romance/drama is not yet at its crescendo. From this moment, however, his ***look*** toward her conveyed ***love*** as his intention.

■ 5 Translation can be straightforward:

> *Sustain me with raisin cakes;*
> *Support me with apples;*
> *For sick (because) of love am I.*

Sustain translates a *pi'el* form of *sāmak*, "cause me to lay/rest myself," that is, **sustain me**, by bringing me raisin cakes. *Support* translates the *pi'el rāpad*, "cause me to spread out," "to be supported" (or "support myself") **with apples**. The verb is extended metaphorically; rather than the literal support of a couch, she asks for the **support** [i.e., **strengthening fuel**] of apples (NIV: **refresh me**).

The third line, *For sick (because) of love am I,* crystallizes the interpreter's dilemma throughout the Song. The woman certainly did not mean she was ill and needed a physician. Did she mean, then, "I am 'sick' ['faint,' 'languishing'] from the intensity of my desire to make love, knowing we cannot yet"? Or did she mean, "I am 'sick' ['luxuriously languorous'] in the joyous afterglow of our lovemaking"? Either meaning is possible; both are plausible. Much of the Song is similarly difficult on this point.

■ 6 **Arm** (or **hand**) is not in the Hebrew text of either line; they read literally *his left . . . and his right.* We may supply one or the other; nothing else makes sense. This is one of the classic poses of lovers lying together. The verse is not a wish, as some translations would have it, but a description. Her unelaborated report of her lover's intimate embrace emphasizes her glad acceptance of him and of their lovemaking, as a train of adjectives could not do.

Her phrasing is more artfully suggestive because she did not pursue additional detail. We could translate the second line, **His right** [arm, or *hand*] *clasps me*. Like English **embraces**, Hebrew *ḥābaq* encompasses a broad semantic range, suggesting many possible actions, especially since the reference could as well be to his **hand** as to his **arm**. This may be one of the reasons for the young woman's cautionary admonition that follows (v 7).

■ 7 This verse is repeated exactly at 3:5, and in a shorter form at 8:4. With most commentators, we take all three occurrences as spoken by the woman; these are not the words of the man or of bystanders ("the chorus"). On **Daughters of Jerusalem**, → 1:5*a*.

I charge you translates the Hebrew *šaba'*, which refers to the swearing of an oath. Here, noting the woman's use of a *hip'il* perfect, we could translate, *I am causing you to swear [take an oath].*

In many other contexts, oaths are sworn in the name of Yahweh, as the impartial witness to its performance. Here, the woman evoked *the gazelles or the does of the field* as witnesses. Later in the Song, the man depicted the woman's breasts metaphorically as **gazelles** (4:5; 7:3 [4 HB]). Proverbs 5:19 speaks of the wife of one's youth as "a loving doe, a graceful deer," and mentions "her breasts" in the succeeding line. This metaphorical linkage, perhaps together with a reluctance to invoke Yahweh's name in an oath involving sexual love, may explain this unusual construction.

Do not arouse or awaken love; the woman used two forms of the same Hebrew root, *'ûr* (*hip'il*, then *po'lel*). Alone, either form could be translated **arouse**, **awaken**, *stir up, incite, excite, stimulate*, and so forth. However, using the two sequentially, the woman made her entreaty stronger even than invoking an oath would do by itself. We will not make it too strong if we paraphrase a bit expansively: *I charge you, O daughters of Jerusalem, asking you to swear by the gazelles or by the does of the open field, not even to awaken, and certainly not to excite love to greater arousal, until it is pleased, until it is delighted [to be awakened and further aroused]*.

The woman spoke of **love** itself, not of "my love," as some older versions have it. The reference is not to the man, but to love *as* love. Sexual love is instantly exciting and powerful, and carries the potential for lasting joy. Wisely, the woman recognized that such a power is best handled with deliberate care.

Noting that some have argued for this as a request not to bother the lovers when they are together, *and* that it is repeated twice more (3:5; 8:4), Hess asks, with wit and some asperity, "In the most important repeated refrain in this greatest example of love poetry in the Bible, what is more likely to be the repeated message: a caution about the evocation of erotic love or a 'Do Not Disturb' sign?" (Hess 2005, 83, n. 92).

FROM THE TEXT

Throughout this dialogue, the lovers revel, enjoying and celebrating their erotic intimacy. The dialogic form itself, the nearly equal division of lines, and their exuberance and wit are implicit reminders that God created humans equally in God's image. God's gifts of love—speech, attention, the mutuality of intimacies, initiative and response—are not reserved to one gender.

The woman's admonition in 2:7 does not forbid altogether the joys of sensual love; the whole of the Song urges otherwise. Rather, this is a reminder that sexual love is not simply, and only, copulation. It is a much greater and more potent gift than that, and with potential for great good and great joy comes also the possibility of disappointment, even of harm. Such a great gift warrants care in its awakening, in its progression, in its full enjoyment. The final word, *until it pleases, until it delights to come*, is an assurance that love's time does come, and that love's own time is worth waiting for.

III. PRESENCE AND ABSENCE: WAYS OF LOVE: SONG OF SONGS 2:8—3:5

OVERVIEW

As in the Song's first section, the woman speaks first here, announcing her lover's approach and arrival outside her windows (2:8-9). Verses 10-13 represent a departure: for the first time, she reports words he had spoken to her (she will do it again in 5:2).

Verse 14 reports the man's words; less certain is whether the woman still is quoting him. A decision is not crucial to interpretation, but a sense of immediacy in word and tone leads us to take vv 14-15 as spoken directly by the man, his ardor emboldened by the lush verdure of the countryside in spring.

Verses 16-17 are the woman's words, echoing the passion of the classic lovers' walk, each basking in the presence of the beloved. As with many passages, we cannot be sure whether she speaks of a love-making just past, or imagines a consummation not yet realized, but soon to be.

In 3:1-5, the woman reports searching the city for her lover, when she could not account for his absence from her side.

131

A. He: Come with Me! (2:8-15)

BEHIND THE TEXT

Israel enjoys a Mediterranean climate: a winter rainy season followed by a rainless summer. In Jerusalem, the literary center of the Song, the rains usually begin mid-to-late October. The heaviest rains fall from late November through February, about 70 percent of the yearly total. In March, the rains taper off, and normally are gone by the end of April. May and September rains are rare; rain in June, July, or August is virtually unknown.

A comparison will help us comprehend the man's energetic joy in this passage. London, England, and Jerusalem, Israel, both receive an average of twenty-four inches of rain per year (we have no numbers from antiquity, but we know they were not markedly different). London averages almost two hundred rain days per year. For Jerusalem, the same amount falls in about fifty rain days per year, most of them December through February. The weather pattern sets the time of year in the Song at about mid-spring.

IN THE TEXT

■ **8** We translate, quite literally,

> *The sound of my beloved! Behold, here he comes!*
> *Leaping upon the mountains, springing over the hills!*

The woman heard her lover before she saw him. **Sound** here can refer to his running, to his call as he approached, or to both. The Western reader does well to recall that for most of history, and in parts of the world down to the present, the most common mode of travel is by foot. A young man running to see his love after a night apart would have surprised no one. Her excitement in hearing him, then watching him bound across the hilly terrain, matched his exuberance in running to her.

The man's arrival is reported seamlessly, which serves as evidence that public segregation of the genders is not a feature of the culture(s) reflected in the OT. Reading rigid, public gender separation into ancient Israel's agrarian, subsistence economy and culture is anachronistic. On **My beloved**, → 1:13.

Mountains . . . hills reminds readers that Jerusalem, where much of the Song is set, is near the ridgeline of the Judean-Ephraimite hill country, ancient Israel's heartland. Even Moses, who never entered it, knew it as a "land . . . [of] valleys and hills" (Deut 8:7).

■ **9** *My beloved resembles* translates a participle from the same root as *děmût*, "(our) likeness," in Gen 1:26. In the speed, strength, and surefootedness of her lover's joyous strides, the woman saw the graceful beauty of the **gazelle** or the **young stag**. Here, the Hebrew *șěbî* vividly conflates two nouns, spelled exactly the same: **gazelle** and "beauty." Pope correctly observes, "The swiftness and agility of the gazelle, and its beauty are all intended in the present passage" (1977, 390).

2:8-9

The first three (Heb.) words of Song 2:9*b*, ***Behold! Here he stands,*** form an exact parallel with the end of v 8*a*. Her designation of the place, **behind our wall,** announced the moment of his arrival. She heard, then saw, his passage across the hills; now, he **stands** at his destination.

The **wall** likely comprised the border of the family compound. The young man did not enter uninvited, but stood where the wall was low enough, and the distance to the house short enough, that she could see him **gazing through the windows,** trying to locate her within.

Looking through the lattices uses both a verb and a noun that occur only here in the OT, but the parallel with the first half of the line establishes the meaning. Wooden latticework, mounted and fastened much as shutters are, still is a feature of homes in older sections of many Near Eastern cities. It allows people to see out without being seen from the street, while providing airflow, and a structure for shady vines to climb.

Gazing and ***looking*** are more apt than "peeking," "peering," and the like in some translations. The fact that **windows** and ***lattices*** both are plural has led some to picture him stepping (or scurrying) from window to window along the wall of the house. As long as the connotation is of eager anticipation, rather than a peeping Tom, this might be the case.

Finally, the KJV rendering, "he looketh forth at the windows," suggests the young man was inside, looking out. However, the woman just reported him coming to her across the hills and standing at the outside wall of the compound. Moreover, the Hebrew preposition *min* is not used of looking out a window from the inside (Pope 1977, 391).

■ **10** The woman's delight in the voice of her beloved resonates in her tone. The first word, *ʿānāh*, usually is translated ***answered,*** but the previous verses (3-9) record no words addressed to him. We may translate, ***He responded, and said to me;*** that is, he **responded** to seeing her as she opened the lattice (v 9), and began speaking to her.

Arise . . . come with me. On the often-sound principle that the simpler explanation is the better one, the man's invitation is clear and unambiguous. We avoid imposing non-Semitic categories on Semitic languages, if we take *qûmî lāk* (**Arise**) and *lĕkî lāk* (**come**) as examples of what we may call an idiomatic variation from the more usual reflexives, the *hitpaʿel* and *nipʿal* stems. The verbs are imperatives, but the man's tone is invitation, with no hint of command. (**With me** is not in the Hebrew text; with others, we take it as implied.)

On **My darling** → 1:9. **My beautiful one** is the same root and expresses the same admiration and wonder as the man's exclamation, "How beautiful you are," in 1:15.

Chiasm is a frequent and effective device of biblical poetry and prose. Here, a simple "grammatical" chiasm (Hess 2005, 91) enhances the literary beauty of the man's invitation: **Arise:my-darling::my-beautiful-one:come.**

■ **11** The particle *kî* connects his invitation with reasons he deemed persuasive. Together, vv 10*b*-11 convey his buoyant, joyful urging:

> *Arise, my darling!*
> *My beautiful one, come!*
> *Because—Look!—The winter has passed;*
> *The heavy rain is over and gone!*

The winter is past by mid-March in Jerusalem, because the heaviest **rains are over and gone**. Carr puts it aptly, "The three verbs almost personify the winter rains as a traveler who has passed through and has gone" (1984, 97). In antiquity, one effect was that roads (most, we would call "paths" or "trails") were passable again. One could venture beyond the edge of town without risk of serious injury on the muddy winter roads. Even setting aside other factors, we need not wonder at the young lover's timing.

■ **12** **Flowers** are literally, *the blossoms*, or even *the little blossoms*, if Carr is correct that this is a diminutive (1984, 97). These are the wildflowers whose blooms form a brilliant, springtime carpet of color on uncultivated hill country slopes throughout the Levant. Flowering trees and vines are not excluded but are not the primary focus.

The season of singing has come; because **the cooing of doves** follows immediately, we take **singing** as the primary meaning. However, a second Hebrew root, *zmr*, means "prune." Taking his cues from Isa 18:5 and the Iron Age I Gezer Calendar, Pope prefers "pruning time," but notes, "The poet was aware of the possible ambiguity . . . and used it deliberately" (1977, 395-96). Creaturely **singing** can encourage and celebrate creaturely fruitfulness. Pruning fosters and increases fruitfulness in many trees and vines. As this *is* poetry, taking both meanings together here is a sensible option.

The cooing of doves; Hebrew *tôr* is the turtledove, a migratory wild pigeon that passes through the Levant from Africa in April, en route to its European breeding grounds. Its arrival in Israel is yet another sign of spring. This is the only occurrence of *tôr* in the Song. Other references to "dove" in the NIV (e.g., 1:15; 2:14) translate *yônâ*, a dove resident in the land year-round.

■ **13** Of the fruit trees of ancient Israel, the **fig** was second to the olive in importance. The **early fruit** ripens in May or early June, thus functioning as another harbinger of spring. (A second crop is part of the "summer fruits" of August and September.)

The fig was important in sacred contexts around the Mediterranean and across much of Asia, including as a symbol of divine favor on human and other fertility. Yahwistic faith taught Israel they did not need to beg, bribe, or cajole, as their neighbors thought necessary. Rather, God is the Original Designer of all fertility, and imbued creation with self-perpetuating fertility. The fig did become in Israel a symbol of God's shalom (wholeness and security).

In spring, also, the **blossoming vines** of the grape **spread their fragrance**. Vineyards were ubiquitous in ancient Israel, and many homeowners had the vine and the fig tree in the open courtyards of their homes (1 Kgs 4:25 [5:5 HB]). Vines, grapes, and wine are even more deeply symbolic of love and fertility than the fig. The vine's fragrant blossoms are a fitting finale to this homage to spring, with its promises of love. As Hess notes, Song 2:13 carries a progression forward from v 12; its sensations are enjoyed close up, not from a distance (2005, 95).

Verse 13b is identical with v 10b (→). Its repetition here forms an inclusio. Of course, the man repeated his invitation in hopes of increasing its persuasive power; he *wanted* her to go with him into the countryside. The second member of an inclusio also functions as an ending. What follows, follows naturally, but is not integral to *this* song (vv 1-13); it is its own vignette.

■ **14** We take v 14 as a further appeal, prompted by the man's fervent desire. This new appeal, he based not on what she would experience if she ventured out, but on what he wished from her. Previously, he had noted her manner with the metaphorical, "Your eyes are doves" (→ 1:15). Here, he called her, **My dove**. On one level, it is an intimate term of endearment. More than that, though, this pet name avers that she embodied love for him.

This is the rock dove (*yônâ*); it resides in the land year-round. The man described its nesting places in two parallel phrases: *in the retreats* ["cliff crannies"; Pope 1977, 400] *of the towering rock refuge* (*sela'*), and *in the secret place of the rocky defile*. Mountain cliffs with their crevices, crannies, and cave openings describe the former. *Sela'* (not *selâ* of the Psalms) is a bulwark of rock, high and somewhat separate from its surroundings, providing a safe refuge. Edom's fortresses, including Petra, are described this way (Jer 49:16; Obad 3). The normal **mountainside** was not so inaccessible, but the crevices and small openings of its narrow, stepped ledges also provided ready nesting sites for the **dove**.

We may visualize the man standing in the garden, looking to the lattice behind which she was hidden from his view (see v 9). Extending the metaphor with which he just addressed her, he asked—in terms of the dove's natural habitat—that she come out to him from her "secret place" within the house.

When the dove is apprehensive or frightened, it does not emerge from its sheltered refuge; if it peers out, it is the picture of timidity. Given the woman's previous boldness, we need not project the shyness of the dove upon her. We need not infer timidity or coquettishness. We note, instead, that the corpus of love poetry from this part of the world (both ancient and modern) suggests that convention may have required her to delay her coming out, to give him time to demonstrate his skill as a maker of love poems.

Whatever the case, he wanted her with him, and told her again in a small, elegant chiasm of the ABB'A' pattern:

> *Let me gaze upon your appearance;*
> > *let me hear your voice.*
> *For your voice is sweet,*
> > *your appearance is desirable.*

2:14

The woman had described herself as *desirable* (1:5). The man had used the same term of her cheeks (1:10). Now, he echoed the whole of her self-assessment, praising her whole *appearance* as *desirable* (NIV: **lovely**).

■ **15** This verse has been problematic through most of its exegetical history. Verse 14 comprises the man's words; in vv 16-17, it is the woman speaking. Between those speeches, this verse begins, **Catch for us.** But who is speaking? The man? Perhaps. The woman? Maybe. Both? We cannot be sure. Some have suggested the "friends" of other passages, or other bystanders. To whom is the command to catch **the foxes** addressed? We think it most likely the speaker here is the man.

On a "literal" level, the picture is not so unfocused. Hebrew *šûʿālîm* can refer to foxes or jackals; **foxes** are more likely to be destructive of vineyards. Their burrowing can destroy the stone walls and uproot the vines inside. Unchecked, a vixen with her den of kits could **ruin** a vineyard in short order.

However, in the Song, a "vineyard" is not just a hillside of grapes, though it can be that. A "vineyard" also is variously the couple's mutual love and the woman's capacity both for sexual union and fruitfulness, especially here, where the vineyards are said to be **in bloom**, that is, beginning the seasonal cycle of fruit-bearing. The woman "is" the vineyard; the couple's love "is" the vineyard.

What then of the fox? Keel provides a plausible understanding, "In ancient Egyptian love poetry, 'fox' or especially 'young fox' is a metaphor for a great lover or womanizer" (1994, 110). The woman as a "vineyard" may prove irresistible to other "young foxes." If not prevented, such an interloper would **ruin** the "vineyard" of the couple's love, just as they are beginning to plant it together. Common sense alone teaches that a third-party seduction early in a courtship almost certainly will be fatal to young love. Young lovers will ward against **the little foxes.**

FROM THE TEXT

In the little metaphorical song about the young foxes, the command to "catch" them is addressed to anonymous others: "[*you all*]" catch is plural in the Hebrew text. Ultimately, however, it is for each couple in a faithful union to guard their own "vineyard" together. No "fox" can trespass on the sanctity of a marriage forged in love, sustained by the mutual trust in and admiration for each other that we see in these young lovers, and anchored in the faithful lovingkindness of God.

B. She: My Beloved Is Mine and I Am His (2:16-17)

BEHIND THE TEXT

Of the place name Bether (v 17), Carr says, "Kirbet el Yahudi, seven miles south-west of Jerusalem . . . is another possible site. . . . A small town and fortress surmount a hill surrounded on all sides by deep canyons" (1984, 103). The LXX (though not the MT) includes Bether as one of the hill country towns of Judah (Josh 15:59a).

IN THE TEXT

■ **16** This declaration is powerful in its straightforward simplicity. The woman affirms what many lovers discover: the mutuality of treasured belonging is key to a lasting love of health and integrity. She will say it again in 6:3, with the order reversed. Here, she references him first, **my beloved is mine and I am his**. The insight is the same; the reversal of her expression in the two locations is another way of illustrating mutuality. In the first instance, he "belongs" first, then she; in the second, she "belongs" first, then he. This subverts any ideas of women "belonging" to men, either then or now.

He browses translates a Hebrew participle, *the one feeding*. Grammatically, two possibilities are open. The verb *rāʿâ* is often used transitively; here, that option would mean, "He [causes his flock] to feed/pasture." It also is used intransitively; here, it would mean, *He [himself] browses/feeds among the lotuses*.

The Song's intertextuality and the interweaving of its imagery is decisive. Already in 2:1, the woman had called herself, metaphorically, "the lotus of the valleys." In 6:3, she repeats exactly the imagery introduced here. In 4:5 and in 7:2-3 [3-4 HB], her lover praises her breasts as twin fawns of a gazelle, and speaks of lotuses in both contexts. Here, her lover—not his sheep and goats—*browses among the lotuses*.

■ **17** **Until the day breaks**; literally, *breathes*. Construals of this as the arrival of dusk, rather than dawn, founder on the metaphor. Winds and breezes tend to subside, not pick up, as day turns to night. Nor can this be the refreshing sea breeze characteristic of many summer days in Jerusalem and the hill country, generally. The roots are different: the sea breeze is *rûaḥ* (e.g., Gen 3:8); this verb is from *pûaḥ*.

Rather, the day's "breathing" is the displacement of the dead calm just before dawn by the rustling of early morning breezes. With the increase of the morning light, **the shadows flee**; that is, what was shadowy and indistinct becomes clearly visible. The woman requested that her lover **turn**, but **until** early *morning*, not **until** early *evening*.

The verbs are imperatives; we translate the woman's request/command:

Turn; resemble, my beloved, the gazelle
Or the young one of the hart/stags
Upon the mountains of Bether.

(→ 2:9.) **Bether** as a place name is reasonable, and another example of double entendre. Picturing her lover as a gazelle or young stag of Bether's rugged terrain attests the young woman's poetic sensibilities. As a verb, *bâtar* means "cut in two"; the geographical name, **Bether**, references its rugged terrain. Allusively, it suggests the woman's breasts ("cleavage" is analogous), or her pudenda, perhaps both.

2:16-17

137

Our interpretation turns on *her* use of "turn" (*sōb* [2:17]). Was she inviting him? "Turn to me, and be to me tonight as the stag is to the doe." Or was she sending him away? "Turn from me for tonight, until the day breaks again, because our time has not yet come; go from me for now—for the night—as you came to me, running across the hills like the gazelle or the young stag."

Taking this speech (vv 16-17) at face value and echoing the tone of most of the Song leads plausibly to the conclusion that this is an invitation for a night of love. Interpreters reading the Song as exhibiting a plot line probably will see this speech as the woman's decision to avoid a premature night together, by sending her lover away.

Wesley on 2:17

Wesley is one of many who was inspired by the first line of v 17, "Until the day breaks": "Until the morning of that blessed day of the general resurrection, when all the shadows, not only of ignorance, and sin, and calamity, but even of outward administrations, shall cease" (1975, 1933).

C. She: Where Is He? (3:1-5)

BEHIND THE TEXT

Verses 1-4 comprise the woman's second "narrative report," her words addressed, in effect, to the hearer/reader, rather than to her lover or to any of the Song's minor personae. Each of the first four verses features the woman calling her absent lover, ***the one whom my nepeš loves***, "the one whom I love with all my life, with all my being."

"Seeking" and "finding" are the dominant themes of this pericope. Twice in each of the first two verses, the woman spoke of seeking her absent lover; both times she reported, but she "did not find him." Next, she reported (v 3), "the watchmen found me," and in v 4, ***I found the one my nepeš loves***.

IN THE TEXT

■ **1** The Hebrew noun is plural; the NIV's **all night long** probably is correct, but it also may mean ***night after night***. The two are not mutually exclusive. This **bed** is the one located in the woman's bedchamber; it is not the "couch" of 1:16.

Again, one's view of the whole governs one's understanding of this scene. If they have not consummated their relationship, why would she expect to find him in her bed? If the lovers are married, or if the Song is an anthology of love lyrics, however arranged, the reader does not wonder at the woman expecting her lover to be in their bed with her, and anxious for him when she discovers his absence.

Some settle this dilemma by taking these words as reporting a nightly dream: she misses her lover from her bed, though he does not yet rightly "belong" there. In her dream, she leaves her house, seeking him until she finds and brings him home with her. Her regular dream anticipates the coming reality. Similarly, but without the facilitation of a dream, Pope suggests her words mean, "Even when I reclined upon my nocturnal couch, I could not give him up; I still sought to find him" (1977, 415).

■ **2** A cohortative can function as an emphatic, **I will get up now**. It may indicate self-encouragement, as in "Let's do this." We may render, *Let me arise now*. We need not choose; essentially, these are two ways of emphasizing the same determination to act. The next two verbs also are cohortatives: [*I will*] **go about/*Let me now go about*; *I* will *seek/Let me seek*.**

Go about the city uses the same verb as the woman's command/request (2:17) for her love to turn away and leave her for the night, a small but effective literary connection. Here, it signals her intention to be thorough, to go *around* the various sectors of **the city**, not just to walk the length of a main street or two. This is reinforced by the proposed scope of her search, *in the streets and in the intersections* (squares). Which **city** is this? The logical candidate is Jerusalem.

Besides the dense interweaving noted above, the second and third lines (NIV) of vv 1 and 2 are identical, except for the tenses of the first occurrence of "seek" in each: v 1, **I looked for**; v 2, **I will search for**. The outcome was the same; she found him neither beside her (v 1), nor in the city (v 2).

Pope observes, "Many critics have felt that the scene cannot be real" (1977, 418). This reading assumes, rather paternalistically, that neither a chaste maiden nor a faithful lover would be out and about in the city at night, alone. Yet, there is no hint of apprehension in this young woman's proposal and her prompt enacting of her plan. She was not afraid, and to hint at impropriety on her part would be to assert that words have no meaning. If this woman was not faithful to her love, the Song is nonsense.

The explanation lies in a *sitz im leben* and an ethos largely lost to the modern world. Ancient cities were tiny, by our standards. The archaeology of the Iron Age I "City of David" shows a population for Solomon's Jerusalem of about 4,500. Hezekiah's Jerusalem (two hundred years later) was no more than twice that size. If the Song is postexilic, the city was smaller than in Hezekiah's day. On such a scale, anyone seeing her likely knew her, or recognized her as belonging to the family of someone he or she *did* know.

In times of social stability, violent crime is rare in small towns; *all* ancient Israel's cities were small by modern standards. Not even at night was a lone woman likely to be the target of a predatory male. The influence of Israel's faithfulness to Yahweh and Yahweh's precepts (however cyclical) strengthened this norm. A final point: the watchmen's regular patrols (v 3) were an added deterrent. We cannot say the night held no possible dangers for her. We *can* say most cities today are exponentially more dangerous for a lone woman at night than was ancient Jerusalem.

■ **3** Verse 3 is tightly bound with v 2:

> 2c *I sought him, but I did not find him.*
>
> 3a *They found me—the watchmen, the ones making rounds in the city.*

"Find" (*māṣ'ā*) is both the last word of v 2, and the first word of v 3. *I did not find him* is a cry of anxiety, even of pain. By contrast, her question to the watchmen, **Have you seen** [him]?, conveys an eager hope, but with little detail. Given our previous assertion about the connectedness of this small city, Carr may be overstating the case, "The local constables would have no idea who it was she was seeking" (1984, 105). A detailed record of the conversation is simply beside the point. The effect is to convey her breathless search.

This is her third use of *sôb/sābab* (turn/go about/go around) in four verses: 2:17; 3:2, 3. Having told her love to "turn/go away," she proceeded to "go about" the city, but did not find him. Find *her*, the watchmen did, while "going about" the city on their rounds.

The one my nepeš/being/life loves, have you seen? The direct object is first for emphasis. It signals also that the woman was not telling, but asking. Logically, she could not have known whether the watchmen had seen her love. Sometimes context is the marker of the interrogative.

■ **4** **Scarcely had I passed** *on from them*; she had not found her love. The lack of an answer from the watchmen makes it clear they had not seen him. Rather than turning (again!), she **passed** *on*, continuing to search and—finally!—meeting with success. The fourth occurrence of *māṣ'ā* (**I found**) in these four verses is climactic.

I held him; this is the same verb ('*āḥaz*) used in 2:15, "Catch for us the foxes." In both places, the Hebrew verb is considerably more forceful than the NIV's "catch"/"held." Carr expresses well the woman's determination reflected here in both her verbs; she "clutched [him] and refused to slacken her embrace" (1984, 106).

It is important to note that **held** ('*āḥaz*) here is a perfect form, while **would not let him go** (*rāpâ*) is an imperfect. If our understanding is correct, she had sent her love away (2:17) as night fell. Immediately, then, she had begun missing him, upon her bed, even before venturing onto the city streets to search for him. Now, having found him, she resolved not to be parted from him again. In light of all this, we may translate:

> *I have taken hold of him, and I will not release him*
> > *Until I have brought him to the house of my mother,*
> > *Even to the bedroom of the one who conceived me.*

My mother's house (*bêt 'em*) is a rare variation on the common phrase "father's house" (*bêt 'āb*), referring to the household unit or the family of origin, not a literal building. The few other texts where **mother's house** occurs also revolve around love and marriage (8:2; Gen 24:28; → Ruth 1:8), suggesting that such momentous decisions involved mothers too.

■ **5** Verse 5 is identical with 2:7. Here it highlights the intensity of young love, which suffers when enduring separation.

FROM THE TEXT

The woman's nighttime scene of failure turned success expresses two potent realities. First, God's gift of love between a woman and a man is compelling in its beauty, joy, wonder, power, complexity, and potential; it drives us to pursue the beloved. Second, wisdom unwraps such a gift only with the utmost care and respect, each for the other and both for God, the Giver.

IV. CELEBRATING AND CONSUMMATING LOVE: SONG OF SONGS 3:6—5:1

OVERVIEW

This third of the Song's five major divisions features three pericopes, with a two-verse coda. If any section of the Song evokes a progression of events, it is this one. The first pericope details the appearance and progression of the grand palanquin of "Solomon" (3:6-11), closing with reference to a wedding (3:11).

The second pericope (4:1-7) is a song in praise of the woman, composed by the man, a song known in Arab cultures as a *wasf* (→ Introduction: Literary Forms and Features). She is apparently adorned in a veil (4:3) and jewelry (4:4), suggesting she is prepared for a wedding. The third pericope (4:8-15) comprises a separate invitation/song, also spoken by the man to the woman, and is the very epitome of verbal foreplay.

The "coda" consists in the woman's invitation (4:16), followed by the man's expression of his joy in their coming together (5:1). Sensuous beauty and mannered delicacy mark the woman's explicit invitation to this consummation. Having accepted, the man matched her with a frank but circumspect delight in her and in their lovemaking.

143

A. Friends: Who Is This? (3:6-11)

BEHIND THE TEXT

This passage evokes the spectacle of a royal procession. More in praise of the escort and the royal palanquin than of the person they carry along, it seems oddly placed between the tale of the woman's search for her lover (3:1-5) and the man's extended poem praising his beloved (4:1-15). Some have argued that it *is* misplaced or that it does not belong to the Song at all. We take it as authentic to the Song, properly placed and contributing to its movement, even if "plot" is too strong a word for that movement.

Identification of the speaker(s) varies widely. Some (e.g., NIV, NRSV) take this section as a continuation of the woman's speech from 3:5. This makes sense, as the person who steps out of the palanquin at the climactic moment is none other than Solomon, a figure of the male lover. She has "conjured" him with her words, inviting her audience to watch his approach, as she has done before (2:8-13) and will do again (5:10-16).

IN THE TEXT

■ **6** **Who is this coming up?** Both the pronoun (**this**) and the participle (**coming up**) are feminine singular, referring to the "carriage" of v 7, which is a feminine noun. If the vehicle itself is the referent, we might normally expect the question in Hebrew to be "what" (*mâ*) rather than "who" (*mî*). However, *mî* can also be translated as "what" (see Judg 13:17; Mic 1:5).

Coming up (*ʿōlâ*) is the usual term for going to Jerusalem from any place in Israel (or beyond), regardless of one's location relative to the compass points. Near Jerusalem, the **steppe** (**wilderness**) comprises the highlands east of Jerusalem, sloping down to the western edges of the Jordan Valley, today's Judean Desert.

The Hebrew text has the noun in plural form, **like *columns* of smoke**. Some take this as **smoke** from burning the **myrrh and incense** mentioned in the next line. This is a simile; the first sign of the palanquin with its procession in the distance was the dust they raised **like *columns* of smoke**. Several columns of dust like far-off smoke signaled a significant retinue.

The mention of **myrrh and incense** here, before onlookers could have discerned their distinctive fragrance on the wind, is poetic license. On **myrrh**, → 1:13. **Incense**, or "frankincense," is a fragrant resin from the gum (drying sap) of trees called today Boswellia. Israel's major source was southern Arabia. Its Hebrew name is *lĕbônâ* ("white stuff," "whiteness"), from its usual whitish color. Frankincense was/is expensive; in the OT, these are the only direct references outside the cultic contexts of tabernacle or temple offerings, or in medicinal usages.

Pope translates **All the spices of the merchant** as, "All the peddler's powders," a reminder that many cosmetic ingredients were expensive imports from far away (1977, 412). "Powders" reflects the Hebrew *ʾabĕqâ* more precisely than **spices**; in antiquity as today, many cosmetics were prepared and applied as powders.

■ **7-8 Look!** translates again the Hebrew *hinnēh* (→ 1:15). **Solomon's carriage** is a little misleading; the Hebrew is "couch, bed" (v 7). The logic of the passage seems to require that this is the conveyance described in vv 9-10 (→), but using a different noun.

The expected revelation did not happen: the "honor guard . . . blocks the view of the litter before one can see who . . . is being brought" (Keel 1994, 128). Whatever the onlookers knew, the suspense continues for the reader: Who is this?

Sixty warriors *surround it*, to guard and honor the occupant. In Israel, David had formed the first unit of the Thirty, an inner circle of elite warriors and leaders (2 Sam 23:23-39). This honor guard escorting the conveyance to Jerusalem comprised **sixty** men, that is, twice thirty.

The prowess of the **sixty** is carefully noted. A literal translation paints a vivid picture:

All of them *are possessors of the sword,*
> *schooled in battle.*

Each man [has] his sword [strapped] upon his thigh
> *because of* [prepared for] *the dread by night* (v 8).

Possessors entails owning and **wearing** a sword, but implies much more, namely mastery. *Schooled in battle* makes that explicit: the life-or-death of battle had honed their study, drill, and sword exercise, made each into a superb warrior. Sword ready to hand, each was prepared not only to fight by day but also to ward against the more visceral *dread by night* (lit. "dread in the nights").

■ **9-10** Here, **the carriage** (v 9) translates a different Hebrew noun than in v 7. This is *ʾappiryôn*, a loanword possibly from Greek (*phoreion*) but ultimately from Sanskrit (*paryanka*), the source also of English **palanquin**, a litter-chair (or bed) borne on two poles by four men, each supporting one end of one pole on his shoulder. A *palanquin* could be open or enclosed by a curtained frame. Its seating could be an upright chair, a sedan chair, or a bed/couch for reclining; any of these would have been secured to the base to prevent it from sliding and spilling the occupant onto the ground.

Because this was Solomon's personal transport, we are not surprised by the luxury. The **wood from Lebanon** may be constructed of cedar; if not cedar, it was cypress (→ 1:17). Verse 10 lists some materials for the palanquin's fittings, but not all of them, nor does it discuss design and construction. The **posts** were **silver**, meaning either a metal alloy containing mostly silver (see 1 Kgs 10:27) or a pole of wood overlaid with silver. Pure silver is not strong enough for this; it would bend and collapse.

Its base; the Hebrew root means "spread"; in the OT, the noun occurs only here. If it means the occupant could "spread out" on it, it was a back or arm rest or perhaps a "bolster" (Pope 1977, 443). It was made with **gold** inlay or overlay or with a fabric covering of gold-woven cloth. Others see here the canopy "stretched out" above the interior, protecting the occupant from the elements. On the royal palanquin, this canopy also would have been woven with gold (Carr 1984, 112).

Seat translates Hebrew *merkāb*, a masculine noun form occurring only three times in the OT. In its feminine form (*merkābâ*), this noun means "chariot." If its underlying referent was the seat or platform upon which the charioteer sat or (more normally) stood, it follows that the masculine form here denoted the seat of the chair or couch upon which the occupant sat within the palanquin. **It was upholstered with purple**, a purple-dyed fabric covering. This dye was obtained by a labor-intensive process from the purple-shaded shell of a murex common in antiquity along the shores of the eastern Mediterranean. The dye's cost meant only the palace, the temple, and a very few others could afford to wear or decorate with "the purple."

Its interior denotes the "passenger compartment" of the palanquin. **Inlaid** is a passive participle (*rāṣûp*), ***was/has been inlaid***. A noun from this root, *riṣpâ*, means "pavement," that is, "what has been fitted together," as paving stones and mosaic floors are laid.

The last piece of *this* mosaic is the Hebrew *'ahăbâ*, **love**. Everything else in this inventory is a tangible material or object: **wood**, **posts**, **base**, **seat**. In such a context, **love** also must be something tangible, observable as part of the palanquin. Considered by itself, **love** may be an abstraction, but here **love** is the *subject* of the inlaid pieces. We may translate, ***Its interior is inlaid with scenes of love***. These inlaid works of art—often created with ivory, ebony, and other exotic materials— were tangible, as were the other objects included in this list.

■ **11** An incorrect word division muddies the last line of the Hebrew text. The NIV translation is correct; its footnoted alternative cannot be. The problem: the Masoretes attached *mêm* as a prefixed preposition to *běnôt* (**daughters of**), but it belongs as a suffix of the prior word; read *'ahăbam*. This is not a masculine plural suffix marker but an enclitic *mêm*. Its grammatical effect here is nil; it serves for emphasis (see Pope 1977, 446). We translate *běnôt* without the *mêm* (which we have attached as a suffix to *'ahăbâ*, where it belongs), and arrange the line as the ABB'A' chiastic unit it was composed to be:

(A) Daughters of *Jerusalem*,
(B) come out
(B') *And* look,
(A') [you] daughters of Zion.

Daughters, as those invited to "come and look," works logically and poetically. The women came out as the news spread of the palanquin's arrival in Jerusalem. Potentially, **daughters** includes all the city's women, young and old, naturally curious for a glimpse of the majestic arrival.

Solomon's crown would have completed his attire on his wedding day but, grammatically, **the crown with which his mother crowned him** stands in apposition to the rest of the verse. It could have been given him at coronation by his mother, but worn also on his wedding day. If the man here is the rustic lover, portrayed as royal in his lover's word picture, his mother could have placed a crown or garland on his head in preparation for the day's festivities. In that scenario, his wedding day and his "coronation day" were one and the same.

Some puzzle over the *wāw* beginning the last clause of the verse; the NIV leaves it untranslated. Here, it means "even," or "that is." The line reveals the emotional state of the groom. He wore the crown with which his mother had crowned him

On the day of his wedding,

Even on the day of his heart's rejoicing.

The poet wanted the reader to know this truly was a day of joy for the man of the Song.

FROM THE TEXT

This is the Song's only "public" scene. The woman introduces the procession, evoking universal interest; the royal escort is celebrated; the women of Jerusalem are invited to come to the square, and *look*—to watch "Solomon" in royal array on his wedding day.

At many places, the Song endorses and celebrates the normal human inclination to keep private the intimacies of lovemaking. *This* scene is the Song's reminder of another truth: love, the well-being of lovers, the enduring societal health of love itself, all these and more are public business too.

Much follows from this, but we will highlight a single implication. Any love of integrity and health is publicly acknowledged. The secrecy of the average "love affair" is one of the factors working against its long-term survival. Those who indulge in pornography and prostitution, illicit acts in secret, commit a host of wrongs against many persons. All parties to such commercial uses of sex depart cheated and deeply wounded. The nonchalance of "hooking up" or of "friends with benefits" yields the same hurtful result; only the economic component of the transaction is missing. One of the signals that a love has integrity, is healthy, and has a chance to last, is that it is publicly acknowledged and celebrated.

B. He: How Beautiful, My Darling! (4:1-7)

BEHIND THE TEXT

On the form of this and the other *wasf* poems in the Song, → Introduction: Literary Forms and Features. The choice of the beloved's features to be celebrated, and the poetry of their presentation, demonstrate a lover's skill (or lack thereof) as a *wasf* composer. The structure of this *wasf* is masterful, a thematic movement from eyes and hair at the top of the beloved's head, downward to the perfection of her breasts, with its crescendo in the awed exclamation, "Altogether, you [are] beautiful, my darling!" This final word also functions as an inclusio for the whole, mirroring the "Behold, you [are] beautiful, my darling!" of v 1.

The metaphors ring strange to readers from urbanized, commercialized cultures. However, each is a perfect choice for celebrating *this* attribute of *this* woman's beauty in *these* lovers' small-town agrarian social context. We, too, will understand her as "altogether" beautiful, as we comprehend the comparisons her lover intended.

IN THE TEXT

■ **1** Verse 1*a* is almost identical with 1:15 (→). The only difference is that here the phrase **behind your veil** is added at the end of the Hebrew line. As noted, Israelite and Judean women wore the veil only on special occasions. If, as we suggest, this section of the Song traces the outlines of a wedding and wedding night (→ Overview above), we need not wonder at this addition. Keel's explanation of the "doves" metaphor leads to the conclusion here that the man could see the woman's welcome in her eyes, even behind her veil. An expanded paraphrase could read, "As we stand here, the looks you give me are messengers of love, even though I can see your eyes only through your veil."

Your hair . . . Gilead; this line is in praise of the woman's long, thick, glossy, wavy black hair. How does this simile accomplish that? First, this was not a single goat, but **a flock of goats**. Many of the goats of western Asia were/are black; a flock exclusively of black goats is plausible. The sheer mass of black hair in such a flock is also part of the simile; her hair was long and thick.

Second, this flock is pictured as **descending from the hills of Gilead**. The slopes of Gilead contained abundant pastureland. We have seen flocks of goats moving down such slopes. Whether grazing, or shepherded at a quicker pace to a lower elevation, they tend to bunch more closely than when on level ground. The visual effect of a black-sheened flock undulating across a slope is vivid and beautiful, an apt metaphor for the luxuriant loveliness of the woman's long black tresses.

■ **2** In the lover's *wasf*, the beloved's teeth are next in consideration. Sheep were more numerous even than goats among the domestic animals of ancient Israel. Everyone would have understood the two specific points of this metaphor:

> **Your teeth are like a flock of *the shearling ewes***
> ***which are* coming up from the washing;**
> **Who—*all of them*—have *twinned*,**
> ***and among whom—all of them*—no [*twin*] *is not*.**

Sheep are washed in preparation for shearing; clean wool is a biblical emblem of pristine whiteness (Isa 1:18). Likening her teeth to a flock of newly washed ewes and lambs is vivid praise for the woman's (perhaps exceptional) dental health. Sheep breeders expect a single lamb in a ewe's first lambing, and usually twins thereafter. If the ancient reality was similar, twins from every ewe is plausible. The simile emphasizes that, of the twin lambs coming up from the washing, not one was missing (*no* [*twin*] *is not*); *all* were alive and healthy.

Uniformly robust health among lambs is remarkable. Reaching marriageable age with every *tooth* still having its (upper or lower) "twin"—not having lost even *one*—was so unusual as to be almost miraculous. This woman was a notable beauty, indeed!

■ **3** As today, women of antiquity used cosmetics to emphasize natural beauty, but we cannot be sure whether this one did. Scarlet is a bright, intense red; the woman could have applied scarlet "lipstick" to enhance her lips for this special occasion, or her natural coloring was eliciting the simile, **like a scarlet ribbon** (or *thread*). The *wāw* introducing the second clause has a causal function: **Your lips are like a scarlet ribbon,** *so that* **your mouth is lovely** [or: *making your mouth comely*].

Mouth is not the usual *peh/pî*; rather, this is the only OT use of the noun *midbār* ("word") to denote the "mouth" (lit. "wordmaker," i.e., the organ of speech). This *phrase* is "wordmaking," too, prompted partly by the artistic needs of poetic meter and accent, but also by this lover's valuation of an attribute of his beloved not often remarked. *Wordmaker* expresses at least two realities he loved about her. For one thing, the sound of her voice delighted him. More importantly, her voice expressed words that endeared her to him, whether words of love, wisdom, companionship, constructive dialogue—whatever the occasion called for. They talked together as equals (see Keel 1994, 143).

We will understand the simile of the next line if we translate, *Like a slice of the pomegranate is your temple behind your veil*. On the last phrase, → v 1. **Temple** is from a root meaning "thin." The noun applies to the temples as the thinnest bones of the skull (see Judg 4:21-22; 5:26). As often, the man's reference to one **temple** encompasses both sides of the woman's face. Moreover, he probably intended her temples and cheeks together, an area of the face where blushing rosiness was/is admired, and sometimes emulated with rouge. In the man's eyes, the woman before him was the picture of radiant health and loveliness.

■ **4** This **tower of David** is not the "Tower of David" in today's Old City of Jerusalem; that structure is Herodian (30s-20s BC). This was part of the defensive wall of David's Jerusalem, on the ridge called today (Mount) Ophel. Strength, endurance, proportional symmetry, beauty, and grace are qualities of a well-built tower. The first hearers of this simile would have thought in these terms, deepening their admiration both of the woman and of the man's poetic inventiveness. It is not helpful to correlate every part of the tower to a woman's anatomy, as may be appropriate with the poet's other metaphors; rather, the whole is admirable.

Occurring only here in the OT, *talpîyôt* occasions many translations, but only something like **built with courses of stone** makes sense. An Iron Age method of laying stone walls and towers—what archaeologists call "stretcher and header" construction—accounts both for **courses of stone** here and for the imagery of the following line. Architectural elegance was one result; more importantly, this method interlocked the courses of a wall, multiplying its inherent strength.

From a distance, this stretcher-and-header method of construction could suggest shields hanging on a wall. It is doubtful that kings or commanders ever ordered battle shields hung on the outside of a city or tower wall. The NIV's citation of Ezek 27:11 is misleading (Pope 1977, 468). Solomon hung golden shields—decorative and ceremonial—within his "Palace of the Forest of Lebanon," not on the outer walls of his defensive towers (1 Kgs 10:16-17). The look of shields fastened to a tower wall was a mental comparison prompted by an artistic masonry pattern of tower walls in their ascending courses.

Now we have the point of the simile: The woman's neck was strong and graceful, like Jerusalem's **tower of David**. We should see more than beauty here. The woman's neck was both an aspect and a symbol of her strength. As most countrywomen in the ANE could expect to carry heavy loads on their heads regularly, a strong neck was a real asset.

As the tower was built in elegant masonry, so her neck was adorned with layers of elegant (and costly) necklaces. The strands a woman wore around her neck on special occasions often represented a significant deposit of wealth: gold or silver, along with precious and semiprecious stones. Her necklaces, conjured as **a thousand shields**, represented a material contribution (real and potential) to the union. She was beautifully adorned, but that very adornment also testified she would not be a junior partner, financially.

■ **5** The man climaxed this *wasf* with a line in praise of the woman's breasts. The appositive, *feeding among the lotuses*, is imported, probably by a later copyist, and probably from 2:16. As it does not belong here (→ 7:3 [4 HB]), we leave it aside. Sentence structure and vocabulary emphasize the symmetry of the woman's breasts. A translation reflecting Hebrew word order is helpful; note the two occurrences of the numeral "two," as a noun, followed by the noun "twins":

> *The two of your breasts are like two of* [female] *fawns,*
>   *twins* [female fawns] *of a gazelle doe.*

In the OT, as in all the ANE, the female breast is associated with sensuousness and sexuality, but also with fecundity and the necessary, all-encompassing nourishment of the infant. It profits little to try to set these functions against one another, or to deny the one and emphasize the other. Both are present; both are important.

The man's present interest, however, was in her beautiful sexuality. The comparison with fawns emphasizes also her young womanhood and the liveliness of her awakening sexuality, a prospect of pleasure and joy they would explore, experience, and learn together.

■ **6** Verse 6a is identical with 2:17a (→). On the identities of **myrrh** and **incense**, → 1:13 and 3:6, respectively. **The mountain of myrrh** and **the hill of incense** are not geographical locations. This verse moves from description toward contemplated action.

When the man came to focus on his beloved's breasts, his desire moved him to lay aside the simile—breasts *like* twin fawns—in favor of a metaphor: they *were* **the mountain of myrrh . . . the hill of incense**. These were exotic luxury goods from faraway places, with erotic associations of their own on many levels. Moreover, the woman had likened *him* to "a sachet of myrrh resting between [her] breasts" (1:13). Now his desire elicited a declaration, **I will go to the mountain of myrrh and . . . of incense**; he would move from praise to action. His meaning, "I am not content only to talk; I/we will enjoy our lovemaking all night long."

■ **7** Verse 7 serves as a coda, summarizing and confirming the specific praises of the *waṣf.* The first clause reprises the avowal already voiced four times: **You are beautiful!** (twice in 1:15 [→]; twice at the beginning of this song [4:1]). With 4:1, this iteration defines an inclusio, framing the song at the beginning and the end.

This articulation brings the series to a crescendo with a superlative **all**: **You are altogether beautiful.** We should take this two ways; it means both, **All of you is beautiful**, and also, **In every way, you are beautiful.** On my darling, → 1:9.

Rendering the original word order of his last fervent exclamation is less literary in English but preserves the vivid force of the Hebrew: **Moreover, a flaw there is not in you!** The noun *mûm* (**flaw**) occurs elsewhere in cultic contexts; a flaw rendered an animal unfit for sacrifice (e.g., Lev 22:20-21). Of course, animal sacrifice was the furthest thing from this man's mind. He was celebrating her perfection "in every way." That such assessments of a beloved may list a bit toward subjectivity does not make them, or those who hold and voice them, any less admirable.

FROM THE TEXT

In our day, some may be tempted to dismiss this and the other similar poems of the Song as sexist, perhaps even as demeaning. If the song here and in the next pericope were sung in public, that is a justifiable response. But there is nothing in the text to suggest that! We may imagine them as private love-talk, verbal foreplay behind closed doors. Between two who love, respect, and trust each other fully, they are the opposite of demeaning. On that score, ours, not theirs, is the sick culture, in need of healing. Especially in considering these and similar pericopes, it will aid the reader greatly to keep this always in mind. God is the Author of all beauty; praise of the beloved honors God, as well as the one receiving the praise.

C. He: Come with Me! (4:8-15)

BEHIND THE TEXT

The man addresses his beloved as his bride only in this section of the Song: five times in this poem (4:8, 9, 10, 11, and 12), and once in 5:1, which closely follows. To those who consider the Song a "quasi-story" or more, this is the wedding night (Garrett 2004, 193). The man's use of "bride" here, and *only* here, is one of the stronger evidences for taking the Song to be (or to be structured as) a story.

Even more important on some levels is that the lover addressed his beloved as "my sister" only five times in the Song. Four of the occurrences are here, in the phrase "my sister, my bride" (4:9, 10, 12; 5:1). The fifth occurrence follows immediately in 5:2, "my sister, my darling."

Carr on "Sister"

Family terms such as "sister" (5:1) or "brother" (8:1), and royal designations such as "king," "queen," "prince" or "princess" are frequent epithets in the love poetry, although the Song uses only "sister" and "king" directly of the protagonists. Many commentators take these words in their literal sense in these poems, but it is obvious from the literature generally that this sort of vocabulary is merely a convention for expressing the high regard the lovers have for each other. (1984, 38-39)

Wesley also understood the gist of this endearment, "So he calls her to show the greatness of his love, which cannot sufficiently be expressed by any one relation" (1975, 1937).

A small point: the possessive suffix pronoun ("my") does not appear with any of the man's six references to his "bride." However, it *is* attached in all five occurrences of "my sister," and four of these precede four of the six occurrences of "bride." Therefore, it is reasonable to infer his meaning as "my bride," also, in each instance.

IN THE TEXT

■ **8 Lebanon,** the mountainous Mediterranean coastlands north of Israel, comprises a coastal range, Mount Lebanon, and an inland range, the Anti-Lebanon Mountains, divided by the Beqa, the "Valley" in Arabic. **Amana, Senir,** and **Hermon** refer to significant mountain peaks. In antiquity, several regions of Lebanon were home to **lions** and **leopards,** though neither of the big cats typically approached humans or human settlements.

These regions lie well to the north of Shunem/Shulam, thought by many to be the woman's hometown. If that conclusion is correct, Shulam was the northernmost location of the Song, except for those mentioned here. Why, then, would she have been in **Lebanon,** for him to plead with her to come from there?

The repetition in the first line is important: *With me from Lebanon,* [*my*] *bride, with me from Lebanon, come. Descend from . . .* We find the proposed emendations and alternative readings unconvincing. The repetition rules out understanding the feminine singular imperative forms (**come** and **descend**) as commands. Rather, they are the lover's invitation. He speaks figuratively here.

She was his heart's desire, but she also retained her freedom of choice. What if she remained in her "mountain" fastnesses, among **lions' dens** and **haunts of leopards**? What if she declined to **descend** to him? In short, this verse is the groom's invitation-cum-request for his **bride** to accede to his expressed intention (v 6), "I will go . . . ," that is, to consummate their union.

■ **9 You have stolen my heart**; repeating it twice, the man expressed amazement at her effect on him, seemingly with so little effort: **one glance . . . one jewel!** The verb is from the same root as the noun, **heart** (*lēb*). We could translate, *You have* *"hearted" me*. Across the centuries, translators and commentators have taken it in both of its opposing possible meanings. Taken as, "You have heartened me," it means (with the NIV), **You have stolen my heart**, that is, "You have captured my heart with love for you." "Heartened" also means "encouraged"; her love for him encouraged and strengthened both his feelings and his actions of love.

Others have taken "hearted" in a more negative sense, "You have *dis*heartened me." Grammatically, it is possible, but nothing else in the Song suggests the woman said or did anything to cause the man to be discouraged, disheartened, or in despair. Perhaps construing this statement as "disheartened" stems from misunderstanding or misapplying the imagery of his request in v 8.

In v 4 the man praised the beauty of her neck adorned with multiple jewels in layered strands. Yet now he declared them superfluous, saying, **You have stolen my heart . . . with one jewel**, perhaps a single stone on a pendant (Carr 1984, 121). He made himself vulnerable with complete honesty: **You have stolen my heart** and, as you know, it wasn't that difficult for you! Will you have me?

On **my sister, my bride**, → Behind the Text above.

■ **10** **How delightful is your love**; by contrast with 1:15-16 and 4:1, the Hebrew particle here is *mah* (How). **Delightful** is a plural perfect of *yāfâ*, also the root of the adjectival forms in these verses. The basic meaning is "handsome/beautiful"; delightful, *desirable*, even "sweet," are reasonable renderings.

Your love (vv 10*a*, 10*b*) is plural, as it is in 1:2, 4, and 5:1. In each place, *loves* (*dôdîm*) means "lovemaking." As with current English usage, it often connotes coitus but can refer to other acts of love. This is affirmed by its use in 1:2*b*, where loves/lovemaking refers to the "kisses" of the previous line (1:2*a*). On **my sister, my bride**, → Behind the Text above.

On **How much . . . than wine**, → 1:2*b*. The particle and denominative verb of 4:10*b* serve also for v 10*c*; including them, we translate, [*How much better is*] **the fragrance of your oils than any** [or: all] **balsams**. First Kings 10:2, 10 reports that the Queen of Sheba brought balsam to Solomon. In all these contexts, and in the six references in the Song (4:14, 16; 5:1, 13; 6:2; 8:14), the Hebrew noun is *bōsem*; its root is the source of the English noun "balsam."

Judean Balsam

Excavations at En Gedi above the western shore of the Dead Sea locate balsam plantations there from the reign of Josiah (seventh century BC), or perhaps a bit later. In the first century BC, Herod the Great and Cleopatra VI—*the* Cleopatra!—were bitter enemies, in part because Mark Antony gave Cleopatra Jericho's profitable balsam plantations. Sometime after his victory over the doomed pair at Actium, Octavius Caesar granted them to Herod. In the following century, Josephus declared balsam sap the most valuable of all Judean products, and Pliny the Elder said Romans preferred balsam to all other fragrances (Keel 1994, 165).

The man specified **balsam** because it was the most desired and costliest of all perfume ingredients. *The fragrance of your oils* reflects the practice of mixing perfumes with oil, before application (→ "Perfume in the Ancient World" Sidebar at Song 1:3). As we know today, many fragrances can react uniquely with the skin of individual wearers. The man's point with these comparisons: *whatever* perfume creation she wore, the fragrance *her* body gave to it made it more delightful to him even than **all balsams**, and in 4:14, even than **all the greatest [best] of balsams**.

■ **11** On my bride, → Behind the Text above.

Your lips drip flowing honey. This is the honey (*nōphet*) that flows when a honeycomb is lifted from the hive. The ancients considered this the best, most desirable of sweets, a perfect metaphor for the lips of the beloved.

Of **milk** King and Stager note, "Goats were the primary milk producers in the ancient Near East; goat milk is richer in protein and fat than sheep and cow's milk" (2001, 103). Richness, sweetness, and abundance are the point of the comparison, with respect both to the rich milk of the goat and the incomparable sweetness of the **honey** from the bee. The poetic parallelism makes sense only if this also is a reference to bee honey.

Bees Produce Honey

Scholars increasingly have accepted the identification of the Hebrew *děbaš* ("honey") with the Arabic *dibs*, a sweet, thick syrup processed from dates or grapes. The two words *are* Semitic cognates, and the Bible nowhere references beekeeping. Moreover, chance finds such as Samson's (Judg 14:8) mean bee honey could not have been a common sweetener, even for the well-to-do.

However, in the Song, the lover's two references *are* to the honey (*děbaš*) dripping from the comb (*nōphet* [4:11]), and to the comb (*ya'ar*) and honey (*děbaš*) together (5:1). In its context, the *děbaš* of Ps 19:10 [11 HB] can refer only to bee honey. Exodus 3:8 is the first of twenty OT references to "the land of milk and honey" (*děbaš*), which makes sense only if this is the honey produced by bees. The land's innate fertility showed in abundant grazing for sheep and goats, and in riots of flowering plants for bees. Still today, in nonurbanized landscapes, one sees in springtime this perfect habitat for production of milk and honey.

Beginning in 2005, archaeology revealed definitive evidence. Excavations at Tel Reḥov, in the Jordan Valley three miles south of Beth-Shean, uncovered a commercial apiary of about 180 cylindrical hives of unfired clay. The bees from such a quantity of hives produced far more honey and beeswax than the local population could have consumed. Not only was bee honey a "normal" product of Israel's agriculture, but it was a commodity exported at least as far as Egypt, and perhaps beyond (Mazar and Panitz-Cohen 2007, 202-19).

In Song 4:10-11 the man noted, first, the scent of his beloved's body enhanced by her *oils* (perfume) and, last, **the fragrance of** her **garments**. Within this inclusio of fragrance, he experienced the delightful taste, smell, and touch of her **lips** and **tongue**. In this context, to wax rhapsodic over the **honeycomb** of her lips and the **milk and honey** under her **tongue** was to employ metaphor, but this is no euphemism. It is, rather, the memory of prolonged kissing.

As we have noted, **Lebanon** and *lĕbônâ* ("incense") are from the same root. Mingling the two via a pun in this passage displays the man's poetic skill. Here, **Lebanon** is not a scribal miscopying of *lĕbônâ*. It is an extension of the natural comparisons—the metaphors of milk and honey—to a new simile, **like the fragrance of Lebanon**. With **Lebanon** in his song already, he evoked the smells of its cedars: the resin; the needles, aloft and underfoot; even the timber of their trunks and limbs. Invigorating as such a forest is, her captivating scent energized him more.

■ **12** On **my sister, my bride**, → Behind the Text above. With numerous major textual witnesses, we read, *A garden locked, my sister, [my] bride, a garden locked [you are], a spring sealed*. An understandable misreading of the final *nûn* as *lāmed* accounts for the MT reading *gal* (**fountain**), rather than a correct second occurrence of *gan* (garden). Poetic repetition from the beginning of the line, rather than juxtaposition of two entities ("pool" and **spring**) merely because they belong to a common category, also clarifies the ending of this line, while maintaining its poetic integrity. **You are** does not occur in the Hebrew text. We rightly infer it from the lover's address, *my sister, [my] bride*.

Throughout the OT period, Israelite cities were surrounded by fortification walls, with the ubiquitous vineyards and olive groves located outside city walls. These often were enclosed within further stone walls for protection against both two- and four-legged thieves (see Isa 5:5). Orchards of fruit or nut trees, and gardens of vegetables, melons, herbs, and so forth, normally were protected by stone walls too. A built-in gate, with lock and key, granted (or denied) access to most gardens. This metaphor declares the person of the beloved similarly protected. In the words of C. S. Lewis, "When a thing is enclosed, the mind does not willingly regard it as common" (1996, 19).

Those towns of ancient Israel's highlands blessed with natural water sources regarded them as community property. Often, a stone casing was built where a spring emerged from the earth to protect surrounding soil from erosion. A removable stone or wooden cover prevented small children and animals from falling into the spring, and made fouling the water (by accident or by intention) more difficult. The covering "sealed" the spring, as a clay or wax seal on a rolled-up scroll prevents its unauthorized opening. The lover recognized the person of his beloved as such a *spring sealed*.

If this chapter is concerned with the wedding night, the public declarations had been spoken; the bride and the groom "belonged" to each other. Yet still he depicted her metaphorically as **a garden locked** and a *spring sealed*. By law and custom, he had acquired the "right" to enter "his" garden, to drink from "his" spring. This man knew better. The right to allow him to "enter" and "drink" still belonged to the bride. Law and custom disallowed others; that did not, ipso facto, authorize him. That privilege remained to her to grant, as he acknowledged with these vivid metaphors.

■ **13-14 Plants** disrupts the metaphor (v 13). We translate, ***Your groove is a paradise***. The noun *šĕlāḥayik* ("your canals," a plural of superlative) is a euphemism for vagina (see Pope 1977, 490-91; Keel 1994, 174-75). Having pictured his beloved as "a garden locked" (v 12), the lover sustains the metaphor. Not every Hebrew "garden" (*gan*) is a ***paradise***, but here the terms are synonymous. Anticipating full sexual intimacy, the lover waxes lyrical in itemizing the bounty of exotic delights awaiting him at her invitation to enter her **garden**, her ***paradise***.

In v 13*a*, the NIV's **orchard** is too restrictive; "orchard" trees bear fruits and nuts, but this list mentions only one fruit tree by name, the pomegranate. In addition, Hebrew *pardēš* is the same Persian loanword as English ***paradise***. Finally, ***paradise*** reflects the man's intention in offering this catalog. The woman's love is a paradise more to be desired than the exotic fruits, aromatics, and spices of the garden (also often "paradise") of the wealthiest, most discerning king, even of Solomon himself.

Symbolizing fertility, **pomegranates** heads the list. This fruit's symmetry, together with its dark red rind, accentuates its beauty. On the inside, fleshy seeds bursting with sweet-tart juiciness multiply the metaphorical aptness. Poetic intuition chose the pomegranate here as the exemplar of **choice fruits**; further enumeration would have been redundant.

On **henna and nard**, → 1:14 and 1:12, respectively. Among the plant products that follow in this list, our identifications of **saffron**, **cinnamon**, and **aloes** are not universally accepted. Most alternate proposals are based on these plants' geographical origins.

Saffron is the only biblical reference to this member of the crocus family. The yellow or orange-yellow styles and stigmas of the flower were dried and powdered for flavoring and coloring foods, and as a dye for textiles. Its value is indicated by the fact that more than four thousand blossoms go into producing one ounce of saffron spice (Carr 1984, 125). On **myrrh**, → 1:13.

Hebrew *qāneh* (**calamus**) simply means "reed." In this context of perfumes and spices, the reed in question is *Calamus aromaticus*. Though called also "sweet cane," this is not a sugar cane. Rather, it has the smell and taste of ginger; crushing the stalk yields gingery oil.

Our English noun **cinnamon** transliterates the Hebrew (or a cognate Semitic) noun. This cinnamon probably was the dried and powdered inner bark of *Cinnamonum zelanicum*, a species of the laurel family originating in Sri Lanka. If a fragrance is intended, rather than a spice, it may have been the oil extracted from the cinnamon bark. On **incense tree, with myrrh**, → 3:6 and 1:13, respectively.

Aloes is not aloe vera, the small succulent. Neither is it an eaglewood or a sandalwood, though both are proposed. The wood of both is itself aromatic, and neither the wood nor other parts were used as (or in) perfumes. Carr proposes *"Aloe succotrina*, a spicy drug . . . from the . . . leaves of a large shrub native to the island of Socotra at the southern end of the Red Sea" (1984, 126). Ancient Egyptians used it in embalming. On **all the finest spices**, → 4:10.

■ **15** The man continues and enhances the metaphor begun with v 12. Here also, **You are** does not occur in the Hebrew text, and the lover does not even refer to his beloved as "sister" or "bride." However, this is the sixth line in the Hebrew text (vv 12-15); the metaphor is firmly established.

This line is three nominal clauses, each adding its own vivid imagery. The first is, literally, ***a fountain of gardens***. As the woman is metaphorically both garden and fountain, ***gardens*** (pl.) has "an intensifying function" (Keel 1994, 180).

The second clause titles her ***a well of living waters***. In the ancient world "living water(s)" denotes water flowing naturally and continuously from its source. A spring is a natural example of "living water." Some wells (*bĕʾēr*) tap into water under pressure, making it in effect a flowing spring; the woman is pictured as such, a new source of "living water." Today, English speakers call these "artesian wells" or, in some U.S. regions, "flowing wells."

Streaming down from Lebanon; the NIV does not render it, but the Hebrew text of this third clause begins with *wāw*. Usually rendered conjunctively ("and") or disjunctively ("but"), *wāw* sometimes means "even." Pope views the participle *nōzĕlîm* as "a poetic synonym for water" and renders it, "cascading" (1977, 496). Taken together, the occurrences of *nāzal* demonstrate that the action of this verb focuses on the downward movement of liquid, rather than on its volume; "cascading" fits here. The image of waters cascading down the mountains of Lebanon most naturally evokes the seasonal torrents of the spring snow melt.

Putting all this together, we propose, as an expansive and expositional translation, [***You are***] ***a fountain flowing vigorously, enough to water many gardens, a flowing well of living waters, even the torrents cascading from the Lebanon in springtime!***

On this understanding, the lover's delight in his beloved, with his enthusiasm for his intertwined metaphors of garden and fountain, crescendos throughout these four verses. Verse 15 is its fitting climax. Neither the fountain spring, nor the flowing well, nor both together, do her full justice. Inviting her to come away with him, he invoked Lebanon's majesty (v 8). Now, to Lebanon he goes to find the sparkling, torrential snow-melt cascades of an essence and purity to represent her faithfully in his chosen metaphor of abundant, pristine waters. Carr summarizes it well, "The imagery is not of the wide-ranging activities of the girl, but of the abundance of her beauty and fruitfulness when the sealed fountain is opened and the locked garden unbolted" (1984, 126).

FROM THE TEXT

Proverbially, brides may be anxious about the wedding night, often over whether (or how much) being "taken" in marriage will hurt, humiliate, or embarrass them. There would be no "taking" this woman without her active consent and partnership in their lovemaking. Here, as elsewhere, the Song celebrates sexual union as a true partnership, and a truly equal partnership. Any other arrangement *is* only an "arrangement," less than God's best for the woman, for the man, and for all the human family.

D. She/He: Invitation to Joy (4:16—5:1)

BEHIND THE TEXT

These are the only lines in the Song that cannot be interpreted, by normal exegetical canons, as referencing anything other than, or less than, consummation of sexual intercourse. The woman invites (4:16); the man reflects on the event (5:1*ab*); friends congratulate the happy couple (5:1*c*).

IN THE TEXT

■ **4:16** Following as it does upon a multiplex of poetic inventions, the woman's invitation bemuses and attracts with its gentle lyric simplicity. Personifying the cardinal winds north and south, she invokes their attendance upon her and commissions them as messengers to her lover.

Already twice in 2:7, and twice in 3:5, the woman used the verb **awake**, charging the women of Jerusalem *not* to awaken love, yet; she will do so again in 8:4. In this larger context, her use of the same verb to call the north wind is an indication of *her* readiness for love.

Calling on **north wind . . . south wind**, the two from opposite bearings, is an example of merism, pairing two terms that may be opposite, to connote the whole. Examples in English would be "for better or for worse" or "night and day." In naming two winds, she invoked all winds, from any and all directions. To attach further significance to **north** and **south** is to add more weight than this line will carry (see comment in Pope 1977, 498-500). However, Davis observes that in the whole of the Bible, this woman is the only person other than God to command the winds; her response to the man's invitation is thus "a remarkable assertion of personal power" (2000, 272).

Her lover just pictured her as a garden locked, and she adopted the image herself. Using the possessive pronoun, **my garden**, she affirmed what he recognized, that her garden—she herself—was hers to unlock, as she chose and to whom she would. The winds spreading her **fragrance** will initiate the unlocking of her garden.

The line ends literally, *that its balsams may cascade*, or, *let its balsams cascade*. This was the final verb of her lover's speech (v 15). As torrents cascade in Lebanon's mountains, so the woman called on the winds to cascade her fragrance over and around her lover, to immerse him in the sensual power of her presence.

In v 10, the man compared balsam with his beloved's perfume; balsam itself, most desired of fragrances, is the point of his comparison. Here, the woman used synecdoche; the best of the class (balsam) signifies all perfume fragrances, **balsams**.

The second Hebrew line is the substantive invitation. A marvel of understated directness and simplicity, it conveys the pure ardor of her welcome to astounding effect. In six lyrical Hebrew lines (vv 12-15), her lover described her as a garden. He had refrained from claiming her as his own, knowing her "garden" was hers to give—or to retain unbestowed—as she wished. Now, she freely gives herself to him with the simple invitation to **come into his garden**.

The power of her invitation is underscored and multiplied by the artless grace of her pronoun exchange. Her first line has **my garden**; her second line has **his garden**. She gave herself unreservedly, joyfully, without constraint.

Her lover had pictured her charms as a "*paradise of* choice fruits," exemplified by the pomegranate (4:13). Reflecting the image back to him, she invites, [*let him*] taste its choice fruits. Grammatically, ***Let him taste/eat his choice/excellent fruits*** also is a viable translation. We need not choose. She gives herself as **his garden**; its **choice fruits** are now his also, to their mutual enjoyment.

■ **5:1** As we have seen in the woman's invitation, one of poetry's evocative powers lies in adroit use of understatement. Here, the lover responds in kind, with four straightforward, declarative statements: **I have come**; **I have gathered**; **I have eaten**; **I have drunk**. Each encompasses multiple levels of meaning, but as a grammatical declaration each is a model of concision.

Each of the four Hebrew verbs ends in *tî*. Multiplying this poetic effect, in terms of the aural reception of spoken poetry, all the other words in the verse are singular nouns, and all but one end with the 1cs dependent (suffix) pronoun, *î*. Thus, only one word in the verse does *not* end with the long vowel *î* ("ee").

I have come, the "normal" rendering of the Hebrew perfect, seems most appropriate here. His beloved has invited him; he has accepted. **My garden** is the third reference to "garden" in these three successive lines. Continuing with his image of her as a garden (4:12-15), the woman first claimed it as her own, "my garden" (4:16*a*); then offered herself to him, "his garden" (4:16*b*). Accepting her gift, he now referred to her as his own, **my garden**. On **my sister, bride**, → Behind the Text at 4:8-15.

I have gathered; this verb occurs only here and in Ps 80:12 [13 HB]. In the psalm, it refers to plucking grapes. In the garden metaphor, generally, "gathering" can refer to any or all aspects of lovemaking. *My myrrh with my balsam* represent and symbolize the whole of the woman's sensuous attraction for him. → on **myrrh** at 1:13, and **balsam** at 4:10.

To the objection of some that **honeycomb** should not appear before **honey** in this sequence, we note that poetic variation is sufficient explanation. (→ 4:11 and "Bees Produce Honey" sidebar, at Song 4:11, above.) **Honeycomb** is Hebrew *ya'ar*; a related noun means "thicket." In some ANE love poems, "thicket" is a reference to a woman's pubic hair. Wild honeybees locate their hives (nests) containing honeycombs with honey in difficult locations, sometimes in thickets of dense shrubs or thornbush. In ancient love poetry, both the lips (see 4:11) and the vagina are figured as possessing the sweetness of honey.

For a poet of love, these relationships are too abundant and complex to edit out and, even for the chaste reader, the allusions are too obvious to ignore. Such images, scattered as they are through the Song, aid the reader in building appropriate discernment between attitudes and actions that truly are chaste, and others that only appear so.

Wine and **milk** are not often paired as being drunk together. Naming **wine**, though, the man did not mean the fruit of the vine, but the varied charms of his beloved as they came together in lovemaking. Given the many references to breasts in the Song, **milk** here likely alludes to love-play involving her breasts (though we need not imagine lactation!).

Honey, wine, and **milk** are the focus of the final two statements here, **I have eaten . . . I have drunk.** Honey and the fruit of the vine are two of the "goodly products" of the land of Canaan/Israel (Deut 8:8). We have noted the phrase "milk and honey" as a symbol of the land's bounty (Song 4:11). The couple's lovemaking is set largely in the verdancy of the out-of-doors. Linking the land's promised fruitfulness with the extravagant joys of love is an intended effect of this and many other statements and allusions of the Song.

For clarity here, rather than poetic style, we translate the last Hebrew line, *Eat, friends; drink, Even become drunk on [your] lovemaking*. Most commonly, this line is treated either as the end of the man's speech, or as a short speech by friends or onlookers. One observation should settle the issue. If this line were spoken by the man, it could mean only that he invited friends or onlookers to enjoy his beloved as he just had done. This line is a benediction upon the happy couple by their friends and companions, who naturally address them as **friends.**

Vocabulary leads some to confuse what the companions were urging. Two different imperatives instruct the couple, **drink.** In the first, *šĕtû*, what is imbibed may be alcoholic or nonalcoholic. This verb—not often, but a few times—is used of drinking to excess, becoming drunk. The second, *šikrû*, when used literally, always means to be or become drunk on an alcoholic beverage, normally wine in Israel's cultural sphere.

It is almost the definition of Semitic poetry that it uses two words, phrases, metaphors, or sentences together to express an idea, the second always advancing in some way the entity, event, or idea introduced by the first. Here, this poetic sequencing is *šĕtû*, **drink** . . . *šikrû*, **become drunk.** Wine was a major feature of wedding feasts in ancient Israel; drunkenness was known. (This does not prove this was the couple's wedding.)

But this is poetry, saturated with metaphor. On *what* were the lovers to become drunk? The answer is the last word, *dôdîm*. The noun *dôd* means "love/lover/beloved." In the Song, as we have seen (e.g., 4:10), its plural (*dôdîm*,

5:1

160

"loves"), means "love*making*." The friends were not urging the couple to become drunk with wine. They were encouraging them to become "intoxicated" with each other in and from their lovemaking. Carr phrases it becomingly, "Thus the third division of the poem ends with the couple's companions and guests rejoicing with them and encouraging them to drink their fill of ecstasy and joy in each other's arms—and bed" (1984, 129).

FROM THE TEXT

Our overhearing of the Song's whispered intimacies grants access for the sake of *torah* (instruction) in this most personal and private of God's gifts. Each metaphorical expression of an act of love in the Song is a statement: "We did this specific act together." "We made love together in this specific series of acts." These statements are in the biblical text. Though in some cases their specific import is obscure to us, because of our distance from their time and culture, it was plain to the ancients who first heard or read the Song. These statements appear without stint, without blush, and without apology. They contribute in essential ways to the central purpose of the Song. Together, these literary, anthropological, and theological realities of the Song constitute vital testimony to the importance God places on the expression and enjoyment of human sexuality.

In the Song, integrity of relationship is assumed, rather than expounded. Decisions about the propriety of given acts belong to the couple, jointly. God's intention in creating humans for sexual union was, and is, mutual pleasure and joy on every level, in a couple's generous offering of love's "choice fruits" to each other.

V. ABSENCE AND PRESENCE: VICISSITUDES OF LOVE: SONG OF SONGS 5:2—8:4

OVERVIEW

This longest section of the Song is marked as a discrete unit by the refrain, **Do not arouse . . . desires** (8:4), used previously at 2:7; 3:5. It begins with the second episode of the woman's searching the city for the man (5:2-8). Two further *wasfs*—the first, the woman celebrating the man (5:10-16); the second, the man's second celebration of the woman (7:1-9*a*)—and a briefer variant on the man's first *wasf* (6:4-7) comprise the greater part of this section. The woman's renewed ardent invitation, essentially in two parts (7:9*b*-13; 8:1-3), brings the section to the refrain (8:4).

A. She (with Dialogue): I Am My Beloved's and He Is Mine (5:2—6:3)

BEHIND THE TEXT

The text offers no transition between the benediction of the friends and the woman's next words. This is evidence of editorial minimalism at work. If the Song exhibits at least the outlines of a plot (and especially if 4:16—5:1 mark a consummation of marriage), the reader reasonably wonders why no change of time or setting is mentioned. The woman sleeps; unbeknownst to her, her love departs; his knock announcing his return wakens her.

Following Exum, we notice striking parallels between this pericope and the events in 2:8—3:5 (2005, 186-87). In both sections, the man arrives at the woman's door and she reports his words of invitation. Both include her statement of loverly solidarity, and both involve the woman searching in the night-bound city for her absent lover. Finally, both function on multiple levels at once: neither journalistic play-by-play of narrated events, nor misty dream sequence, both sections explore the anticipations and disappointments of young love, with good doses of double entendre. In the commentary below, then, we have tried to avoid overly literalistic readings of the "action," while still trying to make sense of the speakers' interactions.

In 5:10-16, the woman answers the daughters of Jerusalem with a *wasf*, such as we have heard from the man in 4:1-7. In the broad arena of Near Eastern love poetry, ancient or modern, a *wasf* in praise of a man is not nearly as common as one in praise of a woman. Hers begins with a general statement (v 10), then progresses from the top of his head downward to his legs and feet (vv 11-15*a*). Technically a conclusion, v 15*b* is a second general statement, but she cannot resist another line in praise of her lover's kisses, before her "real" conclusion, "This is . . ." (v 16).

Compelled by the *wasf*, the friends offer their help in finding the missing lover (6:1). That the entire exchange (5:8—6:3) operates at several levels is evidenced by the woman's reply (6:2-3), though it is less enigmatic than it might have been, as its imagery has appeared in the Song previously.

IN THE TEXT

■ **5:2** We translate *I was sleeping*, but my heart/*mind* was awake. Some take the participial forms as evidence the woman was dreaming. More likely, it describes the half-awake, half-asleep state that precedes full slumber. Given her tepid response (v 3) to his plea for entrance, it is not likely dreamy or drowsy anticipation on her part. **Awake** (*ʿēr*) is the same root the woman used to caution the women of Jerusalem not to awaken love until it pleases (2:7; 3:5; 8:4). Now at least, if not earlier, she herself has been awakened to love, even if she is not fully awake yet this night.

Hebrew *qôl* ("voice/sound") not being used as an exclamatory particle, we read the next hemistich, ***The sound of my beloved knocking***. His knock roused her from her sleeping or drowsy state; then she heard his voice outside the door. This is the only place in the Song where either lover uses four terms of endearment in succession. The effect here is to signify his great urgency to see her. The irony hardly can be accidental, then, that this also is the only vignette without an immediate positive response from the lover.

My sister: → Behind the Text on 4:8-15.

My darling: → 1:9.

My dove: → 2:14.

My flawless one uses the Hebrew word *tām*, which most famously identifies Noah and Job as persons of blameless integrity (Gen 6:9; Job 1:1, 8). Given the man's lavish praise of her person, it is reasonable to infer that his use of *tām* here includes the integrity of her physical essence and appearance, along with recognition of her moral and ethical righteousness.

Drenched translates a phrase that literally means ***full of dew***; the second hemistich reads, ***my locks with the dewdrops of the night***. In the late spring and early summer months, the hill country experiences sharp fluctuation from daytime high temperatures to nighttime lows. Most nights, this produces very heavy, late-night and early-morning dews.

As with other details of this scene, the woman kept much to herself, telling the reader neither why her love was absent from her, nor what he was doing outdoors. Whatever the reasons, his string of endearments following his vigorous knocking displayed his eagerness to rejoin her; the disclosure of his chill dampness revealed his urgency.

■ **3 My robe**, or *tunic* (*kūtōnet*), is the (usually) one-piece inner layer of clothing worn next to the skin. It was a shin- or ankle-length shirt with sleeves, donned by pulling it over the head. These commonly were of wool; a linen one marked the wearer as comfortably well-off. The woman had taken off her tunic for the night and was lying in bed without clothing.

I have washed my feet; we are used to picturing foot washing, in biblical narrative, as done when entering a home. However, home flooring of hard-packed earth or plastered surface did not keep sandaled feet clean. Both cleanliness and comfort made washing one's feet before getting into bed a prudent routine.

Must I . . . must I? translates the Hebrew, ***How should I . . . How should I?*** Was the woman posing straightforward questions, indicating impatience with her lover, or even simple disinterest, or are these rhetorical questions intended as teasing coyness? Importantly, we assume her questions were followed by actually donning the tunic again; she would not likely walk from her sleeping place to the outer door of the house without it.

If the reader sees her here as impatient, this response comes as a surprise in the Song. Elsewhere, both lovers express ardent desire for each other. She holds her own in the boldness of their words; she speaks more often, and at greater length, than he. Against that backdrop, a peevish response here would seem jarring, out of character, off key.

Many lovers adopt a coy, teasing approach from time to time. If this was her pose here, she intended the tone of her questions to increase his desire for her, by delaying him a little longer than necessary. While we see no petulance or impatience in this initial response, we cannot with certainty opt either for initial disinterest or for a teasing coyness on her part; either is possible. Whichever was her reason, the outcome was quite disappointing.

■ **4-5** Profoundly intimate double entendre begins here. The "literal" meanings are clear. The metaphorical meanings are clear and vivid enough in their suggestiveness that they cannot be accidental; the poet intended both. The purpose and genius of double entendre, though, is to obscure and tantalize with words and images that, encountered on either level separately, would be perfectly clear. The Hebrew text reads:

> *My beloved put forth his hand into the hole,*
> *and my womb [belly] was thrilled because of him.*
> *I rose to open to my beloved,*
> *and my hands dripped myrrh.*
> *My fingers (dripped) liquid myrrh*
> *upon the handles of the bolt.*

The man reached through the hole of the latch in the door (in most dwellings, only the outer doors would have such a latch; thus our assumption that she greeted him there, not at the bedroom door). Keys were large and made of wood. Without the key, one could extend one's hand through the keyhole, but could not open the door from the outside. By this time, his presence just beyond the door was making the woman eager to admit him. Whatever his gesture, her reaction was visceral. She began to open the door, her hands already anticipating the physical joys of lovemaking as she grasped the bolt to raise the latch and let him in.

What does this scene look like when we "decode" the double entendre? First, **hand** is one of several euphemisms for penis, both in the Bible (see Isa 57:8, and possibly Jer 5:31; 50:15) and in other ANE sources. The next Hebrew noun is **the hole**. He put his "hand" into the "hole"; they enjoyed a(nother) tryst in her bed. Similarly, the woman *rose to open to [her] beloved. What* did she open? The door? Herself? Both in turn?

On **myrrh**, → 1:13. On the literal level, **flowing** (or liquid) **myrrh** evokes the fresh sap as its flows from the cut bark, or the hardened resin softening and melting from body heat, when applied as a perfume or worn/carried as a sachet. If the woman had anointed herself in anticipation of his coming, her fingers may have left a residue of myrrh as she opened the door to admit him into the room. Euphemistically, sexual activity produces various "myrrhs" of quite a different kind, but even more desirable to lovers. Inescapably, her fingers would have left "myrrh" on the "handles" of [his] "bolt."

These two verses picture the woman in her house, with her lover outside the door. They also provide the outlines of a lovers' tryst. In addressing her friends, she intended them to understand both. Regarding the tryst, however, this is not her report of that evening, as it turned out differently (v 6). It is her skilled description of the natural rise of amorous desire, *before* opening the door to find him gone.

■ **6** If the woman meant to continue the suggestiveness with **I opened for my beloved**, carrying out the intention she had expressed in v 5, her mood was rudely shattered. Her pathos may be more nearly reflected if we translate, *But my beloved had turned away; he had passed on* [*from me*].

My heart sank employs the Hebrew noun *nepeš* (see 3:1-5); the verb usually is rendered, "go out." **At his departure** reflects a seldom-attested meaning of *dbr*, but it fits this context. The NIV note, "when he spoke," is less plausible, as it is too far removed in the text from the man's request at the door (v 2). A literal translation is, *My life went out* [*from me; i.e., I fainted*] *at his leaving* [*me*]. More colloquially, Carr gets it exactly, "I nearly died when I found he had gone" (1984, 136). She spoke similar words in 2:5, but languorously. Davis says of her plaintiveness here that this "declaration of lovesickness is at the same time a declaration of her soul's strength. It bespeaks the wise anguish of someone who now knows what it means to lose what matters *absolutely*" (2000, 279, emphasis hers).

I looked for him but did not find him reports an identical effort, with an identical result, as at 3:1, 2 (→ Behind the Text above). This third time, however, reflects increased anxiety and pathos, as she added, **I called** *to him*, **but he did not answer** *me*. The reader is left to wonder at his leaving. Did he not hear her calling? Or did he ignore her and continue on his way?

■ **7** As happened the first time she ventured out to look for her lover (3:3), **the watchmen found** her instead. Except for a missing vowel letter here, the lines are identical (→ 3:2-3). This time, though, the watchmen did not give the woman opportunity to ask about her absent lover (see 3:3*b*). We may read,

> *They struck me;* they bruised me.
> *They lifted* [*stripped off*] *my mantle from upon me,*
>> *the* watchmen of the walls.

It is important to note, first, the three verbs in succession: *They struck me;* they bruised me; *they lifted*. Three or more verbs strung together are a narrative signal of intense activity, a sudden, purposeful quickening of the pace.

Hebrew *nākâ* means "to strike," without reference to number of blows, or to results. Moses struck the Egyptian overseer; possibly only a single blow, but it killed him (Exod 2:12). Here, one or more blows (perhaps with fist or staff) **bruised** the woman.

Mantle (NIV: **cloak**) translates *rĕdîd*, from the root *rdd*, used of hammering gold into an overlay, gold leaf; for example, 1 Kgs 6:32 reports such a beaten gold overlay upon the cherubim and palm trees carved into the two doors opening into the holy of holies. This mantle was sewn from fabric similarly thin and fine, and

167

usually worn over a tunic, which as stated above we assume she was wearing. They did not strip her naked, but removed her outer wrap (contra Carr 1984, 137).

This startling encounter is hard to read. Why did the watchmen treat her so? They (or their comrades) had met her previously and allowed her to go on her way (Song 3:3-4). Any explanation is conjectural, but Hess suggests, "This may be the rough treatment she receives while being pushed along, back to her home, by guards who feel they have more important things to do" (2005, 176). Her reference to these men as the **watchmen of the walls** is new here, and the noun (sg., *hômâ*) otherwise occurs only at 8:9, 10, both metaphorical uses. We take it in the literal sense of city walls here.

■ **8** The woman turns her attention now from a recital of what has happened, to her hopes for what may. **I charge you**, or *I cause you to swear [an oath]* is the first word of the Hebrew text; it is a *hip'il* (causative) of *šb'*, "to swear [an oath]." The final word of 5:9 is the same, except it is 2fs, "you charge us/you cause us to swear." Together, these "chargings" constitute an inclusio, framing vv 8-9. One literary effect is that vv 8-9 together provide a transition between the woman's longer, differently focused speeches of vv 2-7 and vv 10-16.

Her charge begins with an implicit instruction to her friends (→ **daughters of Jerusalem** at 1:5a) to look for her lover, or at least to be on the lookout for him: **if you find**. If they were successful in locating him, the logical question would become, what message did she wish them to convey?

To understand her tone here, and arrive at her meaning, we need to remember that her lover had left after coming to her, because she had been slow to open to him (5:2-6). We have noted also that the section immediately prior to this (4:16—5:1) represents a consummation of their relationship. In such a circumstance, both would have been left wondering. As Keel points out, this is a common dynamic in relationships, "the missing of the opportune moment, the painful recurrence of feelings out of phase: when he wants to, she does not; when she wants to, he does not" (1994, 186). It need not be fatal to their bond.

The question is straightforward, **What will you tell him?** Her answer, the message she wanted these women to deliver to her love if they found him, seems open to interpretation. We note first that the NIV's **tell him** beginning the next line is not in the Hebrew text and unnecessarily complicates the issue.

We have seen this line previously (2:5). In both contexts we should read, *Weak/faint/languishing (because) of love am I*. The circumstances differed, however. There, at some point in the intimacy of lovemaking, the woman's statement had been prompted by the *presence* of her lover (→ 2:5). Here, exactly the same declaration is occasioned by the *absence* of her lover.

Carr takes 4:16—5:1 as the lovers' consummation. A short time later, finding herself without him, the woman used her previous words to reassure him of her continuing love. Carr says, "She challenges her companions: 'What are you going to tell him? That I am worn out . . . with lovemaking?' . . . The question is almost rhetorical. 'Don't be foolish. How could I not want more?'" (1984, 138).

Another reading also is plausible. The issue was love, but she was *languishing* for *want* of love(making) because he was not with her.

The Presence and Absence of the Lover

The final line of 5:8 repeats 2:5 but under different circumstances. . . . As with his presence, so with his absence . . . The passion for love in this section becomes an ideal: the intensity of love does not change when the object of that love has left. His absence may alter the way in which the love is expressed, but it does not affect its power. (Hess 2005, 178)

■ **9** The friends' response was not a settled refusal, but the interested challenge of a group whose curiosity she had piqued with her charge. Though skeptical—for what prior reason(s) would they have put themselves out for her and her lover?— they were willing to hear her out.

The initial hemistiches of these lines are identical: *What is your lover compared to [any other] lover . . . ?* On **most beautiful of women,** → 1:8. In this context of their twice-voiced question, the women's use of her lover's epithet for her is jocular irony. Given their role throughout the Song, we think of them as speaking here with amusement, but not with malice or hostility.

■ **10** The woman's response is a *wasf,* beginning with a two-word observation: her lover's appearance was **radiant and ruddy.** Today we are more likely to describe a bride as **radiant** in her wedding dress, but the broader import is that anyone pictured as **radiant,** *dazzling, brilliant,* or *glowing*—we may translate the Hebrew ṣaḥ with any of these—is the picture of health, vitality, and vigor.

Ruddy translates ʾādōm, an adjective from the same root as ʾādām, "human." In Israel's cultural world, ideal human skin tones signifying beauty and health were vibrant reddish-browns. Both Esau (Gen 25:25) and David (1 Sam 16:12) are described with a related adjective, David in a context of lavish approval. "Radiantly, glowingly handsome" is an apt paraphrase of the woman's words here.

Outstanding among ten thousand; employs again the root *dgl* (→ discussion of the noun *degel* in 2:4). Given the basic meaning of the root, "to look," in this context it means *the one looked at among a myriad.* In Hebrew as in Greek, **ten thousand,** or *myriad,* does not express a precise numerical value, but a multitude. Among a numberless company of handsome and admirable men, the woman said, **my beloved** would be the one looked at by everyone. Strictly speaking, this part of her opening assessment was subjective.

■ **11** In a crowd, head, face, and stature are more likely than other features to compel attention. Thus, it was natural for the woman to begin her more detailed praise with her lover's **head.** From there, she moved down his body to his feet, figured as bases or pedestals also of **gold.** In toto, then, 5:11-15 portrays him metaphorically as the prized work of a sculptor's genius.

The NIV's **His head is purest gold** reflects a traditional view of the two nouns *ketem* and *pāz*. However, both nouns are infrequent, and this is the only time they occur together. *Ketem* means **gold**, but recent identifications of *pāz* have shifted from an idea of "pure gold." *Pāz* probably was topaz or a similar semiprecious gemstone, "chrysolite" in its original Greek meaning of "golden stone" (Carr 1984, 140). We may translate, a bit expansively, *His head (is) finest gold or, if you prefer, a perfect tone of topaz.*

His hair is more specifically, *his locks*; some suggest forelocks (bangs). If **wavy** is correct here, this adjective suggests, not unruly randomness, but a tasteful, ordered styling. Hair **black as a raven** framing and contrasting with the "golden" face of a man radiant and in vigorous health was the beginning of a striking sculpture, indeed.

■ **12** On **His eyes are like doves**, → 1:15. Here, the woman requited the loving notice expressed there. Adding **like** here is a literary variation, from his formal metaphor to simile, a subset of metaphor.

Doves favor nesting places in cliff walls above ravines (**water streams**) (→ 2:14). Here, we note the focus on the stream, rather than on the cliff. No hill country water source flows year-round, but this phrasing reminds the reader the lovers were enjoying the springtime together, when streambeds do carry water.

The vocabulary of the second line is reasonably clear, but its import has proven elusive. Two points are decisive: The second line reveals the comparison is to doves, not to doves' eyes. The participle *yōšĕbôt* (*sitting*, rather than the NIV's **mounted**) modifies doves, not the lover's eyes. With these clarifications, we translate the verse (partially following Pope 1977, 502):

5:12-13

His eyes [are] like doves by the *watercourses,*
Splashing in [their] milky spray,
   sitting by [their] riffling pools.

Doves, often grayish or darker in color, like to sit on stream banks where pools reduce the current's strength, splashing/bathing in the edge of the water, the spray turned "milky" by the light's diffraction of the water. Just so, the dancing liveliness of the lover's dark pupils sparkled in "milky" pools, the whites of his eyes.

We noted that this *wasf* is framed in terms of a sculpted male statue. **Mounted like jewels** is a product of doubtful inferences arising from that total image. Verses 12-13 depart from the sculpture metaphor, perhaps because the woman did not deem even precious metals and other luxury materials adequate to convey the perfection of her beloved's face.

■ **13 His cheeks** refers to the cheek and/or the jaw, that is, the "sides" of the face from bottom to hairline, where facial hair grows.

Given the nature of the hill country, it is reasonable to envision these **beds of spice**, or plots, as terraces down the slope of a hillside, a small detail of association with the "vertical" plane of the human cheek. **Spice** is Hebrew *bōśem*, *balsam* (→ 4:10).

Yielding perfume is suitably ambiguous; it can reflect either the MT or the LXX reading. The Hebrew *gdl* means "to be/become large." The MT points this form as a noun, "towers," that is, strongholds storing and guarding the perfumers' arts. The LXX takes it as a *pi'el* participle, that is, "growing [the aromatic plants from which] the perfumes [are derived]." Here, the LXX is the better reading. Like the line above, this metaphor compares "organics"; her lover's face was a "bed" of the plants from which perfumes were manufactured. This line is metonymy, substitution of the source (bed of aromatic plants) for their product (the perfumes the lover applied to his face and beard).

His lips (are) lotuses, dripping flowing myrrh; on *lotuses* and **myrrh**, → 2:1 and 1:13, respectively. The *lotus* is not a source of **myrrh**, but in the back-and-forth of memory and anticipation, the woman's juxtaposition of metaphors is neither a poetic nor a logical problem.

Lips feature in eating, in speaking, and in kissing. Certainly, the lovers enjoyed all these together, but we agree with Carr, "The frequent use of the 'kissing' image in the Song (*e.g.*, 1:2) suggests this as a better interpretation here" (1984, 142). His kisses were liquid **myrrh**.

■ **14** Moving down from his face, the woman resumed the image of a sculpture. **His arms** translates Hebrew *yādāyw*; in this context, both **arms and hands** are indicated. **Rods** is from the root *gll* ("roll"), referencing both their cylindrical shape and their manufacture. A smith could make a rod by heating a mass of metal to soften it, then rolling it into the desired shape. This *waṣf* is a figurative portrayal of her lover's worth in the woman's eyes. Though the arms of real statues would have been gold-plated, she would not have pictured his arms as anything less than solid **gold**.

Set with topaz (*taršîš*) is a better guess for the identity of the gem than many, as topaz and gold are complementary in color. However, though *taršîš* is a gemstone in this and some other contexts, we cannot be sure which stone she intended. The point lies elsewhere; picturing golden arms inlaid with semiprecious stones emphasized both value and beauty.

The Hebrew noun *mē'îm* is more specific, more restricted than **his body**. Translating "loins," Pope comments, "The term 'loins' includes the lumbar region, front, back, and sides" (1977, 543). Elephant **ivory** was used decoratively in temples and palaces, and in the homes of the wealthy. Ivory was an inlay decoration in furnishings and carved into figurines and other small objects. Here, the woman sustained her lavish description of her lover by choosing ivory as the material for such a large area of his physique as his "loins," his entire lower torso.

Lapis lazuli is a semiprecious stone, usually an intense azure blue in hue. It is often referenced in written descriptions of statuary (as here), often represented artistically on human and "divine" figures, and is common as a decorative element of jewelry. Here, the azure of the lapis contrasts to great effect with the ivory it accented, and also with the gold and marble featured in other lines of the *waṣf*.

5:14

■ **15** **Marble** is actually a limestone crystallized by metamorphism. Its strength and durability, the complex patterning and coloration of its veining, and its lasting retention of a high polish combine to make marble a highly prized building material through all historical epochs. Thighs and lower legs support the human body as we stand upright; characterizing her lover's as **marble**, a stone of enduring supportive strength, is poetic and suitable.

Discussing v 11, we suggested that, rather than **pure gold**, the Hebrew *pāz* may mean topaz or a similar semiprecious stone. Here, **pure gold** would not be strong enough for **bases**, or pedestals, to support a statue, but the same is true of topaz. The "problem," though, is hypothetical. Presenting her lover as an admirable statue, the woman could complete the metaphor referring to his feet as **bases**, without acknowledging the physical limitations of sculpting a real statue.

On **Lebanon** and **its cedars**, → 4:8 and 1:17, respectively. Just as many regard the sequoia as the most majestic of North American trees, so in antiquity the **choice** among all the trees known in western Asia and the eastern Mediterranean was the cedar of Lebanon. The profile of the living tree; the fragrances of its greenery and its wood; the beauty, strength, and durability of the timber milled from it—all informed the woman's estimation of her lover, **choice as** Lebanon's **cedars**.

This woman spent most of ten Hebrew lines comparing her love to the work of skilled human artisans. Yet it does not surprise the observant reader to find her reverting to natural-world splendors for her summative comparison of his appearance. Mere human artistry could not convey all she saw in him, knew of him, enjoyed with him.

■ **16** The woman's *waṣf* focuses most of its descriptors on her lover's appearance; the sense of sight is pervasive. Other senses may be inferred, but they are backgrounded. Other women were not expected to interact with him in ways that involved the other senses intimately.

At the end of her poem, though, one could say she gave up on sight, finding sight inadequate to convey all she intended. Already we have seen this woman act with boldness (see 3:2). Here we see it again, as she conjured a picture of her lover's kisses. How is he better (5:9)? Imagine his touch, his taste and smell, the feel and sound of his breath on your neck! Now do you understand why I praise him so?

It can be difficult to render idioms of such matters from one language into another. Merely translating the words usually is not sufficient, and a literal translation often is too wooden in the receptor language. Sometimes, however, it is worth the effort:

> *His palate (is)* [*the essence of*] *sweetnesses,*
> *And all of him (is)* [*the essence of*] *desires/delights.*

It goes without saying that kisses referenced this way are deep, passionate, "soulful." In this very public utterance, the woman celebrated them as good, right, virtuous.

The woman's final word is a marvel of eloquent simplicity. As in many cultures, she could have rendered no greater endorsement, no greater praise, than to call him both lover and **friend**: companion, confidant, soulmate. On **my beloved**, → 1:13. On **my friend**, → 1:9. We noted there that *ra'yātî* ("my beloved") is the man's preferred endearment for the woman, but not hers for him. **My friend** here is not *ra'yātî*, but from the same root. On **daughters of Jerusalem**, → 1:5*a*.

■ **6:1** In response, the women posed a question framed as a perfect parallelism:

Whither did your beloved go . . . ?
Whither did your beloved turn . . . ?

On **most beautiful of women**, → 1:8; 5:9. Whereas the context of 5:9 suggests the women may have quoted this epithet insincerely, this use draws the reader to conclude that the woman's *waṣf* had won them over. Now they repeated it with sincere admiration, ready to join and assist in her quest.

■ **2-3** The woman's answer is unexpected. If she knew where to find him, why had she asked friends for help? Taking the "garden" as metaphorical, rather than as a physical locality, merely moves these questions to another plane. Two interpretations are plausible. Some read this as the woman reporting her lover's return; while the friends were out looking, he returned on his own. If this is the case, then they resumed their lovemaking immediately, and she recounts their reunion here. As poetry is not required to report every move, this is perfectly feasible.

Keel suggests another satisfactory option (1994, 210). He argues that she expressed faith in his return, based on their previous consummation. Rather than an announcement that he already *was* back, she had recovered her confidence and was sure he *would* return, because he already **has gone down to his garden** once, and thus they were one. If this is the case, the reversal of clauses at v 3*a* is striking at this moment of vulnerability: in spite of his absence, she affirmed *first* that she was his, before claiming him as her own.

In 4:12-14 (→), the man had lavished praise on his lover as a **garden** (→ 5:1). The woman's answer here shows her pleasure in this metaphor of their love. **Spices** have figured repeatedly in these poems (→ 4:10). **Beds of spices** was last used by the woman to praise the man's "cheeks" (5:13), and now she appropriated that praise to her own person. The verb **to browse** is intransitive here. The man was not pasturing his flock; in the manner of the gazelle or stag to which she has compared him, he himself "fed" in the "garden" she had given him (4:16; → 1:7-8 and 2:16). **Lilies** here is *lotuses*, as at 2:1, 16. Except for the reversal of the two clauses of the first line, 6:3 is identical with 2:16 (→).

FROM THE TEXT

These two sections together, 5:2-9 and 5:10—6:3, open with the lovers parted (5:2), and close with them either reunited or on the brink of reunion, with the woman recalling the intimacies and solidarity of their lovemaking (6:2-3). If we are reading the Song on its own terms, as poetic considerations of the experiences of young lovers, this section seems fairly true to life. Great desire and longing between lovers sometimes go unfulfilled. Since the text gives no plain indication for what separated these lovers in the first place, we would do well to refrain from working too hard to construct a narrative explanation. In the Song, as in life, trusting the bonds of love and the faithfulness of the beloved lead to reunion. Even considering their separation, and her peril in the street, the overwhelming emphasis here is on the deep thrill of loving and being loved by another.

B. He (with Dialogue): Lovely as Jerusalem (6:4-13 [6:4—7:1 HB])

BEHIND THE TEXT

Whether the couple was reunited in 6:2-3 or not, they certainly are together in this next section. The man praised his beloved in vv 4-9 (incorporating some lines from the *wasf* of 4:1-3), and then dialogued with the listening friends (6:10-13). A comment on versification will be helpful here. Chapter and verse divisions were not implemented in the biblical text until the Middle Ages. The MT of the Hebrew begins ch 7 with what the English (via LXX tradition) calls v 13 of ch 6, "Come back, come back, O Shulammite . . ." We will discuss the import of these decisions below, but for now it will help the reader to know that the brackets in the following verse references note the Hebrew versification.

IN THE TEXT

■ **4 Tirzah**, about forty miles north of **Jerusalem**, lay at the head of the largest wadi leading to the Jordan Valley from the hill country. After establishing independence for the ten northern tribes, from Solomon's son Rehoboam of Judah, Jeroboam I made Tirzah the capital of the new northern kingdom, Israel (ca. 920 BC). Fifty years later (ca. 870 BC), Omri built his new capital, Samaria, about ten miles west of Tirzah.

That this man compared his love to the beautiful city of Tirzah is considered very strong support by those who date the Song early. A Judean poet is not likely to have mentioned Tirzah before—and on an equal footing with—Jerusalem, once the northern tribes rebelled successfully against rule from Solomon's capital. At a minimum, we may conclude, with Carr, "A Solomonic date for this part of the Song is most likely. . . . The parallel between the two cities—one the capital, the other a northern 'garden city'—is in keeping with the royal/rural elements in this unit" (1984, 147).

On **my darling**, → 1:9.

Following Solomon's magnificent building projects, **Jerusalem** would have seemed the loveliest of cities to any Judean. The man had compared his love favorably with natural wonders on the grand scale of the mountains of Lebanon (4:8-15). It was fitting that when comparing her loveliness with the work of human hands, he should include Solomon's masterwork.

This line was prompted by the comparisons with the splendid cities, Tirzah and (especially) Jerusalem. She was awesome, wondrous, as their walls and towers were awesome, wondrous; this was beauty on a **majestic** scale. In its day, the KJV's "terrible" was appropriate. Today, it is archaic, its old import lost.

Troops is not in the text, but imported from the presence of the following root *dgl*, a form of which is translated **banners** elsewhere (→ 2:4). This form is *nidgālôt*, a feminine plural *nip'al* participle. The basic meaning of *dgl* is "to see." Here we take the *nip'al* as passive, rather than reflexive, "the things seen/looked at/marveled at." Translating expansively for clarity, we may render, [**You are**] *as* **awesome as all of the wonders** [**that are**] **marveled at** [**in these two wondrous cities, even all their walls, gates, towers, and battlements**].

This was a woman of integrity and wholeness in every way (→ "my flawless one" at 5:2). Moreover, she was, to her lover, the personification of physical beauty. To deem such a woman as awesome ("terrible" in the KJV's old sense), majestic as the fortified royal city of Jerusalem, is to hold her in positive regard.

■ **5a** A bit woodenly, but quite literally, we may translate 6:5a, ***Turn aside your eyes from facing me, because they cause a storm of disturbance within me***. Why should the woman's direct gaze have disturbed the man? One clue is that this request follows immediately upon his comparing her beauty with the majestic aspects of a fortified city, naming Tirzah and Jerusalem. From without, fortified cities are imposing. Just as an approaching army may be abashed at the sight of a beautiful and strongly fortified city, so a man may be abashed by a beautiful woman of strong personal confidence and assurance, such as this woman; the NIV's **they overwhelm me** captures that nuance.

A woman's gaze may abash (**overwhelm**) a man for more fundamental reasons than proud resistance to would-be conquerors. In 1:15 (→), the man said, "Your eyes are doves," meaning, "Your glances/looks are messengers of love." Setting aside the metaphor, he may be saying here simply that her direct gaze of inviting love was momentarily too much for him. Even the wholly loving gaze of a woman wholly beloved can **overwhelm** a man.

■ **5b-7** This poem as a whole is not itself a *wasf*, in that it extends beyond the woman's physical attributes. However, these lines do reprise several lines of the man's first *wasf*, 4:1c-3 (→). That "just shorn" of 4:2a is omitted here (6:6a) is not significant; it could be assumed here. A more substantial omission is the line about her lips and mouth, which occurs in the first *wasf* at 4:3a. This poem simply has different emphases.

■ **8-9** **Queens** and **concubines** begin and end these three lines, an inclusio marking them as a distinct unit. Verse 8 reads, literally, ***Sixty queens they, and eighty concubines, and young women without number***. Several note that **sixty** and **eighty** are threescore and fourscore (Pope 1977, 568). They present a fulsome multiplication (3x20, 4x20) of the traditional "three—yes, even four" formula we see, for example, in Prov 30:15, 18, 21, 29.

Queens were not just anywhere; to imagine sixty of them is a remarkable number. Ancient Near Eastern kings, nobles, and other wealthy men regularly had **concubines**, but they were not just servant girls to whom the master had sexual access. A concubine had rights; essentially she was a secondary wife. It would have been a wealthy man indeed who could support eighty.

The NIV's **virgins** as a translation of 'almâ is indefensible (Song 6:8). The Hebrew 'almâ denotes **young women** of marriageable age, regardless of marital status or sexual experience. Depending on the situation, any woman between the ages of about twelve and twenty-five or so might have been designated an 'almâ. As a demographic set of ancient Israel, they would have been **beyond number**.

These three groups of women are introduced here as theoretical constructs, not as belonging to Solomon's harem chronicled in 1 Kgs 11:3. The Song does *not* say here that Solomon had experience of all these women, in his harem, only to find them wanting once he found the Shulammite. The Song *does* affirm that the man found his beloved unique among all women, represented poetically by **queens, concubines** and **young women**. A literal translation of Song 6:9 will demonstrate:

> **One is she, my dove, my perfect one.**
> > **One is she of her mother;**
> > **Chosen is she of the one who bore her.**

My dove: → 2:14.

My perfect one: → 5:2. This is the second, identical occurrence of these endearments together; the first is at 5:2. We could imagine the lover saying today, "Don't bother me about sixty, or eighty, or a countless crowd of women, no matter their 'quality.' She's my one and only; she's the one for me!"

6:10The man's reference here to her mother does not require us to understand his beloved was an only child. In 1:6, the woman spoke of her "mother's sons," and the speech of 8:8-9 is attributed to persons calling her their "little sister." Here, the matter could be as simple as the exuberant poetic license of one convinced that surely everyone must think as highly of his beloved as does he. It also could assert that his beloved was cherished by her mother; as this was not always the case for daughters in the androcentric cultures of the ANE, it is another mark of her merit.

Young women in 6:9 translates the Hebrew bānôt. Usually it is rendered "daughters," but here it is a synonym of 'ălāmôt in v 8. We think it makes sense to read this Hebrew line as not containing a definite article, and translate,

> **Young women saw her,**
> > **and they blessed her;**
> **Queens and concubines [*saw her*],**
> > **and they praised her.**

This closing of the inclusio reverses the order. Ordinary women all together, young women without number, acknowledge the worth of this woman. Then women of privilege, queens and concubines generally, not just specific individuals—whom we may have expected would assume themselves superior—instead join in praising this one.

■ **10** Though not obvious in English, the Hebrew text makes clear that these words describe the woman. The demonstrative (**this**) is feminine singular, as are the participle (*looking forth*) and the adjectives (*beautiful, shining, majestic*). The answer to the speaker's rhetorical **Who** is the woman, as also at 3:6 and 8:5.

These lines may have been spoken by "Friends" (with the NIV's heading); if so, they exemplify the praises of the women noted just above. Depending on the identity of the speaker of 6:11, this verse could have been spoken by the man. The laudatory intentions may be rendered vividly:

> **Who is this woman, the one peering forth**
> **like the dawn, beautiful as the moon,**
> **Shining like the sun, majestic as the starry hosts?**

All the possibilities of beauty in the heavens are inherent in this catalog, appointed to every potential and desirable effect.

First, the **dawn** peers forth, her pale glow coloring to rose and illumining every corner. In naming the heavenly bodies, neither **moon** nor **sun** is the usual Hebrew noun; we may say the speaker opted for more poetic usage. The **moon** ("the white one") is **fair**, exquisitely luminous, *beautiful*, as the man has portrayed his love multiple times already in the Song. The **sun** ("the hot one") shines so brilliantly no one can regard it full on, like that which had driven the man to ask his love to look away (v 5).

The phrase we have translated *majestic as the starry hosts* is identical with the Hebrew we rendered at v 4, *awesome as the things marveled at* (→ comments on *dgl* at 6:4 and 2:4). Here, in the context of **the dawn**, **the moon**, and **the sun**, *the things marveled at* can be only *the starry hosts*, including, as usual, the five planets visible to the naked eye.

Israel's neighbors regarded all these phenomena, including the dawn, as deities. The sun and moon were identified by some as male, by others as female. This is another reason the usual names of the sun and the moon are not used here, and the stars are subsumed under a single adjectival participle, "the starry hosts." Majestic and beautiful as all these are, faithful Israel knew they were not gods, but God's. For this same reason, the man's catalog here is a comparison of beauty with beauty, not a cunning ploy to designate his beloved a "goddess."

■ **11** These two Hebrew lines may have been spoken either by the man or by the woman. They contain no grammatical or syntactical clues to the speaker's identity, and the statement would be plausible coming from either.

The answer to the, "Who is this?" of v 10 must be "the woman." It would be natural, then, to identify her as the speaker in this verse, responding by saying where she was going. The sexual imagery of the **nut trees**, together with **the vines** and **the pomegranates**, support this reading.

Alternatively, to this point in the Song, the *garden* has been a metaphor for the woman, and the man has been the one to go there (e.g., 5:1; 6:2). The sexual imagery here can just as well refer to the woman as to the man, or even to both, enjoying together the springtime **new growth** and fruitfulness.

On the "literal" level, the verse is straightforward. **Grove of nut trees** (Heb.: *ginnat ʾĕgôz*). *Ginnat* is a synonym for "garden" that often denotes great wealth (see

6:11

Esth 1:5; 7:7-8). *'Ĕgôz* is the walnut, perhaps not native to the southern Levant, but reasonably inferred as one of Solomon's introductions (1 Kgs 4:33 [5:13 HB]). Two springs on the western edge of the Kidron Valley, Gihon and Rogel, provided ample water for royal gardens in that part of the valley. Perhaps from ancient memory, that section of the Kidron Valley, "between the Temple Hill and the Mount of Olives, . . . is still called by the Jerusalem Arabs *Wadi al-Joz*, 'Nut Valley'" (Pope 1977, 579). Pope also cites abundant evidence from western Asian and Mediterranean sources of the sexual associations of the walnut (and other nuts). The walnut is especially prominent because of its visual resemblance to both male testes and female vulva.

Longman on Song 6:11

The whole nut represents the male gland (even down to contemporary English slang), and the open nut, the woman's vulva. In any case, the verse as a whole is a coy suggestion of intimate relations between the man and the woman. When she talks of exploring the grove, she means that she will be exploring the man's body. Thus, whether we understand the imagery to refer to the place of lovemaking or the lover's private parts, or perhaps both, we understand the speaker to say that intimate union is in mind. (2001, 185)

The reference to **the new growth**, followed by mention of **the vines** and **the pomegranates**, is a reminder that a garden dominated by one species does not necessarily exclude others. In **the valley** were walnut grove, vineyard, and pomegranate orchard, contiguous with one another. Though this is the first mention of the nut in the Song, the lovers have spoken previously of the vine (→ 2:15) and the pomegranate (→ 4:13). As we have seen, these also have both erotic connotations and associations with fertility.

6:12

■ **12** As virtually every exegete has noted, the Hebrew of this verse is well-nigh intractable. For a detailed discussion of the issues, see Pope (1977, 584-92); Longman is more concise (2001, 185-87). Most take these as the woman's words. If they are, they probably belong with 6:11 as hers, also. One cannot make sense of this line without emendation, but adopting the smallest emendation possible, the deletion of a single *yôd* (the smallest letter of the Hebrew alphabet), we translate,

> *I did not know*
> *My life set me*
> *Chariotry*
> *With a noble man.*

We take this to mean: "Without my realizing it, my fancy/my desire set me in a chariot with a noble man."

If the woman spoke vv 11-12 in answer to the question of v 10, her statement of v 12 is a response to event(s) of v 11. In the Song, the woman is the "garden," but gardens also are the idyllic venues of the lovers' trysts; in v 11, this is **the grove of**

nut trees. This time, the lovemaking evoked for her a martial image: a horse-drawn chariot, expertly driven by a brave, skilled, and noble warrior.

The chariot was the ancient "tank," a fast and nimble archer's platform. The charioteer drove two or three horses for maximum speed and mobility; the quick-firing and deadly accurate archer wreaked havoc on foot soldiers within range of his bow. With her lover as vital partner in a swift and regal ride, experiencing the immediate rush both of pursuit and of triumph—this is a credible analogy for the mutual joys of lovemaking.

Desire translates the Hebrew *nepeš*. Its basic meaning is "life"; here the context calls for the nuance, "my self," that is, "my own desire, my inner self/imagination, roused by our lovemaking." (→ 1:7 and Behind the Text at 3:1-5.)

We have deleted the *yôd* in *ʿammî-nādîb* partly because retaining it and translating **my people** leaves *nādîb* with no cogent function in the sentence. We do not find it a credible move to combine the last two words as the proper name Amminadib or Amminadab. Here, *nādîb* is singular and functioning as a common noun; even if it were adjectival, it could not modify the plural "chariots."

Though *nādîb* means a **royal** [**man**], **a noble** [**man**], or **a prince**, this does not prove the man was Solomon. As noted previously, such terms often are used in love poetry to convey the loving regard of the speaker. Of royal blood or not (he may have been), in the eyes of the woman this was **a noble man**.

Any solution to the difficulties of this Hebrew line requires conjecture, and a suitable humility in the offering. We are confident in these proposals, but we do not imagine them to be the last word on Song 6:12.

■ **13 [7:1 HB]** If, as most agree, the friends called out the first line, **Come back**, this verse belongs with the dialogue of 6:10-12. However, there is plausible argument also for tying it with 7:1 [2 HB], as the last words of the one verse, **the dance of Mahanaim**, are followed immediately in the next by an exclamation on the beauty of the woman's "sandaled feet," the beginning of another *wasf*. The verse functions as a hinge between what comes before and what comes after.

Come back is a single Hebrew word, the imperative of *šûb*, "turn, return, come back." Repeated four times by the friends, it may be a call for the woman to come back from her imagined chariot ride with her lover, just mentioned (6:12). If, however, we translate *šûbî* as *Turn!* it becomes a simple request from the women for the Shulammite to turn herself more fully toward them, so they may see her better. Only now have they begun truly to appreciate this woman for all she is, as the man said they would (v 9).

That we may gaze on you affirms this understanding. This is not the usual word for "see" or "look." The Hebrew root is *ḥzh*, often used to speak of prophetic visions (see Num 24:4; Isa 30:10). If they could **gaze** intently on her—we almost may say, "study her"—they would enjoy the further opportunity of admiring, understanding, and praising her (Song 6:13). As Mark Twain opined, we love to stand in the reflection of greatness; that is not always a weakness.

The Hebrew definite article can have a vocative force, as it appears to, here: **O Shulammite**. The definite article precludes the possibility of taking this as the woman's personal name. From among the varied suggestions, probably it is a gentilic, designating her as a native of Shulam/Shunem, a town at the eastern edge of the Jezreel Valley. This naturally leads to the question of whether this woman was Abishag the Shunammite (1 Kgs 1:3; 2:17). Opinions are strong on both sides: This *must* be the same woman; this *cannot* be the same woman. As the only evidence for identifying them is this gentilic, we think this woman probably was *not* Abishag, though it is not impossible.

We think it more likely the *woman* spoke the next line, **How will you gaze?**, rather than the man, as the NIV has it. It is in direct response to the request of the women for her to "turn"; it would be more natural for the woman to evince this hesitation with the women, than for the man to do so, since he has anticipated they would do just that (Song 6:9).

With Pope, we think **Why** an infelicitous translation of *mah* (1977, 601). **How** retains the deliberate ambiguity of the question: "What will be your attitude as you gaze upon me?" "Do you need to stare at me more than you already have?" "Please do not stare at me anymore." All these and more are possible implications of **How will you gaze?** Perhaps she was reluctant to become a spectacle, no matter how sympathetically and admiringly regarded. In any case, if *she* asked this question, it is the perfect setup for the man's second full *wasf*, which follows.

In the MT, the last phrase is, literally, **as the dance of the two camps**. Jacob named the place of his wrestling with God "Mahanaim"/**the two camps** (Gen 32:2). Because of this, some have identified this verse as a reference to an otherwise unattested festival at Mahanaim, on the order of those noted in Judg 11:40; 21:19. Again, as the appropriation of a common noun as a place name is the only evidence, it hardly constitutes proof.

More likely is the suggestion of Carr and others, "the dance of the two groups" or "hosts" (1984, 155). On an occasion such as this, the two "hosts" were not armies (to which this noun often refers) but two groups (perhaps one of each gender, or one of each family) performing a counterpoint dance as a traditional feature of the wedding festivities. It will help us visualize the celebration to which she referred if we translate, **the dance of the two companies**.

FROM THE TEXT

The awesome majesty of the woman's presence, appearance, persona, is a major feature of this section. The man compared her to the great and beautiful cities of Tirzah and Jerusalem (v 4), even begging her to turn her overwhelming gaze from him (v 5). The "friends" considered her the equal of exquisite dawn, luminous moon, brilliant sun, and the entire heavenly host of stately planets and constellations.

By contrast, across much of history and through many cultures, gender relationships are marred, diminished, rendered sterile by men's denigration of women, by means ranging from colossal to trifling, as any woman could attest. What transformations might we see in homes, congregations, and the culture at large, if Christian men began to relate to the women they profess to love as the Song models and encourages? How greatly might love blossom and flourish? How quickly could the multiple forms of abuse and their resultant heartaches diminish, even disappear? These are not rhetorical questions. Learning to embrace the Song's assessments as reflecting God's intentions for gender interactions of comprehensive integrity is within the reach of men and women committed to following God in all things.

C. He: How Beautiful! How Pleasing! (7:1-9*a* [2-10*a* HB])

BEHIND THE TEXT

This section comprises the man's second full *wasf*, the songs in praise of the beloved. Given the woman's question referencing **the dance of the two companies**, it is fitting that this one begins with her "sandaled feet" and moves upward to her hair (7:5), before breaking to a more focused praise employing an extended metaphor. This reverses the order of his first *wasf*, (4:1-7), and of hers (5:10-16), which both began with consideration of the beloved's head. On differences in verse numbers, → Behind the Text at 6:4.

IN THE TEXT

■ **7:1 [2 HB]** We may translate either, *your feet in the sandals*, or *your dance-steps in the sandals*. Ornate sandals may have heightened the visual sensuality of the dance (see Jdt 16:9). Because this dual possibility directly follows the woman's mention of **the dance of the two companies** (6:13 [7:1 HB]), many take these lines to be reporting an actual dance performed for the man, with the onlookers as an additional audience.

While a dance here is not impossible, neither is it necessary. It seems more natural to take the woman's dance reference simply as an apt comparison with the onlookers' desire to gaze upon her, rather than as a report of her dancing. Beginning his *wasf* with her feet rather than with her head is first, then, a sign of attentiveness not only to her person but also to her words.

As in 6:12, *nādîb* ("prince") does not necessarily denote a person of royal or noble birth, though it may. Whether or not born into a noble household, in his eyes this was a noble woman, a **prince's daughter**.

We should translate the second line:

The curves of your thighs are like ornaments,
the work of the hands of a [consummate] artist.

This comparison of the human form with the work of a master sculptor we saw first in the woman's *wasf* in praise of the man, especially at 5:14-15. Only the finest jewelers could craft *ornaments* (jewels) of perfect symmetry in their curvature. Only the finest sculptors could craft a human likeness of perfect visual symmetry. This woman's thighs did not resemble jewels, nor were they adorned with ornamental jewels or precious metals. The point of this comparison is the curvilinear symmetry of her hips and thighs.

Hess on the *ʾĀmmān*

The term for "artist" (*ʾāmmān*) occurs only here and is never used for the Creator in the biblical text; yet the principle of one who forms what is beautiful is applicable (Ps 19). Thus there is an indirect allusion to God here. In fact, it is the allusive nature of the reference to God that serves the theological purpose of the Song. . . .

The language is about royalty and peasantry, about those who long for love and those who have found it, about the natural world and the supernatural sphere. The delights of the male in admiring his lover's curves fully embrace the carnal, but they do so in the recognition that this is good because it is more than carnal. . . . It points to God himself. Yet within the rules of such poetic language it cannot do this by naming the divine. Instead, the language of the joys of creation can never reach very far behind created things because it must always remain close to the carnal, the subject of the poem. Hence the male is still concerned for his lover even when he sees her beauty as part of a larger drama. Nevertheless, he remains enchanted by her so that the praise directed to her physical appearance becomes an expression of gratitude for the One who has made it all. (2005, 213)

■ **2 [3 HB]** Continuing upward, the man moved from simile (*like ornaments*) to metaphor: her **navel** was **a rounded goblet**; her **waist** was **a mound of wheat**. We do well to remember that metaphor conveys primarily a single emphatic comparison, at a point of vivid likeness, between two essentially unlike entities. Here, that central point of comparison in both metaphors is abundant fruitfulness, joyous plenty.

Several commentators take *šōr* (**navel**) as the vulva, citing a potential Arabic cognate, *sirr* (Pope 1997, 617; Carr 1984, 157). However, the arguments from various Semitic cognates is equally strong on both sides. Rather than argue from philology, then, we take **navel** as a euphemism for the vulva (following Longman 2001, 194-95). Again the point of comparison is critical to interpretation, which here is the containing of liquid (**wine** in the **goblet**). As Longman observes, "The navel is not a particularly moist location, whereas the vulva is, at least when sexually excited. . . . The description of the woman's aperture as containing wine implies the man's desire to drink from the sensual bowl" (2001, 194-95). A second compelling argument is the progression of the *waṣf*: the order upwards is *thighs*, *šōr*, **waist** (*beten*/**belly**). The vulva lies between the thighs and the waist.

Blended wine is a reasonable guess at the meaning of *mezeg*, a *hapax*. A probable cognate, *māsak*, always refers to mixing wine "either with water to dilute it or with spices and honey to strengthen it" (Carr 1984, 158).

Your waist translates the Hebrew *beten*, which means specifically, "womb"; here, it is an example of metonymy. We need not be so literally minded that we envision the woman carrying excess belly fat, and certainly this woman was not pregnant. Taken by itself, the lower torso of a reasonably fit woman is more or less rounded, precisely because of the womb.

In the agricultural context of the ANE, the comparison with **wheat** is significant. **Wheat** was the preferred grain for human consumption, yet after two or three generations of cultivation, many Mesopotamian regions had to switch from wheat to barley. Barley tolerates the increases in soil salinity caused by irrigation; wheat does not. Due to the annual inundation of the Nile, this was less of a problem in Egypt. Because the hill country required no irrigation (see Deut 8:7-8), wheat was an important export of both Israel and Judah (Ezek 27:17). **Wheat**, the staple of the daily diet, represented all the bounty of the land.

As throughout the Song, **lilies** should be *lotuses* (→ 2:1, 16; 6:2-3). They have already been associated with the intimacies of the breast (4:5). As the breasts are the subject of the next verse, this imagery continues here, as well. The lotus also adorned festive tables in Egypt and elsewhere, a connection further enhancing the image of fruitful plenty.

■ **3 [4 HB]** → 4:5.

■ **4 [5 HB]** **Like an ivory tower** is the third instance of the man praising the beauty of his beloved's neck (1:10; 4:4). In the previous verses, he mentioned the jewelry highlighting her natural loveliness. Here, the comparison of her unadorned neck with the smooth texture and luminescent tones of fine **ivory** intimates that such beauty really needs no embellishment.

Heshbon lay across the Jordan from Jerusalem. Excavation has uncovered reservoirs at the foot of Tel Hesban, the probable site of ancient Heshbon. The small tributary of the Jordan beside which the city was built provided ample water to keep them filled.

Pools translates the Hebrew *běrēkôt*, larger than wells, deeper than springs, connoting not so much the *source* of water as those do, but the *storage* of water. Deep, still pools (reservoirs)—their stone- and/or plaster-work perhaps adorned by artistic masonry—were a suitable metaphor for the woman's limpid and loving eyes. She already had intimated the sparkle of his eyes in comparing them to "doves by the water streams" (5:12). His metaphorical identification, **your eyes <u>are</u> the pools** of water, both alludes to and advances her earlier praise of his eyes. Such apt and thoughtful reciprocity of expression permeates the Song.

By the gate of Bath Rabbim has attracted many suggestions. The preposition *'al* offers a way forward; in some contexts, its connotation is similar to English "over against"; hence the NIV **by** is helpful. Pools/reservoirs could be located beside or near city gates, for the same reasons cities often grew up beside springs and wells. As defensive concerns arose, some cities enclosed their water sources, though Heshbon does not seem to have done so. This even may account for the visual aptness of the lover's metaphor: these beautiful pools were admired by everyone entering and exiting the city.

Bath Rabbim (lit. "the daughter of the many") may be the name of one of Heshbon's several city gates. If so, it could refer to the precinct of the city just inside the gate; to the area just outside the gate; to an otherwise unknown town or village, to which the road from the gate led; to the fact that many citizens exited and reentered through this gate every day; or to some other persons, place, or factor undiscoverable at this late date.

Hess on "Your Eyes Are the Pools"

The eyes provide a powerful magnet. . . . Like the pools, their reflection and beauty promise an abundant life. However, this is not to be enjoyed by all. Hence the pools themselves, like the eyes of the female, need to be guarded by the strongest towers possible. . . . Although [she is] alluring and desirable, the lover's description of his beloved values characteristics that suggest a personality at peace with itself and an internal strength of character. (2005, 216-17)

The line, **Your nose is like** a **tower**, jarring to Western readers, has elicited widely divergent interpretations through the centuries. Most we set aside, and note first that the point of the simile cannot be an outsized proportion of the nose to the woman's face, the image the modern mind is prone to leap to. The Hebrew phrase is naturally rendered, *like a tower of the Lebanon keeping watch toward Damascus*, a tower such as Solomon's architects certainly incorporated into his military outposts in the Lebanon mountains and elsewhere (1 Kgs 9:19).

A tower built on a mountain is not too large, but small in proportion to its mountain, to compare with a well-proportioned nose enhancing the beauty of a striking woman. The diversity of cultural beauty norms so often appealed to on this point is nowhere nearly broad enough to accommodate that interpretation in any culture. The metaphorical nicety lies elsewhere. Whatever its subsequent profile, a tower is built straight. So, too, whether seen face-to-face or in profile, a straight nose, unmarred by accident or disease, is regarded as comely.

■ **5 [6 HB]** This first segment of the man's *wasf* culminates in praise of the crown of her head. The MT pointing, *like the Carmel*, is reflected in the NIV's **Mount Carmel**. As many of the geographical *topoi* of the Song are northern (e.g., 4:8; 6:4), this reading is correct; he did not have in mind the southern (Judean) town of Carmel. Moreover, **Mount Carmel** is the crown and glory of the highlands south of Galilee. Its name, "the vineyard of God," reflects its status as Israel's garden spot. As Mount Carmel is perpetually forested, or lavishly productive in cultivation, so the beloved's head, her "crown," is gloriously adorned.

The Hebrew behind the NIV's **your hair** indicates unbound, unplaited tresses—combed but not restrained—flowing naturally to the beloved's neck and shoulders, a picture of life, health, and youthful vitality. The Hebrew 'argāmān can suggest the NIV's **royal tapestry**, but that is perhaps too interpretive. As the name of a color, 'argāmān often denotes purple, but it also can indicate shades of hair from crimson to reddish-brown, whether naturally colored or henna-dyed. It even may refer to the highlights of brown or black hair brought out by sunlight or moonlight.

Though the Hebrew text lacks the article, the NIV's **the king** is plausible. Elsewhere, he is called "the king" with no necessary reference to Solomon (→ 1:14). To confess being **held captive by** the beauty of her **tresses**, or perhaps with his fingers entwined in them, is a pleasant metaphor.

■ **6 [7 HB]** The man's praise of individual features of the woman's person has moved from her "sandaled feet" (v 1) to the "tresses" of her hair (v 5). It is feasible, as some do, to regard this verse as a summary exclamation of praise closing the *waṣf.* Others read it as the man's introduction to his proposal (vv 7-9a) to move from words to action. We need not choose; this is a transition verse, a hinge, serving both functions.

Thrice in 1:15-16, and twice in 4:1, the NIV translates the man's exclamation, "How beautiful you are . . . how beautiful!" (→ 1:15). Elsewhere, too, when speaking of the woman herself, the man and the "friends" use the adjectival form (1:8; 2:10, etc.), though not again with **Behold**/How (*hinnēh*). The woman also uses it of the man, once (1:16). Here, the Hebrew reads, **How beautiful you are**. The adverbial particle **How** aptly translates the Hebrew *mah*; here, **beautiful** is a verb, not an adjective. This also is the last time the root occurs in the Song; it is climactic.

This is poetry, employing stratagems both overt and subtle. Feminine forms of *yāpâ*, "beautiful," occur fifteen times in the Song; as noted, this is the climactic fifteenth. We cannot prove the poet's intention, but the reader may note that this is twice seven, plus one. In Hebrew thought, seven is a number of perfection, or completion; twice seven is doubly perfect. Twice perfect, plus one, is one step better, as Prov 30 famously demonstrates. The poetic framing is brief, elegant; the expository expansion, cumbersome, "How beautiful, both outwardly and inwardly, you are: twice perfect, and beyond!"

The second short clause is perfectly parallel, exhibiting also the adverbial particle followed by the verb, **How pleasant [delightful, lovely] you are!** It affirms both the beloved's physical beauty, and the reality that genuine beauty really is much more than skin deep.

My love, with your delights! is a plausible translation of the final two Hebrew words, but not the only one. Pope renders, "O love, daughter of delights" (1977, 593); Hess has, "O love, O daughter of pleasures" (2005, 218). These reflect a small, realistic, and defensible emendation, dividing *battaʿǎnûgîm,* "in/with delights/pleasures," into two words, *bat taʿǎnûgîm,* "(O) daughter of delights/pleasures." This can make sense.

7:6

185

We offer a new proposal. The verbal root of the second noun (*'ānōg*) means, "be soft, delicate, dainty." A woman's body is often experienced by her sexual partner as "soft, delicate, dainty." Her body parts are not themselves the **delights** or "pleasures," but catalysts for them, for both partners together. Moreover, perfectly good Hebrew words are available had the lover wanted to reference either **delights** or "pleasures." Thus, translating the plural noun *ta'ănûgîm* as **delights** or "pleasures" represents an interpretive move: not the "softness," "delicateness," or "daintiness" itself, but its putative outcome for the lover in the act of lovemaking.

For our part, setting aside the traditional move, we do not read this noun clause as referencing his own **delights** and "pleasures," or even theirs together, in the intricacies of their lovemaking. Rather, he truly celebrated his beloved, for herself, in her own right, in language of exquisite intimacy, tenderness, celebration, and tact. We translate the whole, ***How beautiful you are! Yes, how delightful (pleasant, lovely) you are, [my] love, in your softnesses.***

■ **7-8a [8-9a HB]** We translate:

> ***This, your stature (your bearing), is like the palm tree,***
> ***And your breasts [are like] clusters of fruit.***
> ***I said [to myself], "Let me climb the palm tree,***
> ***Let me grasp its fruit."***

The demonstrative (***this***) emphasizes the following noun (most basically, "standing," insufficient here). The mature date palm is tall and slender, epitomizing beauty in its profile and "stance." Her regal bearing emphasizes and enhances her beauty.

Keel demonstrates that feminine beauty and fertility have been symbolized by date palms and date clusters in the Middle East, virtually since the beginning of historical records (1994, 241-47). Modern-day Iraq (ancient Mesopotamia) cultivates more than one hundred varieties of dates, and date groves are nearly ubiquitous in Egypt's Nile Valley. We may assume dates were cultivated, as they are today, in the Jordan Valley from the Sea of Galilee to the shores of the Dead Sea. En Gedi and Jericho were (and are) noted for their palm trees (→ 1:14).

Dates grow in clusters; as the dates in a tree's several clusters enlarge and ripen, they bend downward on their fruit-stalks and hang suspended below the circle of fronds crowning the tall, slender trunk. The man compares his beloved's breasts with the shape of the entire cluster, not of a single date. In reference to dates, the Hebrew *'eškōlôt* (**clusters**) occurs only here; elsewhere, it usually means clusters of grapes. The sensual sweetness of the date also informs the metaphor.

Let me climb . . . let me grasp; here, the man is not asking the woman's permission to caress her breasts, though we may be sure this man would not do that without her assent. The verbal form expresses his internal decision to initiate this intimacy with her if, indeed, she does assent. Even when lovers are accustomed to intimacy, the initiative of one or the other usually occasions its renewal. Celebrating his love in the common metaphorical comparison with the prized date palm, he determined to take the initiative, to **climb the palm tree** and **grasp its fruit-stalks**, that is, move to caress her, and see what transpired.

■ **8b-9a [9b-10a HB]** The English verse division does not take into account the change of speaker at v 9b [10b HB]. This masks the progressive shortening of the man's last three lines, a device expressing here the building intensity of his longing. We translate:

> *Now may your two breasts be, I pray, like clusters of the grape,*
> *And the breath of your nostril like the apples,*
> *And your palate like the best wine.*

In the second and third lines, respectively, the NIV's **the fragrance of your breath**, and **your mouth**, express the lover's meaning. We have translated a bit more literally to underscore our point that the increasing intensity of his desire for her impels him to increasing urgency in his requests, causing and reflected in this shortening of his successive lines.

Of course the man hoped, after his initiative in v 8a, that they would make love. His image of date **clusters** high on the palm tree began a train of thought; here he altered his metaphor slightly, to **clusters of the grape** on the vine.

From **clusters of grapes**, the metaphorical chain naturally lengthens to include the apple, another common symbol and accessory of love (→ 2:5). As free-flowing thought will do, the metaphorical association reverts a step to wine, the most important of the several sensual products of the vine.

The fragrance of your breath like apples is a plausible rendering of a Hebrew line following in a natural parallelism with the previous line, and without apparent textual issues, despite some views to the contrary.

We have said 7:9a records the man's as-yet-unexpressed intent to initiate lovemaking. These lines express that intent, three spoken requests addressing her directly. As usual in Hebrew syntax, the first word is a verb, here followed by the common particle of entreaty, ***Now may they [your two breasts] be, please/I pray [you]***. Moreover, it also functions elliptically as the verb of the following lines, ***And [may] the breath of . . . [be, please,] like . . . ; And [may] your palate [be, please,] like***. The intensity of the man's ardor here equals that expressed by both lovers in various places throughout the Song. These lines stand as further assurance that coercion played no part in this relationship. Her response would determine what transpired.

In 2:3, the woman compared her love with the apple tree among the trees of the forest. In 2:5 (→), she appealed for the sustenance of "raisin cakes" and of apples. Here the man made his own use of traditional associations of grapes/wine/raisins and apples with love. Taking them up again, he also acknowledged his appreciation for her use of that same imagery in those earlier lines; what first was hers, and now was his, became the richer for both as "theirs."

FROM THE TEXT

Two revealing, helpful questions may occur to the reader:

1. Have I praised my love recently? In my own voice, but with something like the lavish poetic imagery of these lovers' praise for each other?
2. Do I emulate these lovers in practicing respect and noncoercion when I am the one to initiate lovemaking?

D. She: I Am My Beloved's! (7:9b [10b HB]— 8:4)

BEHIND THE TEXT

The woman's invitation, which drives this pericope, need not be read as only an excuse for time alone with her man (though it did provide that!), with no intention of observing the progress of the henna, grape, and pomegranate buds and blossoms. Modern readers often are several stages removed from direct daily contact with nature. Lines like these are a salutary reminder that the health and progress of crops and livestock have been necessary human concerns throughout history. Inattention or catastrophes always meant prolonged hardship and sometimes even death. All ancient Israelites (and others) observed, evaluated, and acted as necessary, whatever other interests may have brought them to their fields, orchards, and vineyards. They could not have done otherwise.

Verses 9b-13 [10b-14 HB] contain the woman's invitation to the man to join her for an outdoor tryst. Chapter 8 begins with an aside, a longing reflection that drives her to action. The section closes with the final instance of the woman's caution to the daughters of Jerusalem.

IN THE TEXT

■ **9b [10b HB]** Verse 9b [10b HB] is transitional, the woman's decidedly positive response to the man's requests, reflecting back to him his climactic metaphor of wine. Her own proposals follow, affirming his decision to speak.

With the NIV, we take the MT as preserving the correct reading, except that the initial *yôd* of the final word should be emended to *wāw* (as small a change as possible, correcting an understandable copyist's error). It follows that this is the woman's speech; she uses the term of endearment **my beloved** (*dôdî*) nearly thirty times throughout the Song, always of her lover. The group of "friends" echo the term back to her several times, but the man never uses it. (His endearment for her is **my darling**.)

In v 9a [10a HB], the man's requests end with the words, **the best wine**. Her response, following immediately, comes almost as an interruption, not actually using the term "wine." Representing the possibilities as literally as we can in English, she said, *It will go to my beloved straightly, flowing smoothly over [his] lips and teeth*. He asked for **the best wine**, here a metaphor for lovemaking. We take this as her response to him; given her Hebrew syntax, it is impossible to overestimate its nanosecond immediacy. His "May it be like . . . ," she greeted with, in effect,

"It's yours," or better, "It's ours." As we shall see (v 11 [12 HB]), she followed with, "Let's go!"

■ **10 [11 HB]** This four-word line is a literary/theatrical aside, spoken not to her beloved but to the hearer/reader. The first of its two clauses, **I belong to my beloved,** the woman had voiced twice before, though not identically (→ 2:16 and 6:3).

And his desire is for me closes her statement of confident solidarity this time. Many have noted that *tĕšûqâ* **(desire)** occurs only thrice in the OT. The first climaxes God's statement to the woman in Eden of consequences stemming from the alienation they had introduced. God's last words to her were, "Your desire will be for your husband, and [*but*] he will rule over you" (Gen 3:16). As we have discussed elsewhere, the man would turn her sexual desire for him against her, using its thrall to abrogate the equality of relationship for which God created humans (Coleson 2012, 138-39).

■ **11-12 [12-13 HB]** **Come, my beloved** returns her attention again to her lover; the woman's next lines unmistakably invite him to take what he asked for (v 11 [12 HB]. The first verb (*lĕkâ*) is imperative, 2ms, except that its suffix makes it akin to a cohortative. This both softens the imperative force, away from "command," and strengthens its loving urgency, **Come!**

The next four clauses all begin with 1cp verbs. Simply stated, she proposed an overnight trip into **the countryside:** *Let us go out,* **let us spend the night,** *let us rise early, let us see*. All are cohortatives (***Let us***), corresponding to the imperative in the second person, and affirming our understanding of **Come**, noted above.

The countryside (Heb.: *śādeh*), usually translated "field," meaning arable land surrounding and between towns and villages. This was not the "wilderness," as some suggest; that was *midbār*, which sustained only the grazing of sheep and goats. Confirming this within the passage is her stated purpose in going out: to check early development of grapes on the vine and pomegranates on the tree, fruits grown by settled agriculturalists.

The NIV note, "the henna bushes," fits the context; **villages** does not: **Let us spend the night** *among the henna shrubs*. Ancient Israelites did not say, *Let us go out to the field* (NIV: countryside), to arrive at a village. The woman proposed leaving human dwelling behind, so they could be alone and make love without being disturbed. As shepherds (→ 1:7-8), these two knew how to guard against (or thwart) attack by nocturnal predators, should any happen by.

Twice previously, the woman had mentioned henna (*kôper*), a common shrub in the eastern Mediterranean, growing as tall as ten feet high (→ 1:14). Whether cultivated grove or wild copse, a stand of henna shrubs in springtime would have been a perfect lovers' bower.

Let us go early; again, the verb form is cohortative, 1cp (7:12 [13 HB]). This verb, *rise/go early* (*šakām*), lends emphasis and urgency to the action proposed or taken; the woman was eager to do this. **To see** is the fourth and last of this cohortative verb chain. This and the next two lines we translate,

Let us see whether the vine has budded,

189

[whether] the blossom *[of the vine]* has opened,

[whether] the pomegranates have put forth *[their]* blossoms.

Certainly, this stated purpose lends "respectability" to her proposed excursion into *the field* (countryside). Yet, this hardly is the woman's purpose in issuing her invitation. The central message of the Song is that loving intimacy between a woman and a man free to commit to each other—expressed in ways that maintain and enhance their integrity, and that of their relationship—needs neither justification nor a veneer of respectability. It is, ipso facto, just and justified. On the vine and pomegranate in springtime, → 6:11.

There I will give you my love; this final line of the woman's invitation, proper, seems straightforward. If Hebrew *dôday* (plural noun with suffixed fs pronoun) is correct, we may read the plural, *my loves*, as singular (with NIV), and take it as a fulsome expression of her hope and intention, as the plural noun form is capable of projecting. Some ancient versions read, "There I will give you my breasts." In light of and by comparison with their same reading at 1:2, 4; 4:10, we conclude that "breasts" is possible here, but hardly plausible.

■ **13 [14 HB]** In Scripture, **mandrakes** are named only here and in the story of the "contest" between the sisters Rachel and Leah (Gen 30:14-16). The Hebrew name of the plant and its fruit, *dodai/doda'im* (from one of the roots meaning "love"; also called "love apple"), reflects its reputation as an aphrodisiac. It also forms a wordplay with *dôday* ("my loves") in v 12 [13 HB]. The mandrake blossoms in early spring, as noted here; the hazelnut-sized fruit ripens in late May-early June (see Gen 30:14).

Delicacy translates the Hebrew *mĕgādîm*, "excellence/ies," which is always used of the good things God provides in and through nature/creation (see Deut 33:13-16). That the woman spoke of these as lying **at our door** reflects the abundant fertility of the fields to which she was inviting the man for their tryst. As with many images of the Song, this also is a purposeful double entendre: their outdoor lovemaking would be the greatest natural *excellence* of this place. Her wordplay continued with her use of **door** (*petaḥ*: "door," "opening") as she offered herself to him. Lovers are permitted bold and vivid language with each other.

Speaking of the bounties of the field, the woman referenced the **new** yields of springtime: barley, leeks, greens, and other fresh plant foods, possibly even veal and lamb. **Old** certainly included wine, nuts, and dried fruits. Moreover, her phrasing, **every delicacy [*excellence*], both new and old**, also continues her celebration of their own lovemaking. Continuing to delight in each other, lovers treasure and re-experience their old ways, even as they learn more of each other, and together discover new and differently exciting ways of loving.

■ **8:1** In the context of their private rendezvous in the vineyard, v 1 expresses the woman's longing for a contrasting reality. She wished they could embrace in public, but that was an affection only allowed between siblings (or cousins, Gen 29:11). Even betrothed or married couples would be **despised** for kissing in the street.

7:13—
8:1

Her wish that the man was **like a brother** is a clever play on his repeated endearment, "my sister" (4:9, 10, 12; 5:1, 2; → Behind the Text at 4:8). The woman longed to inhabit such a permissive space with her beloved. **Nursed at my mother's breasts** designates the full-blooded connection most likely to result in such sibling affection; children from the same father but different mothers more commonly experienced rivalry than natural warmth.

■ **2** Moving from wishing to action, the woman determined to take him home. With Exum, we leave the optative ("I wish . . . I would") behind in v 1, and translate the verbs of v 2 as the future imperfects they are: *I will lead you . . . I will bring you . . . I will give you to drink* (2005, 246). On **my mother's house**, → 3:4.

The exact import of **she who has taught me** is elusive. What had her mother taught her: the ways of love? Of hospitality? The refreshments mentioned convinces some of the latter, but this refreshment is clearly euphemistic. Teaching the skills of love-play is a concept foreign to the Song, and as Exum observes, this young woman needed no such instruction (2005, 247). It could as easily be a reference to the general instruction mothers gave in preparing daughters to manage a household. Pope follows the LXX, emending the Hebrew from *tlmdny* to *tldny*, "she who bore me." It makes sense in the context of the passage, and also brings this into tighter parallel with the text of 3:4, "brought him to my mother's house, to the room of the one who conceived me."

Spiced wine is a luxurious elevation of the "regular" wine referenced as a fruit of love throughout the Song (1:2, 4; 4:10; 5:1; 7:2, 9 [3, 10 HB]). When coupled with **the nectar of my pomegranates** (→ 4:3, 13 and 6:7), it is clear the man was being offered a decadent, figurative treat, the gifts of the woman's body as she offered herself to him.

■ **3** This aside opened in v 1 with a wish. It continued in v 2 with the woman planning to take action. As throughout the Song, the movement between anticipation of lovemaking and its fulfillment is fluid here in these three verses, but now the lovemaking had become present tense. This verse repeats 2:6 (→) exactly.

■ **4** On **daughters of Jerusalem** → 1:5. This verse is a shortened version of the woman's urging at 2:7 and 3:5 (→ 2:7). Here she omitted the "guarantors" of the oath, "by the gazelles or by the hinds of the field," by which she had bound the women previously.

Carr anticipates Exum in proposing that the smaller textual difference is more significant (1984, 168). The negative particle *'im*, occurring twice in the last line on both previous occasions, here is replaced twice with *mah*. Most commentators take *mah* here in (an uncommon) negative sense, and retain the traditional reading, *Do not arouse and do not waken love until it desires/pleases*. This third repetition of the "instruction" concludes another major section of the Song.

FROM THE TEXT

The Song's celebration of nature, in the context of and including human sexuality (as in 7:12 [13 HB]), stands as a corrective to the (ultimately) pantheistic polytheism of Israel's neighbors, to which Israel also was constantly succumbing. It also corrects the Platonic Gnosticism that plagued Second Temple Judaism and much of the early church, and that continues as a major heretical stain and stumbling block upon and within the church today.

The Shulammite's delighted declaration (vv 9b-13 [10b-14 HB]) is a reminder that not all is lost. God's intention in creation is unconstrained sexual (and other) reciprocity between a man and a woman, committed to each other and relishing the expression and fulfillment of their mutual desire. The Song—implicitly throughout, explicitly in this simple, yet profound, statement of her satisfaction in his desire for her—announces that God's redemption reaches to the innermost secrets of human intimacy. Moreover, as with much else in God's redemptive action, this joy need not wait; here, it is begun already.

Trible on "For Me Is His Desire"

In Eden, the yearning of the woman for harmony with her man continued after disobedience. Yet the man did not reciprocate; instead, he ruled over her to destroy unity and pervert sexuality. Her desire became his dominion. But in the Song, male power vanishes. His desire becomes her delight. Another consequence of disobedience is thus redeemed through the recovery of mutuality in the garden of eroticism. Appropriately, the woman sings the lyrics of this grace: "I am my lover's and for me is his desire." (1978, 160)

VI. ENDURING LOVE, HERS TO GIVE: SONG OF SONGS 8:5-14

BEHIND THE TEXT

The Song ends with a series of short speeches that establish the couple in their love. The friends greeted the returning couple with a familiar question, "Who is this?" (8:5a). The speaker shifts mid-verse to the woman, who didn't answer her friends but addressed her lover directly, invoking their lovemaking, and that of his own parents, with a cherished outdoor bower as witness. She pronounced over him the power of love to give and protect life (vv 5b-7).

The woman's brothers attempted to intervene in vv 8-9. She responded directly in v 10, continuing in vv 11-12 with the assertion that her vineyard was her own to give; they had no say in the matter. For its time, this is a bold assertion, indeed, but when throughout the Song has this woman not been her own person? Hearing the exchange, her love entreated her to speak to him (v 13). She responded (v 14) in the erotic imagery of their dialogue throughout, a fitting curtain to the written romance, at once tender and adventurous, which is the Song.

■ **5** The first line of this question has been asked before in the Song, **Who is this coming up from the wilderness?** In 3:6, it turned out to be a magnificent equipage bringing the man in the guise of Solomon. A second time, the friends asked, "Who is this that appears like the dawn?" and it was the woman in all her majestic beauty (6:10). Now the friends asked again, observing the couple returning to town after their rendezvous. They knew full well who she was this time, and likely what the lovers had been up to.

In using the term **beloved**, the friends bring a satisfactory closure to their observation of the couple throughout the Song. They have teased the woman with, "How is your beloved better than others" (5:9), and then asked, "Where has your beloved gone?" (6:1). Now the friends signal their benevolent acceptance of the pair, receiving them home as it were.

The apple tree and its fruit enlivened the couple's love talk at several points (2:3, 5; 7:8 [9 HB]). In this passage, she could be citing their most recent assignation; an apple tree would make for a fragrant bower. The woman's reference to the man's **mother** conceiving him in the same place where his lover **roused** him is jarring to modern readers, who want to keep any idea of parental sexual activity as far from their own as possible. Ancient cultures were not as squeamish; it was an effective way to express an implicit hope for conception, in a previously fortuitous location. Its full significance will be made clear by the next two verses.

8:5-6

The last two lines build up a striking emphasis through the use of an artful chiasm in synonymous parallelism that is obscured in most English translations. The verb in question is *ḥbl*, which in the *pi'el* stem means either "conceive" or "travail (in labor)." With Longman, we see "conceive" as the most natural connotation in the context of erotic poetry (2001, 207 n. 12). Instead of the NIV's **conceived . . . was in labor**, and maintaining Hebrew word order, we translate both occurrences as *conceived* to restore the parallelism:

| *There* | *your mother* | *conceived you,* |
| *There* | *she conceived you* | *who gave you birth.* |

■ **6** The woman continued her admonition with what many identify as the most resonant verses in the whole Song. This is the only place where the Song diverges from the particular love of two specific people to consider the essential nature of love. She called on the one to whom she'd given herself to cherish their love, using the metaphor of a **seal** (Heb.: *ḥôtām*, from the same root as the seal over the spring in 4:12). Levantine seals are known in two forms: engraved cylinder seal and flat, stamp-like signets, worn variously threaded on string around the neck (i.e., **over your heart**), or as a ring or bracelet (**on your arm**). It was the guarantee of the holder's identity, their seal of approval, their signature on contracts. The woman called her lover here to make her the signifying feature of his identity, to keep her close and to be known by his relationship to her.

This was not, as some have argued, an attempt to stake her claim upon him, like a gaudy tattoo to warn away interlopers. That is a tragic diminishing of their love, often read into the passage due to mistranslating the word *qin'â* in the next line as **jealousy**. Instead, the seals worn on one's person, "with their ornamentation, symbols, and portrayals of the gods, functioned as amulets" (Keel 1994, 272). The seal of their solidarity would give him strength and protection, like an amulet. With her on his **heart** and **arm**, he would be protected by **love** itself.

The astonishing capacities of love are what she had in view here. It is ***stronger than death***; though the typical Hebrew comparative construction is missing here, the poet cannot mean only **as strong as death**. What good is love that is only as strong as its opponent? These two lines form another synonymous parallelism, often obscured by a misleading translation: the synonyms are *'ahăvâ* (**love**) and *qin'â* (ardor). We translate:

> **For stronger than death is love**
> **Fiercer than Sheol is ardor.**

Though *qin'â* can mean **jealousy**, the English word has alarming connotations for modern readers. The woman's whole point was that love is mighty, powerful against even the forces of death. Jealousy may give a temporary surge of angry strength, but it has no power to sustain in the long run and most often leads to the death of love, not its preservation. (As studies in domestic violence have shown, jealousy in romantic partnerships leads, tragically often, to abuse and even death.) *Ardor*, on the other hand, is the connotation of the noun in passages where the Lord himself defends his beloved people (Isa 9:6 [5 HB]; 42:13; 63:15).

In OT thought, **Sheol** (the grave) is the morally neutral destination of the dead. It is the Hebrew forerunner of the Greek concept of Hades but has no attending sense of judgment or punishment. It represents the end of life, the thief of joy, and the fate of fading into obscurity, but ardor is stronger and more determined than this most inevitable of human experiences.

The last line characterizes love as a **fire**, using the uncommon noun *rešep*, which names the part of a fire that reaches out: ***flame*** (Ps 78:48), ***spark*** (Job 5:7), or ***lightning bolt*** (Ps 78:48). The final word of the sentence has elicited much discussion: *šalhebet* is the even rarer noun **flame**, occurring only here and in Ezek 21:3 and Job 15:30. Here its extra syllable, *šalhebetyâ*, is the focus of the debate. *Yâ* is a shortened form of the divine name of Israel's God, Yahweh, and could render the noun, ***flame of Yah***. But sometimes Hebrew appends the divine name as an intensifier, thus the NIV **mighty flame**.

There is no other mention of Yahweh in the Song. Does this verse intend to invoke Israel's God here, as the crowning source of love's power? Or is the poet continuing the pattern of the Song, what Longman calls "a conscious avoidance of specific reference to God" (2001, 213 n. 34)? Is this an intentional wordplay to *prompt*, rather than *answer*, questions about love? The latter certainly aligns with the purpose and method of wisdom literature generally: to prod, to explore, to consider questions, without ever settling too absolutely on an answer.

Augustine on 8:6

> When death comes, it cannot be resisted. By whatever arts, whatever medicines, you meet it; the violence of death can none avoid who is born mortal; so against the violence of love can the world do nothing. For from the contrary the similitude is made of death; for as death is most violent to take away, so love is most violent to save. Through love many have died to the world, to live to God. (Wright 2005, 365)

■ **7** The metaphor of love as a mighty fire is extended into this verse. Fire is famously susceptible to water, but the fire of **love** cannot be quenched, even by **many waters**. Even the water of multiple **rivers** would be insufficient to extinguish its flame with *flooding* (NIV: **sweep . . . away**).

Such a durable power as love, she argued, is worth more than **all the wealth of one's house**. Death, the grave, water, even money: the most powerful forces in the human realm will fail before they defeat love.

With the whole short speech in view, the import of love and conception under the apple tree (v 5) now is clear. The power of love brought her beloved into life under the apple tree. It will now protect him even against death and all the chaos between conception and the grave. Love is therefore his most valuable possession.

■ **8-9** This may be the woman quoting an earlier family assertion that begins, literally, **We have a** *young* [little] **sister**, *and she has no breasts* (v 8). If, however, this is "real time" dialogue, her siblings are speaking for themselves, not actually having noticed her in some time, and still thinking of her as prepubescent. As is well-known, girls in the ancient world were considered ready for marriage at puberty, which could happen around age twelve or thirteen, though usually it occurred a bit later.

Given their earlier anger (1:6), her siblings' query and their proposed "solution" could reflect their fears for the family reputation. Alternatively, they may have been expressing a genuine care for her. They regarded themselves as responsible to protect her and also to protect the family from any too-early sexual expression on her part. The import of their query is, **What shall we do for** [or, *to*] **our sister** [to keep her a virgin] until **the day she is spoken for?**

Their proposals (8:9) consist in precisely parallel lines:

If a wall she (is), we will build upon her a silver turret;
If a door she (is), we will secure upon her cedar planking.

Keel rightly notes that **door** here translates *delet*, the (usually) wooden flat structure closing an opening, not *petaḥ*, the opening itself (1994, 279). This would seem to confirm that the parallelism here is synonymous, not antithetical. Both lines emphasize the siblings' resolve to protect their **little sister** from too-early sexual experience, whether or not she wanted to open her "door" before she was spoken for (v 8).

Literal walls can be breached; ancient builders often used stone turrets or battlements of varied design to buttress the defenses of city walls. Just so, the siblings thought to ensure against the **wall**—their little sister—being "breached" before her proper time. Though a turret would not have been wholly of silver, any silver ornamentation would have embellished the beauty of the walls, and thus of the city itself (see the "shields" of 4:4).

Door, though a different metaphor, offers the same meaning. Closed doors prevent entry; open doors allow it, and may be regarded as invitation. The siblings envisioned reinforcing the existing "door" with **cedar** planking (lit. board[s] of cedar), doubling its thickness and strength. Their little sister, and the family honor, would be well protected.

■ **10** The woman ended the matter by declaring emphatically, **I am a wall**. She was a mature woman; her **breasts**, which they thought hadn't developed yet, were in fact **like towers**. That these "towers" stood upon the "wall" is her assertion not only of mature womanhood ready for marriage, but also that, as a "wall," she had not been breached. The metaphor maintains its consistency; towers anchoring city defenses do not stand proudly unscathed as a city is conquered. If this woman had known her lover (as so many earlier passages intimate), it was not because he "conquered" her. She had accepted him willingly and joyfully.

Her statement also is a confident assertion of her beauty and desirability. Her lover had praised the perfection of her breasts (4:5, 7; 7:3, 7-8 [4, 8-9 HB]). Here, rather than demurring out of a false or misplaced modesty, she agreed.

Thus . . . contentment is not just an implication; it is a statement to the woman's siblings that she had chosen her own man. **I have become** translates the Hebrew verb as a stative, **I have become *and I continue to be***. **In his eyes** is idiomatic, "This is who and what I am to him." An obvious implication: not only he, but she also, was glad of that.

One bringing contentment reads *môṣ'ēt* as a *hip'il* (causative) participle from *yāṣā'* ("to bring"). We also may read *mots'et* as a *qal* participle from another weak verb, *māṣā'* ("to find"), and translate **one finding shalom**. We are not forced to choose. Not only does grammar allow for both readings, but this is poetry; the "ambiguity" is intended. The woman brings *shalom* to the man; she finds her *shalom* in him. We need not be surprised to find this reciprocity here; the lovers have insisted on it throughout the Song.

Contentment renders Hebrew *shalom*, most often translated, "peace." However, *shalom* is more than absence of conflict. Its basic sense is "completion": nothing needed for wholeness or well-being is lacking. The woman brought to the man, and herself experienced, **contentment**, fulfillment, wholeness, total well-being, *shalom*.

■ **11-12** At face value, these verses rebuke the wealthy and powerful Solomon. Sovereign though he was, he possessed no right to the woman, who already in 1:6 had identified herself metaphorically as a "vineyard." Interpretive differences lie in

8:10-12

identifying the speaker and in discerning what is "literal" and what is metaphorical (see Pope 1977, 686-93).

If Baal Hamon is a geographical location, the most likely candidate is Belemoth/Ibleam in the Dothan Valley; it would have been one of Solomon's royal estates in the north. Because "Baal Hamon" can be translated "Lord of the many (or crowd)," some take this as a reference, not to viticulture, but to Solomon's harem, numbering seven hundred wives and three hundred concubines (1 Kgs 11:3).

Whether vines or women, the point of reintroducing Solomon here is that he could not have cared for such a vast "estate" by himself; thus, the need for **tenants** (Song 8:11). If the reference is to vines, for the portion of the vineyard he leased, each **tenant** was to pay an annual rent of **a thousand shekels of silver**. If Hebrew *notĕrîm* bears both meanings—**tenants** (v 11) and **those who tend its fruit** (v 12)— then each **tenant** also paid day laborers about two hundred shekels in toto to work the vineyard, pruning, harvesting, and so forth. Thus, each tenant's annual cost was twelve hundred shekels; any harvest value above that was profit.

If **vineyard** is a metaphor referencing Solomon's harem, numbers are not so easily assigned. However, the presence of guards, overseers, and other male functionaries in and for royal harems is a widely known phenomenon. Moreover, these men were less often eunuchs than is commonly assumed today. The dangers to Solomon's ownership and control of such a "vineyard" are as self-evident as the fact that he could not personally tend a working vineyard of grapevines by himself.

The first three words of v 12 are the crux of the matter. We may translate, accurately if not elegantly, *My vineyard, which is mine, is before me. Before me* means not only in front of me, within my sight, but also "in my possession, to do with as I will." Solomon could not do all he wanted with his vast "vineyard," whether grapevines or wives, simply because there were too many. The speaker, who reintroduced Solomon here precisely to make this point, *could* dispose of **my own vineyard** as he or she pleased.

So, who is the speaker? Some say the man, citing his publicly proclaimed preference for this woman over an infinite number of others, whether of high estate or low (6:8-9). We lay greater emphasis on the woman's declaration early in the Song that her vineyard was her own (1:6). She retained total control over her "vineyard," to withhold or bestow as she desired. She had bestowed, and no one—not Solomon, not her brothers—could reverse her decision. Her emphatic declaration, *My vineyard, which is mine, is before me [to do with as I please]*, is a quintessential declaration of God-given right and rights, more than two millennia before King John's Magna Carta acknowledgment in 1215 that, under God, royal power has real limits.

■ **13** If vv 8-12 present a real-time exchange between the woman and her siblings, the reader may envision the man (over)hearing, and responding to her emphatic declaration of their love. For this scene, the NIV's **dwell** is too permanent an image. We translate, *Oh, you who are sitting within the gardens [i.e., at home], with [your] friends in attendance, cause [i.e., please allow] me to hear your voice.*

This pair had ventured out, both separately and together; establishing their relationship had not been easy. Now, finding her at home among her friends, having heard her declare her resolve to her siblings, the man expressed only the longing for permanence: to be at home with her, to have her at home with him.

■ **14** The woman's response was simple, elegant, fraught, "a reprise of many of the longings of earlier passages in the Song" (Carr 1984, 175). It recalls 2:17, without repeating it verbatim. *Dôdî* had been the woman's endearment throughout; of course, she would call him **my beloved** one final time.

Come away is scarcely powerful enough. "Bolt" (Pope 1977, 654) conveys the intended vigor of the woman's invitation: "Run to me with all the power and speed you can summon." Moreover, the verb (*bāraḥ*) carries another double entendre: to bolt can be to run through or into, and a bolt can enter or pierce. When he accepted her invitation, she would be ready for him.

Be like here is not the preposition, *kĕ*, but an imperative verb form, *dĕmeh*, the same root as in Gen 1:26, "resembling us; according to our likeness." She urged him to "resemble" the buck of the **gazelle**, or the **young stag** of the deer in its speed across the mountains. She had used this image of him already in Song 2:9, 17.

On **the spice-laden mountains**, → 4:10.

FROM THE TEXT

Some interpreters wonder at this "abrupt" end to the Song. We remind ourselves again that the Song is poetry. A poetic composition *may* have a plot; if it does, it also may have a tidy ending. Most poems, however, do not feature readily discernible plots. In this regard, the Song belongs in the company of "most poetry." The reader is invited to embrace the conviction that the man accepted this final invitation with alacrity. Her invitation as the closing of the poem (and the door upon all bystanders) is, then, simply another way to frame that happiest of endings, "And they lived happily ever after."

The appeal of that formula in fairy tales is precisely that we understand it can be so, and it should be so. The Song is one of the many witnesses in Scripture that God's redemptive purposes make it so for those who put their trust in God. If the love portrayed in the Song proves to be only a foretaste of that love the redeemed will experience with God eternally, then of course the fullness must be greater than the foretaste, and we cannot, will not, be disappointed in that.

ESTHER
Elaine Bernius

DEDICATION

This book is dedicated to my mother, Edwina Marie Case Davis,
a true transmitter of relief and deliverance in this world;
and to my children, Todd Matthew, Asher Elizabeth,
Ruth Edwina, and Lydia Elise—
may you grow and flourish in the shadow of
her beautiful heritage.

ACKNOWLEDGMENTS

As Esther has taught me, I write this as a record of remembrance of all of those who have walked with me on this journey of discovery and growth.

First, I acknowledge the love, care, and sacrifice of my family. Thank you, Brian, for being my steady rock, my sounding board, my biggest fan, and my sure haven. I am so thankful to share all of life with you. Todd, your precious gift of encouragement lifts my heart so many days. I pray you will always shine that light into this world and that this work may nurture your love for your Lord. I give my thanks and love to my girls, Asher and Ruth, whose delight in stories of all kinds keeps bringing me to the word with wide-eyed wonder. May you both grow to know and treasure your cherished place in this ultimate story more than any other.

There are so many who have read portions of this work along the way, who have let me process my ideas aloud, and who have dug into the text alongside me to share perspectives and insights. I am so grateful for your generous contributions and your loving corrections. My thanks to my editor, Alex Varughese, for his wise counsel and guidance and for entrusting me with this project. To my brilliant colleagues who made this work so much better along the way—Brian Bernius, Keith Drury, Ken Schenck, Lenny Luchetti, Steve Lennox, Amanda Drury, and Chris Bounds. This was all given from extra time that none of you have. Thanks for that sacrifice. It is a joy to minister alongside you and learn from you. To dear family and friends who read from different perspectives and brought so much richness of insights—Chuck Davis, Juli Harmon, and Deven Swan. To John Harmon who gave many hours to the tedious work of checking my Hebrew, providing fabulous suggestions along the way. Any mistakes that are still in here are all on me, John! To many classes of students at Indiana Wesleyan University who were gracious in listening to longer lectures about Esther and driving me back to the text and to my knees, and in particular to Devin Drake whose enthusiasm for Esther and all biblical literature truly inspires me. To Bible study groups at Marion First Church of the Nazarene, you pushed me to get to where the rubber meets the road. It is my privilege to share life with you as the family of God.

Finally, I give all praise to the Lord God, Father, Son, and Spirit, who has delivered me from the bondage of sin and self and has brought me into his abundant life of rest and relief.

BIBLIOGRAPHY

Anderson, B. W. 1954. Esther: Introduction, Text, Exegesis, and Exposition. Pages 822-74 in Vol. 3 of *The Interpreter's Bible*. Edited by George Arthur Buttrick. New York: Abingdon-Cokesbury Press.

Arnold, Bill T. 1998. *Encountering the Book of Genesis*. Grand Rapids: Baker Books.

Arnold, Bill T., and John H. Choi. 2003. *A Guide to Biblical Hebrew Syntax*. Cambridge: Cambridge University Press.

Baldwin, Joyce G. 1984. *Esther: An Introduction and Commentary*. Tyndale Old Testament Commentaries. Downers Grove, IL: InterVarsity Press.

Bechtel, Carol M. 1989. *Esther*. Interpretation: A Bible Commentary for Teaching and Preaching. Louisville, KY: John Knox Press.

Ben-Dov, Jonathan. 1999. A Presumed Citation of Esther 3:7 in 4QD^b. *Dead Sea Discoveries* 6:282-84.

Bennett, Stephen J. 2010. *Ecclesiastes/Lamentations: A Commentary in the Wesleyan Tradition*. New Beacon Bible Commentary. Kansas City: Beacon Hill Press of Kansas City.

Bergey, Ron L. 1984. Late Linguistic Features in Esther. *The Jewish Quarterly Review* 75:66-78.

Berlin, Adele. 1983. *Poetics and Interpretation of Biblical Narrative*. Sheffield, England: Almond Press.

_____. 2001. *Esther*. The JPS Bible Commentary. Philadelphia: Jewish Publication Society.

Bickerman, Elias. 1967. *Four Strange Books of the Bible*. New York: Schocken Books.

Blumenthal, David R. 1995. Where God Is Not: The Book of Esther and Song of Songs. *Judaism* 44:80-92.

Branson, Robert D. 2009. *Judges: A Commentary in the Wesleyan Tradition*. New Beacon Bible Commentary. Kansas City: Beacon Hill Press of Kansas City.

Briant, Pierre. 2002. *From Cyrus to Alexander: A History of the Persian Empire*. Translated by Peter T. Daniels. Winona Lake, IN: Eisenbrauns.

Brower, Kent E. 2013. Scripture, Wesleyan Approach to. Pages 488-89 in *Global Wesleyan Dictionary of Theology*. Edited by Al Truesdale. Kansas City: Beacon Hill Press of Kansas City.

Bush, Frederic W. 1996. *Ruth, Esther*. Word Biblical Commentary. Waco, TX: Word Books.

_____. 1998. The Book of Esther: Opus non gratum in the Christian Canon. *Bulletin for Biblical Research* 8:39-54.

Cameron, George G. 1973. The Persian Satrapies and Related Matters. *Journal of Near Eastern Studies* 32:47-56.

Cherry, Constance M. 2010. *The Worship Architect: A Blueprint for Designing Culturally Relevant and Biblically Faithful Services*. Grand Rapids: Baker Academic.

Clapper, Gregory S. 2013. Scripture, Theology of. Pages 486-88 in *Global Wesleyan Dictionary of Theology*. Edited by Al Truesdale. Kansas City: Beacon Hill Press of Kansas City.

Clines, David J. A. 1984a. *The Esther Scroll: The Story of the Story*. JSOT Supplement Series 30. Sheffield, England: JSOT Press.

_____. 1984b. *Ezra, Nehemiah, Esther*. New Century Bible Commentary. Grand Rapids: Eerdmans.

_____. 1990. Reading Esther from Left to Right: Contemporary Strategies for Reading a Biblical Text. Pages 31-52 in *The Bible in Three Dimensions: Essays in Celebration of Forty Years of Biblical Studies in the University of Sheffield*. Edited by David J. A. Clines, Stephen E. Fowl, and Stanley E. Porter. JSOT Supplement Series 87. Sheffield, England: JSOT Press.

_____. 1991. In Quest of the Historical Mordecai. *Vetus Testamentum* 41:129-36.

Collins, Kenneth J. 2007. *The Theology of John Wesley: Holy Love and the Shape of Grace*. Nashville: Abingdon Press.

Conti, Marco, ed. 2008. *1-2 Kings, 1-2 Chronicles, Ezra, Nehemiah, Esther*. In Collaboration with Gianluca Pilara. Vol. V of Ancient Christian Commentary on Scripture. Edited by Thomas C. Oden. Downers Grove, IL: InterVarsity Press.

Craig, Kenneth M. 1995. *Reading Esther: A Case for the Literary Carnivalesque*. Louisville, KY: Westminster John Knox.

Creach, Jerome F. D. 2003. *Joshua*. Interpretation: A Bible Commentary for Teaching and Preaching. Edited by James Luther Mays, Patrick D. Miller, and Paul J. Achtemeier. Louisville, KY: John Knox Press.

Daube, David. 1946. The Last Chapter of Esther. *The Jewish Quarterly Review* 37:139-47.

Day, Linda M. 1995. *Three Faces of a Queen: Characterization in the Books of Esther*. JSOT Supplement Series 186. Sheffield, England: Sheffield Academic Press.

_____. 2005. *Esther*. Abingdon Old Testament Commentaries. Nashville: Abingdon Press.

Dorothy, Charles V. 1997. *The Books of Esther: Structure, Genre, and Textual Integrity*. Sheffield, England: Sheffield Academic Press.

Driver, Godfrey Rolles. 1954. Problems and Solutions. *Vetus Testamentum* 4:225-45.

Drury, Keith. 2005. *With Unveiled Faces: Experience Intimacy with God through Spiritual Disciplines*. Indianapolis: Wesleyan Publishing House.

Edlin, Jim. 2009. *Daniel: A Commentary in the Wesleyan Tradition*. New Beacon Bible Commentary. Kansas City: Beacon Hill Press of Kansas City.

Feldman, Louis H. 1970. Hellenizations in Josephus' Version of Esther. *Transactions and Proceedings of the American Philological Association* 101:143-70.

Fox, Michael V. 2001. *Character and Ideology in the Book of Esther*. 2nd ed. Grand Rapids: Eerdmans.

Gehman, Henry Snyder. 1924. Notes on the Persian Words in the Book of Esther. *Journal of Biblical Literature* 43:321-28.

Gershevitch, Ilya, ed. 1985. *The Cambridge History of Iran*. Vol 2: *The Median and Achaemenian Periods*. Cambridge: Cambridge University Press.

Gordis, Robert. 1976. Studies in the Esther Narrative. *Journal of Biblical Literature* 95:43-58.

_____. 1981. Religion, Wisdom and History in the Book of Esther: A New Solution to an Ancient Crux. *Journal of Biblical Literature* 100:359-88.

Green, Joel B. 2010. *Reading Scripture as Wesleyans*. Nashville: Abingdon Press.

Hadley, J. M. 2005. Hebrew Inscriptions. Pages 366-80 in *Dictionary of the Old Testament: Historical Books*. Edited by Bill T. Arnold and H. G. M. Williamson. Downers Grove, IL: IVP Academic.

Hallo, William W. 1983. The First Purim. *Biblical Archaeologist* 46:19-26.

_____, ed. 1997. *The Context of Scripture*. Associate editor, K. L. Younger. Leiden; New York: E. J. Brill.

Hamilton, Victor. 2001. *Handbook on the Historical Books*. Grand Rapids: Baker Academic.

Herodotus. 1920. Translated by A. D. Godley. 4 vols. Cambridge, MA: Harvard University Press.

Huehnergard, John, and Harold Liebowitz. 2013. The Biblical Prohibition against Tattooing. *Vetus Testamentum* 63:59-77.

Humphreys, W. Lee. 1973. A Life-Style for the Diaspora: A Study of the Tales of Esther and Daniel. *Journal of Biblical Literature* 92:211-23.

Jobes, Karen H. 1999. *Esther*. NIV Application Commentary. Grand Rapids: Zondervan Publishing House.

Josephus, Flavius. *The Works of Josephus: Complete and Unabridged*. 1987. First pub. 1736. Translated by William Whiston. Peabody, MA: Hendrickson Publishers.

Keener, Craig S. 2012. *Acts: An Exegetical Commentary: Introduction and 1:1-2:47*. Vol. 1 of *Acts: An Exegetical Commentary*. 4 vols. Grand Rapids: Baker Academic.

Kershaw, Ian. 2008. *Hitler: A Biography*. 1st American ed. New York: W. W. Norton & Co.

King, Thomas J. 2013. *Leviticus: A Commentary in the Wesleyan Tradition*. New Beacon Bible Commentary. Kansas City: Beacon Hill Press of Kansas City.

Knight, Henry H., III. 2013. Wesley, John, Theology of. Pages 564-66 in *Global Wesleyan Dictionary of Theology*. Edited by Al Truesdale. Kansas City: Beacon Hill Press of Kansas City.

Koehler, Ludwig, and Walter Baumgartner. 2001. *The Hebrew and Aramaic Lexicon of the Old Testament (HALOT)*. Study Edition. 2 vols. Subsequently revised by Walter Baumgartner and Johann Jakob Stamm. Translated and edited by M. E. J. Richardson. Leiden: E. J. Brill.

LaCelle-Peterson, Kristina. 2008. *Liberating Tradition: Women's Identity and Vocation in Christian Perspective*. Grand Rapids: Baker Academic.

Laniak, Timothy S. 1998. *Shame and Honor in the Book of Esther*. Dissertation series 165. Atlanta: Society of Biblical Literature.

Lennox, Stephen J. 2015. *Joshua: A Commentary in the Wesleyan Tradition*. New Beacon Bible Commentary. Kansas City: Beacon Hill Press of Kansas City.

Levenson, Jon D. 1997. *Esther: A Commentary*. The Old Testament Library. Louisville, KY: Westminster John Knox Press.

Lewis, C. S. 1948. *The Screwtape Letters*. New York: Macmillan.

Longman, Tremper, III. 2001. *Song of Songs*. The New International Commentary on the Old Testament. Grand Rapids: Eerdmans.

Millard, A. R. The Persian Names in Esther and the Reliability of the Hebrew Text. *Journal of Biblical Literature* 96:481-88.

Moore, Carey A. 1971. *Esther*. Anchor Bible. Garden City, NY: Doubleday.

_____. 1985. Esther Revisited: An Examination of Esther Studies over the Past Decade. Pages 163-72 in *Biblical and Related Studies Presented to Samuel Iwry*. Edited by Ann Kort and Scott Morschauser. Winona Lake, IN: Eisenbrauns.

Niditch, Susan. 1993. *War in the Hebrew Bible: A Study in the Ethics of Violence*. Oxford: Oxford University Press.

Oden, Thomas C. 2009. *Classic Christianity: A Systematic Theology*. Previously published in three vols. 1987, 1989, 1992. New York: HarperOne.

Olmstead, A. T. 1948. *History of the Persian Empire*. Chicago: University of Chicago Press.

Oppenheim, A. Leo. 1965. On Royal Gardens in Mesopotamia. *Journal for Near Eastern Studies* 24:328-33.

Peterson, Eugene H. 1980. *Five Smooth Stones for Pastoral Work*. Grand Rapids: Eerdmans.

_____. 2006. *Eat This Book: A Conversation in the Art of Spiritual Reading*. Grand Rapids: Eerdmans.

Reid, Debra. 2008. *Esther*. Tyndale Old Testament Commentaries. Downers Grove, IL: IVP Academic.

Schenck, Kenneth. 2015. Why Wesleyans Favor Women in Ministry. 8-27-2015. Online. https://www.wesleyan.org/62/women-in-ministry.

Strawn, Brent A. 2013. Hiddenness of God. Pages 233-34 in *Global Wesleyan Dictionary of Theology*. Edited by Al Truesdale. Kansas City: Beacon Hill Press of Kansas City.

Talmon, Shemarayahu. 1995. Was the Book of Esther Known at Qumran? *Dead Sea Discoveries* 2:249-67.

Tomasino, Anthony. 2009. Esther. Pages 468-505 in *1&2 Kings, 1&2 Chronicles, Ezra, Nehemiah, Esther*. Edited by John H. Walton. Vol. 3 of Zondervan Illustrated Bible Backgrounds Commentary. Edited by John H. Walton. Grand Rapids: Zondervan.

Tov, Emanuel. 2008. The LXX Translation of Esther: A Paraphrastic Translation of MT or a Free Translation of a Rewritten Version? Pages 507-26 in *Empsychoi Logoi—Religious Innovations in Antiquity: Studies in Honour of Pieter Willem van der Horst*. Edited by Alberdina Houtman, Albert de Jong, Magda Misset-van de Weg. Leiden: Brill.

Voigtlander, Elizabeth N. von. 1978. *The Bisitun Inscription of Darius the Great: Babylonian Version*. Part 1, Vol. 2 of *Corpus Inscriptionum Iranicarum. l. Inscriptions of Ancient Iran*. London: Lund Humphries.

Wells, Samuel. 2013. *Esther*. In *Esther & Daniel*. Brazos Theological Commentary on the Bible. Grand Rapids: Brazos Press.

Wenham, Gordon J. 2000. *Story as Torah: Reading the Old Testament Ethically*. Edinburgh: T&T Clark.

Wesley, John. 1765. *Explanatory Notes upon the Old Testament*. Made available by Wesleyan Heritage Publishing. 8-28-2015. http://wesley.nnu.edu/john-wesley/john-wesleys-notes-on-the-bible/.

Westbrook, R. 1992. Punishments and Crimes. Pages 546-56 in vol. 5 of *The Anchor Bible Dictionary*. Edited by D. N. Freedman. 6 vols. New York: Doubleday.

Wright, N. T. 2014. *Surprised by Scripture: Engaging Contemporary Issues*. New York: HarperCollins Publishers.

Yamauchi, Edwin M. 1980. The Archaeological Background of Esther: Archaeological Backgrounds of the Exilic and Postexilic Era, Part 2. *Bibliotheca Sacra* 137:99-117.

_____. 1996. *Persia and the Bible*. Grand Rapids: Baker Books.

INTRODUCTION

A. Methodology

The methodology of this commentary can broadly be considered literary criticism, which focuses on the "literary artistry of the biblical text" and "begins not with the who and when, but with the why and how of a text" (Arnold 1998, 186). By all accounts, Esther is a grand piece of literature—a beautiful, captivating story. Not discounting its beautiful, captivating heroine, the book has been crafted by an expert storyteller who has dramatically incorporated all the elements of the most suspenseful of tales—a setting in a lavish, exotic palace; a tyrant king whose whim governs all; a loving, honorable godfather; a formidable opponent of pure evil; and a series of nail-biting twists and turns that keep the ultimate outcome ever in doubt.

For all of these elements, however, we must not be tempted to think that this story is complete. It cannot be pulled from an array of dazzling princess storybooks, read, and then reshelved among the rest. Rather, this story is part of an even grander story—the story of God's redeeming and restoring work in this world (→ From the Text, ch 1). It is only in light of this larger narrative, a narrative that both precedes and follows this story, that the tale of Esther, Mordecai, and their people—God's people—can be rightly understood, experienced, and then passed on to the world in various contexts of time and place.

Eugene Peterson, best known as author of *The Message: The Bible in Contemporary Language*, clarifies for us that story is not only our "most accessible form of speech" but also the most significant form of communication as it "invites our participation" (2006, 40). Since the book of Esther has come to us today in story form, it is imperative that the story remain ever before us in order both to maintain its accessibility and to continually invite our participation. Therefore, this commentary, particularly in the In the Text portion of each section, has been written to maintain the narrative flow of the biblical text. Though we will stop and carefully examine details in "the discipline of attending to the text and listening to it rightly and well" (ibid., 50), as readers we must always return to the story. Only when we respond to its literary cues can this book reveal its purposes, allowing us to see the truth in the text and be changed by it. As Peterson has so eloquently reminded us:

> Stories suffer misinterpretation when we don't submit to them simply as stories. We are caught off-guard when divine revelation arrives in such ordinary garb and mistakenly think it's our job to dress it up in the latest Paris silk gown of theology, or to outfit it in a sturdy three-piece suit of ethics before we can deal with it. The simple, or not so simple, story is soon, like David under Saul's armor, so encumbered with moral admonitions, theological constructs, and scholarly debates that it can hardly move. There are, of course, always moral, theological, historical elements in these stories that need to be studied and ascertained, but never in spite of or in defiance of the story that is being told. (Ibid., 43)

It is most vital that we understand *what* story is being told here in Esther. This is not a romance that ends, as Hollywood so often depicts, with the camera fading out on the silhouette of the macho-yet-virtuous king embracing his dazzling-yet-daring queen. In fact, there is little in that last sentence that should even be imagined about Esther and Xerxes as presented in the biblical story. This also is not a rags-to-riches story of the underdog Jews winning against the powerful Persians, or a moral tale proving the value of fasting, obedience, or other virtues. Rather, this is a small portion of the larger story about God and about how God works in this world to fulfill his purposes.

We meet in the pages of Esther a God who is eternally loyal to his covenant promises and his covenant people, gracious to those people despite their past choices of disobedience, and ever-present in his efforts to bring them into lives of "relief and deliverance" (4:14). At the same time, he is hidden, seemingly absent at times, choosing to bring about the salvation of his people through those very people in need of saving. This is that bigger story, "that God put his wonderful world into human hands; that the human hands messed up the project; and that the human hands of Jesus the Messiah have now picked it up, sorted it out, and got it back on track" (Wright 2014, 35). In the interims, both before Jesus came and now after he has come, there have been many other human hands involved—the hands of his people Israel, including Esther, and now the hands of his people the church, including you and me. Let us now dive into the pages of Esther together with our hands open to all that the Holy Spirit will have us receive.

B. Placement in the Canon

In the Christian canon, the book of Esther appears as the final book in the portion often labeled "history" (Joshua—Esther). Together, these books follow the Israelites from entry into the promised land, through the establishment of and subsequent split of the monarchy, and eventually into exile.

In the Hebrew Bible (or *Tanakh*), Esther appears in the third and final section known as "Writings" (*Ketuvim*, which follows *Torah* and *Nevi'im/*"Prophets"). Within this grouping a subset has developed known as *Megillot*, "Scrolls," which includes the five shortest books of the section—Song of Songs, Ruth, Lamentations, Ecclesiastes, and Esther (often in that order). These five books are read throughout the year on specific festival days, with Esther being read on Purim.

Interestingly, Esther is the only book of the Hebrew Bible that is not quoted or recorded among the Dead Sea Scrolls (the oldest copies of the OT, with fragments dating from the second century BC to the second century AD). They do contain, however, an Aramaic fragment known as "4Q Tales of the Persian Court," which seems to carry some of the same themes as the book of Esther. Based upon this fragment and an extensive linguistic survey of the Dead Sea Scrolls from Qumran, S. Talmon has concluded that "the authors of [the Qumran] texts knew the Esther story, and that some of them were actually familiar with the biblical Book of Esther" (1995, 265).

The fact that the book of Esther doesn't appear in any of the Dead Sea Scroll fragments may allow us to conclude that "while the Book of Esther was well known in the late Second Temple period, when most if not all Qumran manuscripts were penned, it had not yet achieved 'canonical' status, viz. was not yet recognized as part of Hebrew Scriptures" (266). This is further supported by the fact that Purim is not celebrated at Qumran. As Talmon has summarized, "But since the Book of Esther had not attained the status of 'Holy Writ,' Purim was not seen at Qumran as a festival anchored in the biblical tradition. Like Hanukkah, Purim was considered to be 'beyond the pale,' and neither of the two is ever included in any one of the numerous calendrical rosters of the" Qumran Community (267). Jesus' own celebration of Hanukkah (John 10:22-23), and presumably also of Purim, demonstrates that this view of the Jews of Qumran was not the only, and was likely the minority, Jewish perspective on these festivals at the time of Christ.

C. Versions of Esther

The translation of the book of Esther with which most Protestants are familiar, and upon which this commentary is focused, is based upon the Hebrew version preserved in the Masoretic tradition (MT). Other versions, though they are less familiar to us, contribute to our understanding of the developing interpretation of this book throughout history and will be considered briefly as needed throughout the commentary.

The Old Greek version (Septuagint, abbreviated LXX) of Esther derives from a Hebrew precursor, which may have differed to some degree from that preserved by the MT. The Greek translation, which is fairly free, also inserts "six large narrative expansions" consisting of over one hundred verses, the origins of which are unknown (Tov 2008, 508). Most striking to us is the explicitly religious nature of these additions. God is mentioned liberally, extensive prayers are voiced, and God is acknowledged as the unequivocal source of the Jews' salvation.

Concerning the compositional nature of these additions, Clines succinctly summarizes, "We do not know at what time or by what means [the additions] became incorporated in the text of Esther that is now commonly called the Septuagint" (1984a, 69). By the time of Saint Jerome's translation of the Bible into Latin (the Vulgate) in the late fourth century AD, these Greek additions were accepted; however, he collected them at the end of the book in 10:4—16:24 in order to maintain the form of the Hebrew version. In modern translations, these portions of Esther can be found in Catholic and Orthodox editions of the Bible (e.g., the New American Bible, the NRSV Catholic Edition, or the Eastern Orthodox Bible) where they are usually integrated into the book, following the tradition of the LXX. The contents of each of these additions are presented briefly here.

Addition A (Vulgate 11:2—12:6): Mordecai has a dream that foreshadows the coming crisis of the book, though he does not understand it. He also thwarts an assassination plot (either previous or identical to the one in ch 2) by two eunuchs against Xerxes and thereby incurs the wrath of Haman. (Placed before 1:1.)

Addition B (Vulgate 13:1-7): This addition includes the text of the edict of Haman mentioned in 3:12-13. Along with pronouncing their destruction, this edict also expands the accusations against the Jews. (Placed after 3:13.)

Addition C (Vulgate 13:8—14:19): This largest addition (thirty-seven verses) contains the prayers of Mordecai and Esther following Esther's command for fasting. Mordecai begins with a strong prayer of praise to God in which he describes his refusal to bow to Haman as his humble declaration of the glory of the Lord. The prayer concludes with his request for God's mercy and deliverance of his people. Esther's prayer, carried out in the appearance and posture of mourning, is a distressed plea for divine intervention on behalf of both her and her people. She recounts the story of God's hand in sustaining his people throughout history, reminding him of his covenant and acknowledging the failures of the people and her own continued faithfulness in her circumstances. (Placed after 4:17.)

Addition D (Vulgate 15:1-16): This variant version of Esther's approach to Xerxes presents Esther as frail and agonized. Upon seeing her, Xerxes is angry, but when Esther delicately swoons from fear, his heart melts, he rushes to her side and holds her, and they speak to one another comfortingly. (Placed immediately after C above; replaces Hebrew 5:1-2.)

Addition E (Vulgate 16:1-24): This section presents the text of the edict of Mordecai mentioned in 8:9, 11. Much like Addition B, it includes a development of the accusations against Haman along with an acknowledgment of Jewish innocence and right to defense. (Placed after 8:12.)

Addition F (Vulgate 10:4—11:1): This additional ending revisits Mordecai's dream from Addition A and interprets it as predictive of the events of the story. The final verse of the book in the LXX identifies "Lysimachus son of Ptolemy, one of the residents of Jerusalem" as the translator of the letter of Purim into Greek. (Placed after 10:3.)

Another ancient witness to Esther is the Greek Alpha Text (AT), which is significantly different from the LXX. This text, which "is preserved in five Greek [manuscripts] dating from the tenth to thirteenth centuries C.E." (Fox 2001, 255), has been influenced by and incorporates the additions of the LXX. However, many textual critics contend that its original form is based upon a Hebrew version that preceded the MT (ibid.; also Clines 1984a, 140). Therefore, its witness, though limited, is valuable.

A third important Greek witness to Esther is provided by the ancient Jewish historian Flavius Josephus, who wrote in the first century AD. One of his major works, *Antiquities of the Jews*, recounts Jewish history from the beginning of time until the beginning of the Jewish War in 66 AD. Thus, Josephus endures as both a major early Jewish commentator on the biblical text and a primary source of information about the intertestamental and NT periods. Josephus's version of the Esther narrative, found in book 11 of the *Antiquities*, is a paraphrase that appears to make use of multiple sources, including and excluding material as fits his purpose. Feldman characterizes the work as follows: "In his retelling of the Biblical book of Esther, Josephus has made a number of changes which would render his work more attractive to his Greek readers and which would defend the Jewish people against anti-Semitic propaganda" (1970, 143).

D. Historical Setting and Chronology

Every story has a setting that provides its backdrop and framework in (or out of) time and space. The story of Esther is no different. Many of the intricately developed historical and cultural details of Esther's setting will be discussed in detail throughout the Behind the Text portions of the commentary.

Here I would like to address the larger question of the historicity of the Esther story. Many biblical scholars today would hold that, though its setting is authentic, the account itself is not. Clines' treatment (1984b, 257-60) contains a fairly comprehensive and extensive discussion of factors *against* Esther's historicity, factors he identifies as "implausible." It is important to note that he does provide a counter interpretation that allows for a historical consideration for each of the factors. However, the factors discussed are extensive, covering both literary and historical elements. The historical arguments of this view rest primarily on the fact that we have no extrabiblical confirmation of the story of Esther, and some would hold that we even have contradictory information. For example, the Greeks only preserve for us the name of one of the queens of Xerxes who is neither Vashti nor Esther, though generally unsuccessful attempts have been made to equate the extant name with both of these (ibid., 258-59).

There are also scholars who would argue for the historicity of Esther, to varying degrees. Clines' commentary mentioned above, for example, also contains a succinct discussion of factors *in favor* of Esther's historicity, finally determining, "No clear conclusion emerges from this survey of the evidence" (1984b, 256-61; see also Yamauchi 1996, 239; Tomasino 2009, 471; and Baldwin 1984, 23-24, for varying affirmations). Scholars of this view may utilize phrases such as "historical novel" or "fictionalized history" to describe the significant latitude in literary embellishment that was acceptable for ancient historians, even those writing biblical material. At the very least, there is broad consensus among scholars from both views that Esther's setting reflects historical reality. From the portrayals of Persian life and a historical timeline that correspond to Greek representations, to the inclusion of Persian terms and seemingly authentic Persian names, there is no doubt that the author of Esther was intimately acquainted with his setting.

Though I place myself in this latter interpretive camp, I would argue that one need not feel threatened by the former. The truth of a biblical story is not ultimately based in its historicity. Or said another way, the story of Esther is true, whether or not it is fully historical. Indeed, the term "story" itself need not imply fiction, à la bedtime stories. My children ask me to tell stories from when I was young all the time. They aren't asking me to fabricate a fantasy of me fighting dragons; they want to hear what I did in school in first grade. They want true stories, at least to the extent my memory allows. Here again, the term "true" when applied to stories presents difficulties. For example, are stories such as the prodigal son (Luke 15:11-32) and the good Samaritan (Luke 10:25-27) true? On the one hand, when compared to stories of my childhood, no. The stories of my childhood happened; the prodigal son and good Samaritan did not. Yet we must affirm that those stories are true in a way and to a depth that most stories of my childhood can never be. Joel Green, in his book *Reading Scripture as Wesleyans*, speaks to the truth of Scripture this way: "How do we know if the Bible is 'true,' then? If it shows us the way to heaven" (2010, ix). Likewise, N. T. Wright affirms, "The Bible does what God wants it to do when, through the power of the Spirit, it enables people to believe in Jesus, to follow him, and to share the work of the kingdom" (2014, 29). Everything that is truth must, by virtue of being true, ultimately point to the one who is truth (John 14:6). Therefore, there is no truer story than the overarching narrative of God's activity in this world, told with stories of all kinds, real and imagined, both in the revelation of the biblical text and in the ongoing revelation of his body the church.

It is my hope that this discussion has alleviated rather than produced anxiety for you, my reader. For many years, the threats of Scripture's potential inauthenticity held me captive to a relentless search for historical proofs. What a cunning ploy of the evil one. As long as I am distracted by looking outside of Scripture to validate it, I am not resting inside of Scripture as a means for God's grace to flow into my life. It is my prayer that you read the book of Esther as the truth of God that it is, encountering in its pages its author—the one who is truth.

E. Theological Themes

I. Reversals (Peripety)

At first glance, one may not see how a topic like "reversals" can be a theological theme. However, salvation history is really all about reversals—reversing the effects of the fall in our lives and in the world. The life, death, burial, and resurrection of Jesus Christ marks the ultimate reversal, when death itself is reversed and true life becomes possible. This greatest reversal had been preceded by a series of reversals in what may be termed a "universal pattern of history" (Bickerman 1967, 198). In this way, God was demonstrating to humanity, time and again, the necessity of a complete overturning of this world in order for us truly to experience him and the lives he created us to live. The OT, for example, shows us that in true life slaves are set free, the powerless defeat the powerful, the foreigner becomes family, the homeless wanderer inherits a great possession, and the childless become ancestors to countless descendants.

Jesus expands upon this pattern of reversals, teaching us that his kingdom operates on principles that overturn the order of this fallen world. The last become first, the poor out-give the rich, mourners become the joyful ones, the sick and sinful are made whole and healthy, and real living happens when we die to ourselves. In order for us to become his agents of bringing his kingdom to this world, we must experience and embody this life of reversals, this life of redemption.

This kingdom principle of reversals is woven into the literary fabric of the book of Esther. Many of these reversal moments will be noted throughout the commentary; however, it is important for several reasons for us to approach the story anticipating this recurrent motif. First of all, an understanding of the author's literary use of reversals helps us to avoid potential misinterpretation or overemphasis. For example, one can overdevelop the Vashti character if her role is not seen primarily as providing the reversal of queenship to Esther (→ In the Text for Esth 1:12). Likewise, the details of Mordecai's decree in ch 8 are rightly interpreted only as the complete reversal of Haman's decree in ch 3 (→ In the Text for 8:11-12).

Second, and more importantly, this theme provides the framework for the overarching theological theme of the book—redemption. Knight describes Wesley's view of the "larger story of redemption" this way: "Ultimately the entire created order will be transformed in holiness and manifest God's love, renewed to a greater degree than its original state" (2013, 566). How true of the microcosm of Esther's world, as we compare the Jews of Persia at its beginning and end! Esther herself is a picture of the reversal women experience from the oppression of the male-dominated world of ch 1 to the co-ruled world of chs 8—10. Reversal, transformation, redemption, renewal—all of these terms capture our author's primary message in slightly different ways and provide insights for how we may appropriate it into our lives.

2. Divine Hiddenness

The trivia fact often known about the book of Esther is that it is one of only two books of the Bible, the other being Song of Songs (Longman 2001, 116; Blumenthal 1995), that does not contain the name of God. In many ways, this is a very unsettling idea. Where is the God of the burning bush who revealed himself and gave his name (Exod 3), or the God of the wilderness whose presence was always apparent in the pillars of cloud and fire (Exod 13:21-22; Num 14:14)? Has he abandoned his people now that they are experiencing the consequence of exile? While biblical authors often use the metaphor of God "hiding his face" as an indication of withdrawal from humanity in judgment for sin (e.g., Deut 31:17-18), this is not always the case. As Strawn affirms, "[God's hiddenness] is a real part of humanity's experience of God (Ps 22:1; Matt 27:46)" (2013, 233).

The question of God's presence or withdrawal from his people is really at the heart of the story of Esther. And the answer the book gives is resounding. Not only has God *not* abandoned his people, but he remains abundantly loyal to his covenant promise—his people *will* be preserved, relief and deliverance *will* rise (4:14)! At the moment in the history of Israel when we could think that his people are farthest from him, the Lord confirms his continued faithfulness on the grandest scale, with a deliverance that rivals the Passover and Exodus. But he doesn't stop there. He goes on to commission, for the first time since Leviticus, an annual festival of remembrance that will be a perpetual reminder of his unquestioning presence in this world! Where is God in Esther? Where he has always been—dwelling among his people (Gen 17:7; Exod 6:7; Lev 26:12; John 1:14).

There is something about God's hiddenness in this book that resonates with modern, Western audiences. We are a people who rarely encounter God in any physical way, who have likely never experienced a supernatural display of his power against the forces of nature, and who are immersed in cultures as foreign to the kingdom of God as Persia was to the promised land. Yet God is active; he is here. We can know it as surely as Mordecai and Esther did. We experience his relief and deliverance in our own lives, and we become the place from which relief and deliverance come into this world. God's seeming hiddenness in our world today is uncovered in us and by us, just as it was in and by Esther, Mordecai, and the Jews of Persia.

3. Divine Providence

The theme of divine providence, or sovereignty, is always a focal point of discussion by Esther commentators and is closely linked to the theme of God's hiddenness. As Wesley recognizes, "The name of God is not found in this book: but the finger of God is, directing so many minute events for the deliverance of his people" (1765, Preface). He goes on to reference the hand of God at the following points in the text—Esth 2:10; 3:7; 5:3, 8, 10; 6:1-3; 7:6; 8:9. A Wesleyan view of divine providence views this activity not as cosmic manipulation by a heavenly puppeteer, but as the divine commitment to actively work all things for the good of his people (Rom 8:28). God, the sovereign, omnipotent Creator, can and will align details for his purposes, and the ultimate outcome is assured because of his incontestable, unlimited being. However, those purposes are not imposed upon humanity, and participation in the final outcome is left in the hands of individuals. This is the distinction made by Wesley and explained by Collins as "the absolute freedom and power of God in terms of creation" that God himself graciously limits to become his "restricted freedom and power that makes room for the human beings (reflective of the divine image) that [he] has actually created" (2007, 38).

The interplay of divine hiddenness and divine providence in Esther becomes essentially a call to faith. Will we, as the Jews of Persia, trust that God is faithful to himself and, therefore, to his promise to his people? As Fox so pointedly states, "The willingness to face history with an openness to the possibility of providence—even when history seems to weigh against its likelihood, as it did in the dark days after the issuance of Haman's decree—this is the stance of profound faith" (2001, 247).

4. How to Live in Diaspora

This theological theme is often obscure to modern readers; however, it indicates a foundational shift in how God's people viewed themselves and their function in relation to the world around them. From the beginning, God's relationship with humanity has involved a spatial element. First there was the garden where humanity had full, unhindered access to God. After that space was lost, God called Abraham to another space—a land he would show him (Gen 12:1). That space, the promised land, was to become, in some ways, a re-creation of Eden. It would be the space in which the people of God would learn to live in relationship with him, having access to his presence in their midst, free from the snare of the gods of the nations (Exod 23:31-33). From this space, they would shine as a light to all those around them, fulfilling the ultimate purpose of God's covenant with them—bestowing the blessing of God's presence upon all nations (Gen 12:3; Isa 49:6; Gal 3:8).

However, due to the choices of the Israelites, this plan was never fully realized (Judg 1:19-36; 2:3). Though God remained faithful to dwell among them in the land (e.g., 1 Kgs 8:10-13), they continually become ensnared by the religions around them, being drawn away from God rather than drawing others to him (e.g., 1 Kgs 11:1-8). Their concept of themselves as a chosen, blessed people became bound up with possession of the land, though God warned them that it was their covenant relationship, not the land, that defined them as his people (e.g., Mic 3:9-12). If they continued to rebel against him, they would lose the land. This is exactly what happened, first to the northern kingdom of Israel (722 BC) and then to the southern kingdom of Judah (586 BC). And this is why the Jews now find themselves living in exile in the book of Esther.

Living in the wreckage of their choices against God's plan, what does the covenant look like now for God's people? How will they live in relationship with him, much less bring others to him, when they have no space where that happens? The books of Ezra and Nehemiah show us a picture of God's people returning to the land, though living there intermingled with non-Jews. They reestablish worship in the temple, read and celebrate the law, and seek to live according to its direction. This minority of Jews produces the population that is living in the land when Jesus comes to this world.

However, the majority of Jews never return to the land, and the book of Esther contains no hint of a summons to return. As Victor Hamilton states, "Esther is about the shift from exile as one way of life (temporary relocation outside Israel) to diaspora as another way of life (permanent relocation outside of Israel)" (2001, 544). In this postexilic period, the space in which God will live in relationship with his people is no longer physical nor is it isolated. Rather, his people are now called to experience relationship with him in the spiritual rather than the physical realm, and to be distinct and set apart wherever they are. Esther, Mordecai, and the Jews in Persia begin to show us what this will look like. It will involve community and character, strength and strategy, prayer, fasting, and without a doubt, the ever-present help of the one who will never leave them or forsake them.

COMMENTARY

I. QUEEN VASHTI DEPOSED: ESTHER 1:1-22

BEHIND THE TEXT

As the curtain opens, we see displayed before us the royal court of Persia, in all its grandeur and opulence. The king mentioned is Xerxes (in Greek), which corresponds to Hebrew *'Ăhašwērôš*, Persian *Khšayāršan*, and English Ahasuerus. Reigning from 486 to 465 BC, he inherited from his predecessor Darius I (522-486 BC) the extensive Persian Empire that stretched "from India to Cush." The name translated "India" (Heb.: *hōdû*; mentioned only in Esther in the biblical text) demarcates the southeastern boundary of the Persian Empire and refers to the northwestern portion of the Indus River valley, which lies in modern-day Pakistan (Yamauchi 1996, 154). "Cush" indicates the southwestern limit of the empire and references the upper Nile region of ancient Egypt, which today would be located in southern Egypt and Sudan (ibid., 114). This locale is mentioned elsewhere in the Bible, often in parallelism with "Egypt" (e.g., Ps 68:31 [32 HB]; Isa 20:3-5; Ezek 30:4-5, 9; see also 2 Kgs 19:9; Isa 37:9).

The Persians and Medes both were "Iranian peoples, springing from the same Indo-Iranian stock" who arrived jointly from the steppes of Russia into the Zagros Mountains of modern-day Iran around 1000 BC. Their paths after that point, however, diverged significantly (Briant 2002, 25-27). The Medes occupied the area around their capital of Ecbatana in the Zagros Mountains of northwestern Iran (Yamauchi 1996, 31ff., 305ff.). As for the Persians, though there is little clarity related to their precise movements after their entrance into the region (Briant 2002, 20), it is agreed that eventually they overtook the Elamite kingdom with its capital Susa, located in the southwest corner of modern-day Iran in its Khuzestan province (Yamauchi 1996, 20).

While the Medes exercised varying levels of control over the Persians at different times, it was the Persians who gained final superiority at the beginning of the reign of Cyrus the Great (also known as Cyrus II; 550-530 BC). The politically astute Cyrus drew upon his half-Median heritage and took steps to incorporate himself into the Median royal family. Thus, biblical authors refer six times to the empire of "the Medes and the Persians" (Dan 5:28; 6:8, 12, 15 [9, 13, 16 HB], 8:20; Esth 10:2; note the common modern appellative "the Medo-Persian Empire"), though more commonly the author of Esther refers to the Persians and the Medes (1:3, 14, 18, 19). Cyrus and future Persian kings utilized the strategic Median capital of Ecbatana (modern-day Hamadan) as a summer capital city, with the historic Elamite capital of Susa serving as the location of the "royal throne" (Esth 1:2) primarily in the winter months (Yamauchi 1996, 41, 305; Briant 2002, 33).

Though first excavated before modern archaeological techniques, the excavations of Susa have revealed significant information about the Persian city of Susa, including a massive palace structure (covering nearly ten acres!) built by Xerxes' father, Darius I. On the western side of the palace is the royal gate structure enclosing some 12,000 sq. ft. with a square before it (see Esth 4:6). On separate mounds are the acropolis, the palace area, and the "royal city," all fortified by Darius, while another mound contains the unfortified "village of artisans." It is possible then that biblical references to "the citadel of Susa" (*šûšan bîrāh*; Neh 1:1; Esth 1:2, 5; 2:3, 5, 8; 3:15; 8:14; 9:6, 11, 12; Dan 8:2) indicate the fortified portions including both the palace structure and the royal city, while references to "the city of Susa" (*hā'îr šûšan*; Esth 3:15; 8:15) designate the unfortified area for artisans (cf. Moore 1971, 5), with general references to Susa including both (→ Esth 3:15; 9:6).

Areas within the palace complex have been tentatively identified as "the outer court (6:4), the inner court (4:11), the house of the women (2:9), and a second house of the women (2:14) for concubines," as well as **the courtyard of the garden of the king's *bîtan*** (1:5; also 7:7, 8) (Yamauchi 1980, 110). Concluding his investigation of terms related to *bîtan* outside of the biblical text, Oppenheim suggests that this location should be understood as "an open structure, probably a colonnaded open hall," perhaps "used for certain prestige purposes, in fact reserved for royalty . . . such as the kings and the heirs apparent" (1965, 330-32).

The Persian Empire was also known for its intricate, highly efficient administrative network. Its division by Darius I into twenty satrapies governed by officials known as satraps (see Ezra 8:36 ["satraps and . . . governors"]; Esth 3:12;

Dan 3:2; 6:2) is discussed by the Greek historian Herodotus, whose *Histories* include significant information about the Persians due to their position as the chief enemy of the Greeks. Additional imperial divisions are discussed in the extrabiblical sources in terms of "nations" (*ethnē*), numbers of which reach totals of forty-six (Yamauchi 1996, 179).

Briant concurs that "the creation of satrapies did not cause the preexisting political entities to disappear" (2002, 64), with leaders of varying ranks holding Persian administrative authority. A possible categorization of the understanding of the Persian administrative system by the author of Esther is given in 3:12, where the king's decree is sent to his satraps (*'ăḥašdarpênîm*, presumably twenty), governors (*paḥôt*) of provinces (*mĕdînôt*), and officials (*śarîm*) of peoples (*'ammîm*). Here in Esth 1:1 mention is made of 127 provinces (*mĕdînôt*, a term that can also be translated "city" in Aramaic). This number corresponds closely to the 120 "satraps" mentioned in Dan 6:1 (which reads 127 in the Septuagint, i.e., the ancient Greek edition of the Hebrew Bible). Scholars debate whether these numbers in the biblical texts are meant to give accountings of particular subdivisions of the Persian Empire, to reflect an early period of administration development, or simply to characterize the Persian administrative system as exhaustively comprehensive. In any case, the vast expanse of the Persian Empire is clearly on display in this opening feast of the king.

The imperial delivery system connects this vast empire. Evidence of the practice of disseminating edicts in multiple languages has come to us through the monumental Behistun Inscription of Darius, which records his ascent to the throne. In that inscription, written in three different languages, Darius notes that he had the inscription copied and sent to every province. In fact, a translation of the Behistun Inscription into Aramaic has been found in Elephantine, Egypt, verifying that the command was carried out (see Briant 2002, 507-10).

Finally, the extravagance of life in the Persian royal court was to such excess that Greek authors were absolutely fascinated with providing detailed accounts of it. In particular, details about Persian feasting are abundant, with descriptions of gold and silver cups for drinking, couches overlaid with gold, silver, and precious jewels for reclining, and brightly colored tents and curtains of luxurious fabrics for astounding Persian guests. The abundance of wine at these feasts is also a common theme of the Greek portrayals. (For a full discussion of Greek accounts of "The Great King's Table," see Briant 2002, 286-97.)

IN THE TEXT

A. The Stage: Persia's Court (1:1-4)

■ **1-2** The book of Esther begins with the temporal phrase **This is what happened during the time of** . . . Though modern translations may not reveal it, this is the same construction that appears in Gen 14:1, Ruth 1:1, Isa 7:1, and Jer 1:3, all of which specify the time setting of their respective accounts in relation to the person or persons ruling. The common narrative form *vayyĕhî* (**This is what happened**) that begins this story is ubiquitous in Hebrew narrative and is used within past time sequences to move the story line from action to action. By beginning this tale with that form, which also appears at the beginning of the narratives of Joshua, Judges, Ruth, 1 and 2 Samuel, and Jonah, the author has situated his drama in the flow of the story of God's people, Israel.

This common introduction also creates a striking literary effect. The opening lines of a story set the scene and prepare us for what is to come. Indeed, when one reads the account in Genesis or Isaiah that begins with this same opening phrase, the character in whose time the story is set is himself a primary character of the story. So also in the opening lines of most of the historical books, the author grabs our attention by immediately turning our focus to the main character. In the book of Esther, however, the author uses this common literary device to his advantage by turning it on its head. He introduces Xerxes the king, causing us immediately to assume that he is the principal player in the story, when in fact he is a fairly minor, stock character whose royal court provides the stage for the unfolding drama and whose persona as the tyrannical ruler produces challenges for the protagonists. This same technique is utilized in Ruth as the audience's initial response is to expect a story about Elimelek and his sons, only to be quickly redirected to the drama's principal players—the women (Ruth 1:1-5). In ancient manuscripts that did not carry the title headings that our modern texts contain, the effect of this literary turn would have been quite jarring and delightful for the audience.

Xerxes receives brief mention elsewhere in the biblical text in Ezra 4:6, where it is stated that they (the *'am-hā'āreṣ* [*people of the land*] mentioned in 4:4) "lodged an accusation against the people of Judah and Jerusalem." This statement follows the account of the persistent conflicts that the surrounding enemies had instigated previously against the Jewish returnees who were rebuilding the temple in Jerusalem during the reigns of Cyrus and Darius.

While the Ezra passage reveals to us neither the content of the accusation nor the response of Xerxes, it does tell us that the complaint was submitted at the beginning of his reign, presumably sometime near 486-485 BC. Therefore, we know that Xerxes was made aware of the Jewish populations who were living in his empire from very early in his reign. The book of Esther opens "in the third year of his reign" (v 3; 483 BC), though it is several years before Xerxes takes a Jewish wife (though not knowing her ethnicity). (See discussion in Edlin 2009, 147-48, concerning the "Xerxes/Ahasuerus" of Dan 9:1.)

■ **3-4** The drama of Esther is often set around a table. The **banquet** (*mišteh*) here is the first of six specified royal banquets (1:3, 5, 9; 2:18; 5:5; 7:1), with much feasting occurring at the end of the book (8:17; 9:17-19, 22) (see Clines 1990, 37-38, for an evaluation of the structure of the banquets, which he numbers at nine by including the *sitting down to drink* of Haman and Xerxes in 3:15). This theme of festival that is woven throughout the book reflects its ultimate purpose—the establishment of a new annual festival for the Jewish people. Nevertheless, the frivolity of the setting creates significant dissonance for the audience as banish-ment (1:19) and genocide (3:13) are casually ordered amid the excess of court life. Indeed, it seems to be precisely for the purpose of flaunting **the vast wealth of his kingdom** *and the glorious honor of his greatness* that Xerxes has assembled all the highest officials of his realm (1:4).

The number of attendees possibly rivaled the Persian banquets feeding up to 15,000 that are documented by the Greek author Athenaeus (IV.146c). With its length of 180 days and the inclusion of *the army [ḥêl] of Persia and Media* (probably meaning its officers), this feast may well correspond to the gathering of Persian officials for a war council in preparation for the impending offensive against the Greeks launched by Xerxes in 481 BC (Yamauchi 1996, 201; Herodo-tus VII.8). For our author, however, it is the gluttony of royal merrymaking rather than the sobriety of military strategizing that dominates this scene.

Alternatively, one may translate Hebrew *ḥêl/ḥayil* as **the aristocracy** (*wealthy land owners*) *of Media and Persia*. Consider, for example, the applica-tion of the term to Boaz in Ruth 2:1. Cast in this light, the purpose for this feast may then be better understood as the wedding feast of Ahasuerus and Vashti, as indicated by the Septuagint (1:5, *hai hēmerai tou gamou*, **the days of the wedding**).

B. Let the Feasting Continue! (1:5-9)

■ **5-6** How else would these lavish Persians celebrate the ending of a six-month feast than with another feast! *When these days were over, the king gave—for all the people found in the citadel of Susa, for those from the greatest to the least—a banquet* . . . The most significant distinction between this feast and its precursor, as emphasized in the Hebrew wording shown here, is in the guest list, extended to all in the citadel, presumably including commoners. While its length is substan-tially shorter as well, one can only assume from the description in v 6 that its décor was no less magnificent. That the choices of white (*ḥûr*) and blue (*těkēlet*), white linen (*bûṣ*) and purple ('*argāmān*) signal royal prestige is confirmed in 8:15 when we view Mordecai, emerging triumphantly from the king's palace "wearing royal garments of blue [*těkēlet*] and white [*ḥûr*] . . . and a purple ['*argāmān*] robe of fine linen [*bûṣ*]." The description of the feast is laden with rare and exotic words, caus-ing even modern readers to feel overwhelmed in their presence! **Porphyry** (*bahaṭ*) is a purple-red igneous stone, anciently quarried in Egypt, though the Septuagint translates *smaragditēs*, which is a green-colored precious stone, perhaps emerald.

■ **7-8** The author does not stop with a description of the decorations. The sump-tuousness of the drinking vessels is rivaled only by the quality and quantity of the wine they hold. While drunken feasts punctuated by the use of ornate vessels may call to mind the feast of the Babylonian king Belshazzar in Dan 5:1-2, and indeed in Jewish interpretation, it was often suggested that the vessels used in Esther are also to be understood as those taken from the temple in Jerusalem, there is noth-ing in the Esther text to suggest that specific insult. Rather, this description of the lavishness of Persian feasting accords well with what we know from Greek texts (→ Behind the Text above).

The wine served at this drinking feast (Gk.: *potos*) is **royal wine** (*yên malkût*) and is served in abundance, **in keeping with the king's liberality** (*kĕyad hammelek, according to the hand of the king*) (Esth 1:7). Such a description of the king's openhandedness with his subjects appears again in 2:18 in regard to the gifts given to the guests at Esther's wedding banquet, as well as in 1 Kgs 10:13 to describe King Solomon's abundant bestowal of gifts upon the Queen of Sheba. However, this is not necessarily a sudden departure from Xerxes' ostentatious exhibition of himself to this point. The more generic translation *according to the king's bounty* (ESV, NASB, NRSV) perhaps better emphasizes the abundance from which the giving comes rather than a particular personality trait of the king himself. The following comment related to the king's **command** (*dāt*) in regard to drinking **with no restrictions** ('*ên 'ōnēs*) may also be understood not as the king's generous open-bar policy (so CEV: "Drink all you want!"), but rather as a release for each guest from any obligation to drink as much or as long as common Persian practice (*dāt*) expected (Esth 1:8). Thus, both excess and restraint are allowable (→ 9:5). Alternatively, the common practice that is perhaps being disregarded is that the **royal wine** (*yên malkût*), which is usually reserved exclusively for the king, is in this case allowed to be consumed by all (Berlin 2001, 10). (The Persian term *dāt*, used here in the first of twenty times in Esther, will be discussed further in 1:15 [→].)

■ **9** This introductory section of feasting ends with a simple footnote regarding a third *mišteh*, about which we are succinctly told its location, guest list, and host. This feast (again, Gk. *potos*) is held in the **royal palace** (*bêt hammalkût*), apart from the king's festivities "in the enclosed garden of the king's palace" (→ v 5). It is explicitly stated that it is King Xerxes to whom the *bêt hammalkût* belongs, though our understanding of the layout of the royal residence does not allow us to pinpoint precisely what area is meant. We do know that this banquet is held in the same place where Xerxes is sitting upon his throne as Esther awaits to approach him in 5:1; thus, we may translate **throne room** or **royal hall**. That a room the size of the throne room would be needed for this gathering may indicate that the guest list for the **banquet of women** included all of the wives of the men in attendance at the king's feast. However, it is also to the *bêt hammalkût* that Esther is taken for her initial presentation to the king in 2:16. There is nothing in ch 2 to insinuate that this presentation was a formal one that would have taken place in a throne room; therefore, it may be best to understand the *bêt hammalkût* simply as an indication of the king's personal areas of the palace, in which a throne room or other such public greeting area may have been situated. Whatever the case, all of this may go unnoticed or ignored as one is caught by the first three words of the verse—***Also Vashti, the Queen . . .*** Though she is introduced almost as an afterthought in Hebrew syntax, it is now to the Persian queen that all eyes turn.

C. The King Demands and the Queen Defies (1:10-15)

■ **10-11** As the feast is reaching its finale, it is not surprising that we find the king in an intoxicated condition (*ṭôb lēb . . . bayyāyin*, **high in spirits from wine** [v 10]). This same description appears in Judg 16:25 (without explicit reference to wine) and 2 Sam 13:28 concerning Samson's Philistine captors and David's son Amnon, respectively. In both of these instances, the parties who find themselves in this state are unable to judge their circumstances lucidly, leading to decisions that cost them their lives. Similarly, here we see drunken Xerxes fail miserably in assessing both his context and his queen. Having already spent 180 days displaying (*har'ōt*) his wealth and glory, he now intends to display (*har'ōt*) his (new?) wife. Speculation concerning his motives are useless considering his state of mind, though the reason he would want to parade her is obvious—Vashti is beautiful. Women of such renown as Rebekah (Gen 24:16; 26:7), Bathsheba (2 Sam 11:2), and Esther herself (2:7) are also considered *lovely of appearance* (*ṭôbat mar'eh*).

The **seven eunuchs** (*sārîsîm*) by whom the king sends his message are listed. The designation *sārîs* originally meant simply "the one (positioned) at the head (of the king)." Therefore, throughout the biblical text, it is most often translated "official" (e.g., Gen 37:36; 1 Sam 8:15; 1 Kgs 22:9). By the Persian period, the Hebrew word had come primarily to indicate a eunuch (i.e., castrated male), and that does seem the most probable understanding within the book of Esther. Note, however, that these servants function not only as guardians of the royal harem (Esth 2:3, 14) but also as guardians of (2:21) and messengers for (1:12, 15) the king. Here, the eunuchs are functioning as mediators of a conversation, the content of which is given in utter brevity, between an all-powerful male and a powerless female. Elements of this mediated conversation will be both mirrored and reversed in ch 4, when again a eunuch mediates a conversation between a male (Mordecai) and female (Esther); however, in ch 4, it is the female who is in the position of power, though she is as yet unaware, and the male who is in the position of powerlessness.

■ **12-15** While the reason for the king's request seems obvious, the reason for the queen's refusal remains obscure. Some early Jewish interpreters suggested that the command that she appear "wearing her royal crown" (v 11; *běketer malkût*) meant wearing only her crown and nothing else. If so, her refusal is a comment on her modesty. Josephus, the Jewish historian of the first century AD, reports that her refusal was based upon Persian law, which would not allow her to be seen by strangers. In that case, the king's response to her refusal provides the first of many ironic turns in this book—Vashti refuses to break a law at the king's command, though later he cannot command that a law he made be broken. Others have observed that her refusal demonstrates her clear-mindedness in the face of the king's drunkenness. She is aware, if he is not, of the vulnerability of a woman entering into a mob of men at the end of seven days of drinking. Whatever the case may be, the reality of the text as we have it is that the biblical author felt no need either to tell us the reason for Vashti's refusal or to develop her character, for good or ill, beyond her quiet entrance and exit. Vashti exists as a character in the story solely to vacate a position for Esther to fill, though literarily her queenly actions do provide a contrast to Esther—the one refuses to come when summoned; the other agrees to go when not summoned. (See Jobes 1999, 70-75.)

While this episode clarifies little about Vashti's character, it puts to rest any remaining doubts concerning the arrogance of Xerxes. Perhaps one could attempt to explain the emotion of Xerxes' response (he **became furious** [*yiqṣōp*] and **burned with anger** [*ḥāmātô bā'ărāh*; v 12]) as due to the public nature of the rejection. However, the irrational course of action, so disproportional to the offense, he pursues clearly reveals him to be an egomaniacal autocrat who sees an affront to his person as an affront to the entire kingdom he rules. Thus, he summons another seven about whom we are told their names along with several other pieces of information. They are **the wise men who understood the times** (*ḥăkāmîm yōdĕ'ê ha'itîm*), **experts in matters of law and justice** (*yōdĕ'ê dāt vĕdîn*) (v 13), those **closest** [*haqqārōb*] **to the king, nobles** [*śārê*] **of Persia and Media with special access** [*rō'ê pĕnê hammelek*] **to the king, who *sit first* [*hayyōšĕbîm ri'šōnāh*] in the kingdom** (v 14).

This is no trivial assemblage! These nobles (*śārîm*) have been present throughout both feasts (1:3, 11), and it is specifically before "the people and nobles" (v 11) that Xerxes intended to display Vashti's beauty. The idea of seven royal advisers is known from Persian history (given to us through the Greeks). According to Briant, "Herodotus often calls the Seven *prōtoi* (III.68-70, 77)," meaning "first," a position indicated in the biblical text, and this "small group of *prōtoi* was often convened by the king in times of peace or war." The existence of a royal council is expected. The phrase used here (*rō'ê pĕnê hammelek*, translated **special access** or ***those who see the face of the king***) is found in 2 Kgs 25:19, informing us that the kings of Judah also retained a royal council.

The designation of **wise men who understood the times** is also echoed in Israelite history when David gathered around him men from the tribe of Issachar known as ***men who have an understanding for the times*** (*yōdĕ'ê bînāh la'itîm* [1 Chr 12:32]); however, Chronicles goes on to say that the purpose of their understanding was for ***knowing what Israel should do*** (*lāda'at mah-ya'ăśeh yiśrā'ēl*). Such noble intentions are not present in these Persian advisers. According to Briant, this council was commissioned and convened "solely on the pleasure of the sovereign. Most decisions were made by the king alone, who received advice from these 'confidants' who owed him everything" (2002, 128-30). It would seem that Xerxes's supposed pursuit of law and justice is simply a pretense for gathering those whose primary role was to stroke the royal ego rather than seek honest rulings.

How are we to understand this **law** (*dāt*) that Xerxes is consulting and that Vashti has allegedly transgressed? The term itself is a Persian one, appearing in the Hebrew portion of the biblical text twenty times in Esther and once in Ezra (8:36), as well as fourteen times in the Aramaic portions of Daniel and Ezra. As it is used several times in Esther (e.g., 1:8; 2:12), it implies nothing more than "practice, custom." The Greek author Herodotus, for example, lists proper Persian practices (*nomoi*, "custom"; "law") for everything from lying and leprosy to birthdays and burials (I.131-140). In its most formal sense, usually expressed in phrases such as "the laws of Persia and Media" (Esth 1:19; Dan 6:8), *dāt* is probably meant to indicate something akin to a Persian law code. However, Ezra 7:26 uses *dāt* to refer both to the Jewish law ("the law of [Ezra's] God") and to Persian law ("the law of the king"), both punishable by the Persian judicial system. Thus, Jewish law governs Jewish people, becoming in essence their law code as Persian citizens, though no one would expect non-Jewish Persian citizens to obey those laws. Likewise, the laws of Persia and Media governed the Jews only in regard to significant issues of the empire, such as "loyalty and tribute" (see Briant 2002, 511), though not in Persian practice. That King Xerxes is unable to judge between the two—practice and law—displays his own ineptitude as a leader and neuroses as a person.

D. Memukan's Speech (1:16-20)

■ **16** The speech of the adviser Memukan is the longest monologue in the book, displaying in its length the excess to which we have grown accustomed in the royal court. The fawning nature of his position is also highlighted, as he begins and ends the opening of his speech in v 16 precisely where we would expect—with the focus on Xerxes (so the Hebrew, **Not against the king alone has Vashti the queen done wrong**). The verb "to do wrong" (*'āvāh*) appears in this form only in Dan 9:5, in a list of many terms used to describe different types of wrongdoing. However, for Memukan, the focus is not on the perceived wrong done but on the persons who have been wronged. Of course, the king is chief among those, but following in a close second are **all the nobles** (*śārîm*, of whom Memukan is "first" [Esth 1:14]) **and all of the peoples who are in all the provinces of King Xerxes**!

■ **17-18** The offense now becomes clear—Vashti has publicly shamed her husband (Laniak 1998). His advisers now fear household anarchy will erupt throughout the kingdom, with Vashti's actions causing **all wives** to **despise** [*lĕhabzôt*] **their husbands** (v 17) with similar refusals (implying, of course, royal support for similar demands!). While this scenario is framed as universal, there can be no doubt that Memukan is primarily concerned with his own household, emphasizing in v 18 that it is the **noble ladies** (*śārôt*), presumably those present at the queen's banquet, who will immediately (**this very day** [*hayyôm hazzeh*]) begin to follow Vashti's lead in responding to their **noble lords** (*śārîm*). The repetition of particular Hebrew forms in v 17 highlights the irony here—the mere telling (*'mr*) of Vashti's act will cause (Hebrew causative stem) defiance in all wives everywhere yet the king's telling (*'mr*) could not cause (Hebrew causative stem) his own wife's obedience.

The Hebrew root (*bāzāh* [vv 17, 18]) that describes the wives' actions is often translated "to despise, scorn" and carries connotations of rejection. This root frequently refers to Israel's rejection of God or his ways (e.g., 1 Sam 2:30; 2 Sam 12:9, 10; Ezek 22:8), yet it is also used to describe God as one who does not reject those who turn to him (Ps 51:17 [19 HB]; 102:17 [18 HB]). Haman later will *reject* (Esth 3:9) the idea of seeking revenge on Mordecai alone and choose rather to seek annihilation of all of God's people. ***There will be no end of rejection and fury*** (1:18) is the cycle of common domestic interactions that, if not stopped, will continually reenact this royal one—following Vashti, wives will reject (*bizzāyôn*) their husbands, and following Xerxes, husbands will become furious (*qāṣep*; see v 12)! (also Wesley 1765, 1:18).

■ **19** Memukan's solution to this situation is simple—an unbreakable royal decree (*dĕbar malkût*) should be issued. That this is to be done ***if it seems good to the king*** (*'im 'al hammelek ṭôb*) appears to be the appropriate way to make a suggestion to a Persian monarch (so Nehemiah to Artaxerxes I in Neh 2:5, 7). However, a comparison of the requests brought to the king for approval in Esther is striking. Here, Memukan asks for the king's pleasure to settle the score for a trivial party incident, while in Esth 3:9, Haman asks for approval to annihilate the entire Jewish population. In all of the other uses, Esther is speaking, issuing the seemingly mundane request for the king's attendance at a feast (5:4, 8), yet following that with her true entreaty for her life and the lives of her people (7:3), and for permission for her people to defend themselves against attack (8:5; 9:13).

The king's affirmative response to Memukan's request here confirms to the audience that he is a self-absorbed tyrant for whom any request that strokes the royal ego is good. His following acceptance of Haman's request bodes much worse, indicating that he has no discernment and may view any request as good to him at any given moment. Thus, the author heightens the tension of the later requests brought by Esther. Are her initial requests, whose apparent value are only to stroke the royal ego, actually a cunning tactic? But will her true requests turn the royal head, or will his total lack of ability to discern aright thwart the response she desires? As yet, the audience does not know.

The notion of the inalterability of the laws of the Persians and Medes is one found only in the biblical text. In Dan 6:8, 12, 15 [9, 13, 16 HB], two Aramaic verbs are used to describe these laws. The root *'dy*, commonly meaning "to pass away" but also "to transgress," is the equivalent of the Hebrew *'br* used here and elsewhere in Esther (e.g., 3:3; 9:27, 28). The other is *šny*, meaning "to change" or "to violate." The first implies the laws' perpetuity and immutability, while the second emphasizes their inflexibility and the strength of punishment to be brought upon violators (though each verb also conveys some of the other's meaning). Most would agree that the further elaboration in Esth 8:8 that laws issued by the king and sealed by his ring are *'ên lĕhāšîb* (not to "be revoked") brings clarity that the first meaning above is to be understood in Esther, and presumably in Daniel. However, clearly the second meaning would be assumed within that understanding as well (see further Clines 1984b, 282; contra Fox 2001, 177).

The absurdity of this entire course of action is crowned by the absolute ridiculousness of the royal decree. The decree itself does nothing to correct the queen's behavior or address Memukan's concerns; rather, the law simply states Vashti's punishment—that she may not **enter** [*lō' tābô'*] **the presence** of the king (*lipnê hammelek*), precisely what she refused to do in the first place (v 12). Furthermore, this *děbar malkût* (**royal decree**) deprives her of her *malkût* (**royalty**), which Memukan in essence has already stripped from her by referring to her only as **Vashti** without her royal title. That honor will now be bestowed upon **someone else who is better than** [*haṭṭōb min-*] **she**. This phrase echoes with the words of Samuel to King Saul in 1 Sam 15:28, when his kingdom is ripped from his hands and given "to one better than" (*haṭṭōb min-*) he, David. The contrast of sins, however, could not be more stark, once again emphasizing to us the lavish triviality of the Persian court.

■ **20** As Memukan concludes, he is generous in his piling on of flattery. He is sure to comment on the greatness (*rabbāh*) of the king's kingdom (*malkût*, that which he just deprived from another), while assuring the king that his **edict** (*pitgām*) will indeed produce the desired effect—the rejection (*bāzāh*) of Esth 1:17 will be replaced with the honor (*yěqār*) that the king had displayed before all his nobles in v 4 but had been so publicly marred by Vashti's snub. The scope of the effect, profiting husbands *from the greatest to the least*, intentionally mimics the scope of Xerxes' guest list (v 5), playing to what may be the king's self-appraisal as a generous and benevolent ruler to all. Thus, Memukan confirms that, while he may not be one who knows the times, he is no doubt one who knows his king.

E. Vashti Deposed (1:21-22)

■ **21-22** Not surprisingly, this proposal, which makes every man **ruler** [*śōrēr*, related to *śar*, "noble"] **over his own household** (v 22), does **seem good** (*vayyîṭab*) to the king and his nobles. Thus, all the administrative power of the Persian Empire is mustered to broadcast the ruling. To the presumed extent of the effect of Vashti's actions on "all" the kingdom (v 16), the **dispatches** (*sěpārîm*) are sent **to all of the provinces** [*mědînôt*] **of the king**, to each and every one (of the 127!) and to each and every people group (*'am*) therein. Moreover, it is to go out in every **writing system** (*kětāb*) and **language** (*lāšôn*) of the empire. Thus, the reader becomes attuned to the immense diversity of populations within the Persian Empire, though for now, we remain unaware that scattered throughout the realm exists a fairly insignificant, small group of exiles—the Jews.

FROM THE TEXT

Learning from the Persians: How can I read this chapter about the lavish debauchery of the royal court of ancient Persia and find anything at all that could be relevant or applicable to my life? This question is at the heart of understanding how Christians today can go about reading stories in the Bible as Holy Scripture. The term "scripture" can be defined as a set of authoritative texts for a community. The Bible, both the Old and New Testaments, are those texts for Christians. If so, what kind of authority for my life can I find in this chapter of Esther?

As its primary objective, the Bible is "the story of God's seeking and loving engagement with creation as its Creator and Redeemer." The need both for God's seeking and his redeeming of humanity, his highest creation, rests in another central part of the story contained in Scripture—"the catastrophic account of human disobedience" (Brower 2013, 489). It is precisely because of human disobedience that the Jews of Susa have found themselves here in Persia, outside the land that God gave to them as the space in which they would learn about and faithfully live out holy love in relationship with him. Within that space of the promised land, God's people were to live separated from the people who surrounded them, people who lived contrary to the laws of God. These people were not permanently excluded from relationship with God, as illustrated by the stories of the Moabitess Ruth (book of Ruth) and the Canaanite Rahab (Josh 2, and 6:25) who became part of God's people. Rather, God's choosing of Israel (the Jews) was to bring them into right relationship with him so that eventually all peoples in the world could be brought into restored harmony with God as well (Gen 12:3), a plan that was fulfilled in the life, death, and resurrection of Jesus Christ (Rom 3:22-24). However, the Jews' rebellion against this plan in the OT had led to the exile they were now experiencing in Esther among the Persians.

These Jewish exiles, however, have begun to learn something that God had been attempting to teach them for years. The Persians among whom they are living paint the picture of lives lived against the will and law of God. Throughout their history, the Israelites had encountered these types of people (e.g., Moabites in Num 25, Canaanites in Judg 17—21, Phoenicians in 1 Kgs 16:31), and their unholy practices had more often than not become a snare to God's people. It was precisely for this reason that God placed in his law commands against marrying anyone who was not a follower of him (Deut 7:3-4; Ezra 9:14). These laws had nothing to do with race or skin color; quite the contrary, in fact. Most of the people with whom Israel came in contact throughout their history would have looked just like them. No, these decrees were about protecting the hearts of his people, to keep them from being lured away from him.

Can I learn from the Persians precisely what the Jews were meant to see? Indeed! When I read the narratives of the Bible, I read them in light of this bigger story of God and his relationship with humanity. In this light, I am not meant to understand every action in these stories as ones to be emulated. Even without direct critique of actions by the biblical authors, the story of God with his people shows me that one way God teaches us how to live rightly with him is by presenting those who do *not* live rightly. Along with its primary function of teaching me about God, the Bible also serves to provide "moral guidance" to our lives—teaching me how a child of God lives (Clapper 2013, 487). In their lives of excess, arrogance, and egotism, the Persians provide the contrast to the life I desire—a life lived for, with, and in God.

Seeing the Marginalized: It is difficult (I hope, impossible) for us as readers to dismiss the character of Vashti as quickly as our author. Though her literary purpose is merely to create space for Esther, as she is quite literally moved to the text's margin, as a person she tugs at both our imagination and our heartstrings.

Esther commentators throughout the centuries have framed Vashti in every possible light, from spoiled to oppressed to noble and pure, each of those requiring very different views of Xerxes and his motives. However, as Clines notes, regardless of her character or that of Xerxes, the only act that Vashti commits in the story is simply to assert "her human right to say no," to determine where, when, and under what circumstances her body may be seen (1990, 32).

This is the first of several places in this book named for a woman where the situations and realities faced by women are brought to our attention (→ From the Text for 2:1-20 and 10:1-3). The functional purpose of Xerxes' decree in this chapter is to silence women and empower men in imperially sanctioned dominance. This legislated practice remains a reality for millions of women across our world today, while the functional attitude is experienced by women even in free societies (and even in our churches!). A Wesleyan perspective speaks directly to this type of oppression, affirming that all humanity, male and female, are created in the image of God (Gen 1:27) and all are one in him (Gal 3:28). The effects of the curse (Gen 3:16) have been fully eradicated by the work of Jesus Christ, and this eradication can be fully realized in this world by the power of the Holy Spirit working through the lives of God's people. The challenge set forth by LaCelle-Peterson rings so true here, "We cannot accept the brokenness and sinfulness of post-fall humanity as 'just the way things are' if we are people seeking to live out God's design for us" (2008, 41; see also Schenck 2015).

For all Christians and hopefully for Wesleyans in particular, exposure to the violation of any person in any circumstance must stir in us unrest and spur us to the righting of wrongs and bringing of justice to this world (Luke 4:18; Isa 61:1-3; 58:6-9). We are compelled to hear Vashti's story with those ears and see with those eyes, even though this probably was not our author's intent. As Clines continues, "Living as and when we do, we are bound . . . to resist the author's intention as the only possible meaning, and bound to enrich the story by reading it in different modes, or dimensions, or contexts" (1990, 32). Christians cannot look on the oppression of women (a given throughout much of time and culture) or any group as a norm to be accepted, but as an injustice that will not exist in the world to come and that, therefore, requires our work to overcome. As we partner with God to bring his kingdom to this earth as it is in heaven, we can do no less.

II. ESTHER MADE QUEEN: ESTHER 2:1-20

BEHIND THE TEXT

Following ch 1, which clearly defines the roles of women throughout the kingdom as subordinate to men, ch 2 presents the life of women inside the palace—a life fully devoted to the whim and pleasure of the king. The Persian harem is known from Greek sources as being, as we might expect, decadently excessive in both its size and lavishness. Though Briant notes the difficulty in separating "fact from Greek interpretation," the classical Greek authors provide much evidence related to the Persian harem, including the practice of gathering women from throughout the kingdom as a payment of tribute to the king, the division of the harem into separate houses for women of varying categories, the provision of servants for the royal wives and concubines, assessment of the unsurpassed beauty of the royal women, the absence of royal wives from the king's drinking parties, and even stories of a Persian king's enchantment with a singular woman in his royal harem (2002, 277-86). In all of this, the details from Esther that are attested in the ancient sources confirm our author's keen awareness of and familiarity with Persian court life.

A close look at the names of Mordecai's ancestors presents another important facet of the background of this story. The names of his grandfather Shimei and great-grandfather Kish are prominent ones in the history of the tribe of Benjamin, particularly in the clan of Saul. The name Shimei is known best to us from the account of King David's flight from Jerusalem in the face of a coup by his son Absalom (2 Sam 16:5-14). There, this Benjamite from the clan of Saul curses David for **the blood of the house of Saul, in whose place [David] had reigned** (16:8). Shimei's life is spared by David (2 Sam 19:23 [24 HB]) but eventually taken by Solomon (1 Kgs 2:46). Kish is renowned as the father of Saul, first king of Israel. While we are not told that Mordecai himself descends from Saul's line, these patronymic allusions to notorious figures within Benjamin, the tribe of Saul, begin to draw out connections with this part of Israel's history in the minds of the audience. These connections will become a vital link in the ensuing plot.

Some, as far back as early rabbinic interpreters, have argued that the Shimei and Kish of Mordecai's ancestry are actually those historic personages of Benjamite fame, giving Mordecai an authentic royal, though rejected, pedigree, and solidifying a direct descent from Saul (though Clines correctly notes that it is impossible to descend from both "the Kish and the Shimei from the books of Samuel" [1984b, 287]). It is the case that the use of kinship terms such as father (*'āb*) and son (*bēn*) to communicate more distant relationships are not problematic in biblical accounting (see, e.g., Gen 28:13, where God identifies himself to Jacob as "the God of Abraham your father," when in fact Abraham is Jacob's grandfather). However, if the author's primary purpose were to communicate that Mordecai was a descendant of Saul, why would he choose Kish as the ancestor to highlight and not Saul himself? Furthermore, the antecedent to the relative clause "who had been carried into exile" (Esth 2:6; *'ăšer hoglāh*) is ambiguous, most typically referring to the initial individual, that is, Mordecai, though potentially referring to the final individual, that is, Kish. Due to the fact that this clause applied to Mordecai would create a chronological difficulty for Mordecai's age in 486 BC, some 111 years after the exile of Jehoiachin in 597 BC, it seems best to apply this clause to Mordecai's great-grandfather Kish. Seeing that the clearest way of reading the genealogy is as direct descent and that the purpose of connecting Mordecai to Saul is fulfilled in this reading without creating the additional chronological difficulty, that interpretation is to be preferred.

This is not the only connection that exists between the tribe of Benjamin and the Esther story. In Judg 21, the Israelite tribe of Benjamin is saved from extinction when four hundred young virgins (*na'ărāh bĕtûlāh* [Esth 2:2 below]) from Jabesh Gilead are spared from the massacre of their city and given to the Benjamites as wives. Clearly, this forceful taking and giving of innocent young women parallels the Esther story. However, there is a further resonance here.

Branson points out that Jabesh Gilead reappears in the biblical account in 1 Sam 11 where the Benjamite Saul saves the inhabitants of this city (apparently descendants of those who had escaped the Judges massacre). It is quite possible that Saul's allegiance to this city is born out of his own lineage as a descendant of a man of Benjamin and one of the young virgins from Jabesh Gilead (2009, 185). Thus, in these very subtle ways, we are introduced to the family of Mordecai and Esther, a family of Benjamin whose salvation came by means of a group of young virgins (→ 2:2 and From the Text).

Collectively, God's people are called "Jews" (*yĕhûdî*) in Esther. This term originally designated only Judeans from the tribe of Judah, as used eighteen times in the OT (e.g., 2 Kgs 16:6). However, in the Persian period (539—330 BC), the term referred broadly to the community who traced their origin, however distant physically or temporally, to the Persian province of Yehud, surrounding Jerusalem. The author of Esther embraced this designation, utilizing it fifty-two of its sixty-four total times with this sense in the OT (first in Esth 2:5). Other biblical authors of this period exhibit acceptance to varying degrees, with Ezra decisively preferring "Israel" over "Jews" and Nehemiah somewhat less so. Zechariah 8:23, also from this period, expresses the returned exiles' hopefulness in God's full restoration of his people, the Jews, saying, "This is what the LORD Almighty says: 'In those days ten people from all languages and nations will take firm hold of one Jew by the hem of his robe and say, "Let us go with you, because we have heard that God is with you"'" (see Bush 1996, 361).

In this chapter, the setting of the book progresses rapidly from the third year of Xerxes' reign (Esth 1:3) to the seventh year in 2:16. Esther is brought before the king in the tenth month (*ṭēbēt*), which in the Persian calendrical system would coincide with our December-January. Persian years begin in Nisan, which coincides with our March-April, and a king's years are dated from the first New Year (March-April) of his reign. Therefore, though Xerxes came to power in November 486, his first year does not end until March 484, due to the fact that year one began to be counted in March/April of 485. Based upon this accession year system, the tenth month of the seventh year would correspond to December-January, 479/478 BC, soon after Xerxes returned from his failed campaigns in Greece (Briant 2002, 161, 535; Clines 1984b, 260-61, 275, 290).

IN THE TEXT

A. The King's Regret and Another Edict (2:1-4)

■ 1 It is not stated how long *after these things* ('*aḥar haddĕbārîm hā' ēlleh*) it takes for the king's fury (*ḥēmāh*) to subside (*šākak*), though we know from 2:16 that Esther comes to the king in the seventh year of his reign (479 BC), which is the year in which he returned from his military campaigns in Greece. Thus, it is possible to conjecture that his fury over Vashti's party snub faded during this time in light of his three humiliating defeats at the hands of the Greeks and the resulting uprising in Babylonia (see discussion in Briant 2002, 541-42). Or perhaps, as early

Jewish interpretation assumes, his regret was much more immediate, happening soon after the effects of the wine abated. Either way, the simplest interpretation of Xerxes' remembering (*zākar*) is to presume that he is regretting the course of action he had taken against Vashti.

■ **2** The significant problem, of course, is that the action that Xerxes is regretting is irreversible. His brilliant royal advisers who concocted the scheme are conveniently unavailable to contend with the effects of their plan upon their sovereign. Instead, it falls to his **personal attendants** (*na'ărê-hammelek mĕšārĕtāyw*) to quickly suggest a solution. Again, quite ironically, it is not the royal advisers, about whom we were told so much, who have the greatest sway over our protagonists, but rather this group of servants who both suggest the plan to acquire Esther and later confirm the need to honor Mordecai (6:3).

The plan proposed here begins the theme of seeking, carried by the Hebrew root *bāqaš*, that pervades the book of Esther. Here, the king's seeking is precipitated by the loss of his wife (ch 1), a loss for which he is the ultimate cause (though Fox notes that the use of the passive voice in *nigzar*, **that which had been decreed concerning her** (2:1), suggests the king's unwillingness to accept responsibility for the action he now regrets; Fox 2001, 26, in Bush 1996, 367). In light of his loss of a beautiful (*ṭôbat mareh* [1:11]) queen, his attendants recommend a search for beautiful (*ṭôbôt mareh*) young virgins (*nĕ'ārôt bĕtûlôt*). This search echoes that made on behalf of the aged King David in 1 Kgs 1:2, though there on a much smaller scale. However, it is in the allusion to Judg 21:12 where this phrase appears that the author begins to paint the ancient backdrop for our story, drawing connections with the salvation of Mordecai's tribe of Benjamin through four hundred young virgins (→ Behind the Text and From the Text). Already in the hatching of this oppressive scheme do we perceive the opportunity for ultimate survival.

■ **3-4** The range of this proposed search will equal that of the preceding royal edict, gathering **all** the beautiful young virgins in **all the provinces of the king's kingdom.** The administration for the process is also as immense, requiring commissioners (*pĕqîdîm*) to gather these women **to the citadel of Susa** (→ Behind the Text for ch 1) where they will be placed **in the house of the women** (*bêt hannāšîm*) under the care of the eunuch Hegai and given **beauty treatments** (*tamrûqîm*). The impulse for this edict is in the end the same as for the last—fulfilling the pleasure of the king. Quite predictably we see for Xerxes that finding a maiden **who seems good in [his] eyes** (*yāṭab bĕ'ênê*) does indeed **seem good in [his] eyes** (*yāṭab . . . bĕ'ênê*). **So he does it** (*'āśāh kēn*). As before, it is the appetites of the king that rule this kingdom, a kingdom in which "the personal has become the political, and both have become laughable" (Levenson 1997, 54).

B. Enter Mordecai and Esther (2:5-7)

■ **5-6** The shift in the Hebrew text is abrupt, with the beginning of the next verse lacking the usual conjunction to connect one thought to another. (This abrupt shift is indicated in the English with **Now . . .** [v 5].) For the first time in our story, the focus of our attention is not the great king, but simply a man (*'îš*), specifically, a Jewish man (*'îš yĕhûdî*). The form of this modest introduction, which begins with the general *There was a man . . .* and moves to the specific *and his name was . . .* , is familiar in Hebrew literary style, appearing with some variations in the introductions of Manoah (Judg 13:2), Elkanah (1 Sam 1:1), Elimelek (Ruth 1:1-2), and even Mordecai's fellow Benjamites Kish and Saul (1 Sam 9:1-2). That this man happens to be in the same location where the young virgins will be brought, **the citadel of Susa**, provides the connection with the preceding verses, though the reason for Mordecai's presence there is not made explicit. It seems safe to assume, however, that Mordecai's presence in the palace complex is due to a position that he holds in Persian administrative service, based upon the fact that he sits "at the king's gate" in 2:21, and that he appears to be among "the royal officials" in 3:2.

At face value, Mordecai's ancestry identifies him as a Benjamite, three generations removed from the Babylonian exile (→ Behind the Text). According to the account of the exile in 2 Kgs 24:8-17, those exiled along with Jehoiachin (also spelled Jeconiah as in, e.g., Esth 2:6; 1 Chr 3:16; Jer 28:4) included the king's mother, attendants (*'ăbādîm*), nobles/officers (*śārîm*), officials (*sārîsîm*), fighting men (*gibbôrê haḥayil*), skilled workers (*heḥārāš*), artisans (*hammasgēr*), and the prominent people of the land (*'êlê hā'āreṣ*). Based upon both this list and the statement in Dan 1:3 that Daniel and his friends were chosen "from the royal family and the nobility," it may be argued that Mordecai's pedigree was one of nobility. However, the 2 Kings passage also states that Nebuchadnezzar exiled all of Jerusalem except "the poorest people of the land" (24:14; *dalat 'am-hā'āreṣ*). Therefore, the text does not require Mordecai's placement among the aristocracy, though it seems likely.

While the genealogy does provide important background for us (→ Behind the Text), it is the fact of Mordecai's exiled status that is being emphasized here above all else. The repetition of the root *gālāh* ("to exile, carry away") four times in Esth 2:6 reveals this emphasis: *who had been* __exiled__ *from Jerusalem with the* __exiles__ *who were* __exiled__ *with Jeconiah king of Judah whom Nebuchadnezzar king of Babylon* __exiled__. The sense of imprisonment that is hammered into the reader by these recurrences portends the coming capture of Esther, introduced in the next verse. "Esther's identity is the identity of the Jewish people"—"vulnerable, with one's destiny in the hands of others and in a land where the rules of engagement may turn out to be significantly different" (Wells 2013, 37-38).

■ **7** Along with being a Jew, a resident of the citadel of Susa, and a Benjamite, Mordecai also became an *'ōmēn*, "nurse or guardian" (see, e.g., Ruth 4:16 and 2 Sam 4:4). While Naomi fulfilled this role for her grandson Obed though his parents were both living, Mordecai filled this role for his uncle's daughter *because she had no father or mother* (*kî 'ên lāh 'āb vā'ēm*). When they had died, he had taken her in *as a daughter* (*lĕbat*). This daughter is known by both her Hebrew name, **Hadassah** (likely meaning "myrtle"), and her non-Hebrew name, **Esther** (either Persian "star" or the Babylonian name of the goddess Ishtar). Evidence for the practice of Jews in diverse contexts appropriating non-Hebrew names to use in foreign venues is found in the OT where Daniel and his three friends have both Hebrew and Babylonian names (Dan 1:6-7), as well as in the NT where the apostle Paul is known in Hebraic circles as Saul (Acts 13:9). The only other information supplied for us concerning Esther is about her appearance. She meets the qualification for all the young virgins in this search in that she is **beautiful** (*ṭôbat mar'eh*); however, Esther is also described as having *a fine form* (*yĕpat-tō'ar*), a phrase used to describe Rachel (Gen 29:17), Abigail wife of Nabal (1 Sam 25:3), and even Joseph (Gen 39:6). That which defines Esther in her introduction will continue to define her for a significant portion of our story, being known only for her outward appearance and by her familial connections. Though concealed initially, however, there is more to Esther than meets the eye.

C. Esther in the Palace (2:8-11)

■ **8-9** After the order is **heard** (*šāma'*) and many girls are **gathered** (*qābaṣ*), Esther is **taken** (*lāqaḥ*) (Esth 2:8). The exile of Esther proceeds with this series of passive verbs that signify helplessness and subjugation. Transferred from the guardianship of one man, Mordecai, to another, Hegai, and awaiting the whim of a third, Xerxes, the future of this girl (*hanna'ărāh*) about whom we know so little seems bleak. Fortunately, in this world that turns on the pleasure of men, Esther **seems good** to Hegai (*yāṭab . . . bĕ'ênāyw*) and **receives his favor** (*nāśā' ḥesed*) (v 9). Though the passive verbs leave one to wonder who is acting here, Wesley sees the ultimate source of the favor Esther receives as "the Divine power, which moveth the hearts of men which way he pleaseth" (1765, 2:9).

The first clause in v 9 (she **seemed good**) is the same used to describe Xerxes' assessment of the proposals made by both Memukan (1:21) and his attendants (2:4). The second clause (**received his favor**) appears for the first time here (with the object *ḥesed*) and is repeated in 2:15 (with *ḥēn*), 17 (*ḥēn vāḥesed*), and 5:2 (*ḥēn*), with the object translated **favor** varying as noted. The most common way to express the idea of finding favor in someone's eyes is with *ḥēn* following the verb *māṣā'* (see, e.g., Gen 6:8; Ruth 2:2; Prov 3:4). Esther herself uses that formation in Esth 5:8, 7:3, and 8:5, all in conditional clauses following **if** (*'im*) and all in the first person. In contrast, only these few verses of Esther contain these objects with the verb *nāśā'*, all in the third person and with the meaning "to receive," rather than its usual "to lift up, carry, bear" (see also Ps 24:5 with this meaning).

As Moore has observed, the uses with *māṣā'* ("find favor") suggest Esther's dependence and passivity while the uses with *nāśā'* ("receive favor") indicate her action and merit (1971, 21). To this point, however, the only quality commended to the reader is that of her outward appearance. In a palace full of all of the youth and beauty of the kingdom, it seems impossible that Esther's appearance alone is so superior to evoke such favor from Hegai (Esth 2:9), from the king (2:17), and from all who see her (2:15). While not yet explicit, the author is subtly exposing an inward character that attracts more attention than an outward shape.

■ **10-11** The concealment of Esther's true character parallels the concealment of her true identity. Mordecai **commands** (*ṣāvāh*) Esther **not to disclose** (*lō' nāgad*) either **her people** (*'ammāh*) or **her kindred** (*môladtāh*). While these two nouns may seem somewhat synonymous, the first clearly indicates her nationality, that is, her Jewishness, while the second could indicate more specifically her family connections, that is, her relationship with Mordecai. Quite humorously, it is Mordecai himself whose actions threaten to sabotage this portion of his own command! **Each and** every day [*bĕkol-yôm vāyôm*] he paces [not just walking (*hōlēk*) but pacing (*mithallēk*!)] **near the courtyard of the harem** *that he might come to know* [*yāda'*] **Esther's well-being** [*šālôm*] **and what is being done** [*'āśāh*] **to her.** Even in this humorous moment, notice again the passive voice used in reference to what Esther is experiencing in this process.

D. Preparation (2:12-14)

■ **12-14** Though it is a luxurious captivity, it is captivity nonetheless. The ludicrous opulence of the Persians is once again apparent in the length of time devoted to beauty treatments in preparation for one's presentation to the king. This twelve-month treatment is **in accordance with the practice of women** (*kĕdāt hannāšîm*, see discussion of *dāt* in ch 1) (v 12). A protocol also exists for one's entry into the king's palace. **All that she asks for** (*kol-'ăšer tō'mar*, note that the Hebrew emphasizes this phrase by placing it before the verb) is **given** [*nātan*] **to her** as she moves **from the house of women to the house of the king** (*mibbêt-hannāšîm 'ad-bêt hammelek*) (v 13). Her "one night with the king" ends with a return, but it is a return to a different place (a second house of women) and to a different guardian, Shaashgaz (who like Hegai is a eunuch and guardian, though over the concubines *happîlagšîm*). There, presumably, ends her identity, as once again she passively waits **to be called** [*qārā'*] **by name**, an occasion that seems quite improbable for this mass of nameless ones and that hinges entirely on the king's **desires** (*ḥāpēṣ*) (v 14).

E. Esther's Ascent (2:15-20)

■ **15-16** The **arrival** [*haggîa'*] **of Esther's turn** (*tôr-'estēr*) brings the final exchange of the passage—Esther is taken (*lāqaḥ*) to the king (v 15). Though the passive voice continues to mark Esther as a captive, these verses give the reader hope! First of all, we are told not only Esther's name, an element that is key (v 14) if she is to escape the utter captivity of a life of concubinage, but also her lineage. She is **Esther, the daughter of Abihail** [*bat-'ăbîḥayil*], **the uncle of Mordecai who had taken** [*lāqaḥ*] **her in as a daughter** (*lĕbat*). While it seems placed at a very odd spot in the story, it is at this pivotal moment in the life of this young virgin, a moment that may damn her to a lifetime of identity-less captivity away from her people and her family, that Esther's full identity is proclaimed. She has a father, and she has experienced a taking of the most precious kind—the provision of adoption. If Esther's past is the precedent, her future is surely not as desolate as it momentarily appears.

2:10-16

Along with her identification, we are told that Esther does not adhere to the protocol that has been followed by all the other young virgins before her. **Esther does not seek** [*bāqaš*] **a thing**. It is a beautiful statement of Esther's character that in her hiding, she does not seek. Though this is the only chance for the taken one (*lāqaḥ* [vv 8, 16]) to take whatever she can, she takes nothing. Rather, as she has always followed the will of her guardian Mordecai, she now follows the advice of her guardian Hegai. **Thus Esther received favor** [*ḥēn*] **from all who saw her**. This statement expresses the result of Esther's choices by the use of the Hebrew imperfect consecutive form (*vattēhî*; for examples of the imperfect consecutive used consequentially, see Arnold and Choi 2003, 85-86). In this way the author communicates Esther's submission in a positive light as well as demonstrates the extent to which these acts distinguish her among her captors and peers.

■ **17-18** Ultimately, however, we have learned that it is only the pleasure of the king that matters; thus, v 17 marks a crucial moment in the text. Succinctly, we are told the king's reaction and the result—**he loved** (*'āhab*) her **and she received** (*nāśā'*) his favor and approval, **so he placed** (*śîm*) the crown upon her, **made her queen** (v 17), and **gave** [*'āśāh*] **a great banquet** (v 18). Yet within this brevity, the author continues his emphasis on Persian superfluity, eclipsing the actions and expectations of the entire story to this point.

His love (*'āhab*) far exceeds the anticipated desiring (*ḥāpēṣ*, v 14). The extent of Esther's enchantment—**more than _all_ the women . . . more than _all_ the virgins**—continues to mimic the extent of Vashti's errant influence (1:16-20). Esther receives both **favor and approval** (*ḥēn vāḥesed*). Thus, that which Vashti refused (the **royal crown** [*keter malkût* (1:11)]) is now placed upon Esther's head, making her queen **instead of Vashti** (*taḥat vāštî*). The story comes full circle with the now indispensable banquet—Esther's banquet (*mištēh 'estēr*), presumably a wedding feast. Like the first, this banquet is **for _all_ his nobles and officials** (v 18), and like the second, this banquet displays the king's abundance (*kĕyad hammelek* [1:7]), though through the giving of gifts (*maś'ēt*) rather than wine (not to say that wine was not present). However, continuing to exceed expectations, this feast, unlike the former, is called **great** (*gādôl*) (though one can hardly imagine how it might surpass the first two), and the **holiday** is extended beyond the citadel of Susa to the provinces. The term **holiday** (*hănāḥāh*) indicates a period of rest, perhaps indicating a royal remission from taxes or an amnesty (so NRSV footnote; contra Clines 1984b, 290), and is a prelude to the ultimate rest from their enemies for which the exiled Jews hope (→ 9:16).

It is important to note that the NIV phrase **the king was attracted to Esther** (v 17) translates the verb *'āhab*, generally meaning "to love." While this verb is often used to describe God's love for humanity, it also expresses human action and emotion. We must be careful neither to assume that these human actions inevitably reflect God's action nor to inject those instances with our modern, Western notions of romanticized love. In fact, as we see in 2 Sam 13, human expressions of *'āhab* can be just as perverted and lacking of God's character in the Bible as they are in today's world. In our context here, there has been nothing in the text so far that would make us assume that Xerxes is committing himself to Esther in an unconditional, selfless love that should be desired or emulated. However, I would argue that the translation "to be attracted to" weakens the overall intensifying effect of these verses. We had hoped that the king might desire Esther, but in fact, he loves her, a statement that at the very least communicates that Esther's situation is now better than might ever have been hoped!

■ **19-20** This narrative of Esther's unlikely ascent to the throne of Persia concludes with a shift of focus back toward Mordecai and a reiteration of Esther's continued loyalty to him (vv 19-20). Though Esther has avoided nameless captivity, the hiding of her identity remains a potentially menacing omission.

FROM THE TEXT

Portraying Purity: For some, Esther's encounter with the king in this chapter may appear as the author's casual indifference toward sexual purity. Linda Day's solution, which makes the encounter nonsexual by stating "exactly what occurs [in vv 16-17] . . . remains a matter of speculation" (2005, 51-52), simply overlooks the most apparent meaning of the text. John Wesley understands Esther with the status of a "wife of lower rank" from the moment she is taken, thereby releasing her from any "sin or dishonour" (1765, 2:13). While this explanation rightly understands both the cultural context and the encounter's sexual nature, it allows Esther to retain her sexual purity only on a technicality.

I would advocate that to define purity sexually is a privileged virtue and valid only in times and/or cultures in which people are granted control over their bodies. Once a person is denied control over her own body, culturally or situationally, her purity can no longer be equated with her sexuality. The reality is, Esther did not keep her virginity; however, she most definitely retained her purity. Esther was a woman who lived a life characterized by obedience, whose inward character more than her outward beauty brought her the favor of all she met, and whose faith in God and sacrificial love for her people brought about their salvation. May these be the qualities for which we remember her and by which she is judged, rather than for those events that happened to her over which she had no control. As Samuel said to Saul in 1 Sam 15:22:

> Does the LORD delight in burnt offerings and sacrifices
>> as much as in obeying the LORD?
> To obey is better than sacrifice,
>> and to heed is better than the fat of rams.

This verse teaches us that one's internal posture toward the Lord is of far more importance than any external, physical representation. That is not to say that the physical is unimportant (God didn't outlaw sacrifices from this time forward!); however, we need only give it its due weight, which in cases of sexual abuse is none at all.

Overcoming: To say that the accounts of the taking of young virgins, in Esther or in Judg 21 (→ Behind the Text and Esth 2:2), is difficult would be a gross understatement. In his commentary, Branson has eloquently addressed the tragedy of the final chapters of Judges, which present "in graphic detail the results of sin as a warning to its readers. God calls for the exclusive loyalty of his people. The worship of other gods leads to spiritual death and social chaos" (2009, 188). The depraved life of the royal court of Persia is social chaos in its most vulgar and absurd condition. It is into this scene of utter godlessness that the Jews have been thrust as a result of their sin—the rejection of God and his covenant.

Just as in Judges where one of the results of sin is the exploitation of women as "commodities to be seized for the benefit of men" (ibid., 188), likewise in Esther, the young virgin Esther is the recipient of this horrific consequence. In neither situation does the Lord step in to stop the mistreatment of these young women, yet in both situations this group ultimately serves as a means of salvation for his people. This is not to say that the Lord directs or condones such behavior. In fact, I would argue that his heart aches in the face of such exploitation and oppression committed by his creations upon one another (see Amos 2:6-16). However, these situations do illustrate for us the working out of God's plan for the restoration of humanity to him in spite of the presence of evil in this fallen world. All situations, no matter how terrible and even with human culpability in their occurrence, can be transformed into tools in the hands of God Almighty to bring about his ultimate purpose in this world! This is as true for Esther and for the women of Jabesh Gilead as it is for Joseph in Egypt (Gen 50:20) and for Paul in Corinth (Rom 8:28) and for us today. Whatever the evil of this world may plot against you, take heart! Our peace comes in knowing the one who has conquered this world (John 16:33).

Bearing God's Image: The book of Daniel (1:3-4) describes the select Jewish male exiles as "without any physical defect, handsome" (the same term applied to Esther in 2:7), but also "showing aptitude for every kind of learning, well informed, quick to understand, and qualified to serve." In contrast, descriptions of Esther in this chapter center exclusively on her physical appearance. I do not want my daughters or any other young woman to take away from the book of Esther the message of her culture and ours—I have to be beautiful to do anything significant in this world. We want the Bible to critique that cultural value, but it doesn't. That is left up to us. The Bible, even the book of Esther, sets us on the proper trajectory to do just that—by ch 9, Esther is a strong queen issuing edicts to her people, with no mention of her appearance. Let each of us continue to live this countercultural message, that through the Holy Spirit our lives are significant because of the image of God we bear rather than for how we appear.

Hide and Seek: Where is God in the book of Esther? This question, springing from the omission of God's name, is an important one (→ Introduction). In this chapter, we begin to see more clearly the author's strategic theme of hiding and seeking that permeates the entire book. The king seeks a new queen (2:2), Esther seeks nothing (v 15), the eunuchs seek to harm the king (v 21), and the plot itself is sought out (v 23). Corresponding to each of these acts of seeking is something that is lost or hidden—a queen, freedom, power, truth. Loss and hiddenness prompt seeking (Luke 15:8). God's hiddenness in this book, and even in our lives, may actually be a strategy that causes our seeking of him. In fact, perhaps we can see God more clearly because he isn't so conspicuously present. Much like Mordecai's connection to Esther is so apparently obvious (Esth 2:11) because of his efforts to conceal it (v 10), so God's presence is unmistakable precisely because of the author's "effort" to conceal him! Continue your search for God's conspicuous hiddenness throughout the book.

III. MORDECAI UNCOVERS A CONSPIRACY: ESTHER 2:21-23

BEHIND THE TEXT

The mention in vv 19 and 21 of Mordecai "sitting at the king's gate" is a reference both to his physical location and administrative position. According to Briant, the king's gate "was actually an imposing building, distinct in Elamite and Persian vocabulary from the gate of a building. The word became a synonym for the palace and the court, as shown by the expression 'Those of the Gate,' which became a sort of court title" (2002, 260; see also Gordis 1976, 47-48). Daniel 2:49 contributes to and confirms this understanding, as Daniel's friends are stationed abroad in administrative posts *while Daniel was in the king's gate*, a phrase translated in the NIV as "remained at the royal court."

Like the histories of all empires, Persian history contains tales of assassination attempts, both successful and unsuccessful. In particular, the involvement of eunuchs in these plots is found in the assassinations of Artaxerxes III (Ochus), Arses, and Xerxes himself (Briant 2002, 269-70, 564). The assassination of Xerxes is recounted by several Greek authors. Those depictions, though differing in details, include conspirator lists involving the king's chief bodyguard and a eunuch (Briant 2002, 564).

The primary court records were "the book of the annals" [*matters of the days*] ["of the kings of Media and Persia"] (Esth 2:23; see this full name in 10:2), a collection of administrative texts, meant to "record important decisions" rather than provide tales of the "battlefield or . . . the hunt" (Briant 2002, 5). Indeed, in 6:1, the text is called *the book of records* [*zikkĕrōnôt*], *the annals*, a description that seems to emphasize this type of administrative focus. Likewise, Ezra 6:2 mentions the "memorandum" (*dikrōn*, same root as above) recording the Persian decision that the Jews were allowed to rebuild the temple in Jerusalem. The notion of royal annals is quite familiar in the biblical text from 1 and 2 Kings where the term is used some thirty-two times (e.g., 1 Kgs 14:19, with one occurrence in Neh 12:23 as well). These works, which contained details of the reigns of the kings of Israel and Judah, were used as source material for the writers of the biblical text, and readers are directed there for further reading. As none of these annals have survived, we do not know their precise nature, whether primarily administrative or historical; however, their existence is supported by the extrabiblical evidence of this ancient royal practice.

The Greek sources preserve for us numerous records of the Persian royal practice of bestowing rewards upon faithful subjects. These sources attest that a record of "the King's Benefactors" was kept in the court (e.g., Herodotus VIII.85), detailing the type of service rendered to the crown and documenting the reward bestowed. Rewards included "positions of authority and seats of honor," upon which an intricate court hierarchy was established, as well as financial rewards involving money, estates, clothing, jewelry, horses, weapons, and so forth (Briant 2002, 302-15). Therefore, the official, written credit given to Mordecai at this moment along with his lack of reward are both quite significant not only for our plot but within Persian culture.

This passage also makes mention of impalement or hanging for the first, but not the last, time in our story (see Esth 5:14; 7:9-10; 9:13-14). The Hebrew verb *tālāh* is variously translated "to hang" (e.g., CEV, NASB, NRSV) or "to impale" (e.g., CEB, NIV, NLT) in English translations. The term most generally connotes the idea of suspending bodies (or body parts) for public display after death, rather than describing a means of execution (e.g., Deut 21:22 and Josh 10:26 speak of *mût*, "execution," followed by *tālāh*, "hanging or impaling"). This distinction is displayed within the book of Esther as Haman's sons are killed on the first day of battle (Esth 9:6-10), but their bodies are not impaled until the second day (9:13-15). Westbrook, citing biblical and extrabiblical sources for the impalement of corpses and body parts, confirms that hanging was "not generally used as punishment in the ANE legal systems" (Westbrook 1992, in Berlin 2001, 32; for Persian evidence, see the Behistun Inscription of Darius, line 19, in Voigtlander 1978, 36). (Note: The noun following this verb, variously translated "gallows," "tree," "stake," or "pole," is the Hebrew *'ēṣ*, which is the generic term for tree or wood.)

IN THE TEXT

■ **21** To this point in the story, the extravagance, lavishness, and decadence of the Persian court have served as a veil, thin though it may be, for its sinister danger. True, life-changing edicts are issued on the monarch's whim, yet that impulsiveness seems easily rendered innocuous, in part by the glut of counselors surrounding him. With these verses, that perception is radically altered.

Another group of characters, revealing yet another layer of Persian administrative classification, is introduced to the story—*two eunuchs from among the keepers of the threshold* (*šĕnê-sārîsê hammelek miśśōmrê hassap*). These who are set in the strategic place to protect the king now seek (*bāqaš*) to do him harm (*to send a hand against*, *šālaḥ yād bĕ-*; see also, e.g., 1 Sam 24:6, 10 [7, 11 HB]). Unbeknown to him, King Xerxes has become the target of the anger (*qāṣap*) that he earlier directed toward Vashti (Esth 1:12). As Clines points out, "Anger lies just below the surface of the bland bureaucracy, and rage is an important motivation in the narrative as a whole (1:12, 3:5, 5:[9], 7:7; cf. 1:18, 2:1, 7:10)" (1984b, 292).

■ **22** Somehow *the plot is made known* [*yāda'*] *to Mordecai* (see the explanation by Josephus [*Ant.* xi:6, 4]), and somehow *he gets word to* (*nāgad lĕ-*) Esther, perhaps through the same channels through which he acquired news of her earlier (2:11). Though Mordecai is clearly the principle character in this portion of the story, Esther's role here is not to be discounted. Here, in the moment she is first called **Queen**, Esther speaks (*'āmar*) to the king. This could be viewed as the first time Esther takes a significant action in the story, rather than being passive or merely evoking a response from others.

The fact that Esther reveals Mordecai as the source of her information is, many argue, "a slight slip in narrative logic" (Fox 2001, 40), betraying their connection and thus Esther's lineage. As noted above, this consequence has, arguably, already been achieved by Mordecai's actions in 2:11. I would contend that the conspicuousness of their relationship is not a failure but a strategy of the author, achieving two results.

First, it confirms our regard of both Xerxes and Haman as utterly self-absorbed and blind to anything that is not personally glorifying. Note that the text is explicit in informing us that both the king and Haman know Mordecai's ethnicity (5:13; 6:10, 13), though neither make the connection with Esther (7:4-6). Understanding this supposed incongruity in the text as an authorial device is a much stronger suggestion than Bickerman's, who sees here evidence of two plots and two tales combined by one author (1967, 172).

Second, this detail advances the book's theme of hiding and seeking, of concealment and exposure (→ From the Text for 2:1-2). The reader is constantly made aware that one's identity as a member of the people of God is a fact not easily hidden. Only to the extent that Esther's identity is "concealed" is God "absent."

■ **23** This matter of the eunuchs' seeking (*bāqaš*) to harm the king is quickly **investigated** (*sought out*, *bāqaš* passive), **verified** (**found to be true**, *māṣā'* passive), punished by impalement (*tālāh* passive), and **recorded** (*kātab* passive). These three short verses are pivotal in the plot of the story as they establish Mordecai's loyalty to the king and provide the means for his coming elevation at precisely the right moment (6:1; Clines 1984a, 105). Furthermore, at each point of these verses, elements of the remainder of the story are anticipated and prefigured—a thwarted murder plot, Mordecai's disclosure of information to Esther, Esther's successful approach to the king, and the impalement of evildoers—all of it a portentous mix!

FROM THE TEXT

Unrewarded Service: Mordecai has recently experienced a severe mistreatment at the hands of Xerxes—having his adopted daughter taken from his home and forced into the king's harem. Although things have turned out as well as could possibly be expected for Esther, Mordecai could easily still consider this king his enemy. When presented with the information that someone is interested in harming his enemy, Mordecai has a choice to make. One could argue that he chose to save the king for the reward expected in Persian culture. However, as we learn here, doing the right thing (such as protecting a life, even the life of an enemy) may not always be rewarded, at least in the short run. In some ways, Mordecai was demonstrating for us the imperatives that Jesus gave to "love your enemies, do good to them, and lend to them without expecting to get anything back. Then your reward will be great, and you will be children of the Most High, because he is kind to the ungrateful and wicked" (Luke 6:35).

Pursuing the values that Christ sets forth here and elsewhere (see Matt 5—7) is difficult; in fact, it is impossible on our own. The world operates against these values because it is not within our fallen human natures to seek the good and well-being of others, particularly our enemies, above our own. It is only by the transforming power of the Holy Spirit in our surrendered lives and hearts that we can set aside the selfishness that pervades our fallenness and respond to those around us—everyone around us—with love, goodness, and justice. We don't do this for the appreciation or thanks it will bring us today; we do it for the one who is our reward.

IV. HAMAN'S PLOT TO DESTROY THE JEWS: ESTHER 3:1-15

BEHIND THE TEXT

Haman's introduction, more straightforward than that of Mordecai in 2:5, contains the same primary pieces of information—his father's name (Hammedatha) and his ethnic identity. Haman is the Agagite (*hā'ăgāgî*). The name Agag (*'ăgag*) with the gentilic ending (denoting ethnic identification; Heb. final *î*, Eng. often -*ite*) appears only in the book of Esther. Jewish historian Josephus (*Ant.* xi:6, 5) explicitly connects Haman's ethnicity with the Amalekites, of whom Agag was king during the time of Saul (1 Sam 15). Thus, with the genealogies of our main characters established, the ancient rivalry is resurrected—Mordecai the Benjamite vs. Haman the Agagite, the Jews vs. the Amalekites.

The Hebrew people first encountered the Amalekites soon after leaving Egypt. Having seen the sea parted in Exod 13 and 14, the only difficulties that have marked their journey have been lack of provisions, details about which they grumbled and for which God provided. However, it is at Rephidim in the Sinai Peninsula that the Hebrew people meet their first enemy—the Amalekites. The famous battle recounted in Exod 17 once again demonstrates the Lord's provision. His people achieve victory clearly due to divine intervention, as they prevail when the hands of Moses are raised but are overwhelmed when his hands are lowered. With the help of Aaron and Hur, Moses' hands stay aloft throughout the battle and the Amalekites are defeated. The Lord then tells Moses in 17:14, "Write this on a scroll as something to be remembered and make sure that Joshua hears it, because I will completely blot out the name of Amalek from under heaven," and Moses goes on to say (v 16), "The LORD will be at war against the Amalekites from generation to generation."

As God's people continue their journey to the promised land and eventually enter it, they encounter many other enemies, including the Amalekites (e.g., Judg 6). However, we learn in 1 Sam 15:2 that the Amalekite attack at the crucial moment of Israel's emergence as a nation from captivity has marked them as the archetypal enemy of God. Thus, God commands the new king of his people, Saul, to "totally destroy" (*ḥāram*) the Amalekites (v 3). The command for total destruction (*ḥērem*) is one that God employs selectively.

As they had entered into the promised land, God had commanded such total destruction of all peoples living there, thereby providing for his people the dedicated space in which they might learn to live in exclusive relationship with him, protected from the lure of other gods who might become a snare to them (Deut 7:16; see discussion in Lennox 2015, 53ff.). However, when his people failed to trust him to take *all* the land from their enemies, the Lord refused to accomplish for them what he intended (Josh 23:13; Judg 2:3), in essence revoking his command of total destruction. At the critical moment of their entrance into the land, *ḥērem* had a specific purpose in God's divine plan for bringing humanity back into relationship with him. Apart from that purpose, it became simply mass murder for its own sake, and God would not allow it.

Not since those commands were given at the entrance into the land has God commanded *ḥērem*, until the Amalekites in 1 Sam 15. Why here? What is the crucial moment in the formation of his people that God is protecting? Saul's reign marks another point of emergence in the life of God's people—their emergence as a kingdom. Thus, with the total destruction of the Amalekites, the archetypal enemy of God, at the hands of God's king, he will establish the archetypal king— one who reflects the will and purposes of the Lord to his people. Just as their initial defeat in the wilderness was entirely an act of divine provision, so this defeat will be one that is entirely an act of divine purpose. Neither the new king nor the people will profit in any way from this destruction. God simply commands an act of obedience (1 Sam 15:19, 22-23). And Saul fails. Agag is spared; the Amalekites are not totally destroyed.

Enter Haman, the Agagite. God's archetypal enemy still exists; thus, his people are in danger. Will a leader arise who will obey, who will trust in God's unseen but promised provision?

Of additional note is the king's signet ring (*tabba'at*), a symbol of authority in the ancient world. The ring would create a seal impression in clay to seal a document (Hadley 2005, 377). Many of these impressions (called bullae) have been found throughout the ancient world, including bullae bearing the name of Xerxes found in Persia (Briant 2002, 412, 447). The biblical text displays the pervasiveness of this ancient practice, documenting the use of signet rings in Egypt (Gen 41:42), in Israel and Judah (1 Kgs 21:8 and Jer 22:24, respectively; utilizing the term *ḥôtām*), and in Persia (Dan 6:17 [18 HB], Aramaic: *'izqāh*).

IN THE TEXT

A. Enter Haman (3:1-6)

■ **1-4** Once again, it is not clarified how much time passes **after these things** (*'aḥar haddĕbārîm hā' ēlleh*; → Esth 2:1), indicating the king's wedding and plot to assassinate him (3:1). Initially, our expectations are raised—**King Xerxes honored . . .** surely Mordecai who has recently rescued him!—only to be dashed. The introduction of Haman (→ Behind the Text above for a discussion of his genealogy) leads to a reconsideration of a brief passage of time. Some five years pass from Esther's presentation to the king (2:16) to Haman's initiation of his plot against the Jews (3:7). Therefore, from the perspective of plot development, it seems probable that the bulk of that time elapsed between the end of ch 2 and the beginning of 3, allowing time for the king to forget Mordecai's faithfulness and (for reasons not revealed to us) to elevate another. Conversely, the time that passes from Haman's promotion (v 1) to the hatching of his evil scheme (v 7) appears quite brief.

Haman's elevation is in the traditional pattern of Persian excess, perhaps intensifying the snub to Mordecai. Xerxes **elevates him and sets his seat above all his fellow nobles** (*mē'al kol-haśśārîm*); so, at the king's command (*ṣāvāh . . . hammelek*), **all the royal officials** [*kol-'abdê hammelek*] **at the king's gate kneel** [*kāra'*] **and bow** [*ḥāvāh*] **to him**. Though in the NIV translation both Xerxes' initial action and the officials' final action are "to honor" Haman, these are two distinct Hebrew roots. As Haman's superior, Xerxes bestows honor by elevating Haman (making him great [*gādal*]), while the officials who are now Haman's inferiors honor him by bowing before him.

This is what Mordecai will not do. Though the royal officials question him, we never hear Mordecai's direct reply. They hound him daily, presumably encouraging him to submit, but he doesn't listen. The reason that we are given for Mordecai's refusal finally comes to us indirectly, in the mouths of the officials, at the end of v 4—**he is a Jew**. There is some ambiguity in the intent of this simple statement.

On the one hand, this action echoes a similar scene in which the exiles Shadrach, Meshach, and Abednego refuse to bow down and worship Nebuchadnezzar's golden image (Dan 3) and are therefore thrown into the fiery furnace. This courageous refusal demonstrates an unwavering adherence to the second command of the Decalogue, which prohibits the making (*'āśāh*) as well as the bowing to (*hāvāh*) and worshipping of (*'ābad*) idols (*pesel* [Exod 20:4-5]). The significant difference in these two situations is that Mordecai is not commanded to bow to an idol, but simply to give honor to a human. Multiple texts provide evidence of obedient Israelites engaging in this very practice (e.g., 1 Sam 20:41, David to Jonathan; 1 Sam 28:14, Saul to Samuel; 1 Kgs 1:23, Nathan to David; 1 Kgs 2:19, Solomon to Bathsheba; 2 Kgs 2:15, prophets of Jericho to Elisha). While some argue that Mordecai's actions shouldn't be viewed as this type of faithful adherence to the law, I would submit that it seems reasonable to view Haman's desire for self-glorification as the equivalent of him setting himself up as an idol (what Wesley terms the requirement of "Divine honour" [1765, 3:2]); thus, Mordecai's refusal demonstrates not only his obedience to the law but also his wise discernment.

Another option is to view Mordecai's appeal to his heritage in relationship to the ancient feud between the Jews and the Amalekites. Thus, he refuses to bow to Haman on the grounds that Jews don't bow to Amalekites—clearly a much more personal motive. Ambiguity in the biblical text need not present either/or alternatives; in many cases, such as this one, both/and provides greater perspective. With both of these reasons, Mordecai's refusal has as much to do with who Haman is as a person and as an Agagite as it does with who Mordecai is as a Jew (→ Esth 4:4).

Clines argues that our story sends a "confused message" to its audience related to Jewish identity, stating,

> The Jewish people find themselves under a death sentence because one Jew [Mordecai] acts like a Jew and tells his people he is a Jew; they escape through the good offices of another Jew [Esther], who has pretended she is not a Jew. If being Jewish is being Esther-like, no tragedy need be expected; if it is being Mordecai-like, no saviour in high places can be counted on. (1990, 48)

Though I would agree that there is no formulaic way in which one gives witness to his or her identity as a child of God, the ultimate message of the book leaves no confusion—a Jew must be a Jew (ch 9, esp. vv 27-28). While different situations require different responses, God's people must bear witness to him.

■ **5** Though the root motivation of Mordecai's stated reason may not be fully clear to us, it seems quite apparent to the officials, who now become informers. Interestingly, since Haman has to be told about Mordecai's actions, it seems that he hasn't noticed the disobedience to this point, though once made aware, he fixates upon it (5:13). The officials pose the situation to their new superior to see if he will accept a conscientious objector status. He doesn't. It appears that the standard Persian practice of religious tolerance only goes so far. Thus, we discover Haman to be a pea in a pod with his sovereign—he is *filled **with anger** (ḥēmāh* [3:5 as in 1:12]) and a personal affront escalates to kingdom-wide magnitude.

■ **6** The absurdity that characterized the response to Vashti's affront in ch 1 and the foreboding of the thwarted murder plot of ch 2 converge to create sheer evil when replicated in Haman's response. He immediately *rejects* (*bāzāh*; also 1:17, 18) the idea of *doing harm against* (*šālaḥ yād bĕ-*; also 2:21) Mordecai alone (*lĕbad*; also 1:16), but rather *seeks* [*bāqaš*; also 2:21] to **annihilate** <u>*all*</u> **the Jews who are in** <u>*all*</u> **the kingdom of Xerxes** (so 1:16, 17, 20). Bickerman argues that it is not Mordecai's Jewishness but simply his offense that sparks Haman's vendetta; had Mordecai been of another race, that race would have been marked (1967, 188). Though this position can be neither confirmed nor denied, the twice-repeated phrase **Mordecai's people** argues against it. Though ambiguous to us, Mordecai's refusal to bow because of his Jewishness seems clearly understood by Haman.

B. Haman's Proposal (3:7-11)

■ **7** Haman leaves nothing to chance as he plots his "final solution to the Jewish question." Far from a game of chance, the casting of lots (Persian *pûr*, translated into Heb. *gôrāl* [9:24]), viewed in the ancient world as a means of direct access to the will of the deity, was even utilized within Jewish law and practice to confirm God's choice in a matter (e.g., Lev 16:8-10; Num 33:54; Acts 1:26; see Keener 2012, 776-79). The difficulties in the wording of the Hebrew in Esth 3:7 as well as discrepancies with the Old Greek text have led to some disagreement concerning whether Haman was casting the lot to determine the day on which to present his plot to Xerxes or to determine the day of the genocide. Based upon the date in the decree of v 13, most assume that the mention of the twelfth month in v 7 should be taken to mean that Haman was casting the lot to determine the most auspicious time for the slaughter (Berlin 2001, 38). The small detail that Haman happens to seek the divine will in the first month—the month of Passover, the celebration of redemption and release—provides the only shred of hope at this moment. The significant amount of time that must elapse from the issuance to the execution of the decree, based upon the casting of lots, marks for Wesley yet another instance of "God's singular providence" in the book by which the Jews are granted "space to get the decree reversed" (1765, 3:7).

■ **8-9** Manipulating the king seems to be a finely honed art form in the Persian court. The manipulation by Memukan, which was clearly self-seeking (1:17), focused on stroking Xerxes' royal ego (e.g., mentioning the greatness of his kingdom and appealing to his self-appraisal as a beneficent ruler) while maliciously dismissing Vashti as expendable. Xerxes' personal attendants who manipulate the king's thoughts away from Vashti (2:1-4) primarily do so in service to the king's desires, though their own burdens may have been eased as well with the lifting of the king's mood.

The manipulation by Haman—self-seeking, fueled by a bruised ego, and most vile in nature—exceeds them both. Its structure is captivating, as Fox has

3:6-9

illustrated, beginning with a true statement, then moving to half-truths, and ending with a lie (2001, 47-51). First, the truth: *There is a certain people* [*'am-'eḥād*] *scattered and separated* [*mĕpuzzār ûmĕpōrād*] *among the peoples in all the provinces of your kingdom* (v 8). With a calculated nod to the expanse of Xerxes' royal power, Haman makes a statement that was potentially true of many ethnic groups once conquered and now living within the vast Persian Empire. The NIV translation **who keep themselves separate** misses the parallelism between the two passive forms *scattered and separated*, thus potentially misplacing emphasis on a seemingly subversive activity. The reality is simply that the Jews (though unnamed to the king) are a dispersed people and their description as *scattered and separated* leaves the impression of triviality—perhaps being so sprinkled about as to seem dispensable.

Haman continues, *Their laws* [*dāt*] *are different from any other people, and the king's laws* [*dāt*] *they do not keep*. Again, the NIV translation doesn't allow us to see that **their customs** and **the king's laws** both utilize the word *dāt*. As noted in the discussion in 1:15, for ethnic groups to follow their own laws and practices was not problematic in the Persian Empire; thus, the first portion of this statement maintains the harmless nature of Haman's speech thus far. The next portion of the statement, however, seeks to destroy. As it discloses that a single Jew, Mordecai, is not following the king's command (*ṣāvāh*) to honor Haman, it is true; as it insinuates that the whole of this people group is disregarding imperial law (*dāt*) by refusing to pay tribute and pledge allegiance to the king, it is a lie (see the similar accusation in Ezra 4:13-15, in Clines 1984b, 296). Haman plays his king perfectly, relying on the paranoia of the self-absorbed monarch to follow the lie. Thus, half-truth takes hold and Haman capitalizes. *It is not worth it for the king to let them remain* (→ discussion of this phrase in Esth 7:4). Without the presentation of a shred of evidence, Haman moves from the insinuation of half-truth to the lie that it spawns. Other groups may be tolerated, but for this particular (dispensable) group, they are not worth the king's tolerance.

Imitating the counselors before him, Haman has a solution prepared to tickle the king's fancy. *If it seems good to the king*—followed by two Hebrew words—*let it be written to destroy them* (*yikkātēb lĕ'abbĕdām*) (v 9). Haman neither lingers nor expounds on his plan; rather, he immediately moves to his final manipulation ploy. Haman offers a bribe. The lack of detail about the proposed genocide is counterbalanced by the specificity of the payment conditions—how much (**ten thousand talents**), to whom (**to the king's administrators**), and where (**for the royal treasury**). The sum is enormous, some argue impossibly so (so Fox 2001, 51-52), though the Old Greek text frames it as merely one-third the price of the king's prized goblet (1:7).

Following Haman's insinuation that the treason of this people is related to their refusal to pay taxes, one could hypothesize that Haman is offering to exact their tax from this group upon their destruction (Berlin 2001, 40-41). The wording in 4:7 as Mordecai relates this information to Esther could be interpreted thus, that the money Haman has offered to pay into the royal treasuries is *by* [i.e., *from*] *the Jews for their extermination* (*bāyyĕhûdiyyîm lĕ'abbĕdām*) (Driver 1954, 238). However, the reality that the text presents is that the king is as unconcerned about the source of the money as he is the identification of the people he will decree to wipe off the face of the earth.

■ **10** Before speaking a single word, the king hands over all authority of the office of the king of Persia (cf. Gen 41:42). Though he was introduced in the story a few short verses ago, Haman's identity is clarified at this momentous moment (so for Esther in 2:15). He is the son of Hammedatha; he is the Agagite; and he now receives a new title that reveals all—he is "the foe of the Jews" (*ṣōrēr hayyĕhûdîm* [NJPS]).

■ **11** There has been much speculation about the perplexing statement the king offers—**Keep the money** (or *The money is given to you*, *hakkesep nātûn lāk*). Why would the king turn down the bribe, seemingly his only profit from the genocide other than the riddance from his kingdom of the alleged freeloaders? The verb *nātan* is extremely common, meaning "to give" most often. L. Day suggests a rendering such as "The price is set for you" (meaning he accepts the terms), using *nātan* in an adaptation of its sense "to set, place" (2005, 72). Possible support may come from Ezek 14:3-4 where men "put [*nātan*] wicked stumbling blocks before their faces" in v 3, followed by the same phrase in v 4 utilizing the verb *śîm*, which commonly means "to set, establish" (e.g., Gen 47:26; Ps 104:9). (The use of *nātan* in Esth 3:14, 15 could be translated accordingly: *A copy of the edict would establish it as law in every province . . .)*

Others compare this exchange with that of Abraham and Ephron the Hittite in Gen 23, in which Ephron both gives (*nātan*) the land to Abraham (v 11) but also receives payment for it (v 16; Moore 1971, 40). Thus, perhaps we are observing the proper etiquette in the offering and accepting of a business agreement. While either are possible, neither seems most probable. I would maintain that Xerxes displays political and economic ineptitude here and is effortlessly swayed by an adviser. This comes as no surprise, his character having been well-established by our author. Xerxes gives Haman a blank check to do with as *it seems good* to him. A kingdom that operates at the whim of an idiot is absurd; at the whim of a madman becomes hell itself (cf. Dan 5:19).

C. Haman's Edict (3:12-15)

■ **12-14** No time is wasted. Within days, the royal scribes are gathered and set to work. There are many similarities between the first edict (1:22), enacted *according to the words of Memukan* (1:21), and this edict, enacted *according to all which Haman had commanded* (3:12). Dispatches were sent . . . to **all** the king's provinces, *in the script of each province and in the language of each people* (v 13). The additional information attached to the second edict—the summons of the scribes, lists of officials, statements of the king's authority (**name**) and seal, and the expansion of its issuance *in every single province*—all add weight to its importance (v 14).

All that Haman left concealed from the king is now brought to its full light. That this is to be a Jewish holocaust is hammered home with three orders—**to destroy** (šāmad), to **kill** (hārag), to **annihilate** ['āḇaḏ] **all the Jews**. The benevolent inclusivity of Xerxes' banquet guest list (1:5) is mocked as the scope of the massacre is revealed—*from young to old, children and women*. In a kingdom where festivals extend for months, genocide requires but a single propitious day, this one eleven months away. The whole kingdom makes ready.

■ **15** As the hoard of couriers surge out of the capital in a deafening roar, the edict rings throughout **the citadel of Susa** (šûšan bîrāh), though it is **the city of Susa** (hā'îr šûšan) that is **bewildered**. One can imagine the panic incited by the sudden unleashing of the administrative communication engine without knowing its purpose. If you have been seeking a tyrannical comparison for Xerxes, it may be found in the end of v 15, which mimics the folk tradition of "Nero fiddling while Rome burned"—*Meanwhile, Xerxes and Haman sat to drink, while the city of Susa was thrown into confusion* (bûk [Exod 14:3; Joel 1:18]). Clines views this as "the fifth and central banquet" of the book, which "marks the point at which Persian success will begin to be overshadowed by Jewish success" (1990, 38). Indeed, the shift of perspective from the palace to the city leads us into ch 4, where Mordecai and Esther once again become the focus of the story.

FROM THE TEXT

Antidotes to Anger: Though perhaps fueled by ancient hostilities, the immediate source of the evil plan against the Jews was Haman's anger. This is not the righteous, controlled anger of God in the OT (Ps 78:38) arrayed against his rebellious people (Ps 78:31; Isa 42:18-25) or those seeking to harm the innocent (Ps 79:1-7; Nah 1). This was a fire of rage that had been kindled with hatred, fanned with utter narcissism, and sparked by a perceived insult. In the post-Holocaust (*HaShoah*) world in which we live, one cannot read of Haman and his "final solution to the Jewish question" without a comparison to Hitler and his policies. Kershaw's description of the inception of Hitler's ultimate plan is chilling in its similarities:

> He had identified his personal fate wholly with that of the German Reich. . . . His searing bitterness and visceral hatred, of a rare intensity, reflected this identification, and was now directed at perceived enemies he had begun to identify years before, scapegoats first for his own ills, now responsible for those of the nation. (2008, 91)

While none of us may be able to conceive of a rage that would drive us to such lengths, we can all perceive in our own lives the seeds of bitterness, hatred, selfishness, and biased perceptions that are the makings of such rage. The psalmist, fully aware of these tendencies in fallen humanity, warns us away from these vices and toward a focus on God (Ps 37:1-9). Likewise, the Apostle Paul addresses the need for us all "to be made new in the attitude of [our] minds," allowing the Holy Spirit to bring forth in our lives kindness, compassion, and forgiveness—the antidotes to anger (Eph 4:20-32).

V. MORDECAI PERSUADES ESTHER TO HELP: ESTHER 4:1-17

BEHIND THE TEXT

This chapter displays the ancient Near Eastern practices of mourning that include the tearing of clothing, wearing of sackcloth, sitting or lying in ashes, wailing, weeping, and even fasting (cf. 2 Sam 3:31-33; 13:18-19; Lam 2:10; Jer 9:16-18 [15-17 HB]; Gen 37:29, 34; Job 1:20; 2:8, 12-13). Evidence for such practices is found throughout the ancient Near East, from Egypt to Mesopotamia, in various forms (Huehnergard and Liebowitz 2013, 62-69). Therefore, though the acts themselves were not exclusively Jewish (thus, the established Persian protocol against sackcloth in the gate), they did serve to identify and unify this scattered people.

(→ Behind the Text in ch 2 for discussion of the king's gate.)

A. Jews Respond with Mourning and Weeping (4:1-5)

■ **1-3** Just as the eunuchs' plot was made known (passive *yāda'*) to him in 2:22, somehow Mordecai **comes to know** (active *yāda'*) **of all that had been done** by Haman and Xerxes (4:1), including details about the exchange of money (v 7). The chaotic **confusion** of the city of Susa (3:15) is illustrated in the actions first of Mordecai, then of the Jews of Persia. Mordecai's acts of mourning (tearing, putting on, going out, wailing, entering) are public, deliberate, and conspicuous, carried out in the area before (*lipnê*) the king's gate, which is the open, public square of the city (*rĕḥôb hā'îr* [4:6]). This is the premium site for public political demonstrations, a fact confirmed to us in 6:11 when Xerxes orders Mordecai honored in this very spot. Though commentators view Mordecai here variously as self-reproachful, manipulative of Esther, or genuinely grieved (Moore 1971, 47), Wesley highlights Mordecai's bravery to publicly "espouse a just cause though it seemed to be a desperate one" (1765, 4:1).

On this day, however, his position in the king's gate, which previously had situated him to save the king's life (2:21), is cut off from him in his grieving. Even the **loud, bitter cries** (*zĕ'āqāh gĕdōlāh ûmārāh*) of this trusted servant cannot penetrate the gilded halls of the Persian court, which are insulated from the tarnish of its subjects' sufferings. The extent of that suffering reaches **to each and every province** (4:3). The Jews mourn with **fasting, weeping and wailing,** just as David and his men mourned the deaths of Saul and Jonathan (2 Sam 1:12). This powerlessness of all Jews intensifies the powerlessness of Esther's passivity and captivity in Esth 2 (Clines 1990, 38).

■ **4** The specific details of which **her attendants and eunuchs came and informed her** are not given. Since Esther asks Mordecai for an explanation at the end of v 5, it appears that she is only told of Mordecai's condition. (It is interesting to note at this point that those closest to Esther seem very aware of her close connection to Mordecai.) In reaction, Esther is **in great distress**. While the Greek text uses the same verb to describe Esther's reaction and Susa's reaction in 3:15 (*tarássō*, **to be troubled, confused, alarmed**), the Hebrew verb here is unique, used only once in this form in the biblical text. Its root *ḥûl/ḥîl* connotes an intensity of activity, describing twisting and writhing in pain (as in childbirth, e.g., Isa 13:8), whirling (as in dance, e.g. Judg 21:21; of a storm, e.g., Jer 30:23), or trembling in fear (e.g., Ps 55:5 [6 HB]). Therefore, we must conclude that Esther's distressed state was a highly agitated one, her mind doubtless imagining endless scenarios that would prompt Mordecai's mourning, each more tragic than the one before. Thus, she sends Mordecai clothing in order that he would put off his sackcloth, but he doesn't accept them.

The text is silent concerning the motivation for both of these actions. It seems reasonable to conclude from the statement in Esth 4:2 that Esther's offer is so that Mordecai might be able to enter into the palace grounds and meet with her. Mordecai's reasons are more obscure, perhaps meant to affirm solidarity with his people or perhaps meant to demonstrate his separation from the power structure that has just decreed his annihilation. Both of these mirror the possible reasons given for his refusal to bow at the beginning of ch 3—one showing his fidelity to the traditions of his people, the other demonstrating his chutzpa. Again, the both/and provides the more complex perception of Mordecai's character.

■ **5** The queen, as Esther was just called in 4:4 (omitted in the NIV), still has no answers; thus, she sends an intermediary, the eunuch Hathak, to come **to know** [*yāda'*] **what is going on and why**. To this point, knowing has been Mordecai's task (2:11, 22; 4:1), with Esther's primary activities (that of hiding her identity [2:20] and reporting to the king [2:22]) proceeding at Mordecai's direction. In contrast, the actions Esther takes here (she **summons** [*qārā'*] **and orders** [*ṣāvāh*]) are powerful ones, an issuing of an edict of her own, of sorts (see these verbs converging again in 3:12 and 8:9). Even in these small acts, we see a queen emerging at this moment of crisis for her people.

B. Mordecai Calls Esther to Act (4:6-8)

■ **6-7** Mordecai is maintaining his sit-in at the city square when Hathak finds him. He seizes the opportunity to get word to Esther, sending back both information and instructions. First, he informs (*nāgad*) her of **all that has happened** [*qārāh*] **to him** (v 7), which is, of course, precisely what she wants to know. The next piece of information signals Mordecai's continued access to insider palace information—the amount Haman has offered to extract from the Jews for their extermination. Mordecai seems to be emphasizing to Esther that the implications of this political deal potentially affect the very economic fabric of Persian society. In a society that clearly values material wealth above individual lives, that makes this the highest of high stakes games and one not easily won. There is nothing hidden here; if Esther chooses to enter before the king, she will do it with eyes wide open and fully aware of what she is asking.

■ **8** The third and final piece of information that Mordecai gives to Hathak is **a copy** (*patšegen*) **of the edict**. With this information, Hathak is then to do three things, all of which have been significant previously in our story—**to show** (*rā'āh* [1:11]) it to Esther, **to inform** (*nāgad* [2:10, 20]) her, and **to command** (*ṣāvāh* [2:10, 20; 3:2]) her in turn to perform three acts. Esther is **to enter** (*bô'*) to the king, **to beg for mercy** (*ḥānan*), and **to plead** [*bāqaš*] **with him for her people**. These three verbs have also had significant touch points within our narrative.

It has already been made known to us that entering into the king's presence is a fickle enterprise, laced with protocol and turning on his whim. Preparations for it have been meticulous, as each of the virgins waited a year **to enter** (2:12); and consequences have loomed large, with Vashti's refusal **to enter** (1:12) and

Mordecai's exclusion **to enter** (4:2). Yet the breaking of protocol has also proven advantageous, with Esther's turn **to enter** (2:15) differing from all the rest and winning the king's favor. Simply the act of entering is a significant command, but Mordecai does not stop there.

The verb translated **to beg for mercy** is built on the same root (*ḥānan*) used to describe the *favor* (*ḥēn*) Esther has received from others (2:15, 17). The same verbal form is translated by the NIV **to beg for favor** in Hos 12:4, and it is used multiple times in Solomon's prayer of dedication for the temple in both Kings and Chronicles (1 Kgs 8:33, 47, 59; 9:3; 2 Chr 6:24, 37). In that context specifically, it is often correlated with prayer and translated "to supplicate," with an emphasis on a pleading for mercy and a return to favor with the Lord after Israel's sin (so 1 Kgs 8:33, 47). Though the sin in this case does not lie with the Jews, the need for mercy and a return to a king's favor is desperate.

Though not readily apparent in the English, the final command is **to seek**. As noted before, this has been a common theme in the book—the king sought a replacement for his lost queen (Esth 2:2), and Haman sought universal revenge for his lost honor (3:6); now the Jews seek mercy for their lost future just as Haman will seek pardon for his lost life (7:7). In the face of what is lost, however, this command brings hope, for Mordecai reverses his command of hiding (2:10) and instead commands Esther **to seek from him** [*pardon*] **for _her_ people**! The beautiful virgin Esther once received the king's favor; will the Jewish queen?

C. Esther Responds with Uncertainty (4:9-11)

■ **9-11** In the next two verses, which tersely describe the cumbersome exchange through the intermediary (paralleling ch 1, → discussion in 1:10), queenly Esther once again **commands** Hathak as she sends her reply to Mordecai. Esther's initial words echo with the superfluity of the Persian court (**_All_** [*kōl*] **the king's officials and the people of the king's provinces** . . . [4:11]). Mordecai, who has been the one to know in the past (2:22; 4:1) and who himself is among the king's officials (3:2), now doesn't seem to know what everyone else knows! The law (*dāt*) is straight-forward—**any** [*kōl*] **man or woman who enters** [*bôʾ*] **the king's presence without being called is put to death** (*mût*). Esther makes it clear that being a woman is no advantage here; there is one law (*ʾaḥat dātô*) for all. An exception does exist for this law, which arguably then places this *dāt* in the realm of practice or custom rather than inviolable law (→ discussion at 1:15; also 1:19), though for the violator, such a distinction would bear little comfort. The exception lies in the king's fancy, in his willingness to **extend** [*yāšaṭ*] **the golden scepter that he (or she) might live** (*ḥāyāh*). The author has prepared us in such a way that these words bring despair. Xerxes is a king whose character cannot be trusted, whose whim can be manipu-lated or purchased, and who ends lives without a second thought.

Our hope lies only in Esther; however, that hope is dashed with the next word in Hebrew—*vaʾănî*, **As for me** . . . The Hebrew sentence structure emphasiz-es Esther's situation in relation to the present circumstance. Just as Sarah couldn't believe she would bear a child since she was old (Gen 18:13; *va'ănî zāqantî*), and Moses couldn't see how Pharaoh would listen to him since he had poor speech (Exod 6:12; *va'ănî 'ăral śĕpātāyim*), so Esther can't see how she can enter before the king since she **hasn't been called** (*qārā'*; → Esth 2:14*)*. This verse feels charged with a frantic dread, and these final words resonate with the hollow reality of Esther's captivity. As Wesley expands Esther's words, I "fear that the king's affections are alienated from me, and that neither my person nor petition will be acceptable to him" (1765, 4:11).

D. Mordecai's Final Charge (4:12-14)

■ **12-13** Just as Mordecai's words were reported to Esther in v 9, now the intermediary reports Esther's words and then returns with Mordecai's reply. In light of the pitiful nature of Esther's words, Mordecai's initial response appears harsh. This entire communication has exposed Esther's isolation—from knowledge of the edict, from the mourning of Mordecai and all the Jews, from speaking face-to-face with Mordecai, and even from seeing the king. With his sharp reply, Mordecai crushes the possibility that she will be isolated from the coming destruction. Though he does not reveal how her identity will be made known, he is firm in his belief that her time of hiding is over; she cannot escape (*mālaṭ*) the annihilation of her people.

■ **14** This verse is undoubtedly the most famous verse in the book of Esther. In response to Esther's response, Mordecai poses a conditional (if . . . then) scenario. However, the conditional (**if**; *'im*) portion of the sentence is not as simple as the English might convey; rather, the verbal construction used here often signals an action that is somehow contrary to the listener's expectations or suppositions. English translations may render this with "indeed," "certainly," or with a verbal intensification (as here, "to be silent" becomes to **remain silent**). A classic example of this construction occurs in Gen 2:17 when God tells the man in the garden that if he eats of the tree, he "will certainly die." Contrary to the man's expectations that the fruit of a lovely tree is harmless to his existence, in actuality that tree will bring death. Likewise, in Exod 3:7 when God suddenly appears to the eighty-year-old exile Moses at the burning bush, he begins by saying, "I have indeed seen the misery of my people in Egypt." God addresses Moses' unstated supposition that God has abandoned both him and his people; rather, God is there to assure him that quite the contrary is true (→ Esth 6:13).

Here, the contrary-to-expectation construction occurs in the condition, with Mordecai addressing what he perceives to be Esther's conflicting suppositions—one, that her silence will condemn her people to destruction, and two, that her silence will keep her safe. In essence, we have here the war between duty to others and self-preservation. Should I act out of guilt or out of fear? The second of these is the impulse for self-preservation and seems a most logical assumption, since we know from the beginning of her time in the palace that Esther has kept her ethnicity a secret. Perhaps Mordecai is warning her that she isn't as hidden as she might think, that her identity is known and she will not be safe in the coming massacre. (That there are those in the most intimate places of the palace who would plot harm has already been established.) The mention of danger to both **you and your father's family** is a rhetorical device meant "to personalize the danger to Esther" (Berlin 2001, 49). Mordecai seeks to break into Esther's insulated world where her first reaction focuses on court protocol and to refocus her thoughts on her family and people suffering outside of those walls.

The first of Esther's assumptions that Mordecai refutes is that she bears the sole burden of the future of her people. On the contrary, Mordecai assures her that the void left by her silence will be filled **from another place** (*mimmāqôm 'aḥēr*), and regardless of her actions, the Jews will receive **relief** [*revaḥ*] **and deliverance** (*haṣṣālāh*). These two nouns are quite rare (each occurring with this meaning but once), but uses of their respective roots are enlightening. Relief from oppression (root *rāvaḥ*) is found both in Exod 8:15 [11 HB], when God brings relief from the oppressive plague at Pharaoh's desperate request, and in 1 Sam 16:23, when Saul finds relief from an oppressive spirit through David's playing. The root of the noun "deliverance" (*nāṣal*) is used ubiquitously to describe God's salvation of his people (e.g., Exod 3:8; 1 Sam 17:37; Ps 143:9). In this moment, the veil hiding the presence of God in the book is most thin, nearly transparent. The people of God know from whence relief and deliverance come; their history, their experience has shown them! The human agents may change, but the divine outcome remains. Wesley points us to Rom 4:18—these are a people who against all hope, in hope believe (1765, 4:14)!

Mordecai has eliminated both guilt and fear as justifiable motives for Esther's choice. In what motivation then should her choice be rooted? One can almost hear the next words in the mouth of a Jewish papa like Tevye in *Fiddler on the Roof*—**Who knows? Perhaps for a time such as this you have come to your royal position**. With a nonchalance that releases pressure in this most pressure-filled of moments, Mordecai suggests to Esther that this may be her unique opportunity to serve God. **Who knows**—the question begs the answer that is so obvious yet never stated. As Bennett points out, this phrase "is usually used in the positive sense of anticipation that some good might come out of the situation (2 Sam 12:22; Joel 2:14; Jonah 3:9; Ps 90:11; Esth 4:14)" (2010, 74). Yet, as with David's situation in 2 Sam 12:22, that good does not always materialize. So with this situation. Though Mordecai is confident in God's deliverance, there is no promise that it will come through Esther; nevertheless, she can choose to serve.

E. Let It Be Done!—Esther's Final Response (4:15-17)

■ **15** The cumbersome information relay is eliminated between Mordecai's words and Esther's reply, giving us the sense of Esther's immediate acceptance of her call.
■ **16** Esther's queenly bearing, which had begun to emerge earlier in the chapter, materializes now with full authority. This series of imperatives is addressed not

4:15-16

to a subordinate (Esth 4:5, 10), but directly first to Mordecai (**Go** [*hălak*], **gather** [*kānas*]—both second-person singular) and then **to all the Jews found in Susa** (**fast** [*ṣûm*]; **do not eat** [*'ākal*] **or drink** [*šātāh*]—all second-person plural). The mourning fast (v 3) is now to be a fast **on behalf of** (*'al*) the queen, as the community gathers both outside of and within the palace for three days, a brief pause in contrast to the gluttonous stretches of time in ch 1. Though not made explicit here, there is an established connection between fasting and prayer (→ From the Text below). Thus, though God is not mentioned, the need for his presence is evident in the seeking posture of his people. "Who knows" but the hope of Joel 2:12-14 may be for them:

"Even now," declares the LORD,
   "return to me with all your heart,
      with fasting and weeping and mourning."
Rend your heart
   not your garments.
Return to the LORD your God,
   for he is gracious and compassionate,
slow to anger and abounding in love,
   and he relents from sending calamity.
Who knows? He may turn and relent
   and leave behind a blessing—
grain offerings and drink offerings
   for the LORD your God.

Esther's words then confirm to us that she is accepting her service and will in fact enter (*bô'*) into the king's presence at the end of the three-day fast. There is no indication that Esther expects to be called, as she is fully prepared to break royal protocol (*lô' kaddāt*, **not according to the law**) and receive the consequences. The formula **if I perish, I perish** (*ka'ăšer 'ābadtî 'ābādtî*) is a "formula of resignation" (Koehler and Baumgartner 2001, 455) found also in Gen 43:14 ("if I am bereaved, I am bereaved") where Jacob releases Benjamin to go with his brothers to Egypt, in hopes that his captive son might be released and his entire family saved. In both cases, the immediate outcomes (perishing and bereavement) are guaranteed and what is risked (a life and a son) is forfeit; thus, the speakers accept the peril as ultimately trivial in view of the greater good.

■ **17** Roles reverse as Mordecai **acts** [*'āśāh*] **according to all that Esther had commanded him**, just as Esther had always followed Mordecai's commands (2:10, 20; 4:8). The author uses the verb *'ābar* (meaning both "to go away" and "to contravene, disobey" [Koehler and Baumgartner 2001, 779]) strategically to indicate another shift in Mordecai—here he **goes away** (*'ābar*) to do the queen's commands, while in 3:3 **he disobeyed** (*'ābar*) the king's commands. (→ discussion at 1:19.) Thus, in contrast to the chapter of the Persians (1) which moved from outlandish feasting to a king's absurd command, this chapter (the chapter of the Jews) moves from sober mourning to a captivating queen ruling her people (though a different people than expected!). And the reversals abound . . .

FROM THE TEXT

The Discipline of Fasting: From its first mention in Judg 20:26-27, fasting coincides with "inquir[ing] of the LORD." In his discussion of Esther 4, Origen, the early third-century AD theologian, places the unmentioned prayer before the mentioned fasting ("the prayer and fasting of Mardochai and Esther," *On Prayer* 13.2, in Conti 2008, 384). Likewise, the fourth-century AD bishop of Alexandria Athanasius states, "When the whole nation of Israel was about to perish, blessed Esther defeated the tyrant's anger simply by fasting and praying to God. By faith she changed the ruin of her people into safety" (*Festal Letters* 4, in ibid., 397). Fasting, to Wesley, connotes eating and drinking "no more than mere necessity requires; that so you may give yourselves to constant and fervent prayers" (1765, 4:16).

Fasting is a spiritual discipline that serves to transform us into the image of Christ. It cultivates in us a hunger for God, an awareness of our dependence on him, and a peacefulness of spirit. The fasting in Esther demonstrates two purposes for which Christians often pursue this discipline—mourning (1 Sam 31:13; 2 Sam 1:12; Neh 1:4; Matt 9:15) and prayer, often for specific purposes such as deliverance from sin, sickness, or danger (2 Sam 12:15-23; also Matt 4:2). Additionally, fasts for repentance (1 Sam 7:5-6; Dan 9:3ff.), identification with Christ, and escape from sensuality also provide contexts in which fasting can serve a transforming purpose in our lives. The perpetual fasting that developed along with the celebration of Purim (→ Esth 9:31) is an example of a fast of remembrance and worship (Luke 2:37; Acts 13:2-3; 14:23) (from Drury 2005, 13-22).

While the fasting that produces individual transformation is vital, it cannot be an exclusive or even primary way of life for God's people. We fast episodically because God calls for fasting that ultimately results in his saving activity in this world. This is the focus of the fasting commanded by Esther, and it is this type of fast that the prophet Isaiah encourages in 58:6-14. In contrast to fasts that are self-focused and result in outward expressions of dejection or outright oppression (Isa 58:3-5; Matt 6:16), this fasting is God-focused and results in outward expressions of joy, healing, and restoration (as in Matt 25:31-46). As we deprive ourselves of food, we become more attuned to the deprivation and suffering of this world, which in turn launches us to act in sacrificial ways on behalf of those in need (as Esther's sacrificial act to save those who could not save themselves).

"For such a time as this": John Wesley's application of this verse is a formidable charge: "We should every one of us consider, for what end God has put us in the place where we are? And when an opportunity offers of serving God and our generation, we must take care not to let it slip" (1765, 4:14). While I can affirm its essence, the nature of statements like this can easily send us (particularly "doers" like myself) into the fear-laced bondage of guilt-laden works.

Perspective is key here. Esther is not indispensable to the progression of God's plan to preserve a people on earth in relationship with him. How many times could we play this out in the history of God's people? What if Noah had refused to build (Gen 6:14)? What if Abraham hadn't gone (Gen 12:1)? What if Moses had never turned aside (Exod 3:3)? What if Hannah hadn't given Samuel back to God (1 Sam 1:28)? What if . . . , what if . . . , what if . . . (Perhaps we could even respectfully imagine people before Abraham, Moses, or Hannah who *did* say no!) In Esther, we find the answer to all of history's "what ifs"—God. If all of those people had refused, denied, or rejected, God would still fulfill his plan to provide restoration to humanity! Period. He has proven that on the cross. So, what does this mean in my life? I can say no to that wondrously worthy outreach project without forfeiting someone's soul. I can give up the guilt in my life! The victimized, "poor me" mentality of suffering under the load that God has given to me and me alone in this world is debunked. God is the major actor in this drama; I am simply an available stagehand.

Far from being too destructive to my self-esteem, this perspective is actually a key to a life of freedom. For you see, though I am not indispensable to God's plan, neither am I dispensable. I can live in the freedom of knowing that I am absolutely essential to God's plan, that in each way I act on God's behalf in this world, I am an *actual* part of the bringing of his kingdom to this earth. The Wesleyan perspective is an optimistic one that affirms that humans work alongside God to bring about the processes of restoration and reconciliation in this world!

Ultimately, "for such a time as this" in my life does not depend on me making all of the right decisions to lead me to the right place at the right time. That certainly wasn't the case with Esther, who was in Persia because of the sin of her people and in the king's harem because of the whim of a tyrant. Rather, "for such a time as this" is about me being transformed into an agent of relief and deliverance in this world. That time can be any and every day of a surrendered life.

VI. ESTHER'S REQUEST TO THE KING: ESTHER 5:1-8

BEHIND THE TEXT

As this scene opens, Esther is standing in the very location that she had identified for Mordecai as forbidden (4:11)—the court of the palace (*ḥăṣar bêt hammelek*), specified here as the inner court (*happĕnîmît*). Xerxes, meanwhile, is sitting upon his throne in what appears to be the royal throne room (→ discussion of palace designations in 1:9; note also 6:4, which indicates another location in the palace, the outer court, perhaps adjacent to this area as well).

IN THE TEXT

A. Esther Appears before the King (5:1-5)

■ **1** Though in our story **the third day** simply marks the end of the specified fast, a broad perspective of God's activity among humanity marks the significance of the third day—from God's first appearance to his chosen people at Sinai (Exod 19:11, 16) to Christ's final conquering of the grave on Easter morning (Luke 24:7, 21, 46), this day is a hopeful one. It is at this most pivotal moment that Esther approaches the king. The Hebrew text helps us to associate the royal position (*lammalkût* [Esth 4:14]) to which Esther has come with the royal robes (*malkût* [v 1]), which she now puts on. In a very tangible way, Esther is taking up her mantle. The scene is laid out like a Hollywood script, the tension palpable as she stands facing (*nōkaḥ*) the palace while Xerxes sits inside on his throne facing (*nōkaḥ*) the palace door.

■ **2** The first time Esther stood in the *bêt hammalkût* before the king (2:16-17), she was taken there by others; this time, **Queen Esther** (notice the title she bears at this critical moment) stands before him of her own accord. Though we are prepared for the worst, his response at this moment replicates his first response—***she receives favor in his eyes*** (*nāśā' ḥēn* [2:17]; → 2:8-9). He signals her pardon by holding out the scepter (4:11), which she **touches**. Again, the Hebrew connects for us the touching (*nāgaʿ*) of the scepter with the attaining of (*nāgaʿ*) her royal position (4:14), thereby confirming for us that it is precisely for such a time as *this* that Esther has arisen.

■ **3-5** The king, immediately addressing her as Queen Esther to quell any protests in the court for his leniency, puts the queen at ease by asking what troubles her (*mah-lāk*; compare Gen 21:17 and Josh 15:18). His second inquiry—**What is your request [***baqqāšāh***]?** (Esth 5:3)—utilizes the now familiar root *bāqaš*, "to seek" (→ In the Text for Esth 2:2, 16-17). Esther has come seeking, and the passive **it will be given you** (*nātan*) thinly conceals a power beyond the king as the ultimate grantor of this request. This greeting alleviates our initial concerns, reassuring the reader that "God in his providence often prevents the fears and outdoes the hopes of his servants" (Wesley 1765, 5:3).

The king, in his predictable thoughtless extravagance, continues by offering her the outlandish gift of **up to half** his **kingdom** (*ʿad-ḥăṣî hammalkût*; which may be understood, as Wesley notes, proverbially, indicating "nothing in reason shall be denied," ibid., 1504). However, Esther, true to her character, does not take what is offered (as in 2:15). Asking for what neither the king nor the reader expects, Esther simply invites the king to a banquet (*mišteh*), extending the invitation, even more unexpectedly, to Haman.

The lack of discernment that the king has just displayed with his offer contrasts the careful maneuvering Esther now employs. Having just defied court protocol, she speaks with the most deferential of language, presenting her request ***if it seems good to the king*** (*'im ʿal hammelek ṭôb* [5:4; also 1:19; 3:9]) and speaking to

ESTHER

5:1-5

the king in the third person. Displaying her awareness of the king's character, she ingeniously shifts focus away from her and to an offering for him, thereby stroking the royal ego and softening his heart toward her request. Taking a bit of wisdom from the movie *My Big Fat Greek Wedding*, if the king is the head of this kingdom, Esther is positioning herself to be the neck that turns the head, a role most recently and maliciously occupied by Haman. The last of her calculated tactics is the inclusion of Haman in the invitation, trusting the old adage "Keep your friends close and your enemies closer." If ever that saying has held true, it most certainly did in the Persian court. This may also have been a maneuver of necessity, since it appears by the king's order in 5:5 that Haman is not present in the court at that time. If Esther is making an adjustment in her plan, it is a contingency for which she had calculated, as the banquet is already prepared.

B. Esther's First Banquet (5:6-8)

■ **6** Now satiated and situated to grant Esther's wish, the king again asks to receive her request, though here "the words are . . . fuller and more formally arranged in a parallelism" (Berlin 2001, 54). Likely, this is Haman's first hearing of the king's extravagant, reckless offer to give up half his kingdom.

■ **7-8** Esther equals the king in formality and in extended parallelism, though remaining evasive. Here, she appeals not only to the king's pleasure (*if it seems good* [v 4]) but also to the **favor** (v 8) she might find from him (*if I find favor* [māṣā' ḥēn]; → 2:8-9). As the king and Haman have done *Esther's bidding* (děbar 'estēr* [5:5]), now she promises to do *according to the king's bidding* (děbar hammelek [v 8]) and make her request, but not until tomorrow. Oh, the difference a day will make!

If, arguably, her first delay was necessitated by Haman's absence in the court, what then is the cause for this second delay? While literarily the delay makes space for the king's upcoming timely discovery concerning Mordecai, Esther's own motivations are hidden. Some commentators have seen the delay as exposing Esther's fear or irresolution. For example, Wesley sees here the "direction of Divine providence, which took away her courage of utterance for this time, that she might have a better opportunity for it the next time, by that great accident which happened before it" (1765, 5:8). However, most commentators, even among rabbinic interpreters, have viewed this delay as strategic maneuvering. Fox, who summarizes the varying views well, has this to say about the rabbinic conclusions:

> The [rabbinic] discussion ends with the report that Rabbah b. Abbuha later met Elijah, who validated all the reasons given. This conclusion recognizes the complexity of Esther's motives and shows that the rabbis respected her as a planner and tactician, not merely as a tool of Mordecai or an attractive charmer. (2001, 72 n. 45)

The Value of Careful Cunning: "See, I am sending you out like sheep into the midst of wolves; so be wise as serpents and innocent as doves" (Matt 10:16 NRSV). Without a reference, these words of Jesus to his disciples could easily be attributed to Mordecai as advice to Esther. It has never been in doubt that in this fallen world, participation in God's plan is a dangerous undertaking for his people (John 16:33; Rom 5:3-5; 2 Tim 3:10-13; 1 Pet 1:6). In those moments when we are "among the wolves," our fallen human instincts tempt us toward flight, meaning we leave or simply keep quiet, or fight, often meaning we plow forward with reckless abandon. I can only imagine that Esther felt those very impulses. After choosing not to flee, how easy would it have been, when the king first received her with such indulgence, to simply make her request for her people and hope for the best? She would have fulfilled her duty and been done with it. However, tactless assaults (often dubbed "direct" and "honest") generally result in much more harm than good. As Jesus advises and Esther demonstrates, a well-planned, calculated maneuver may win more ground and pave the way for future influence.

The caution, of course, is that a serpent's cunning often turns to deceit; therefore, Jesus charges us not to be guilty of becoming like the wolves in our midst, but to retain our innocence (i.e., lack of guilt). In this most dangerous of all circumstances for Esther personally, I am most struck by the way she stays true to her character. Relying on the favor she has and continues to garner and continuing to practice restraint, Esther executes a series of steps she had carefully prepared, perhaps improvising as necessary. This is not to say that she knew exactly what would happen. As Jesus goes on to encourage his disciples, "Do not worry about what to say or how to say it. At that time you will be given what to say, for it will not be you speaking, but the Spirit of your Father speaking through you" (Matt 10:19-20). When faced with hostile situations in our lives, we use the reason, perception, and experience God has given to us, all the while submitting ourselves to the guidance and prompting of the Holy Spirit. This is the example of Esther before the Persian wolves.

VII. HAMAN'S RAGE AGAINST MORDECAI: ESTHER 5:9-14

BEHIND THE TEXT

See the discussion in Behind the Text for 2:21-23 for information regarding impalement. As noted there, the "pole" upon which Haman plans to impale Mordecai is the Hebrew 'ēṣ, the generic term for tree or wood, also translated "stake" or "pole." Its height of 50 cubits is approximately 75 feet, or roughly the average height of a North American red maple tree.

■ **9-10** As he leaves an intimate meal with the king and queen, Haman is described as **happy** [*śāmēaḥ*] **and high in spirits** (*ṭôb lēb* [v 9]). The latter phrase was used in 1:10 to describe the intoxicated condition of Xerxes during the second feast, there with the clarifying information "from wine" (*bayyāyin*). Though the mention of drinking wine occurred here in 5:6, the irrational nature of Haman's response in the following verses suggests that Haman's state is comparable to that of the king's when he requested and then banished Vashti. The object of Haman's *anger* (*ḥēmāh*; compare 1:12) is Mordecai, who has returned to his position in the king's gate but remains adamant in his refusal to recognize Haman. Interestingly, here it is his refusal to rise (*qām*) rather than bow (3:2) that infuriates Haman. Ultimately, though, these verses reveal to us Haman's primary motivation—he wants people to *tremble in terror* (*zûaʿ*) before him. This is not the reverent awe that the Lord deserves and requires from his people (Deut 6:2, 13, 24) and that leads to wisdom (Prov 9:10); rather, this is a deranged lust for complete control over one's victims that the Babylonian tyrant Nebuchadnezzar displayed (Dan 5:19). While it may seem surprising that even in this inebriated state of rage, Haman is able to *restrain himself* (*ʾāpaq*, reflexive), Wesley simply sees here once again "God's wise and powerful providence," which prompts Haman to act "contrary to his own inclination" (1765, 5:10).

■ **11** Parallels to the king's actions in ch 1 continue as Haman calls together his own assembly (his friends and Zeresh, his wife, who does come when he sends for her) for the ostentatious purpose of **counting out** [*sāpar*] **for them** his vast wealth (*kĕbôd ʿošrô*, compare the equivalent phrase *ʿōšer kĕbôd* in 1:4), **his many sons, and all** *about how* **the king had honored him and . . . elevated him above the other nobles and officials.** The repetition of these final two phrases from 3:1 gives the indication that the events of the last two chapters have transpired quite quickly.

■ **12-13** Haman concludes his boasting session with the day's news—**Queen Esther brought no one to the banquet with the king except me, and tomorrow also I am invited** [*qārāʾ*] **by her along with the king** (5:12). The status of being summoned has been significant in this book (*qārāʾ* [2:14; 4:11]). Haman, the called one, stands in contrast to Esther, the uncalled one. The latter received pardon; will the former?

The reversal in Haman's discourse is as sudden as was the reversal in his mood, as he deems **all of this worthless** (*ʾên šōveh* [5:13]), utilizing the same phrase he used to convince Xerxes that the Jews' survival was of no worth to him (3:8). Indeed, here it is the mere presence of Mordecai *as a Jew* that consumes him. Mordecai is the only individual referred to as a Jew singularly (*yĕhûdî*) throughout the book, with this the first of six occurrences of the phrase **Mordecai the Jew** (5:13; 6:10; 8:7; 9:29, 31; 10:3; see also 2:5; 3:4).

■ **14** Haman's wife (who seems to be the principle speaker here, as the verb is in the third-person feminine singular) has the perfect solution to restore her husband's happiness (*śāmēaḥ* [v 9])—simply impale the one whose presence offends you, and do it in the morning, so your party won't be spoiled. In a most grotesque way, this mimics Memukan's suggestion of ch 1 in its size (the **pole** is as absurdly tall as the decree was absurdly broad) and irrevocability, with both of the proposals meant to soothe a bruised male ego in an overt display of power. Just as the absurd proposal of Memukan and the grandiose proposal of the king's servants seemed good to Xerxes in 1:21 and 2:4, so the savage proposal of his wife and friends **seems good** (*yāṭab*) to Haman. So he sets out to do it.

FROM THE TEXT

The Garden Lie: Haman's obsession is a sober warning to us all. He became so fixated on a single annoyance in his life that he disregarded all else. As Wells so eloquently summarizes, "Haman has abundance, but can see only scarcity. He has the opportunity to live out of joy, but instead lives out of envy and pride and fear" (2013, 63). Is this not the temptation of the human heart since the garden (Gen 3)? The one thing becomes the only thing, while the one who is all in all is ignored. I become convinced that the one thing I cannot have will be the only thing that will satisfy—to my own demise. Truly entering into a life of abundance and joy is possible only through the saving work of Jesus Christ (John 10:7-10) and the transforming power of the Holy Spirit in our lives (Gal 5:13-26). I pray that we learn from the sinful example of Haman, in order that we might not become the person whom Wesley identifies: "So ignorant are the wisest men, and subject to fatal mistakes, rejoicing when they have most cause of fear, and sorrowing for those things which tend to joy and comfort" (1765, 5:12).

VIII. MORDECAI HONORED: ESTHER 6:1-14

BEHIND THE TEXT

For a discussion of the Persian royal custom of giving rewards, see Behind the Text for Esth 2:21-23.

The concept of covering one's head or face in grief or shame is found in 2 Sam 15:30 (David's flight from Jerusalem), 19:4 [5 HB] (David's mourning for Absalom), and Jer 14:3-4 (the nation's response to judgment; see also Isa 25:7, in which these effects are reversed by the Lord).

A. The King Battles Insomnia (6:1-6)

■ **1-2** Wisdom from the author of Ecclesiastes could perhaps never be more true than for the incomparably rich Persian king Xerxes:

> The sleep of a laborer is sweet,
>> whether they eat little or much,
> but as for the rich, their abundance
>> permits them no sleep. (Eccl 5:12)

Whatever the source, his riches or otherwise, of his insomnia (poetically phrased in Hebrew, "the sleep of the king fled" [v 1]), its opportune arrival seems suspiciously coincidental. Its cure seems readily found in the reading of the official record of the kingdom (here ***the book of records, the annals*** [*sēper hazzikrōnôt dibrê hayyāmîm*]; in 2:23 and 10:2 "the book of the annals" [*sēper dibrê hayyāmîm*]). However, before the reading can induce sleep, the record of Mordecai's service to the king (2:21-23) is found (*māṣā'*), again a serendipitous moment. As we have seen before (2:8; 5:3), Wesley views this passive verb as the work of "the wise and omnipotent God, who hath the hearts and hands of kings and all men perfectly at his disposal, and can by such trivial accidents (as they are accounted) change their minds" (1765, 6:1).

■ **3** From the beginning (1:4), we have known that this king is obsessed with displays of honor (*yĕqār*) and greatness (*gĕdûllāh*). The sole purpose of Memukan's decree was to restore the king's lost honor (1:20), and the king distributes greatness to whom he will (3:1; 5:11). Thus, his question is not surprising. His attendants, accustomed to their sovereign's moods and outbursts (→ 2:1-2), give the quick reply.

■ **4-5** Ready to remedy the oversight then and there, yet always one to seek out advisers (1:13), the king asks, **Who is in the court** [*beḥāṣēr*]?, supplying the impression that royal officials continually await the king's impulses. The location in the palace where Haman has just entered is mentioned only here, and seems to be an area beyond the inner court, a place that can only be accessed by a summons (see 4:11; 5:1). Like Esther, Haman comes prepared with a request but with no summons (though he fancies himself as one called [5:12]), and his entry is made possible by the king's favor; however, in Haman's case, the king's favor is not directed toward him. Unaware of this, however, he enters the king's presence—always a perilous undertaking (see 4:8).

■ **6** Honor is the overriding theme of this chapter, with seven of the book's ten occurrences of *yĕqār* appearing here. The ***desires*** (*ḥāpēṣ*) of the king had governed the selection of a queen (2:14), and now there is a ***man the king desires to honor***. Haman's recently inflated ego takes over, leaping to the assumption that no one deserves the king's honor more than he. Thus, the great irony is launched.

B. Haman Hatches His Most Honorable Scheme (6:7-9)

■ **7-9** Ah, yes, one can almost see Haman slowly and delightedly turning the phrase over on his tongue—*the man the king desires to honor* (v 7). He repeats it three times in these three verses. The spectacle he unveils is quite intricate and well thought out. The ornaments of this display are the king's own **royal** *robes* (*lĕbûš malkût*, as Esther's garb in 5:1) and horse, identified by its **royal** *crown* (*keter malkût*, as Vashti's and Esther's headpieces in 1:11 and 2:17). Since honor is not an internal quality for Haman, however, it can only be achieved for him through an external dishonoring of others. Thus, the robes and horse that have clothed and carried the king himself simulate a coup, and the humiliation of **one of the king's most noble princes** (*miśśārê hammelek happartĕmîm* [v 9]) achieves the complete control of others that he desires. It is carried out in the most public of places (*the city square* [*rĕḥôb hāʿîr*], where Mordecai mourned [4:6]). The visual spectacle, which proves insufficient, is accompanied by the proclamation (*qārāʾ*) of the king's delight. It is this calling out of the honoree that identifies the ultimate royal acceptance (cf. 2:14; 4:11).

C. Haman's Humiliation (6:10-14)

■ **10-11** Just as he had in ch 3, the king accepts Haman's plan unquestioningly, instructing him to omit nothing *from __all__ he had suggested* (*dābar* [v 10]), just as the edict had been issued *according to __all__ which Haman had commanded* (3:12). In that instance, Haman had concealed the full nature of his scheme until he had the king's approval; here, the king's approval reveals to Haman the true reality of his fantasy. The phrase **for Mordecai the Jew, who sits at the king's gate** is almost the precise phrase that Haman had uttered in disgust a few verses before (5:13). Haman leaves, his request remaining unasked, to carry out his own commands. In contrast to the last chapter filled with Haman's words, Haman is hauntingly silent in his humiliation.

■ **12** The full reversal of the station of these two men is most apparent in this verse. Haman's elevation to his position (ch 3) had precipitated Mordecai's mourning, thereby denying him access to the king's gate (4:2); now, it is Mordecai who is returned to his seat in the gate while Haman scurries away in mourning (*ʾābēl*; → 4:3).

■ **13** Just hours before, Haman had gathered his wife and friends around him to crow over his newly elevated position as intimate associate of the king and queen (5:10). Now, this same group gathers to hear *all that has happened* [*qārāh*] *to him* (implying a negative circumstance, as in 4:7). The response comes not from his friends, but from his advisers, wise men (*ḥākām*) as the king had consulted in 1:13. His wife is also involved, though the plural verb may indicate she is not the main speaker (contrast 5:14).

This group clearly perceives the recent reversals against Haman as ill-omened, explicitly viewing them as the beginning of Haman's downfall (*nāpal*) before Mordecai. Their feeble attempt to offer hope by framing the fact of Mordecai's heritage as conjectural (*if* **Mordecai . . . is of Jewish origin,** translated **since** in the NIV) goes unnoticed against their definitive conclusion—*then you will not prevail against him*. Contrary to every plan, manipulation, and evil scheme—all that Haman had sought (3:6)—he *will fall* [*nāpal*] *before Mordecai* (→ 4:14 for discussion of this contrary-to-expectation construction found both here and there).

■ **14** It seems that Mordecai's honoring happened in the morning (precisely at the time when Haman had planned to execute him [5:14]), for barely had he had time to get home and tell his tale than he was whisked away to the palace for the banquet.

FROM THE TEXT

God's Hand: I don't view every sleepless night as a sign from God; however, some undoubtedly are. God's concealed activity in the book of Esther is clearly demonstrated in the king's insomnia. Saint Jerome, the translator of the Latin Vulgate in the late fourth century AD, directs our thoughts in this way:

> There is no doubt that the mighty sovereign [Xerxes] . . . , after feasting sumptuously . . . would have desired to sleep, and to take his rest . . . had not the Lord, the provider of all good things, hindered the course of nature, so that in defiance of nature the tyrant's cruelty might be overcome. (Conti 2008, 388)

Some of us are more prone to see God's activity in the mundane details of our lives; others of us see his activity less in the execution of the details but in the working together of those details toward his purpose. Quite likely, both are avenues he uses, and I am well served to acknowledge and appreciate both, though careful never to ascribe to him the doing of evil (→ From the Text for Esth 2:1-20).

A Humility That Brings Honor: Once again, Haman offers to us a picture of a life lived contrary to kingdom principles. The words of Christ in Luke 14:11 could as easily apply to this chapter in Esther as it did to the guests in the Pharisee's house that day: "For all those who exalt themselves will be humbled, and those who humble themselves will be exalted" (compare Matt 23:12). Contrary to our human perceptions, honor is not something bestowed upon us; it is something formed within us. As I humble myself before the Lord and submit myself to the work of the Holy Spirit to develop honor within me, the less visions of being honored by humans plague me. "True humility is not thinking less of yourself; it is thinking of yourself less" (often attributed to C. S. Lewis; cf. *The Screwtape Letters*, Letter 14). How many honorable Mordecais and Esthers live quiet lives of humble service around me each day? Let me seek to honor them.

IX. HAMAN IMPALED: ESTHER 7:1-10

BEHIND THE TEXT

For a discussion of the ancient practices of impalement, see Behind the Text for Esth 2:21-23.

IN THE TEXT

A. Esther's Second Banquet (7:1-6)

■ **1** In this final royal banquet of the story, the king and Haman enter into Esther's presence for a second time. The wording mirrors that of 3:15, when the king and Haman again had gathered "to drink" (*lištôt*). Their callousness at that moment looms large in the face of Esther's impending request.

■ **2-3** The words of both the king and Esther in these verses echo their statements from the first banquet (5:6-8). The king's words are almost verbatim, the only differences being one slight shift in verbal agreement and the explicit reference to Esther as the queen. Esther, addressing the king in the same deferential ways (with one addition of a second-person pronoun), eloquently reorders her statement to include only two additional words in Hebrew—**my life** (*napšî*) and **my**

people (*'ammî*), the substance of her petition and request. The request is striking in its simplicity and, as Wesley notes, "very affecting" (1765, 7:3).

■ **4** This second portion of Esther's statement is a brilliant rhetorical maneuver. She succinctly though subtly states the truth of the situation by utilizing the passive voice, *we* **have been sold** (*nimkarnû*), to obscure the accusation against the king, who is himself one of the agents of this transaction. She then lets the hammer of Haman's edict resound three times with the repetition of the exact verbs from 3:13—*for destruction* (*lĕhašmîd*), *for massacre* (*lĕhărôg*), *for annihilation* (*lĕ'abbēd*). The brilliant move comes next as she poses the hypothetical scenario (*'illû*, **if**) that esteems the king's supreme importance while heightening the gravity of the situation. Esther offers the possibility that if, in contrast to the holocaust they face, it had only been *for slavery* (*la'ăbādîm vĕlišpāḥôt*) that they had been targeted, she *would have remained silent*. This final verb reverberates for the readers if not for the king—Esther is *not* keeping silent (4:14)! At this very moment, she is the agent through whom God's plan of redemption for his people is being accomplished!

The final phrase of Esther's speech is ambiguous. The NIV offers the following competing translations: **because no such distress would justify disturbing the king** *or* **but the compensation our adversary offers cannot be compared with the loss the king would suffer** (NIV footnote). The first is perhaps the most straightforward and oozes with a deferential concern for the king's personal well-being. Using the same language utilized by Haman in 3:8 when he argued that *there was no worth/profit* (*'ên šōveh*) in tolerating the Jews, so Esther argues that *there is no worth* in disturbing the king over this distress (*haṣṣār*, i.e., "it's not worth it"). However, the second possibility, admittedly more subtle grammatically yet much more potent, would infer that *there is no profit* from the adversary (*haṣṣār*) that would outweigh the damage done (i.e., this will be financially detrimental to you). Let us not underestimate Esther's brilliance; our confusion may be of her own doing. Perhaps the ambiguity here is intended, offering the king an avenue for plausible deniability. (See Berlin 2001, 64-68, for her fascinating interpretation of this scene.)

■ **5-6** By his response, it would seem that the king seizes upon the second interpretation above, equating *haṣṣār* with a particular adversary of the Jews rather than a general distress over the situation. When expecting a profit, the king condoned the annihilation of a people without even asking for their identity (ch 3); when threatened with ruin, the king wastes no time in seeking out both the name and the whereabouts of the perpetrator. Ironically, of course, the king's demand for *the one whose heart has filled him to act in such a way* (7:5), brings condemnation upon his own actions, much as David served as his own judge and jury in 2 Sam 12:5-6. Likewise, Esther's response is somewhat analogous to Nathan's (2 Sam 12:7), though she exposes only *this evil Haman* as an adversary [*ṣar*] and enemy. Note that in Esth 3:10, the narrator has already supplied the reader with Haman's title, "the foe [*ṣōrēr*, from the same root as adversary] of the Jews" (NJPS). With the king and queen united against him, Haman is terrified (*bā'at*), as were both Daniel before the messenger of God (Dan 8:17) and Job in the face of divine punishment (Job 7:14).

B. Haman's Demise (7:7-10)

■ **7** The grammatical structure of this verse demonstrates the simultaneity of Haman's actions with the king's—*as the king left . . . , Haman stood*. The king's rage (*ḥēmāh*) drives him from the banquet **into the palace garden**, the same place where he had become enraged with Vashti years before (1:5, 12). Anger has consistently led to extreme actions in this book, from Vashti's exile (1:12, 19) to Haman's decree against the Jews (3:5-6) to the construction of Mordecai's gallows (5:9, 14). Thus, with the king's enraged exit, Haman sees that his life is lost. His only hope lies in Queen Esther, from whom he now desperately *seeks* [*bāqaš*] *his life* (→ discussion in 4:8).

■ **8** This verse continues the grammatical structuring of the previous verse, indicating actions happening one on top of the other. Just as Haman had jumped to his feet as the king was storming from the room, now the king returns just in time to see Haman **falling** (*nōpēl*) upon his wife's **couch**. Thus, the prophecy of Haman's advisers and wife is fulfilled and Haman's expectations are completely contradicted as he has quite actually fallen before the Jews (6:13). Haman's perceived assault on the queen has given the king the rope he needs to hang him (though probably not literally), since sentencing him for his acts against the Jews would show the king culpable as well (Berlin 2001, 64). The king's exclamation launches his attendants into action, and Haman's face is now covered in ultimate humiliation (→ 6:12).

■ **9-10** As usual (1:14; 2:2), those around the king supply him with a plan. Harbona had been among the eunuchs in 1:10 whom the king had sent to bring Vashti, and he now provides the king with the information concerning the pole that Haman had erected for Mordecai. In a bit of cunning that rivals Queen Esther's, he is careful to clarify for his forgetful king exactly who it is that Haman has planned to murder—it is *Mordecai, the one who spoke well* [*ṭôb*] *on behalf of the king* (8:9). The sentence rings with the final reversal for Haman. Just as the honor he planned for himself was given to Mordecai, so the death he planned for Mordecai is given to him.

FROM THE TEXT

Fallen Humanity: "We sometimes startle at that evil, which we ourselves are chargeable with. Ahasuerus [Xerxes] is amazed at that wickedness, which he himself was guilty of" (Wesley 1765, 7:5). While we may not want to admit it, each of us can connect with Xerxes in this chapter. How often do our minds, if not our lips, charge then condemn others for their faults and failures, with little thought of our own? Early in Romans (2:1-8), Paul addresses the corruption found in all fallen humanity, including those "who pass judgment" yet "do the same things" (v 1). Likewise, Jesus cautions against self-absorbed hypocrisy like that of Xerxes

(Matt 7:1-5). However, in our Western culture, which exalts the virtue of tolerance above all else, many have taken Christ's command to "judge not" as an indication that we should excuse all actions, making no evaluations of right or wrong. This conclusion not only misses the point of the passage but also misunderstands the character of God in whose image we are created.

In Rom 2:6, Paul makes clear that "God 'will repay each person according to what they have done.'" When we examine Ps 62:11-12 [12-13 HB], from which this quote is drawn, we find that God's repayment for both good and evil comes directly from two aspects of his character. He is strong, therefore he is able to carry out judgment; he is faithfully loving, therefore he is trustworthy to rightly identify human motivations and repay accordingly. In the same way, Jesus calls us to the loving act of pointing out and aiding in the removal of the specks of sin that plague and injure our friends. This is a command. The problem comes with our ability to rightly identify human motivations, both in ourselves and in others. It is only by the strong power of the Holy Spirit to transform us into God's character that we can first lovingly examine ourselves and be cleansed of our own faults and failures, and then reach out in love with humility to help free those around us from the bondage of sin in their lives.

Unchanging God: Even greater than our similarity to Xerxes is God's dissimilarity. Clines has pointed out that here in the story, the king shifts from "Opponent" of the Jews to "Helper" (1990, 36). As readers, we have already been conditioned to expect fickleness in this king, to see him shift whichever way the most promising winds may blow. This unpredictability alongside seemingly unlimited power has made him supremely dangerous. By contrast, God's "divine reliability" alongside his truly unlimited power (omnipotence) make him supremely trustworthy.

In both the Old and New Testaments, God is described as unchanging, without variation, eternally the same (Oden 2009, 67-69; cites Ps 102:26-27 [27-28 HB]; Mal 3:6; James 1:17; Heb 13:8). The Jews of Esther's day had received God's punishment of exile for their lives of rebellion against him, but they also experienced his deliverance, primarily because of his covenant promise to them, but also because of their obedience. Because God's nature is unchanging, I can be assured that he will act in the same way today as he did back then. Lives lived in rebellion to God—whether my own or those of my oppressors—will ultimately receive his punishment. Likewise, lives lived in obedient commitment to him will receive his promise of deliverance. These may not unfold as immediately or dramatically today as they did in the OT, but they are as eternally true. Oden goes on to point out that this unchanging nature is not one of rigidity and inflexibility, but rather one that is always "consistent with his own nature, congruent with the depths of his own essential goodness, stable, not woodenly predictable." Therefore, while I may not know why God seems to be choosing to act or not to act in any given situation, I can trust that his choices are fully good and right, and I can rest in his promise to redeem and restore me.

X. REVERSALS ABOUND: ESTHER 8:1-17

BEHIND THE TEXT

See 1:19 for a discussion of the inalterability of Persian law.

IN THE TEXT

A. The King's Edict on Behalf of the Jews (8:1-14)

■ **1-2** This is the second of four times in the book that Haman's name is followed by the title "the foe of the Jews" (*ṣōrēr hayyĕhûdîm* [NJPS]; 3:10; 8:1; 9:10, 24). The first was as royal authority was passed to his hands; the second is here, as all his possessions pass to royal control, first to the hands of Queen Esther then to Mordecai, all on the very day of Haman's death. Furthermore, the royal authority that had been Haman's is stripped (*'ābar*) from him and passed to Mordecai, with 8:2 echoing the words of 3:10. Likewise, the concealment of Esther's identity is now fully reversed, as she reveals to the king her connection to Mordecai, whom Xerxes clearly knows to be a Jew (see 6:10).

■ **3-4** While the action of the story surrounding the main characters seems to be wrapping up, the audience is quickly reminded that nothing has changed for the Jews. Though the Agagite has been destroyed, the **evil** (*rā'āh*) that he ***intended*** [*ḥāšab*] **against the Jews** is alive and imminent. The wording of this verse brings to mind Gen 50:20, when Joseph assures his brothers that, "You intended [*ḥāšab*] to harm [*rā'āh*] me, but God intended it [*ḥāšab*] for good to accomplish what is now being done, the saving of many lives." (→ From the Text for Esth 2.)

285

Though Esther seems to have achieved security for herself and her father's house (4:14), it becomes clear that this has not been her sole motivation, as there are still many lives to be saved. Thus, she approaches the king, an act that places her life in jeopardy once again (cf. 5:2; Levenson 1997, 107; contra Bush 1996, 444). Falling at the king's feet and weeping, Esther **begs for** the king's **mercy** (ḥānan), thereby completing Mordecai's initial charge to her (→ 4:8).

■ **5-6** Esther is elaborate in the presentation of her request, preceding it with four deferential clauses far surpassing the deference shown throughout the book (e.g., 1:19; 3:9; 5:4, 8; 7:3). The length of this introduction emphasizes the weight of the request—Esther is asking for a de facto repeal of a law of Persia and Media, the ultimate reversal (**overruling**, lĕhāšîb [8:5]). Esther is as specific in her request as she was deferential in its introduction. Leaving nothing to chance or the forgetfulness of Xerxes, she identifies Haman by his full familial title, specifies the nature of what was written (**to destroy**), and clarifies its extent to **the Jews in all the king's provinces**. She ends with a personal appeal for her **people** ('ammî) and her **kindred** (môladtî, → 2:10, also 7:3, when her life was also in jeopardy). In all of this, Wesley notes that Esther "prudently takes off the hatefulness of the action from the king, and lays it upon Haman" (1765, 8:5).

■ **7-8** The king's reply matches Esther's request in both formality and thoroughness. Xerxes and Esther are each identified by royal title, while Mordecai is given the designation **the Jew** (8:7). First used derogatorily in the mouth of Haman (5:13) and then planted ironically in the mouth of Xerxes (6:10), here the narrator seems to have reversed the term into a mark of honor. Indeed, the king's own words highlight the elevation that has occurred in the status of the Jews. In 3:11, the king gave Haman authority **to do with the people as it seemed good** to him, all without asking or knowing their identity. Here, however, as Xerxes uses similar terms to give authority to both Esther and Mordecai (note second-person plural pronouns and verbal forms) to issue a decree **as it seems good** to them, it is specifically a decree **in behalf of the Jews** ('al hayyĕhûdîm [8:8]). Esther and Mordecai have given a face and a name to a faceless, nameless people.

The king states that what will now be written and sealed will be **unable to be reversed** ('ên lĕhāšîb), which ironically proves that irrevocable Persian law is not so irrevocable. That fact, however, is ultimately inconsequential for God's people. We are fully aware, though Xerxes may not be, that the statement he makes is in no way a timeless promise for the Jews. There is no guarantee of no future laws against them, of safety from all foes, of peace and security. These things are as fleeting as is Persian law. However, what is timeless, guaranteed, and unalterable is the relief and deliverance of God's people. Today it came through Esther and Mordecai. Tomorrow it will come through another source. Regardless, the survival of a people of the Lord God in this world is the one thing that **cannot be reversed**.

■ **9-10** Barely two months after the first edict was written and dispersed (3:12), another is written, this one containing **all Mordecai's orders** rather than Haman's (8:9). The description of the dissemination of the two edicts is almost identical, with a few expansions to the second (see chart in Bush 1996, 442-43). Most significantly, the Jews are named twice as explicit recipients of the edict in their own script and language. Additionally, the extent of the kingdom detailed in 1:1 is reiterated here to identify the reach of the edict. Though the time may seem short, it was arguably interminable for the people over whom hung a death sentence for those weeks. Wesley suggests that the delay in time was "for the greater illustration of God's glorious power, and wisdom, and goodness, in giving his people such an admirable and unexpected deliverance" (1765, 8:9).

■ **11-12** The core content of the two edicts is as similar as their modes of delivery (compare 3:13). In both, the right is given **to destroy** [*šāmad*], **kill** [*hārag*] **and annihilate** (*'ābad*) a group of people including its **women and children** and **to plunder** *their possessions* (v 11) all on the same *single day* (v 12). The primary difference, of course, is that in this edict, these rights are granted to the Jews. It is that fact that makes these similarities, issued at the command of Mordecai, so chilling. The Jews as the recipients of these deeds is devastating; the Jews as the perpetrators seems profane. How can we respond?

First of all, this edict must be read in the framework of reversals that permeates the book (→ Introduction). With its significant number of similarities to the first edict, this account is clearly meant to mirror and, therefore, reverse its predecessor. Thus, when we encounter a similarity such as the reference to **women and children**, for example, a mirrored reading would interpret this as a reference to a group approved for destruction, as in 3:13. Reading this, as some do, as a reference to Hebrew innocents also being attacked (thereby further validating the self-defense claim of the edict) fails to read the overall account in its intended framework (compare NIV translation vs. note).

Second, with the similarities simply functioning to emphasize the reversal, it is upon the distinctive commands to the Jews that we should focus and place significance. The first of these distinctions in the second edict comes in the first action to which the Jews are called—not to destroy, but **to assemble** [*qāhal*] **and protect themselves** (*'āmad 'al-nepeš*, **to take a stand for their lives**; → 9:16). Second, the destruction is not targeted at an unarmed, defenseless people but at *any armed force* that initiates violence against them. Clearly, this is the definition of self-defense.

■ **13-14** Again, these verses mirror 3:14-15 in most ways; thus, the differences hold the significance. The initial difference, of course, is the indication that it is the Jews who can now make ready for that day. However, theirs is a qualified rather than an unqualified preparation. They may make ready **to avenge themselves on their enemies** (v 13). While the idea of vengeance seems disturbing to us, it is discussed some seventy-nine times in the OT and is directly linked to the character of God. We tend to be drawn to descriptions of God's character that highlight his grace, mercy, compassion, forgiveness, faithfulness, and abounding steadfast love (e.g., Exod 34:6; Neh 9:17; Ps 86:15; Jonah 4:2). However, a characteristic often listed alongside these is that God is slow to anger. On the one hand, this is immensely comforting; on the other, however, this is a word of caution and warning to those who would live a life of defiance against him, thereby provoking his anger that is slow but not impotent.

In Nah 1:2-3, we see that God is a God who takes vengeance on his adversaries and enemies—those who would thwart his purpose of reconciliation and restoration. However, even to the guilty, to those who deserve punishment, he is a slow-angering God! Descriptions in Nahum of his punishment are followed by another attribute of God—he is good (1:7). God is good, in one part, precisely because he will protect those oppressed and in trouble who take refuge in him *by* punishing their oppressors (see also Isa 61).

Note that here in Esther, of course, this avenging is not petty revenge for any slight grudge; the enemies upon whom the Jews may avenge themselves are those who have come upon them with a fighting force. Those who raise their hands to annihilate God's people are subject to the judgment of the Almighty God who has vowed to protect and sustain his people in this world. (→ "Violence in Esther" excursus at From the Text for Esth 9:1-19 below; also Niditch 1993, 119-22.)

B. Response to the Second Edict (8:15-17)

■ **15** This portion of the chapter continues to reflect images from earlier in the book, but in an equal and opposite fashion. After the first edict was issued, the narrative camera zoomed in on the self-congratulatory royal toasting (3:15); here, it pans to Mordecai walking out of the king's presence. Then, the city was in chaos; here, there is a joyous celebration. Then, Mordecai wore sackcloth and ashes (4:1); here, he is wearing the colors, fabrics, garments, and accessories of royalty. Then, there was weeping and mourning (4:3); now, joy and gladness. Then fasting, now feasting.

In 4:1, Mordecai, "wearing sackcloth and ashes, . . . went out into the city, wailing loudly and bitterly," his actions and his dress representative of Jews throughout the kingdom. One can imagine the scene now as Mordecai emerges from the palace dressed in royal robes to the joyous cheers of the entire city (the grammatical structure of the verse signaling simultaneity of action). Mordecai's clothing harkens back to the description of the royal banquet of 1:5-6 (→). The phrase describing the **large crown of gold** (*ʿăṭeret zāhāb gĕdôlāh*) that Mordecai wears utilizes the more common Hebrew word for crown, different from the word used in 1:11, 2:17, and 6:8 (a noun occurring only in Esther in the Bible). Clines suggests that this crown is simply "the head-dress of a Persian noble," rather than the crown of royalty that Mordecai wore in ch 6 fulfilling Haman's desire (1984b, 318).

■ **16** *To the Jews there was* **light** [*ʾôrāh*] *and joy* [*śimḥāh*], **gladness** [*śāśôn*] *and* **honor** (*yĕqār*). Nowhere else in the biblical text do these terms converge, presenting us with a picture of unprecedented hope among and goodwill toward God's people. Indeed, there are echoes of the most joyous, hopeful passages of the Prophets in these words—a time when joy and gladness reign in place of suffering and sorrow (e.g., Isa 35, 60). Isaiah 60 in particular bursts with light imagery. Light is a sign of protection, of guidance, and of hope (Exod 13:21; Isa 42:6), all of which the Jews have experienced throughout their history, but never more so than here in Esther.

It is the honor that they receive, however, that resonates most loudly throughout this story. Xerxes flaunted it (Esth 1:4) and legislated it (1:20), Haman demanded it and plotted for it (3:5-6), but it was ultimately Mordecai who was the man the king delighted to honor (ch 6) and his people who become the honored ones.

■ **17** The resulting merriment that takes place far and wide, **in every *single*** province (as in 3:14; 4:3; 8:13), is called *a feast [mišteh] and a celebration* (yôm ṭôb). This feast sits in stark contrast to both the flamboyant Persian feasts of ch 1 and the desolate Jewish fasting of ch 4. The celebration is simply a *good day* in Hebrew, though a festival feeling is present and likely underlies this phrase (see its use in 1 Sam 25:8 referring to sheepshearing time, a typically festive occasion). Some translations (including the NASB and NRSV) translate "holiday" both here and in 2:18, which describes the celebration of Esther's wedding, though the terminology in Hebrew is different. In 2:18, the holiday is an official one, perhaps accompanied by some type of release from legislative constraints; here, the holiday is a spontaneous one, the outward manifestation of the joy bubbling up among the Jews.

Accompanying these festivities are what appear to be mass conversions, as **many people of other nationalities became Jews**. While most translations employ **became Jews** for this unique Hebrew verb (mityahădîm), it is most broadly translated *acted in a way characteristic of Jews*, which could encompass cultural, religious, and even ethnic elements. Thus, translations and commentators alike have taken it to mean "declared themselves Jews" (RSV), "professed to be Jews" (NRSV), "sided with the Jews" (Berlin 2001, 80), and even "pretended to be Jews" (GW; for a full discussion, see Bush 1996, 448).

The Greek edition of Esther clearly envisions religious conversion, translating the ambiguous Hebrew with "were circumcised." Debra Reid has expertly navigated to the heart of this situation by focusing on the "parallel . . . with Esther's own journey: she chose to identify herself with her people despite the risks involved; now non-Jews choose to identify themselves with Jews because they see only benefits from doing so" (2008, 138).

Whatever the precise effect, its cause is unambiguous—*for the fear of the Jews had fallen upon them* (nāpal paḥad). Throughout their history, the Jews have experienced the benefits of the coming of fear, both upon their enemies (e.g., exit from Egypt [Ps 105:38]; entry into Canaan [Exod 15:16; Deut 11:25]) and upon their own people (e.g., Saul's rallying the troops [1 Sam 11:7]). In all of these cases, some more than others, the fear was not fully justifiable (e.g., would the Egyptians really have been afraid of a bunch of slaves?). The argument always exists that there is no real reason for said people to be afraid, therefore, a claim of fear when people "shouldn't" be afraid must be false. Thus, Esther commentators debate whether this fear is real or trumped up, rational or supernatural. In reality, all of those possibilities could be quite accurate on some level. To get lost in those conversations can miss the point our author is trying to make that, in some small way and probably for a variety of reasons, exiled Israel has become a light to the nations. It took God's people losing the promise of the land (Gen 12:1) to begin

8:17

to fulfill the ultimate purpose of the covenant—to bring blessing to all humanity (Gen 12:3; contra Wells 2013, 76).

FROM THE TEXT

Vengeance Is Whose? Though very few of us will ever face the annihilation of our people or family at the hand of an enemy, some of us have experienced true evil, and most of us have faced a circumstance that seemed like an armed onslaught against us. In those circumstances, we might wish to claim the edict of Esth 8 as our authority to exact vengeance upon our tormentors. However, as we have seen above, this text doesn't allow for a revenge free-for-all.

In addition, this text doesn't constitute the Bible's sole stance on our responses to evil. For example, after the first eleven chapters of Romans systematically spell out the steps for our reconciliation with God and restoration to his image, the Apostle Paul then shifts in chs 12—15 to the practical implications of that process on our daily lives. In 12:17-21, he specifically addresses the idea of taking vengeance. His conclusion is straightforward, "Do not be overcome by evil, but overcome evil with good" (v 21). Paul also quotes OT passages (from Deuteronomy and Proverbs) in these instructions for the Christian response to evil. Clearly, a life of revenge-seeking has never been a part of God's plan for his redeemed world. Therefore, as Christians, we are called to be bringers of peace and compassion, and to lay the evil that needs to be repaid in the nail-scarred hands—wounds that remind me of my own sins for which I paid no penalty.

Living God's Plan: One reason that I love to read postexilic literature in the OT (e.g., Ezra, Nehemiah, Haggai, Zechariah, Malachi, and, of course, Esther) is it feels like God's people are finally living into God's plan as they had been chosen to do. In their early history, we find individual Israelites following the Lord, but as a whole, his people are just frustrating—constantly disobeying, ignoring the prophets' warnings, and living like the rest of the ancient world. What they weren't doing was being a light to the people around them.

So often in my life, I am very concerned about the plan God has for me, where I'm going to live, work, go to church, send my children to school, and so forth. The reality is that he wants to use everything I do, whatever I do, wherever I am, to accomplish his plan of bringing humans into relationship with him and restoring his image in which they were created. Which is the most important part of that last sentence, the part about me or the part about him? I know, that's not a fair question, but we need this eternal perspective. The details of what I do in my life pale in comparison to the result that God wants to accomplish through those details. So, let's flip the paradigm. Instead of asking our children (and ourselves!), "What are you going to be when you grow up?", let's first teach them what they are made to be—"You are the light of the world" (Matt 5:14). Then we can ask, "So, how can you be *that* in your life?"

XI. THE TRIUMPH OF THE JEWS: ESTHER 9:1-19

BEHIND THE TEXT

As we would expect at the end of this book of reversals, many of the issues that arise in this portion of the text have been treated earlier. See the Behind the Text sections in ch 3 for a discussion related to the keeping of spoils by Saul (9:7-10 below), ch 1 for considerations concerning Esther's request for an additional day of fighting in Susa (9:13 below), and 2:21-23 for a treatment of the public display of bodies (9:13 below).

Yamauchi comments on "the care that the Hebrew scribes exercised in transmitting such foreign names" as those of Haman's sons (vv 7-9), some of which are supported by parallels in the Elamite Persepolis texts (1996, 238). From a literary standpoint, the listing of these names along with their father sets them up as marked enemies of the Jews. This disdain is reflected in the rabbinic commands related to the reading of the Esther scroll at Purim—Haman's name is to be booed and hissed, while the names of his ten sons must be read dismissively in one breath (Levenson 1997, 121-22; see also Gehman 1924, 43).

■ **1** Following an opening temporal phrase such as **On the thirteenth day of the twelfth month**, a Hebrew reader immediately expects a main verb to move the action along (so, 1:3; 3:1; 5:1; 8:1). However, here our author builds suspense by delaying the main action with the interruption of several subordinate clauses describing this particular day. It is the day upon which **the edict commanded by the king was to be carried out** (meaning Haman's edict), the day upon which **the enemies of the Jews had hoped** [*śābar*] **to overpower** [*šālaṭ*] **them**. However, **on this day**, now finally encountering the main verb, **the tables were turned** (*hāpak*). This phrase summarizes a primary theme of the book of Esther. On the day when all hope was lost, the odds were insurmountable, the enemy was poised to strike, and there was no place to turn, "the reverse occurred" (ESV); "the opposite happened" (NJPS); "[it] had been changed" (NRSV); "it was turned to the contrary" (KJV, NASB).

The Israelite exilic community is no stranger to reversal at the hand of God, particularly the reversal that turned light (peace and prosperity) into darkness (mourning and captivity) (Amos 5:8; 8:9-10). However, that same hand now reaches out in faithfulness to fulfill his covenant (Gen 17:1-8), turning their "mourning into gladness" (Jer 31:13; also Ps 30:11 [12 HB]), their captivity into goodness and well-being (*ṭôb* and *šālôm* [Esth 10:3]). There is an equivalence to this reversal as well, with the Jews overpowering (*šālaṭ*) those who had hoped to overpower (*šālaṭ*) them.

■ **2** The Jews *assemble*, in accordance with the king's first permission given in 8:11, the second of which was *to take a stand* [*'āmad*] *for their lives*. This stand produces a reversal in favor of the Jews as **no one** is able to stand [*'āmad*] *before* **them**. The object of the Jews' attack (*sending a hand against*, so 2:21, 6:2; also 3:6; 8:7) are identified in 8:1 as both "the enemies of the Jews" and "those who hated them." They are *those seeking* [*bāqaš*] *their harm* (or evil; see 8:3, *destruction*). Clearly, this is not a passive group, and the threefold designation assures the reader that the Jews are not partaking in a reverse slaughter of innocents. Rather, these are the people who have not responded positively to the *fear* (*paḥad*) of the Jews that had *fallen* upon <u>all the people</u>, as opposed to those who had responded by aligning themselves with the Jews (8:17).

■ **3-4** Here we see an additional positive response as <u>all</u> the administrative force of Persia **helped** [*nāśā'*] **the Jews** (v 3). These particular governmental officials have all appeared in Esther before, yet only here are they all together, perhaps indicating the pervasiveness of the administrative support for the Jews. One group, **the king's administrators,** appears elsewhere only in 3:9, there designated by Haman to receive his proffered bribe. Rather than accountants of Jewish inventory on this day, they end up assistants for Jewish interests. The type of aid all these officials give is unspecified, the Hebrew utilizing the verb *nāśā'* with the meanings (in this rare stem) "to exalt" (as in 3:1, 5:11 referring to Xerxes' elevation of

Haman; also 2 Sam 5:12) or "to offer support" (e.g., 1 Kgs 9:11; Ezra 8:36). As in Esth 8:17, the ambiguity of the act is offset by the clarity of the cause—**fear** (*paḥad* [8:17; 9:2-3]). Here, however, it is the fear of Mordecai, now Persia's most powerful administrative official, rather than fear of Jews generally that motivates the bureaucrats to action. The final verbal construction in v 4 clarifies that Mordecai has not only achieved power but that his power is continuing to grow (see similar constructions in Exod 19:19; 1 Sam 17:41; 2 Sam 3:1).

■ **5** As in Esth 9:1-2, the author here identifies the recipients of the Jewish assault as **their enemies** and **those who hated them**. However, it is the actions of the Jews that draw our attention with their stark brutality. The construction **with the sword, killing and destroying** is unparalleled in the biblical text, even deviating from similar passages in Esther (3:13; 7:4; 8:11) by utilizing very rare forms from the roots "to kill" (*hārag*) and "to destroy" (*'ābad*) and omitting the root "to annihilate" (*šāmad*, so 9:6, 12). We may hypothesize that our author is sketching shades of Isa 27:7 (with some commonality of vocabulary), with its emphasis on the totality of destruction that awaits those who seek the destruction of God's people.

The ability of the Jews to do **what they pleased** may indicate the "free hand" they were "given by the authorities," but that does not consequently imply that the Jews "did not confine themselves to self-defense" (Moore 1971, 90). The phrase **as they pleased** utilizes the noun *rāṣôn* ("pleasure," "favor," "will"), which is also found in 1:8, a context that allowed for either excess or restraint. This appears to be somewhat different from the pleasure of the Persians (usually *'im 'al . . . , ṭôb*) that has motivated many actions, good and bad, in our story (1:19; 2:4; 3:9, etc.). Perhaps the distinction may be demonstrated in a translation *as they willed* here and in 1:8 (also, e.g., Dan 8:4; Neh 9:24), while translating "as it seemed good" elsewhere. The first appears to draw more from one's fixed character, the second from one's fickle perception. Based upon the character of the Jews we know best in this story, readers may anticipate a restrained dealing with their enemies, rather than assuming the opposite.

■ **6** When one sees the reports, however, this idea of Jewish restraint comes into serious question. The death toll from Susa—500 on the first day, 300 the second (v 15)—arrives before the devastating figure of 75,000 killed throughout the kingdom. There is no extrabiblical, Persian corroboration of these numbers, and commentators consistently assert their conflated nature for this time period (see Fox 2001, 110). Both the Jewish historian Josephus and the Greek Alpha Text (AT) record equally large numbers (75,000 and 70,100, respectively), though the old Greek text records only 15,000. Based upon these historical and textual factors as well as the evidence of Jewish restraint throughout the passage, it is best to view these numbers as a literary expression of the extensiveness of the Jewish victory proportionate to the incomparable vastness of the Persian Empire. However, whatever the count might have been, we must view any number as heart-wrenching in the human souls it represents.

9:5-6

■ **7-10** It appears that Haman's ten sons, the only specified casualties on the first day's fighting, were part of the fighting force that had come against the Jews, as the text gives no alternate explanation of their deaths. Though the list of their names is fascinating (→ Behind the Text for Esth 9:1-19, above), it is the reiteration of Haman's title "the foe of the Jews" (3:10; 8:1; 9:10, 24 NJPS) that catches the readers' attention and reminds us of the ultimate cause of this day. With the death of his sons, all of Haman's boasting in 5:11 has been undone—his wealth and position have been given to Mordecai and now his many sons are killed by Mordecai's decree. The reversal is complete.

Further support for the restraint shown by the Jews is displayed in the three-fold occurrence of the phrase that first occurs here—**but they did not lay their hands on the plunder** (*bizzāh*, 9:10, 15, 16). This had been the ultimate failure of Saul against the Amalekites in 1 Sam 15 (→ Behind the Text for Esth 3). Though God had commanded total destruction, Saul chose (though blaming his troops) to keep some spoil (*šālāl* [1 Sam 15:21]). The exiled Jews do not make the same mistake. Though "measure-for-measure retaliation" (Anderson 1954, 866) was al-lowed by Mordecai's edict, it is clearly not embraced by the Jews. Just as Esther showed wise restraint by choosing not to take what was offered her (Esth 2:15), so the Jews here refuse the spoil, though it was theirs for the taking. Thus, Ander-son's claim that the Jews' actions throughout ch 9 are "a case of 'do unto others as they would have done unto you'" is discredited (ibid., 866-68). What "would have been done," at Haman's promise, was not only a full annihilation of all Jewish people but also the enrichment of the royal treasury through the spoils taken from the Jews. The Jews do neither to their enemies.

■ **11-12** The majority of commentators view the king's response to the news from Susa as callous and insensitive (e.g., Fox 2001, 112; Day 2005, 150). His state-ment, **What have they done in the rest of the king's provinces?** (v 12), perhaps even rings with an air of excited anticipation as he roots on his new favored champion in the distant sporting arena of his empire. Others, however, read a sense of stunned disbelief that sends him reeling and seeking advice from the nearest adviser, who happens to be his queen (Clines 1984b, 324). Unfortunately, it is the former that seems most consistent with his character throughout the narrative, thus framing his words to Esther as congratulatory and rewarding for the entertainment her first request has produced. He phrases his offer as before (5:6; 7:2; similar 5:3), though simply asking, **What else** [*'ôd*] **is your request?**, without the now evident qualifier "even up to half the kingdom."

■ **13** Esther's reply, with a shortened form of her assumed deference (compare 5:8; 7:3; 8:5), contains two requests. The first is for a day's extension of the royal permission for the Jews of Susa to defend themselves. Such a request, and a seem-ingly swift one at that, begs the question, why? The first reports that have come in (9:6, 11, 12) confirm the deaths in the citadel of Susa (*šûšan bîrāh*); however, here Esther asks for an extension **in Susa** (*šûšan*). When **Susa** is used against "the citadel of Susa" or "the city of Susa" (→ Behind the Text for ch 1), it seems to be broadly referring to both areas (so 4:8, 16). Therefore, perhaps Esther's request is signifying her awareness of adversaries who still exist throughout the city, a portion of which was not included in the first day's fighting. Indeed, it is in **Susa** broadly where this new decree is then issued and where the additional three hundred are killed (9:14, 15, 18; Berlin 2001, 86). In this light, her second request, for the public display of the bodies of Haman's sons (→ Behind the Text for 2:21-23), may serve as "a deterrent" to those "pockets of resistance" that still exist (Moore 1971, 91), thereby seeking to lessen the second day's death toll.

■ **14-15** These verses succinctly describe the implementation and outcomes of Esther's requests. The *law was established* (v 14; for this translation of the passive of *nātan*, → 3:11), the bodies impaled, the Jews assembled, and three hundred killed, though once again, no spoil is taken.

■ **16** The answer to the king's inquiry in 9:12 is found here. Throughout the kingdom, the Jews had **assembled** *and taken a stand for their lives*, the precise actions allowed by the edict (8:11). The author makes the addition here that they are taking *a stand* not only *for their lives* (*nepeš*) but also for **relief** [*nôaḥ*] **from their enemies**. This final outcome of rest or relief (again in 9:17, 18, and 22) is the fulfillment of the rest begun by Esther's coronation (2:18) and promised by God (4:14, though with a different word there). It also aligns with God's plan to give his people rest, as shown in both in the establishment of Sabbath (Exod 20:11; 23:12) and in the giving of the land (Deut 25:19; Josh 1:13).

■ **17-19** These verses describe the celebration that erupts following the Jews' successful defense, as well as supplying the practical explanation for the discrepancy that developed between the rural celebrations on the fourteenth (following fighting only on the thirteenth) and the urban celebrations on the fifteenth (following two days of fighting). For both groups, the celebrations are called **a day of feasting** [*mišteh*] **and joy** (*śimḥāh* [Esth 9:17]), with v 19 adding *a celebration* (*yôm ṭôb*), words that also described the spontaneous celebration that occurred in 8:16-17 when Mordecai's edict was announced throughout the kingdom.

All of the feasts of the book, along with their fasting counterparts, culminate in these final feasts of the Jews. The *sending portions* [*of food* (*mānôt*)] *to one's neighbors* (so Neh 8:10) also mirrors the gifts given by the king in celebrating Esther's rise to power (Esth 2:18). Thus, the goodness that had been bestowed by the Persians is now bestowed by the community of God's people. As Bechtel rightly observes,

> The experience of receiving God's grace begets more grace. Centuries later another Jew named Paul would describe it this way: 'Yes, everything is for your sake, so that grace, as it extends to more and more people, may increase thanksgiving, to the glory of God' (2 Cor 4:15). (1989, 81)

FROM THE TEXT

As we read this narrative as Scripture, so full of killing and death, we must recognize that "the lesson" to us today "is not, 'Go and do likewise'" (Wells 2013,

77). The fight against evil in this fallen world is real, yet for God's people today, it is a fight—indeed, an entire war!—that is already won. We continue to fight the battles as we await our ultimate and eternal rest, but these are battles "not against flesh and blood, but against the rulers, against the authorities, against the powers of this dark world and against the spiritual forces of evil in the heavenly realms" (Eph 6:12; also 2 Cor 10:4). Therefore, the weapons we use are not those for physical defense, but for both spiritual defense and offense. In Ephesians and elsewhere, we uncover the articles in our arsenal, which include prayer, fasting, and solitude for submitting ourselves to the leadership of the Holy Spirit; truth, righteousness, faith, and salvation for aligning our hearts and minds with Christ and protecting us from the lies and temptations of the evil one; and the gospel of peace, the Word of God, and love (1 Thess 5:8) for confronting our enemies in the likeness of Christ our Lord.

Violence in Esther

Violence perpetrated by God's people in the OT is nowhere more visible and visceral than at their entrance into the promised land in the book of Joshua. In his commentary on Joshua (2015, 53-62), Stephen Lennox precisely and thoughtfully lays out the theological and hermeneutical issues with which we must wrestle when we encounter a passage of violence in the biblical text. Using his work as a template for this discussion of the violence in Esther, one is able to see the Bible's trajectory to move humanity away from an existence of violence toward an existence of goodness and well-being, or following Lennox, away from the kingdom of this world and toward the kingdom of God.

First, any act of violence, whether in the biblical account or on our television screens, must wrench our hearts. May I never perceive these depictions without feeling the heart of a mother who knows she is watching her children turn themselves over to their own destruction. This is but a glimpse of the father heart of our God.

Second, though without trivializing or dismissing the first, we turn to wrestling with this text by approaching it "in its historical context, in light of God's revealed character, and in light of God's redemptive plan" (ibid., 55). The ancient mindset that frames the Joshua narrative is much unchanged in the historical context of the Esther narrative, though the power structures have shifted considerably. In Esther, rather than individual nations battling one another to establish the superiority of their god and thus their divine right to rule a territory, the Persian Empire (along with empires before and after) existed as a testimony in the minds of its people to their established superiority. Within that context, the Jewish religious minority, though tolerated, had to begin to make the shift from experiencing their identity of chosenness externally through territorial possession to the internal experience of goodness and peace (ṭôb and šālôm [Esth 10:3]), fully wrought by the hand of God yet also resulting from their obedience (e.g., Neh 10). In this way, God uses the flow of history to shift his people from a primarily nationalistic view of their relationship with him to a communally interpersonal view of that relationship. Seen in that light, their view of violence as "actions that tear at the fabric of Israelite society by defying the sovereignty of God" (Creach 2003, 15, in Lennox) is further narrowed, operating now only in the realm of a threat to their continued existence rather than a threat to territory or power (→ In the Text for Esth 8 and 9).

The book of Esther has to its advantage over earlier books in the OT a rich revelation of God's character unfolded over centuries. Thus, our author's portrayal of God's character can at once be more subtle (anticipating an alert audience) as well as more developed (building upon that which has come before). God's role as sovereign of this kingless, kingdomless people becomes clearly defined in terms of provision for and protection of the weak and oppressed, those devoid of power, the least. Never since the ordered genocide of Exod 1 have God's people been more oppressed than in Esther.

Moreover, though subtly "hidden" throughout the text, both God's power to deliver and the ultimate source of justice in this debauched dominion are never in doubt. Surprisingly, as God's people have been forced out of earthly power structures, their access to divine power structures seems to have increased. Precisely because military might is no longer available to his people, God is able to refine our perception of his character not by ordering or orchestrating an "aggressive military action" against the Persians, but rather by providing his people with the defense they needed, no more and no less. In this way, God's grace and mercy are extended beyond the Jews in ways more clearly evident than in the past.

Alliances with God's people that happened on a very small scale in Joshua (e.g., Rahab, the Gibeonites), now happen with many (Esth 8:17). There is a very clear choice provided to the people of the land of Persia, with an abundance of time to proclaim their allegiance (nearly nine months from 8:9 to 9:1). In perfect alignment with the revelation of the past, God is bringing clarity to our understanding of who he is, setting us on a trajectory to recognize him when we see him face-to-face in the person of Jesus Christ.

Likewise, his plan to restore humanity to relationship with him gains further clarity in Esther. God's covenant, first to Abraham (Gen 12:1-3; 17) then to David (2 Sam 7:1-17), established his plan to work with, in, and through humans to restore all humanity to unlimited relationship with him as bearers of his full, unmarred image. The Jews, as respondents to rather than co-initiators of this unbreakable promise (Gen 15), regularly throughout history put its fulfillment in jeopardy by their disobedience.

However, the gracious, slow-angering, forgiving God continued to provide opportunities for them to act as agents of its fulfillment. Ultimately, God himself would become human in the incarnation of Jesus Christ for the purpose of securing once and for all the way by which full reconciliation might happen. In the "intermediate" time of preparation for that "ultimate solution," however, God is not stagnant; rather, he is actively at work revealing the fullness of his plan to his people. Therefore, in the book of Esther, we see clear moves God has made to shift his people from an adolescent understanding (having "stooped to the weakness" of their understanding in former days) to a more mature awareness of his unfolding plan. Along with those mentioned above, these are but a few of the steps we can see.

- In the past, the effects of sin in the fallen world permeated the Jews' national structure, at times even necessitating offensive military action; in Esther, those effects are ameliorated to the point that Jewish agency in violence is limited to defensive rather than offensive strategies.
- In the past, Jewish flourishing meant Gentile defeat; in Esther, Jewish flourishing means flourishing for all (Esth 10).
- In the past, the Jews were meant to serve as God's light to the nations emanating from his "city on a hill," the promised land; in Esther, Jews permeate all society of the whole world (from the Persian point of view), and the nations respond. Where his *nation* broadly failed, his *people* broadly succeed.
- In the past, God's primary human agents of restoration within power structures have been males (Moses and Joshua, along with prophets, priests, kings); in Esther, men and women serve as equal human agents in positions of power—a step toward the equality of all image bearers.

The implications for the kingdom of God are clear. Though the OT moves us toward a lessening of violence, it is not until the death and resurrection of Christ, which assures the triumph of God's plan of human restoration, that we can envision the elimination of all violence for any reason. In this kingdom light, God's people now may respond to their enemies with no human defense, knowing that there are no weapons that can be arrayed against us for our annihilation (Matt 5:38-48; 2 Cor 10:3-6). God's plan is that all humanity might experience the fullness of unlimited relationship with him (1 Tim 2:3-4), and the exponential increase of Gentiles who join the cause of God will continue until unimaginable sums are reached in the kingdom of God (Rev 7:9-10). Indeed, in Christ, all can be received into the kingdom as children and heirs without distinction (Gal 3:28).

XII. PURIM ESTABLISHED: ESTHER 9:20-32

BEHIND THE TEXT

Some modern commentaries break the narrative after 9:16, thereby making 9:17-19 part of this section on the establishment of Purim (so Reid 2008, 144ff.). However, the Hebrew Bible places the section break after v 19, completing the battle narrative with a description of the resulting celebration. Those verses then transition us from the narrative of the spontaneous celebration to the legislation of the structured celebration, the one begetting the other.

IN THE TEXT

■ **20-23** *These things* that **Mordecai recorded** (v 20) is "a most ambiguous phrase" (Moore 1971, 93), with suggestions ranging from as much as the entire book of Esther to as little as summary statements similar to vv 17-19 or vv 23-26a. The intent, however, is that this recording might provoke remembering, an act already proven essential in this story of salvation for the Jews (2:23; 6:1-3).

Mordecai asserts himself as one with the authority to establish not only Persian law (8:2, 9) but also Jewish law. Indeed, Mordecai's establishment of this celebration marks the only Jewish festival instituted in the Hebrew Bible outside the Law (Lev 23; though Hanukkah, or "the Festival of Dedication," was established in 1 Macc 4:36-59 and celebrated by Jesus in John 10:22-23). This annual festival, celebrated *each and every year* (Esth 9:21), emphasizes the two major outcomes of the Esther story—relief (*nôaḥ* [v 16]) and reversal (*hāpak* [v 1]). In addition, Mordecai extends the sharing of food among the community (v 19) to include the giving of **gifts to the poor** (v 22). This action permanently frames the remembrance of Israel's past story of oppression within a present context of caring for the oppressed around them, just as the Decalogue given in Deuteronomy reframes the keeping of Sabbath as a remembrance of their own time in forced labor (Deut 5:12-15; compare Exod 20:8-11).

■ **24-26a** Though these verses do provide a brief plot summary, their primary purpose is to explain the name given to the festival that the Jews have just adopted. Therefore, they contain only the plot elements necessary for that purpose. It is the minute detail of the casting of the lot (*pûr* [3:7]) that now proves significant in its connection to the festival's name; thus, the details related to Haman take prominence here—the repetition of his full description (3:10), a succinct accounting of his evil plan, a free rendering of the king's response, and the accounting of Haman's death. Esther appears minutely or not at all simply because she is subordinate to the purpose of these verses. (See summary of opposing views on this interpretation in Moore 1971, 94; for Esther's role, compare the NIV translation [But when **the plot** came to the king's attention (9:25)] versus the NIV footnote [*when **Esther** came before the king*], which offer competing attempts to interpret an unclear Hebrew pronoun.)

■ **26b-28** After this brief explanation, the author returns to his discussion of the establishment of the festival. Though it has already happened in this chapter (v 19), by v 28 the author has clearly moved "us out of the historical context of Esther and the Persian court into his own context, presumably some years later" (Reid 2008, 144). In this way, the broader purpose for the composition of this book is revealed to and impressed upon the reader.

Exceeding the extensiveness with which any action or command of the extravagant Persians has been expressed throughout the book, our author piles on expressions to emphasize that this celebration is to happen among *all* God's people, in *all* places, for *all* time, without fail and without end. "Like the laws of the Persians and Medes, this practice . . . 'shall not pass away'" (Fox 2001, 122), though of course, very ironically, only the Jewish practice and not the Persian law has actually endured.

■ **29-32** These final verses of ch 9 reiterate both the establishment of and the Jews' acceptance of Purim. However, not surprisingly, this unique situation of establishing a new festival does not happen easily or, perhaps, quickly. Therefore, a second letter is sent, this one perhaps primarily composed by Esther (note the third-person feminine singular verb), though sent by Mordecai (9:30, masc. verb), and therefore invoking the full authority of the crown of Persia. Esther is called **daughter of Abihail** (v 29), giving her Hebrew lineage for the first time since 2:15. Then was the moment when she was most in jeopardy; now is the moment when she is most exalted as she confirms the establishment of an eternal celebration for all her people. Likewise, Mordecai is designated **the Jew**, a title bestowed on him three times in these last seven verses of the book. Both of these characters have transformed through a variety of roles in this book, from orphan and caregiver to queen and second-in-command. Only one role, however, has remained unchanged for both—their identity as one of God's people.

This second letter seems to function as an expansion of the first in at least two specific ways. First, it includes the first mention of fasting since ch 4, which some interpret to be the establishment of the Fast of Esther celebrated still today by Jews on the 13th of Adar (so Moore 1971, 96-97). Alternatively, the phrase **their times of fasting and lamentation** (v 31), which **they had established** may reference either the inclusion of this festival into the regular cycle of Jewish fast days or the acknowledgment of the already adopted practice of mourning that the Jews have instituted in remembrance of the Esther story, to which the joyous festival should now be added (Clines 1984b, 330-31).

Second, this letter contains a message of assurance and hope to the Jewish people, sent with *words of well-being and trustworthiness* (*šālôm ve'ĕmet*). The Jewish people can rest as their time of danger is past, and now is a time of peace in the empire. The experience of "peace and security" characterizes God's restoration of his people after their experience of exile in Jer 33:6. Similarly, Zechariah commands the people to embrace "peace and truth" as their response to God's reversal that has turned fasts into "joyful and glad occasions and happy festivals," just as here in Esther (Zech 8:19; Berlin 2001, 92-32). (For discussion of the connection of remembrance and the recorded word [Esth 9:32], see Wells 2013, 87-91.)

FROM THE TEXT

Salvation History as My History: For many readers, their knowledge of the book of Esther has ended by this point, and indeed, it can be quite easy for the modern (particularly non-Jewish) reader to become utterly disinterested in the bureaucracy of this section. The formalities of establishing a new festival accompanied by a rehashing of details from the preceding story seem anticlimactic at best and downright pointless at worst. However, there are key details that a thorough reader must confront and process here. This is not a story to be read and forgotten; it is not even a story meant primarily to be studied and searched; this is a story to be read, remembered, and lived out.

As Thomas King so clearly reminds us in his commentary on Leviticus, the sacred festivals that Israel was commended to celebrate in the Torah were a yearly "reliving of salvation history," through which "God's activity becomes an experienced reality for each new generation" (2013, 244). It is not enough to read and know about God's deliverance of his people; it must be experienced and internalized as a present reality as much as a past reality. While Christians continue our active remembrance of God's activity in the OT, it is in the person of Jesus Christ that we find "God's greatest act of intervention" with humanity. Therefore, Christians celebrate the Christian year, experiencing "the birth, life, death, resurrection, ascension, and return of Jesus Christ" as a "means of living in communion with Christ by making a pilgrimage through the year in contact with his person and work" (Cherry 2010, 205-18).

Reliving *all* of salvation history allows me to see more clearly who God is and how he has been who he is in the lives of his people for all time. As the image of his character (who he is) is developed in me through this active participation, I then experience his faithfulness to be who he is in my life, just as he has shown himself faithful in the lives of his people throughout history. It is through this continual reliving of God's activity that I can have the ability to see his saving hand in those darkest moments of my life, those moments when all seems threatened with annihilation. When I can't see God's activity in my life, I fall back on the communal remembering (Esth 9:27-28) of his activity in this world, and I become assured that he will prove faithful once again!

9:20-32

XIII. THE GREATNESS OF MORDECAI: ESTHER 10:1-3

BEHIND THE TEXT

If the end of ch 9 seemed to modern readers an anticlimactic, drawn-out, redundant conclusion, the existence of ch 10 proves even more confusing, "strictly unnecessary for the purposes of the narrative" (Clines 1984b, 331). Though some view these three verses, often termed a postscript, as an addition by a later editor of the book (ibid.), Berlin sees this chapter functioning as a "coda" that she defines as "a literary device to confirm that the story is complete, its loose ends have been tied up, and that it is valid" (2001, 94).

It is not clear within the Persian governmental system the exact position that Mordecai would have held as "second in rank" to the king (10:2). Arguably, this may be a status tied to particular personalities rather than a position (compare Tomasino's discussion related to Haman's position [2009, 487]).

These verses do raise the question of the story's main character—is it Mordecai or Esther? Based upon the end of ch 9, one might argue Esther, while ch 10 leans toward Mordecai. As Clines notes, these concluding verses may be why Purim was "known, at least in the first century BC, as 'Mordecai's day' (2 Mac. 15:36)" (ibid., 331), though ultimately Esther earned the title role.

IN THE TEXT

■ **I** The world of ch 1 is extended and strengthened in ch 10. The rulers of the world are as strong as ever, with wealth flowing in from **throughout the empire**. One might even argue that Xerxes is even stronger, with emphasis given to his control **to its** [the empire's] **distant shores.** This Hebrew phrase is *'iyyê hayyām*, also translated *coastlands* or *islands of the sea*, indicating the islands of the Mediterranean, "the furthest extent of the dispersion of Israel" (Clines 1984b, 332; Isa 11:11; 24:15).

■ **2 And all his acts of power and might . . . are they not written in the book of the annals of the kings of Media and Persia?** This is a standard biblical summary statement following an account of an event in the reign of a king (e.g., 1 Kgs 16:5, 27; 2 Kgs 13:8, 12). The significant addition, of course, is the inclusion of **a full account of the greatness** [*gĕdûllāh* (1:4; 6:3)] **of Mordecai,** now known as the one *whom the king had elevated* (*giddal*; see 3:1 and 5:11 for this applied to Haman).

■ **3** Just as the extent of the king's greatness now surpasses his previous glory, so Mordecai surpasses even the greatness of Haman. While Haman was elevated to a position *above all his fellow nobles* (3:1), Mordecai's position is second only to the king. Along with his standing in relation to the king, we are also told his standing in relation to **the Jews** and *to the multitude of his kindred.* He is both *great* (*gādôl* as above, **preeminent among** [NIV]) and *accepted* (**held in high esteem** [NIV]).

The inconceivable has happened once again (compare Gen 41:43), with an Israelite serving second only to the king of the greatest kingdom on earth. Just as Joseph's position resulted in a "great deliverance" of God's people (Gen 45:7), now Mordecai's is used for their ultimate **good** (*ṭôb*)and **welfare** (*šālôm*). The immediate rest and relief provided by Esther's coronation (2:18) and the Jewish victory (9:22) becomes a permanent peace (*šālôm*) for the exiled Jews.

FROM THE TEXT

Partnership: As this ending helps us to see, the book of Esther is not primarily a story about a woman's liberation (a "girl power" story, as one of my students called it). It is an account of the liberation of God's people from terror and doom to peace, security, and flourishing in this world. That liberation came by the activity of God, but his activity was not primarily miraculous or supernatural in nature. Rather, God worked out his purposes in partnership with willing individuals who lived *into* the positions and opportunities placed before them. *Both* Esther *and* Mordecai were available at "such a time as this," and both contributed, equally and with mutual dependence, to God's plan of restoration by fulfilling the role given them by their society. The roles themselves are not sacred; their individual participation in the act of restoration is. The takeaway is simple: it is God's will to utilize all available servants—male and female, old and young, Jew and Gentile, slave and free—for the purpose of bringing his kingdom!

CPSIA information can be obtained
at www.ICGtesting.com
Printed in the USA
LVHW081048080122
708030LV00015B/264